Slavery and the Rise of the Atlanti

The inclusion of the New World in the international economy, among
the most important events in modern history, was based on slavery.
Europeans brought at least 8 million black men, women, and children
out of Africa to the western hemisphere between the sixteenth and
nineteenth centuries, and slavery transformed the Atlantic into a complex trading area uniting North and South America, Europe, and Africa through the movement of peoples, goods and services, and credit
and capital. The chapters in this book place slavery in the mainstream
of modern history. They describe the transfer of slavery from the Old
World; its role in forging the interdependence of the economies bordering the Atlantic; its effect on the empires of Portugal, the Netherlands, France, and Great Britain; and its impact on Africa.

SLAVERY AND THE RISE OF THE ATLANTIC SYSTEM

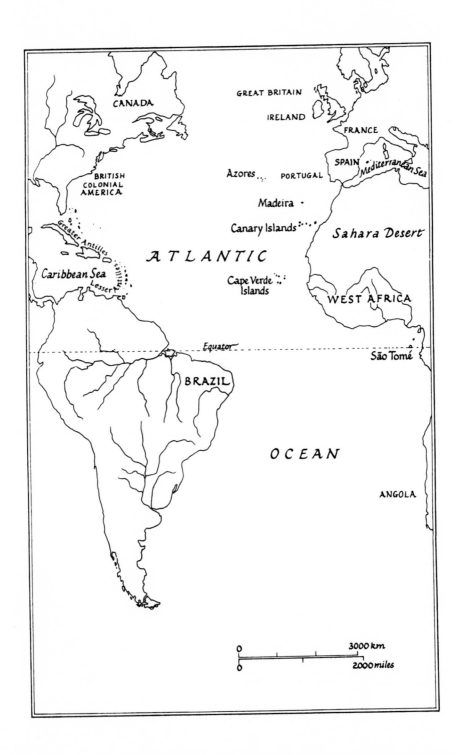

CANADA

GREAT BRITAIN

IRELAND

FRANCE

BRITISH
COLONIAL
AMERICA

SPAIN

PORTUGAL

Mediterranean Sea

Azores

Madeira

Greater Antilles

Canary Islands

Sahara Desert

A T L A N T I C

Caribbean Sea

Lesser

Cape Verde
Islands

WEST AFRICA

Equator

São Tomé

BRAZIL

O C E A N

ANGOLA

3000 km

2000 miles

SLAVERY AND THE RISE OF THE ATLANTIC SYSTEM

Edited by
BARBARA L. SOLOW

CAMBRIDGE
UNIVERSITY PRESS

W.E.B. DUBOIS INSTITUTE FOR AFRO-AMERICAN
RESEARCH,
HARVARD UNIVERSITY

Published by the Press Syndicate of the University of Cambridge
The Pitt Building, Trumpington Street, Cambridge CB2 1RP
40 West 20th Street, New York, NY 10011-4211, USA
10 Stamford Road, Oakleigh, Melbourne 3166, Australia

First published 1991
First paperback edition 1993

Library of Congress Cataloging-in-Publication Data available.

A catalogue record for this book is available from the British Library.

ISBN 0-521-40090-2 hardback
ISBN 0-521-45737-8 paperback

Transferred to digital printing 2002

Contents

Contents

Preface

T HE chapters in this volume were originally presented at a conference on "Slavery and the Rise of the Atlantic System," held at Harvard University on September 4–5, 1988. The conference was sponsored by the W. E. B. DuBois Institute for Afro-American Studies and the Charles Warren Center for Studies in American History at Harvard University and was funded by a grant from the National Endowment for the Humanities.

We are grateful to Randall K. Burkett, Associate Director of the DuBois Institute, Martha Moore, Staff Assistant, and Daniel Miller and Layn St. Louis, graduate students, for their indispensable assistance.

This volume is dedicated to the memory of the late director of the DuBois Institute, Nathan I. Huggins: scholar, teacher, colleague, and friend.

Barbara L. Solow

Contributors

Luis Felipe de Alencastro Centro Brasileiro de Analise e
Planejamento and Universidade Estadual de Campenas, Brazil

David Eltis Queens University, Canada

P. C. Emmer University of Leiden, The Netherlands

S. L. Engerman University of Rochester

David W. Galenson University of Chicago

Franklin W. Knight The Johns Hopkins University

Joseph C. Miller University of Virginia

P. K. O'Brien London University, United Kingdom

William D. Phillips, Jr. University of Minnesota, Twin Cities

Jacob M. Price University of Michigan

David Richardson University of Hull, United Kingdom

Barbara L. Solow Harvard University

Patrick Villiers University of Orléans, France

Introduction

BARBARA L. SOLOW

THE inclusion of the New World in the international economy ranks among the important events in modern history. Slavery was the foundation of that inclusion in its early chapters, and slavery accounts for the growth and importance of the transatlantic trade. The chapters in this volume thus place the study of slavery in the mainstream of international history.

Europeans brought 8 million black men and women out of Africa to the New World between the sixteenth and nineteenth centuries, and slavery transformed the Atlantic into a complex trading area uniting North and South America, Europe, and Africa through the movement of men and women, goods, and capital. It was slavery that made the empty lands of the western hemisphere valuable producers of commodities and valuable markets for Europe and North America: What moved in the Atlantic in these centuries was predominantly slaves, the output of slaves, the inputs to slave societies, and the goods and services purchased with the earnings on slave products. To give just one example, by the late seventeenth century, the New England merchant, the Madeiran vintner, the Barbadian planter, the English manufacturer, the English slave trader, and the African slave trader were joined in an intricate web of interdependent economic activity. Slavery thus affected not only the countries of the slaves' origins and destinations but, equally, those countries that invested in, supplied, or consumed the products of the slave economies.

In the centuries that followed the Era of the Discoveries, Europe turned its face overseas, the Atlantic supplanted the Mediterranean as the center of the international economy, and those nations with ties to the Atlantic forged ahead. In Asia, European powers found they could exploit their conquests by the expropriation of riches and resources, by the imposition of taxes and tolls, by the formation of monopolies, and by systems of forced deliveries. These policies, which were costly to maintain and involved serious disincentives and inefficiencies, were not readily applicable to the undeveloped lands

1

of the western hemisphere. There were few existing rich economies to loot and an insufficient supply of voluntary labor to found new ones. The mining areas of colonial Spain aside, North and South America and the Caribbean languished before the coming of slavery, and trade between them and Europe stood at low levels. Once the productive labor of African slaves was added to the ample land and resources of the New World, economic growth began.

Brazil was founded on plantation slavery. The foreign trade of seventeenth-century New England, based on fur, fish, and timber, never achieved the pace of development that began when merchants started to trade with the slave plantations of the West Indies. To eliminate the economic stagnation of the American South, slaves were "the one needful thing" to grow rice, indigo, and Sea Island cotton and to expand tobacco production. Not one of the Caribbean islands succeeded in establishing a viable society on the basis of free labor; they flourished under slavery. The trade of Spain's Latin American colonies, which declined after the end of the mining era, only revived much later, with the introduction of large-scale slavery into Cuba. Those regions of the New World with few links to slavery remained relatively dormant.

On the other side of the Atlantic, those regions linked to the colonial trade experienced increased demand for their goods and services – manufactures and shipping – and became sources of dynamic growth in their countries. In a reciprocal relationship, European demand for colonial goods, matched by a supply of slave labor to produce those goods, encouraged European development in the colonial period. The chapters in this volume trace this relationship over time and space.

Barbara Solow's chapter argues that the link between slavery and colonial development is not accidental but arises from the inherent difficulties of settlement in regions where land is either originally abundant or has been made so by the expropriation of the indigenous population. Following arguments that go back to the English classical economists, Solow suggests that, at a time of simple agricultural technology, newly discovered countries with abundant land are more likely to stagnate than grow. High incomes are to be had, but only as a return to labor. The poorest Europeans will have an incentive to emigrate but may not have the means. If they do come and settle, they will find it hard to accumulate capital from their small farms and even harder to attract capital from abroad. Potential returns to the European investor will be great – greater than those at home – but they are unrealizable because a supply of labor will not be forthcoming to potential landlords. No one will willingly continue to share the fruits of his labor with a landlord by paying rent when he can capture them all for himself on his own farm.

Slavery solves the problem. Labor comes; the many have no choice but to obey the few; European capital and entrepreneurship can now combine with the labor of slaves and the abundance of land to produce goods for the metropolitan market; with the proceeds of these goods, the "empty" lands can now engage in international trade with that market, to their mutual benefit. Slavery is thus not merely a source of labor: Under the conditions stipulated, slavery is the only source of a permanent supply of labor and of increased capital accumulation. Thus there is nothing accidental about the appearance of coerced labor, whether of slaves, serfs, or convicts, in regions with vast tracts of thinly populated land. Where land was a free good and only labor received an economic return, Europeans garnered the return without performing the labor: by enslaving Africans (or enserfing peasants or importing convicts).

Solow cites Evsey Domar's modern model of this situation. Domar has expressed his conclusions in an especially illuminating way: Of the three elements of this simple agricultural economy, Free Land, Free Labor, and a Landowning Aristocracy, only two but not all three can coexist. Solow argues that this model of economic development with abundant land provides a useful conceptual framework for understanding colonial American history, neither deterministic, simplistic, nor unicausal, and more consistent with the historical record than alternative schemes. Unlike them, she says, it helps explain why two streams of labor, free and slave, came to the Americas and formed two different but interdependent forms of social and economic organization. And, unlike them, it gives slavery a major explanatory role in colonial history.

The passage of slavery from the Old World to the New is discussed by William D. Phillips, Jr. Europe knew slavery from antiquity, both in its small-scale, domestic, and artisanal form and as large-scale gang labor. The latter type, where slaves formed the basis of the labor system, had disappeared by the Middle Ages, and domestic and artisanal slavery followed. In any case, domestic slaves in part represented consumption, not production. Thus, American slavery in its characteristic form involved the reintroduction of a system dormant in Europe for 500 years.

The Spanish and Portuguese conquests in Latin America provided very limited opportunities for looting and legitimate trade. The absence (and destruction) of rich economies and trading networks meant that Europeans, in order to exploit their conquests, would have to devise a new economic and social order to produce profitable commodities for trade. To America's abundant land and resources, labor would have to be added. Spanish efforts to solve the labor problem by the *encomienda* and *repartimiento* systems were ended by royal decree (except in mining), and the demographic catastrophe suffered by the Amerindians ensured that an indigenous labor force would not be forthcoming. By the seventeenth century, labor in colonial Latin America was being supplied by free natives (*naborios*), mestizos, and mulattos; black slaves; and (illegally) coerced Amerindians.

For the first century and a half, Phillips writes, domestic and industrial slavery coexisted in Latin America, but after the middle of the seventeenth century the demand for slaves came almost exclusively from the plantation and mining sectors, and gang labor became the predominant form of slavery in Latin America.

Black slaves in significant numbers came to America embedded in an institution with very old roots: the sugar plantation. Its origins go back to the end of the eleventh century, when the first Crusaders found Muslims growing sugar on plantations in Syria and Palestine. When the last crusader states fell at the end of the thirteenth century, Europeans transplanted the industry to Cyprus, Crete, and Sicily in the Mediterranean and then to Madeira and the Canaries in the Atlantic. According to Phillips, the nearly exclusive reliance on slave labor came only in the Atlantic.

Phillips's chapter thus shows that, before Columbus discovered America, Europeans were growing sugar with mostly free and some slave labor in the Mediterranean; they were also using some slaves in domestic and artisanal occupations; they were acquiring slaves from black Africa and from other sources. But in the New World sugar was slave-grown, slaves were found mainly in gang labor on sugar plantations, and slaves were overwhelmingly black.

The transfer of the slave–sugar plantation to the New World arose because, in the absence of a developed, populous economy, Europeans needed to establish a profitable export crop and provide a labor force to grow it. This labor force would have to be coerced, and the Amerindians had neither the numbers, the skills, nor the discipline to form it. In sugar the Europeans found their profitable crop, in slaves they found the coerced labor force, and in Africa they found a trading network for acquiring the slaves.

"Without African slaves and the transatlantic slave trade," writes Franklin W. Knight, "the potential economic value of the Americas could never have been realized." Knight's chapter discusses the role of slavery in the developing international capitalist system that began in the era of European expansion.

Although slavery antedates capitalism, they were inextricably bound together. European expansion was not motivated exclusively by economic motives, nor did slavery initially have a role in it. Indeed, slavery had virtually ceased as a mode of production in Europe. But in the establishment of the new international capitalist system, Knight finds slavery an indispensable catalyst.

For Europeans, slaves were private property, and slavery fits into the capitalist world of profit-maximizing entrepreneurs who combine privately owned factors of production to produce goods for sale in a market. Besides being a commodity of trade, slaves are also a factor of production. Their introduction to the world economy added a significant amount of productive resources beyond what would have been offered voluntarily. Moreover, Knight points out that there are important backward and forward linkages in obtaining slaves, in combining them with other factors, in processing slave-grown commodities, and in shipping and marketing these products. Thus, Knight concludes, slavery played a role in increasing economic production, in spreading and remodeling capitalist institutions, in inculcating the capitalist mentality and traditions, and in developing and strengthening institutions appropriate to the capitalist world.

The notion that slavery was a noncapitalist or precapitalist institution has survived for a long time. Flavio Versiani, in a paper presented at the conference on "Slavery and the Rise of the Atlantic System" but not available for publication, observes that it underlies an interpretation that attributes the end of Brazilian slavery to the triumph of the capitalist spirit of the southern planters over the non-market, irrational economic ideology of the northern sugar planters. The technical and financial complexity of the slave economy argues against such a view, Versiani says, and the picture of a benign, paternalistic planter class is deceptive, since it is confined to a period when the economy had ceased to be very profitable. In Brazil, the early industrialists, who were organized in family firms and disbursed dividends by custom, not profitability, had a better claim to be called economically irrational or precapitalist.

Versiani sees the end of Brazilian slavery as the result of a politically based movement that fostered and even subsidized free labor immigration. The price of slaves had risen with the closing of the slave trade, and the price of free labor fell with the immigration of the 1880s. Against this background emancipation makes economic sense, and no recourse to economically irrational, noncapitalist slave owners is required to explain it.

Pieter Emmer makes a valuable distinction between the first and second Atlantic systems. The founders of the first system, Spain and Portugal, were at an early level of economic development, lacking the means for effective colonization. The Iberian system retained feudal elements; it was managed by an exclusivist commercial policy characterized by close state control. That policy was not conceived in terms of exploiting the colonies by producing for an international market. Instead it was designed to use the monopoly power of the state to organize the extraction of precious metals with the labor of the indigenous population, and colonial development was directed to sites and transit routes that furthered this policy.

Emmer's second Atlantic system began in the Caribbean in the middle of the seventeenth century and occurred in an open international setting, with the Dutch, French, and English as participants. Almost immediately the French and English moved to restrict Dutch access to their colonies and reserve them for their own nationals. The quick end of the open system did not represent a return to the first Atlantic system for several reasons: First, the northern European nations were at a different level of development than the Iberian system and could provide more of the elements of successful colonization; second, they exercised less detailed state control in their commercial policy; third, both legal and illegal breaches were made in their national policies. There was no exclusivity in capital movements, in the slave trade, or in commodity movements. For example, capital was raised in an international market; the British sold slaves to French and Spanish colonies; New England traded outside the British empire; French sugar was marketed by the Dutch.

From the beginning, Spain and Portugal differed in their circumstances. As Phillips notes, the Portuguese monarchy was more secure and less devoted to religious ends. Spain was more populous, and could expand the kingdom of Castile as a patrimonial state and establish settlements under semi-noble control. More important, Spain found precious metals in its territory much earlier than Portugal did. Spain had the mercury needed to exploit them. In order to hold Brazil, Portugal had to find sources of revenue other than gold and silver.

Portugal's solution was to plant an export-oriented agricultural economy in Brazil. It found the model flourishing in the Atlantic islands. Sugar was the export; African slaves were the laborers; and northern Europeans were the suppliers of capital, shipping, and markets in the absence of Iberian resources. The Dutch role, Emmer shows, was to penetrate the Iberian system and later transfer it to the Caribbean.

Spain's monopoly of sea power in the Caribbean was contested by the Dutch, French, and English, and from the early seventeenth century, Spain was unable to prevent northern Europeans from occupying the Lesser Antilles. After initial experiments with tobacco, indigo, and ginger, grown mainly by free labor, the islands were converted one by one to sugar plantations with slave labor. The colonies of both France and England were at first dependent on the Dutch, and Emmer shows that the Dutch continued to play a role in the nominally exclusivist but actually rather open second Atlantic system.

Emmer's chapter raises directly the question of what were the benefits of Atlantic trade and how were they distributed: Cui bono?

Africa has rarely been portrayed as a gainer, but how badly was it hurt? David Eltis presents some quantitative data useful for answering this question. In his chapter, he estimates first the value of the slave and commodity trade between West Africa (Senegambia to Angola) for five decades: 1680s, 1730s, 1780s, 1820s, and 1860s. African exports are measured c.i.f. and imports f.o.b. in current prices. Total trade increased until the decade of the 1780s; it fell to a lower level in the 1820s and rose to new heights in the 1860s. (However, the series is in current, not constant, prices.) Although the 1860s show trade high in absolute value, world trade had increased by so much more that Africa's share fell. Africa's role in world trade was important in the slave era, not afterward.

Slaves dominated Africa's Atlantic trade until the 1860s, accounting for 86%, 94%, and 81% of the total in the 1730s, 1780s, and 1820s, respectively, but less than 1% in the 1860s. To the 1730s the expansion of trade reflected a doubling of both prices and quantities; thereafter prices doubled but quantities increased only by half. Thus, the slave market was demand oriented, and supply was at first elastic but less so at higher quantities.

Examining the composition of per capital imports into West Africa, Eltis finds that textiles were dominant in every period. Potentially socially destabilizing goods (alcohol, guns, gunpowder) amounted to around 20–30% of the total. Eltis notes that the share in African imports of firearms, alcohol, and tobacco did not differ from that in many other countries and that gun imports in the eighteenth century were lower than in the nineteenth.

A comparison of Africa's total trade (exports plus imports in current prices divided by 2 divided by population) shows West Africa far

Barbara L. Solow

below Brazil, the United States, Great Britain, and the British West Indies in every time period studied. Eltis concludes that this may indicate that European goods could make far fewer inroads into Africa than they could elsewhere: "African textiles, metal goods, and merchandise satisfying psychic wants were simply more competitive in the face of European competition than their counterparts in the Americas." It may, however, merely indicate low levels of income in Africa.

Finally, Eltis examines the value of trade (exports plus imports) between six West African regions and the Atlantic world. The wide geographic dispersion of African trade is well documented. Only the Bight of Biafra and Senegambia weathered the suppression of the slave trade without suffering decreased revenues, and the Bight had consistently the greatest trade contact with the Atlantic, probably from the 1740s. Eltis notes that in no region was the revenue per capita of oceangoing trade significant, though Dahomey has the best claim.

Eltis concludes that his analysis would be interpreted as tending to minimize the significance of the transatlantic slave trade to Africa. His findings have shown, Eltis remarks, that "more than most populations in the nineteenth century world, Africans were feeding, clothing, and sheltering themselves, as well as developing the full panoply of a multi-faceted cultural existence, without overseas economic exchange." May not the self-sufficiency of Africa and the failure of European goods to penetrate its markets show that any supposedly negative impact of the slave trade was illusory? he asks. Nevertheless, he concludes, contemporaries and modern historians will continue to believe that slavery did have a significant impact. Indeed, Eltis's chapter illustrates that wide differences of opinion existed at the conference on the validity and interpretation of his estimates. May not Africa's international position partly be a result of the slave trade?

If Africa was unaffected or adversely affected by slavery, how can we explain Portugal, a great slaving nation and imperial power, yet an increasingly backward economy from the sixteenth to the nineteenth centuries? This is the subject of Joseph C. Miller's chapter.

Miller shows that, from the beginning, metropolitan Portugal was involved only peripherally in developing its Atlantic possessions. Genoese provided capital for Madeira and São Tomé, and Brazilian trade with Europe was dominated first by the Dutch and then by the English. Local trade and plantations fell to colonial elites, Jews, and Afro-Portuguese in São Tomé, Luso-African settlers in Angola, and the American-based planters and merchants in Brazil. Internationally in Europe, from the middle of the seventeenth century, Portugal depended on England to guarantee its national sovereignty and, in turn, granted England access to its markets at home and in the colonies.

Metropolitan Portugal provided administrators for the imperial territories but thus abandoned economic activity there to others. Vain efforts were made to limit foreign and colonial access to the empire, particularly with regard to the rich trade in sugar and gold from Brazil. Angola occupied a distinctly secondary position on the scale of metropolitan development priorities. Miller concludes that to the limited extent that these protectionist policies succeeded, they managed only to protect backward and inefficient sectors of the Portuguese economy, and by the late eighteenth century Pombaline Lisbon had to all but acknowledge its inability to dominate commerce in Angola and Brazil.

If Brazil meant riches for England and brokerage for Portugal, Africa assumed the position of a second-best market, to be fought over by Brazilian colonials and metropolitan Portuguese who were losing out in the main lines of imperial economic development. The low-value rum that Brazil sent to Angola, like its famous trade in third-rate tobacco to West Africa, played a role analogous to the shipments of otherwise unprofitable products of colonial New England: This trade gave a colony an advantageous secondary staple.

In the final analysis, although slavery made Brazil a valuable producer of sugar, source of gold, and market for manufactures and other goods from Europe, the Portuguese empire was not the main beneficiary. Portugal made superficial gains from brokerage, but England sold manufactured goods at higher prices than the Brazilians could otherwise have afforded and received Portugal's tropical products and gold more cheaply than it could have done under other circumstances. England would not have done either on such a scale or made equivalent profits without the secondary, marginal trade in slaves from Angola.

European conquest of foreign lands does not guarantee political sovereignty, and political sovereignty does not guarantee successful economic exploitation. This is the starting point of Alencastro's chapter on the Portuguese empire. The metropole must "colonize the colonies" by consolidating political authority, by ensuring the existence of an economic surplus, and by directing the surplus toward itself. Slavery is the key to understanding how the Portuguese imperial structure managed these problems.

In their Asian dominions, Alencastro observes, the Portuguese neither organized nor invested in productive activity, but entered as participants into the age-old trading patterns of Asia. They tried, with minimal success, to divert the gains to their own account and eventually lost their position in Asia to the Dutch and, later, the English. In East Africa the Portuguese had even less success. In Mozambique they were swallowed up in the ongoing local commerce and became just one group among many in the East African trading system. They were, in Alencastro's word, "kaffirized." On the other side of Africa, Portugal's policy was the diversion of the domestic slave trade to international markets.

In the different Latin American context, without the flow of metalwares, textiles, and spices of the East, the Iberian states sought first to extend their sovereignty and then to control the natives to ensure an economic surplus for Europeans. At first, the metropolis tried to control the colonies through royal officials and the clergy; later, control was exercised by assigning each colony a role in the Atlantic trading system. Where Spain's policy rigidly focused on direct trade between the colonies and the home country, leaving the slave trade to subcontractors, Portugal introduced Africa into its empire from the first.

For Alencastro, slavery is the decisive element in understanding the political and economic structures of the Portuguese empire.

1. The introduction of African slaves solved the contention – dating to the Amerindian period – among crown, clergy, and colonists over control of the labor supply.
2. The slave trade was an important source of revenue for crown and church. Duties, fees, and taxes on slaves and their products provided a mechanism for financing these institutions at colonial expense.
3. By introducing African slaves to the international market, the Portuguese empire moved from what Alencastro calls a "circulation economy" to a "production economy." The extended coercion of Africans added a large labor input to the world economy, resulting in increased commodity production as African labor was joined to the rich, abundant land of Brazil. The British and French were quick to adopt this strategy for generating profit for their own empires.
4. The slave trade tied Portugal's possessions together in a complementary, not a competitive, pattern. Slavery linked the African to the Asian colonies: Lisbon had to remit precious metals to cover the deficit in its Asian balance of trade, and it acquired these metals in Africa by exchanging slaves for them. Brazil was linked to Portugal by exports and to Africa by imports.

Alencastro sees slavery as a consequence of imperial policy in the expanding capitalist world, not as a question of demographic, cultural, or somatic factors.

Thanks to the spectacular growth of Saint Domingue, after the Seven Years' War the French Antilles came to rival the British West

Indies in the output of slave plantation crops and to outdistance them in productivity. French foreign trade rose dramatically over the course of the eighteenth century, growing, according to one estimate, by at least 3% a year between 1717 and 1787. At different times, the share of total trade attributable to the colonies ranged from 34% (1717 and 1721) to over 40% (after 1770) for Bordeaux; around 33% (between 1773 and 1778) for Le Havre-Rouen; and between 15 and 20% (from 1730 through the 1770s) for Marseilles. This colonial trade was primarily to the plantation colonies; neither Canada nor Louisiana was so important, and in any case, both ceased to be French after 1763.[1]

Patrick Villiers presents a critical survey of French trade statistics, beginning with official series from the eighteenth century and continuing with the contemporary work of Jean Tarrade. Villiers supplements the usual sources with data on French fleets. These data have hitherto been of little value for estimating colonial trade in slaves because of ambiguities of tonnage measurement. Villiers has now resolved this problem; his work enables us to make fruitful use of the fleet data.

What effect did this growth in trade have on the French domestic economy? A full-scale assessment remains to be written, especially a comparison with the British case. In his book *La Rochelle and the Atlantic Economy during the Eighteenth Century*, John G. Clark provides many materials useful for considering the question. Professor Clark was unfortunately unable to present a paper at the conference; his work contains valuable hints.

The West Indian trade engaged the bulk of eighteenth-century shipping in the Atlantic ports of Nantes, La Rochelle, and Bordeaux. Even Marseilles, trading mainly with the Mediterranean, and Le Havre-Rouen, trading mainly with northern Europe, experienced added impetus from the colonial trade. Nantes and La Rochelle dominated seventeenth-century Atlantic trade; then La Rochelle's share began to decline and Bordeaux's to rise, while Nantes's share stayed fairly steady; by the 1770s and 1780s, Bordeaux had 25% of all French foreign trade, over 40% of it colonial. These ports were fully integrated into the Atlantic trading system, Clark points out, with links to Amsterdam, London, Geneva, the Hanse towns, Africa, the Indian Ocean, Canada, Louisiana, and the West Indies. Capital, goods, and information flowed increasingly back and forth. Yet the link of France's Atlantic economy to its domestic economy was not strong: France's

---

[1] John G. Clark, *La Rochelle and the Atlantic Economy during the Eighteenth Century* (Baltimore, 1981), p. 40.

advantages over Great Britain in the West Indies may well have been overborne by its disadvantages at home.

Clark describes this dynamic Atlantic economy as yoked to a dormant rural sector and an exploitative state:

Three economies, each with its own special focus and at a different stage of development, coexisted in eighteenth-century France. A subsistence rural economy consisted largely of peasants, most of whom were so marginally integrated with regional markets that the nation was only imperfectly fed. ... The second economy was based on the coastal and major river cities, connected by major waterways, which serviced each other's needs and the markets of the colonies and foreign nations. The primary economic hinterlands of the coastal cities lay overseas rather than inland. ... The third economy – the state – fulfilled its own needs by milking the other parts of the triad. (P. 16.)

The hinterlands of the Atlantic ports consumed only small quantities of the imported goods and were poorly developed sources of exports. La Rochelle, the poorest, had the most meager industrial sector: Aside from sugar refineries, "only a small glass plant, three starch manufacturers, and an earthenware factory" (p. 256). Nantes could draw on the Paris basin, but trade was burdened by feudal tolls on the Loire. Bordeaux had a rich wine-producing interior and was connected by the Gironde to the wheat, lumber, wool, cheese, and coal of a wide area.

Thus, to a larger extent than Great Britain, France had to obtain trade goods from outside of its own economy – from Holland, the Hanse towns, and the Baltic. The Dutch provided cheese and cowries for the slave trade; Hamburg, Lubeck, and Bremen sent manufactures, metalwares, textiles, wood products, and food; the Baltic sent planks, staves, and barrels. The impetus that French colonial production gave the economy had to be widely shared with these northern countries. The same is true of invisible earnings. Clark explains that although French ships dominated in the high-seas merchant fleet – the *vaisseaux de long cours*, trading to the Atlantic, Africa, and the East – foreigners dominated the European trade – *le grand cabotage*, trading to England and Ireland, Holland, Scandinavia, the Baltic, and the Mediterranean. Many Dutch merchants resided at Nantes, and in the early eighteenth century foreign vessels were preponderant at Bordeaux. Clark quotes a Rochellais analysis of *le grand cabotage* in 1783, attributing the Dutch superiority to their lower costs and greater experience in northern waters. The costs were explained by greater efficiency and by regulations that required the French to carry crews twice as large as the Dutch. In any case, the shipping earnings associated with the rise of the colonial trade were shared by the French with others (particularly with fellow Protestants in Amsterdam and Geneva). In a word, the multiplier effects of the expansion of France's plantation colonies were spread beyond France.

Clark stresses the economic burdens imposed by the ancien regime and, consequently, the difficulty of translating *any* economic impulse into sustained development. In his view, the French state not only failed to further the economic interests of the nation, it actually impeded them. The state competed for resources with the private sector and used these resources unproductively; it diminished capital availability; its tax policy, perversely, fell disproportionately on the peasantry and bourgeoisie; and "hardly a commodity moved but a fee was exacted against it" (p. 22). Under the ancien regime the incentives for economic gain were found less in enterprise and efficiency than in seeking privilege, subsidies, and monopoly.

Thus, because of the nature of the hinterland of its ports, of its rural economy, and of its state, France evidently benefited less than Great Britain from the dynamic growth of its plantation colonies. Instead of containing the gains from colonial trade within one integrated commercial system, the way the British empire did, the French situation diffused them over a wider area. French colonial growth encouraged metal and textile manufacturers in northern Europe and shippers, insurers, bankers, and other purveyors of commercial services there. The earnings of these northern Europeans on these goods and services could be spent anywhere, not just in France. In the British case, the circulation remained within one system, one that included the important North American colonies, for which the French colonial system had no corresponding member.

To a certain degree, the trade between France and its rich West Indian colonies represented a trade between northern Europe and those colonies: Colonial produce was in part reexported to northern Europe to pay for the trade goods that originated there. For this portion of its colonial trade, France was a bystander as the sugar and supplies flowed between the islands and the northern countries.

This is not to say that its colonial trade failed completely to stimulate French industrial development. Nantes drew on a wide area of suppliers. Charles Tilly has argued that increased manufacturing for colonial markets in the Vendee, by altering the balance of the rural economy, was part of the background of the counterrevolution there. Behind La Rochelle, textile production for the colonies was initiated in Niort, St. Jean d'Angely, and Saintes. Bordeaux had a more flourishing industrial base and hinterland than either. The dependence of the industry of these regions on international trade, much of it colonial, can be measured by their relapse into agriculture when that trade was cut off during the Napoleonic wars. This "deindustrialization" or "repasturization" suggests the actual and potential importance of foreign trade to French development and of the West Indian trade that was its most dynamic sector.

Patrick O'Brien and Stanley Engerman demonstrate the increasing importance of the Atlantic trade to the British. Tudor England saw a shift of exports from primary raw materials to woolen cloth. Although total exports in Elizabethan times amounted to perhaps 4% of national income, the Tudor wool exports "could have supported and sustained somewhere between 28% and 46% of England's non-agricultural population." O'Brien and Engerman estimate that English domestic commodity exports may have quadrupled between 1560 and 1700; their share of national income rose to 8% or 9% by the end of William's reign, and total receipts from them could have provided functional subsistence for 20% of the population or mere subsistence for up to 32%. About 85% of these exports in 1700 were going to Europe and only 12% to the Americas.

Over the long eighteenth century (1697–1802), the mean annual growth rate of the volume of British exports rose to 1.5%, perhaps 50% increase over the period from 1560 to 1700. But in 1802 manufacturers amounted to 88% of the total, and metals, metalwares, and cotton textiles had substantially diminished the share of woolens. The market for the new exports was across the Atlantic: 95% of the incremental commodity exports were going to North America and the British West Indies. O'Brien and Engerman tell us that this Americanization of exports had already peaked in 1802.

The significance of export growth for the British economy goes beyond these quantitative data. Externalities and feedback and demonstration effects must be considered, and O'Brien and Engerman point out that the most dynamic and innovative industries of the Industrial Revolution were precisely those that led the export market for America.

Having established the quantitative importance of colonial trade for British manufacturing in the eighteenth century, O'Brien and Engerman note that questions of causality remain. Was colonial trade a consequence of a mercantilist commercial policy with government investment in military and naval power securing monopoly rights for Britain? Adam Smith thought so. But O'Brien and Engerman concur with recent cliometric work that concludes that commercial restraints were flexibly administered and did not result in any significant misallocation of resources.

More important, was increased colonial trade merely a passive response to economic forces originating in the metropolis? Obviously, there must have been a demand for colonial products in the home country, and the foreign exchange earned by colonials paid for the English manufactures they imported. Again, O'Brien and Engerman reject the notion that exports are passive. By examining data on export growth and terms of trade, they argue for autonomous foreign demand until about 1790, when a shift away from dependence on foreign demand coinciding with an adverse shift in the net barter terms of trade set in. From 1790 until the turn of the nineteenth century, they say, exports were less dependent on autonomous demand shifts than during the export growth spurts that occurred between 1688 and 1792. Thus, O'Brien and Engerman assign foreign (mostly colonial) trade an independent role in explaining economic growth and structural change in the industrializing British economy of the period 1688–1802.

O'Brien and Engerman consider that contrary arguments may have been erroneous because of the underlying theoretical frameworks of their proponents. They doubt whether the theory of comparative advantage, which assumes (among other things) fixed resources and full employment, is a useful model for eighteenth-century trade. Their preference is for the vent-for-surplus model of Adam Smith.

Adam Smith visualized two routes connecting trade and growth. The first is the familiar role of trade in widening the market, allowing specialization and division of labor, and increasing productivity by overcoming indivisibilities. The second, the vent-for-surplus, turns on the role of trade in absorbing surplus productive capacity for which there is no demand in the domestic economy. Not surprisingly, O'Brien and Engerman say, the gains from trade seem small to those who think in Ricardian terms, with their notions of fixed resources fully employed. But a theory that allows for unutilized land and labor permits output increase with little resource cost. Whereas modern adherents of the vent-for-surplus idea find it a useful description of the initial development of traditional peasant economies in Africa and Asia, where surplus resources are associated with various aspects of low levels of domestic development, O'Brien and Engerman find it an attractive framework for relating trade to growth in the eighteenth century as well.

In arguing for the significance of colonial trade, O'Brien and Engerman do not consider the role of slavery. "Obviously," they say, "in the early stages of opening up territory overseas, the level and growth of exports from Britain to the Empire depended almost entirely on inflows of capital and labor from the metropolis" (p. 194). It is precisely this view of the colonial empire that is challenged by others.

The labor of slaves was critical. The export market across the Atlantic was generated by slave-grown commodities. Economic development in the British colonies had lagged before the coming of slavery, according to Richardson and Solow. Solow argues that the immigration of free labor was slow to develop. Most white laborers came as indentured servants, and two-thirds of the indentures came to areas that were destined to become slave states. The growth rate of the black population in the British colonies exceeded that of the white population in all but two of the decades between 1650 and 1750. Moreover, it was black labor that grew the commodities that entered international trade. Sugar alone provided 60% of British America's exports to Britain before the Revolution. The exports of the British colonies in the West Indies and the American South were overwhelmingly slave produced; 78% of New England's exports and 42% of those of the Middle Colonies went to supply the slave plantations of the British West Indies before the Revolution. The foreign exchange to purchase British goods was earned from the labor of slaves, and it was the American slave who ultimately provided the increased market for the manufactured exports of Great Britain in the eighteenth century.

The importance of this trade can only be established by comparison with an estimate of alternative resource allocations. Whereas the Ricardian view suggests that we ask what the resources embodied in exports would yield if devoted to domestic use, O'Brien and Engerman ask: With lower levels of exports, could internal trade have provided a comparable stimulus for the spread of markets, communications, urbanization, and legal and financial institutions? They doubt it. From the viewpoint of slavery, the appropriate question is: What would have been the economic consequences had immigration from Africa been free instead of coerced and black labor, once here, been voluntarily supplied? What would have been the effective demand in Britain for colonial products if their cost had to be high enough to induce East Anglian farmers to emigrate to perform disciplined labor in the tropics from sunup to sundown? In the context of the vent-for-surplus model, the unutilized land and natural resources were in the western hemisphere; there was little voluntary surplus labor; the institution of slavery supplied the need.

David Richardson presents evidence that wealth and growth in

New England improved markedly around the middle of the eighteenth century, and this improvement coincided with a general upturn in economic activity throughout the entire North Atlantic economy that centered on the expanding trade between Europe and the slave plantation colonies. This buoyant environment, Richardson says, stimulated New England's trade and accelerated its growth.

Richardson bases his conclusions on quantitative estimates of the New England commodity trade and some rough estimates of invisible earnings. New England's imports on a per capita basis did not differ substantially from other colonies' in the eighteenth century, nor did its earnings on exports, if we allow for coastwise trade and invisibles. From Shepherd and Walton's data for 1768 and 1772, it is apparent that New England's imports were dominated by Great Britain. Britain supplied two-thirds of the imports, and the remaining third came mostly from the West Indies. These latter imports made a large contribution to Britain's African and coastwise trade.

The Caribbean dominated New England's exports as much as Great Britain did its imports, and Richardson endorses Samuel Eliot Morison's characterization of the West Indies as the cornerstone of New England's prerevolutionary trade. Richardson documents the marked increase, both in overall and per capita trade, during the third quarter of the eighteenth century. Exports to Africa and southern Europe just barely managed to sustain their per capita levels of 1750, whereas exports to the British West Indies quadrupled. These estimates are not precise, since trade data before 1768 are less reliable. However, Richardson has assembled figures on shipping from Boston, Newport, and Salem that reinforce the general conclusion: In the final twenty-five years of British rule, growth in New England's overseas trade seems to have rested largely on dealings with slave-based economies in the Caribbean.

The shipping and trade statistics understate the importance of the West Indies to New England. Two-thirds of its invisible earnings probably arose from the West Indian trade. In all, New Englanders may have owed as much as 10% of their per capita incomes to commodity and shipping exports to the West Indies on the eve of the Revolution. Whatever annual growth rate in per capita incomes in New England we assume for 1750–75, it is clear that West Indian trade played a large role.

Equally important may be the indirect role of the West Indies in supplying the demand for food from urban New England. In the early eighteenth century New England's food imports were negligible, but a substantial deficit in food grains had arisen by the eve of the Rev olution. The inability of New England farmers to meet the growing demand from the urban classes was offset to some extent by imports from the Middle Colonies, especially New York and Pennsylvania. Richardson argues that New England was able to pay for these imports by shipping West Indian products of sugar, rum, and molasses to the Middle Colonies and the colonies of the Upper South. Richardson concludes, with Klingaman and Shepherd and Williamson, that the slave colonies contributed significantly to supplying the food needs of New England in the second half of the eighteenth century.

David Galenson's chapter looks at the adoption of slavery in the Chesapeake, the first slave economy among Britain's mainland colonies. Chesapeake slavery was securely established in the 1680s, yet slaves were desired by planters from the 1660s. Why the delay? It cannot be explained by changes in the prices of servants or slaves, in planter wealth, in the composition of output, or in production techniques. Galenson points to the likelihood that the increased precision of the legal definition of masters' property rights in slavery of the late 1660s and early 1670s was an important factor in increasing the demand for Africans, thus leading to the large-scale growth of slavery of the 1680s. At that time, changes in the supply conditions of free and slave labor caused a sharp shift to slavery.

The adoption of slavery varied positively with the assets of the plantation owner. Galenson believes that this could be due to imperfections in the credit market, greater ability of large planters to assume risk, and better access of large planters to information. Large planters had less contact with their labor force than small ones, and this may have translated into less reluctance to hire a labor force of a different race.

Jacob Price's chapter offers a rich synthesis of existing scholarship on credit in the slave trade and plantation economies, despite his explicit rejection of such a description. In his own view, his work is just "an explanatory essay suggesting some questions and answers hinted at by our still scrappy evidence."

The abundant land of frontier economies, Price writes, is valueless without capital and labor. An entrepreneur with capital can acquire labor, either of indentured servants or of slaves. In the former case, he lends passage money and is repaid in labor; in the latter, he purchases the slaves and acquires the right to their labor. But the prospects for rapid capital accumulation by entrepreneurial agricultural settlers reinvesting the returns on the labor of existing servants and slaves are not good, and an initial supply of credit would greatly accelerate the development of these regions. Eventually the settlers are able to generate their own capital requirements, for replacement if not for expansion. But, says Price, credit institutions are important, and in the Americas they remained important until the end of slavery.

Price distinguishes three needs for credit: primary credit, for making real capital investment in productive assets; secondary credit, for the transfer of title ownership in existing assets; and tertiary credit, for consumption. The cost of these kinds of credit was an important factor in the working of the plantation economies. Different legal systems evolved different credit institutions, and Price describes a Latin model and an Anglo-Saxon model. The Latin model protects the integrity of the plantation as a working unit and prevents creditors from seizing nonland productive assets like equipment, livestock, and slaves. The Anglo-Saxon model favors the interests of the creditor over those of the plantation unit, and metropolitan interests were usually able to maintain this balance of power over colonial protests that pushed in the direction of the Latin model.

Price begins his survey with the Brazilian experience, an example of the Latin model. He then turns to the British slave trade, first under the Royal African Company and later under independent traders. Finally, he discusses French credit arrangements.

The falling sugar prices of the 1730s induced British planters to seek legislative relief, moving toward the Latin model. The Colonial Debt Act of 1732, which governed debtor–creditor relations until the end of the trade – "truly to be called the Palladium of Colony credit, and the English Merchant's grand security" – provided a uniform system for all colonies in proving accounts for debt litigation and made lands, houses, chattels, and slaves liable for satisfaction of debts due by bond. The 1732 act had brutal implications for slaves; it was offensive to plantation owners, but its effect on the slave trade was probably expansionary rather than restrictive. Price describes the reorientation of the credit institutions of the slave trade after 1732 under the immediate remittance system. His chapter also contains a section on mortgage credit.

Taken together, the chapters in this book describe the evolution of the Atlantic system to which slavery contributed so much. They analyze the transfer of slavery from the Old World to the New (Phillips) and argue that this introduction was not simply fortuitous but resulted from the economic choices available to countries with "free" land (Solow). Subsequent chapters illustrate how the flow of slaves and their products first gave rise to and then integrated the European empires of Portugal (Miller, Alencastro) and Great Britain (Richardson, Galenson, Solow); how a different economic policy delayed

Spain's participation in the system (Knight); and how France's participation developed (Villiers), and was first limited and then "prematurely" ended by, its particular circumstances.

Other chapters bring out the interdependence of the entire Atlantic system as efforts to maintain national exclusivism failed (Emmer): The Dutch were active in Brazil and in the British and French Caribbean; the British were active in the Portuguese empire; British North American colonies traded with the French Caribbean; the Hanse towns were connected to French colonial trade (Emmer, Miller, Clark). The chapters show that the gains from trade were not always distributed to the European power with sovereignty over its colonies, and that returns flowed to providers of goods and services that were determined not by the flag of the imperial power but by economic relations on a broader scale (Miller, Alencastro, Clark). Thus European centers with certain advanced institutions (Price) – the British especially – were in a position to benefit most from the Atlantic system (O'Brien and Engerman), and the provider of slaves, Africa, was perhaps touched least (Eltis).

Finally, from these pages it emerges that the mere existence of imperialism or colonialism does not explain how the metropolis exploited the periphery, as some would have it: It was the coerced labor of African slaves that allowed Europe to benefit so greatly from its conquests in the New World. When we assess the distribution of those benefits, we find that although the race went to the swift, the glittering prize was hammered out by African hands.

CHAPTER 1

Slavery and colonization

BARBARA L. SOLOW

WHEN the elder Hakluyt published his promotional tract for the
North American colonies in 1585, he painted a picture of a thriving
trade in colonial products (woad, oil, wine, hops, salt, flax, hemp,
pitch, tar, clapboards, wainscot, fish, fur, meat, hides, marble, granite, sugar), exchanging for British goods (woolens, hats, bonnets,
knives, fishhooks, copper kettles, beads, looking glasses, and a thousand wrought wares), lowering British unemployment, promoting
manufacturing, and providing advantages to church, crown, and national security. This would require the migration of thirty-one different kinds of skilled workers to America.

If Hakluyt saw any difficulties in achieving this happy state of
affairs, a propaganda tract was not the place to mention them. Certainly, Adam Smith would have seen none. Two centuries later he
wrote, "The colony of a civilized nation which takes possession either
of a waste country, or of one so thinly inhabited, that the natives
easily give place to the new settlers, advances more rapidly to wealth
and greatness than any other society."[1] Yet from the day Hakluyt
wrote until almost the middle of the eighteenth century, economic
growth and progress were barely discernible in the colonies, and the
North Atlantic economy was of negligible importance. It did not develop automatically or in the manner Hakluyt and Smith envisaged.

In Section I of this chapter, I argue that firm and enduring trade
links between Europe and America were not forged without and until
the introduction of slavery; that the eras of privateering, chartered
companies, and the early staple trades were not preludes to development, but rather unpromising beginnings leading to stagnation;
and that colonial development was strongly associated with slavery.
Voluntary labor was slow to immigrate; capital was hard to attract or
generate; promising export crops were slow to emerge; and when
they did, free labor was reluctant to grow them. African slaves pro

[1] Adam Smith, *Wealth of Nations*, ed. Edwin Canaan (New York, 1933), p. 539.

21

vided much of colonial America's labor, attracted a large share of capital investment, accounted for most of the colonial export crops, and (compared with free labor) conferred wealth and income in greater measure on those places and times where slavery was established.

In Section II, I argue that this pattern of development is not adventitious but is explained by the difficulties inherent in colonizing regions where land is relatively cheap and abundant.[2] Placing colonial history in the context of "free" land has a long history: It provides that conceptual framework for the period whose absence is so often deplored by historians. And, as a conceptual framework, it has substantial advantages over the available alternatives, whether older ones like the Imperial School of Charles M. Andrews or contemporary ones suggested by John M. McCusker and Russell R. Menard, Bernard Bailyn, or Jack P. Greene and J. R. Pole.

I

To those who saw colonial development as the inexorable working of the Divine Hand of Providence or the only slightly less Divine Hand of Comparative Advantage, the early period just represented stages of growth, and the repeated failures of colonizing attempts were attributed to ad hoc circumstances. Seeing development as foreordained, and Elizabethan seadogs and Roanoke as stages in an inevitable process, begs the question of providing a conceptual framework that seeks systematically to account for the timing and pattern of growth.

The privateering attacks on Spain, launched by the French, English, and Dutch from the early sixteenth century, have been portrayed as the first stage in developing the Atlantic system and as the opening battle in a war for command of the seas in order to exploit the new discoveries of the western hemisphere. This is an exaggerated Atlantic-centric view. It has been shown that such an interpretation, for example, of the Anglo-Spanish wars, pales before Philip II's interest in crushing heresy and rebellion in northern Europe.[3] Priva-

---

[2] This formulation begs the question of how lands became "cheap and abundant." The process of emptying land by the near extirpation of the indigenous population, by disease, by disintegration of their social and environmental fabric, and by dispossession is an ongoing part of the history of these regions.

[3] R. B. Wernham, *Before the Armada* (London, 1966), pp. 354, 367–8, quoted in K. G. Davies, *The North Atlantic World in the Seventeenth Century* (Minneapolis, 1974), p. 27. Davies's book is an indispensable source, and I am deeply indebted to it.

The harmful effects of European Privateering

teering is better understood less as a prelude to colonization than as an alternative to it. Privateering robs Peter to pay Paul: Whatever the Dutch or French or English gained, the Spanish lost. Worse than a zero-sum game, privateering invites retaliation, increases risk, and discourages settlement and economic activity, which depend upon security from international lawlessness. More plausibly, English governmental policy in the Caribbean turned from encouraging privateering to opposing it when settlement began to promise dividends.

With the notable exception of Massachusetts Bay, chartered companies – Dutch, French, English – failed to found settlements in the Americas. To treat these failures as due to "adverse winds," to having settlers "not of the right stuff," "lack of tenacity," "poor leadership," or "lack of supplies," is to miss the essential difficulties of providing men and capital for colonies under the prevailing economic conditions, which persistence and leadership could not easily overcome. The success of the Massachusetts Bay Colony rested on the strength of its noneconomic motives. The "lack of initiative and vitality" explanation of French colonization does not go far to explain the failure in Canada and the success in the French West Indies.

It is hard to accept that English chartered companies fared badly in America for lack of know-how and entrepreneurial skill when they were demonstrably successful in trading to the Baltic, the North Sea, and the Mediterranean. Here, with abundant land, no labor supply, and no export crop, there would be no surplus for the company. Neither governments nor capitalists were willing indefinitely to invest large sums in colonies under these conditions. The history of failed settlements may thus be more instructive than the history of successes. "Only a small fraction of white immigrants reached the New World under the aegis and at the expense of chartered companies. . . . The age of company-promoted white emigration from Europe was short, over with a few exceptions by the middle of the sixteenth century."[4]

Thus, voluntary settlement for economic reasons was not forthcoming on a large scale in the English colonies or, for that matter, in those of Spain, Portugal, France, or Holland. If settlers came for noneconomic reasons, their progress would be strongly affected by their ability to develop exports and attract capital. But where European demand for American exports *was* forthcoming – for fish, fur, tobacco, and timber – colonial settlement was scarcely more successful.

McCusker and Menard give an excellent description of the theory

[4] Davies, p. 96.

that holds that colonial growth was grounded in the export of certain staple commodities. It is worth quoting at length:[5]

Colonization begins with an increase in demand for staples in the metropolis. ... Given the limited metropolitan supply of natural resources, burgeoning demand produces a sharp jump in staple prices. Those higher prices absorb the high costs of colonial enterprise, raise the rate of return, overcome fears, and increase the incentive to colonize. Capital and labor migrate to the new region, the staple commodity is produced, and trade begins. The metropolis imports the staple and exports manufactures to satisfy the needs of the emigrants. It also exports still more capital and labor to further increase supplies of the commodity.

In McCusker and Menard's version of the theory, equilibrium states are followed by repeated growth cycles, based on new demand shifts or discovery of new staples, thereby continually increasing the size of the colonial economy.

The staple theory story depends upon shifts and elasticity of demand and on the production characteristics of the staple. The European demand for fur and tobacco was inelastic, for timber limited, and the production characteristics of fur and fish made them the enemies, not the progenitors, of settlement.

Overproduction crises plagued tobacco production from the first. Colonial tobacco had to be protected by banning cultivation in Europe. Neither the British nor the French West Indies prospered in the tobacco era, and supply restrictions were enacted well before the middle of the seventeenth century. As Governor Culpeper of Virginia wrote in 1681, "Our thriving is our undoing."[6] The period of growing tobacco exclusively with free labor ended after 1680.

When the demand for tobacco rose after some decades of stagnation, it came not from England but from the continent. Colonial production for this reexport trade responded extraordinarily; it is associated with the spread of slave labor and large plantations. Toward midcentury, tobacco lost its dominance as both great planters and small producers began to diversify into wheat and cattle. Tobacco, which once accounted for almost all the exports of the Lower South, fell to less than 75% well before the end of the eighteenth century. As a share of total agricultural production, it was even lower. This staple was weak; with a free labor force it was even weaker.

---

[5] John J. McCusker and Russell R. Menard, *The Economy of British America, 1607–1789* (Chapel Hill, 1985), pp. 21–2.
[6] Quoted in Davies, p. 176.

Fur also suffered from inelastic demand. Before the end of the seventeenth century, beaver flooded Europe in quantities that could not be absorbed at the going price. Quite independent of the state of demand, the fur trade represented the antithesis of settlement. Beaver is not highly reproductive and does not migrate. Once the beaver was exhausted in a locality, the hunters had to move on. Although furs were important to the Pilgrims and Puritans and the early settlers of Virginia, gradually the area east of the Appalachians became denuded of furs. Canadian fur interests reached the Pacific well before the end of the eighteenth century. The fur trade represented dispersion par excellence. In fact, the fur trade drew men away from farming and settled agriculture.

So long as easy prey were available, fur "production" was carried on by hunter-gatherer techniques, not in settled societies. The Hudson's Bay Company, a profitable enterprise over the long run, exemplifies trade without settlement in the clearest way. The company consisted of a handful of Scots and English in stockaded forts, who dealt with the Indians, served a tour of duty, and rotated back home. The French too understood that, left alone, fur trading would never result in settlement. It was this conviction that impelled the French minister Colbert to adopt a policy of subsidizing colonization by granting monopolies in return for the promise to colonize. French companies conducted a losing struggle to centralize fur trading at Montreal and Quebec: Only then could they collect the revenue to repay the crown for their privilege and make a profit. The traders, of course, wanted freedom to find the best market: It was hard to squeeze monopoly profits out of them without coercion.

Fisheries is another unlikely candidate for initiating settlement. The fishermen of England's West Country managed the industry without settlement and opposed it bitterly. As in the French case, the early colonizing interests were courtiers who sought proprietary monopolies. They could get returns on their investment only by licensing and taxing fishermen. Of course, fishermen would not volunteer for that. Without coercion they would not form settled colonies any more than the coureur de bois would. Only a few thousand people lived in Newfoundland in the eighteenth century; until then there was some doubt about whether it was, strictly speaking, an English colony. Newfoundland had no Anglican church until 1701, no justice of the peace until 1729, and no grammar school until 1799. "The settlement existed largely to serve vessels that came from Europe to buy fish, and became completely dependent on New England for its rum and provisions."[7] If settlers already were established, fish could be an important staple if indeed there was a market for it.

The abundance of timber in America was an important colonial resource. Wood was an especially valuable raw material in preindustrial economies, but American timber products failed to become a major export to Europe because of heavy transport costs. These products benefited from the English wartime demand for ships and masts; generally, however, Baltic supplies dominated the market. American wood products, including ships, faced the same problem fisheries did: There were strict limits on direct trade to Europe because of cheaper alternative European sources of supply. As we shall see, given a closer market, these products (and the services ships could provide) would enter trade on a much larger scale.

Thus neither brigands nor merchants succeeded in founding a permanent colonial economy, and the existence of staple crops was not a sufficient condition for development – though, as McCusker and Menard have persuasively shown, perhaps it can be regarded as necessary for rapid growth.

The reluctance of Europeans to migrate to the western hemisphere is well documented. David Eltis has estimated that down to about 1820, four or perhaps even five Africans were brought here for every European who came, and not until 1840 did European arrivals permanently surpass African. In terms of immigration, Eltis remarks, the Americas were an extension of Africa rather than Europe until the late nineteenth century.[8]

Building on the work of Gemery and Galenson, Stanley Engerman notes that in British North America, two slaves arrived for each white immigrant before the American Revolution. The mainland colonies below the Mason-Dixon line received two-thirds of all mainland white immigrants and nineteen-twentieths of all mainland black slaves. Two-thirds of these southern white immigrants came as indentured laborers.[9] The flow of transported convicts, vagrants, and defeated rebels has fallen beneath the notice of historians until recently; some estimates of convicts go as high as 50,000 for 1718–75.[10] How many

---

[7] Davies, pp. 165–6, and Ralph Davis, *The Rise of the Atlantic Economies* (Ithaca, N.Y., 1973), p. 272.

[8] David Eltis, "Free and Coerced Transatlantic Migrations: Some Comparisons," *American Historical Review*, Vol. 88, No. 2 (1983), p. 255.

[9] Stanley L. Engerman, "Slavery and Emancipation in Comparative Perspective: A Look at Some Recent Debates," *Journal of Economic History*, Vol. XLVI, No. 2 (1986), p. 320.

[10] Bernard Bailyn, *Voyagers to the West: A Passage in the Peopling of America on the Eve of the Revolution* (New York, 1987), p. 294.

indentured laborers were kidnapped or shanghaied or lured by fraud will never be accurately known. But it is clear that only in exceptional circumstances did large numbers of Europeans desire to emigrate in the colonial period.

There is no direct relation between migration and population, of course, since natural increase intervenes. Nor is there a one-to-one correlation between population and labor force, since participation rates and hours worked must be taken into account. And there is no one-to-one correlation between labor inputs and development, since capital, technology, industrial organization, and the division of labor must all be considered. In this wider context, the significance of slavery becomes even more evident.

In 1650, of the nearly 100,000 colonists in British America, there were about 16,200 slaves, all but 1,200 in the British West Indies. The mainland colonies were 97% white and the islands 75% white. By 1750 the mainland colonies were 80% white and the islands only 16% white.[11] If we calculate the percentage rate of population growth per decade from 1650 to 1770, we observe the relative blackening of the colonial labor force. The growth rate of the black population exceeded that of the white one for every decade from 1650 to 1750, with two exceptions, 1710–30 and 1720–30, when slave rates were unusually, low. In 1750–60, the white population grew faster than the black one; in 1760–70 they were about equal; only in the (wartime) decade 1770–80 did white rates decisively pull ahead (Table 1).

The blackening of the labor force exceeded the blackening of the population. Participation rates of slaves were higher than those of free whites because of the participation of women and children (among other reasons); slaves worked longer seasons and longer hours, on average, than whites. We know this from direct observation and from the dramatic shift in the labor supply after emancipation, when free blacks had some control over their participation rates and supply of labor.

With an assured labor supply and the emergence of a dependable staple crop, Europeans began to send capital and organize production in America, and the colonies began to grow faster. The staple was sugar. "After 1660 England's sugar imports always exceeded its combined imports of all other colonial produce; in 1774 sugar made up just half of all French imports from her West Indian colonies; over the colonial period as a whole more than half of Brazil's exports of goods were sugar. Sugar made up almost a fifth of the whole English

[11] For fuller discussion, see McCusker and Menard, chap. 10; Davis, chap. 8.

Barbara L. Solow

Table 1. *Percentage growth rate per decade of black and white populations in British North America*

	Black	White
1650–60	122.8	32.3
1660–70	54.8	41.2
1670–80	47.9	19.9
1680–90	33.7	26.0
1690–1700	23.1	16.8
1700–10	53.6	19.7
1710–20	12.0	37.1
1720–30	23.0	31.7
1730–40	42.1	34.1
1740–50	31.2	22.8
1750–60	28.6	35.0
1760–70	29.0	30.7
1770–80	18.8	29.0

Source: Calculated from McCusker and Menard, Tables 5.1, 6.4, 7.2, 8.1, and 9.4, with the assistance of Rebecca M. Solow.

import bill in 1774, far surpassing the share of any other commodity." Already by 1668–9, London's sugar imports exceeded tobacco's by £300,000 to £225,000, and by 1700 sugar imports into England and Wales were twice the value of tobacco.[12]

If the demand for sugar had the characteristics that made a successful staple, were slaves required to produce it? There is no inherent reason why export-led growth is associated with plantation slavery: Small holders in West Africa produced most of the world's cocoa crop; small Burmese peasants supplied rice to much of Southeast Asia; the wheat of Canada and the wool of Australia were produced on family farms; but these crops came much later. Sugar had production characteristics that gave slave labor enormous cost advantages over free labor. (The same holds true for colonial rice and indigo. For tobacco and coffee the situation is more complicated and slavery's advantages are less marked.) Thus, the importance of slaves in America was not only that they could be coerced into coming when free labor did not, but when they came they did different things. More of them worked, they worked longer, they could not disperse, they attracted investment, and they produced crops for trade and export on a scale unmatched by free labor. The commodity exports of Britain's American

[12] Davis, p. 251; Davies, p. 312.

Table 2. *Share of slave colonies in average annual value of commodity exports from British America, 1768–72 (£ sterling)*

Total exports		Percent produced by slave labor	Percent exported to slave colonies
British West Indies	3,910.6	Nearly 100	
Upper South	1,046.9	Est. 50	
Lower South	551.9	75	
Middle Colonies	526.5		42
New England	439.1		78
	6,475.0		

Source: Calculated from McCusker and Menard, Tables 5.2, 6.1, 8.2, and 9.3. Canada's small share has been omitted.

colonies were to a remarkable extent either the outputs of or the inputs into slave colonies (Table 2).

Slave-grown sugar provided 60% of British America's commodity exports. If two-thirds of tobacco exports were slave-grown, the share of slave crops in commodity exports rises to over 78%. New England sent 78% of its exports to the West Indies. These colonies provided the market for 42% of the exports of the Middle Colonies and 32% of the nontobacco exports of the Upper South. Without slaves, what would American exports and American markets have amounted to? Without slaves, what would American growth and income have amounted to?

We cannot answer precisely, because we have no reliable estimates of colonial growth rates. Lacking data, income has been estimated by indirection, deduction, and shrewd guesses. Wealth estimates have a firmer foundation. They show that regional variations in wealth are associated with the ownership of slaves. McCusker and Menard have summarized the wealth profile of free whites in 1770–5 in Table 3.

This table seriously understates the share of the British West Indies in the total. Jamaica alone, with a free white population of 15,000, is included; but the total free white population of the West Indian colonies was three times that number in 1770 (McCusker and Menard, p. 54). In 1770 the Leewards and Barbados combined to produce nearly as much sugar as Jamaica. If Jamaica represented two-thirds of the West Indian wealth, the relatively few free whites of the British West Indies would have held more wealth than the New Englanders and perhaps as much as the Middle colonists. The southern colonies held over half the total colonial wealth.

The views on colonial income growth are divided. Pessimists argue

Table 3. *Wealth per free white person in British America, ca. 1770–5*
(£ sterling)

Region	Net worth per free white	Total
Continental colonies (1774)	£74	
New England	33	£19,000,000
Middle Colonies	51	30,000,000
Upper and Lower South	132	86,100,000
West Indies (1771–5)		
Jamaica	1,200	18,000,000
	15	

Source: For footnotes and explanation, see McCusker and Menard, p. 61.

that urban and rural poverty were both increasing over the eighteenth
century. Some direct evidence on urban poverty has been offered for
Boston, New York, and Philadelphia. For rural areas, strongly rising
incomes are hard to imagine, whether we visualize immobile colonists, causing overpopulation and diminishing returns, or mobile colonists, replicating their farms on the frontiers. Some rural poor turned
not to the frontier but to vagabondage; some moved to urban centers,
depressing incomes there even further. To the extent that there *was*
a safety valve, it only prevented incomes from falling further. A leading pessimist quotes approvingly the conclusion of Terry Anderson:
"during the first eight decades of the eighteenth century, agricultural
productivity declined [and] real wealth per capita stagnated."[13]

Optimists point to evidence that over this period colonial consumption patterns show marked improvement. From midcentury, the
colonies imported a wide range of English manufactured and semi-
manufactured goods, which were turning up increasingly in probate
inventories north and south. In fact, the colonies were an even more
important market for these "baubles of Britain," as T. M. Breen has
called them, than the British domestic market.[14]

In a recent article, Main and Main have tried, for New England, to
reconcile these improved consumption patterns with the lack of evidence for overall growth in consumption (as measured by the value

[13] For a good exposition of the pessimist view, from which this quotation is taken, see
Billy G. Smith, "Poverty and Economic Marginality in Eighteenth-Century America,"
Proceedings of the American Philosophical Society, Vol. 132, No. 1 (1988), pp.
85–117.
[14] T. H. Breen, "'Baubles of Britain': The American and Consumer Revolutions of the
Eighteenth Century," *Past and Present*, No. 119 (1988), pp. 73–104.

of probate inventories). They argue "that changes in the makeup of these [consumption] goods constitute an improvement in their material standard of living separate from, and additional to, the growth in total estate value."[15] This improved market basket does indeed argue for increased welfare. Main and Main measure the improvement by using an "index of amenities" devised by Carr and Walsh. The inclusion of imported foods, forks, coarse and fine earthenware, linen, silverware, religious and secular books, timepieces, wigs, and pictures in inventories is taken to show increased economic welfare, independently of total consumption estimates.

These amenities must be investigated further. What share of them did the colonies produce? What proportion was imported? If a large share was imported, how were they paid for? This brings us back by another route to the role of slavery. The tea, coffee, sugar, earthenware, linen, silver, books, clocks, and other miscellaneous manufactures the colonists began to consume were not all produced in the colonies; some were imported. Imports had to be paid for by exports, and we know how crucial slave labor was to colonial exports.

McCusker and Menard believe that colonial income growth probably occurred in two spurts. The first took place at the onset of settlement as farms were established in the wilderness; the second, "less pronounced and perhaps less uniform in the several major regions, began during the 1740s and lasted to the Revolution . . . this second period can be attributed to a burgeoning metropolitan demand for American products, although more-strictly internal processes that reflected a widening market also played a role."[16] The metropolitan demand, we have seen, was mostly for slave-grown products; for some regions, the burgeoning demand was from the West Indian slave colonies.

If we disaggregate and consider the colonies one at a time, slavery looms even larger. In the seventeenth century, Barbados in the Caribbean and Virginia on the mainland were the only colonies of continuous progress. Barbados did not thrive until the sugar–slave era; indeed, no British West Indian colony ever founded a successful society on the basis of free white labor. Virginia was a precarious case of touch-and-go until the tobacco settlement was made. The spread of tobacco merely underlined the hopelessness of establishing a colony on the basis of glass, iron, potash, and wine. Maryland too was

[15] Gloria L. Main and Jackson T. Main, "Economic Growth and the Standard of Living in Southern New England, 1660–1774," *Journal of Economic History*, Vol. XLVIII, No. 1 (1988), pp. 27–46.
[16] McCusker and Menard, pp. 60, 268–9.

poor and thinly populated before tobacco production began. The years of growing tobacco exclusively with indentured white labor were not destined to be many.

If we want to visualize Massachusetts without Boston and its commodity and shipping trade to the West Indies, or Rhode Island without Newport and its slave and rum trade to Africa and the islands, we need only look at Connecticut:[17]

> ... during the colonial period Connecticut never developed any single center of mercantile and trading interest to compare with Boston or Newport.... The inhabitants of the towns were more or less isolated, their energies were centered largely upon their own agricultural pursuits, and their lives were in the main peaceful and undisturbed.... Connecticut stands alone, in a class by herself, as something unique among the British colonies of the New World – a small, slow-moving agricultural settlement, occupying but a tiny part of the earth's surface, largely isolated from the main currents of English and colonial life....

In the eighteenth century, Connecticut, with no banks, no credit, a money shortage so severe that salaries, rates, and taxes were paid in kind, exports few, agriculture primitive and unremunerative, contained 150,000 people in seventy towns that remained substantially without industry as late as 1818.[18]

Similarly, South Carolina and Georgia looked different the minute slave crops appeared. If we want to visualize the Lower South without rice, indigo, and Sea Island cotton, we should think of the backward mixed farms of North Carolina.

Billy G. Smith has written that "Some historians, astigmatised by notions of the shortage of labor, the abundance of natural resources, and the general affluence of early America, have not seen much poverty."[19] They have been "astigmatised" by notions like Hakluyt's and Adam Smith's that development would be quick and easy.

II

Adam Smith's optimism rested on the "cheapness and plenty of good land." In settled countries rent and profits eat up wages, but not here. The colonist pays no rent and trifling taxes. He can easily acquire more land than he can cultivate. Indeed, "he can seldom make it

---

[17] Charles M. Andrews, *Our Earliest Colonial Settlements: Their Diversities of Origin and Later Characteristics* (Ithaca, N.Y., 1933), pp. 117–18.
[18] Andrews, pp. 127–9.
[19] Billy G. Smith, p. 108.

produce the tenth part of what it is capable of producing." He will quickly collect laborers and, though wages are high, he will be able to pay them. Of course, his laborers will soon leave him and move on to acquire their own land. Admitting the difficulties of keeping labor, Adam Smith ignores the problem of obtaining it. If rent eats up wages in settled lands, will not wages eat up rent in unsettled ones? The cheaper and more plentiful the land, the harder it is to get the labor; in the limit, it is impossible.

Adam Smith was not really interested in the theory of colonial growth. His concern was the virtues of laissez-faire, and in this connection he wanted to show that the gains from the colonies were overborne by the losses inflicted by a mercantilist commercial policy. In fact, until the Colonial Reform movement of the late 1820s, most British writing on colonization was confined to the effects on the mother country and was not concerned with the growth of the colony. The father of the Colonial Reform movement and the pioneer thinker on colonial development was Edward Gibbon Wakefield.[20]

Wakefield turned Adam Smith upside down. Free land did not cause colonial prosperity; it prevented it. Wakefield had ample leisure to reflect. He spent three years in Newgate jail for kidnapping an heiress. Transportation of convicts, colonization, and capital punishment were no doubt prominent subjects of discussion in Newgate, and Wakefield formed strong views on all three. In 1829 he set some of them forth (anonymously) in *A Letter from Sydney*, purporting to come from Australia but actually originating in Newgate.[21]

Wakefield portrayed himself as a well-to-do Englishman who emigrated to Australia with sizable capital. He planned to buy an estate, build a house for himself, surround it with parks and pleasure grounds, and let the rest of his acreage to tenants, for whom he would also build houses and supply working capital as an English landlord does. He brought 20,000 acres of land for less than 2 shillings an acre. The timber that had to be cleared would have fetched £150,000 in England, but for lack of available labor in Australia, the standing timber represented a deadweight loss of £15,000. The absence of labor, of roads, and of towns and markets rendered his coal and mineral deposits valueless, but at least "being under the surface they can do me no harm. An estate of 20,000 acres, containing rich mines of coal

---

[20] For an excellent discussion of British economic thought on the colonies in the nineteenth century see Donald Winch, *Classical Political Economy and Colonies* (London, 1965).

[21] Edward Gibbon Wakefield, *A Letter from Sydney* in M. F. Lloyd Prichard (ed.), *Collected Works* (Auckland, 1969).

and iron, and covered with magnificent timber, is, no doubt, a very good thing in some countries; but here you will lose money by such a possession."[22] When he tried to sell the estate, people laughed; they could get crown grants at 6 d. an acre.

Abandoning his dream of becoming a landed proprietor, he had to try his hand at farming. The servants he brought from England decamped. He supplied their lack with convicts. They lost his sheep and stole his effects. He called a constable and had them arrested and jailed. He called for their release the next day; it was harvest time. Disillusioned with convicts, he sent to his estate in England for shepherds, cowmen, carpenters, and blacksmiths. He paid their passage and promised them wages. The skilled left for higher pay in Sydney; the rest, in a period of two years, saved enough to stock a small farm and, one by one, departed. He ended in a small house in Sydney, paying twice the rent for half as good a house as he could have had in an English provincial town, living off the returns from his English capital and the pitiful proceeds of the sale of his 20,000 acres.

Countries with abundant cheap land will stagnate, not grow, concludes Wakefield. A poor English farmer can better himself by going to Australia (if he can afford the passage): Higher incomes are to be had, but only as a return to labor. The mere immigration of such people will not ensure economic growth. The immigrants will just replicate their family-sized farms across the vast landscape. Division of labor will be retarded. The surplus of such farms will be small, and there will be difficulties in marketing it. Potential returns to capital *would* be great – rates of return would exceed those current in England – but they cannot be realized without the supply of labor to capitalist landlords that is not forthcoming. No man will willingly continue to share the fruits of his labor with another if he can capture them all for himself.

In Australian conditions, people with capital cannot get labor, few people will come voluntarily, and people with labor who do come cannot easily accumulate or attract capital. "If for every acre of land that may be appropriated here, there should be a conviction for felony in England, our prosperity would rest on a solid basis, but, however earnestly we may desire it, we cannot expect that the increase of crime will keep pace with the spread of colonization," he tells us. "I began to hanker after what, till then, I had considered the worst of human ills – the institution of slavery."[23]

---

[22] Ibid., p. 103.
[23] Quoted in Winch, p. 95; Wakefield, p. 112.

Wakefield understood that the significance of slavery was not that a black labor supply would substitute for a white one, but that slavery under certain circumstances was the sole source of a permanent supply of labor to landlords and the sole source of a sizable accumulation of capital:

What was the sole cause of the revival of slavery by Christians, but the discovery of waste countries, and the disproportion which has ever since existed in those countries between the demand and supply of labor? And what is it that increases the number of slaves of Christian masters, but the increase of Christian capitalists wanting laborers, by the spreading of Christian people over regions heretofore waste?[24]

Wakefield did not, of course, justify slavery but only sought to explain it. His solution to the free land problem was for governments to price land grants and thus prevent the evils of dispersion, lack of markets, and labor and capital shortages. The difficulties of that solution and the history of the Colonial Reform movement are not part of our concern here.

Marx devoted a chapter to Wakefield in *Das Kapital*.[25] He understood well what he and Wakefield had in common: Both believed that capital accumulation depended on the private ownership of the means of production. In Marx, this privatization comes about in the transition from feudalism to capitalism, when landlords first acquire property rights in their estates and the power to exclude laborers from them. In America, such property rights exist legally, but because of the extent of land, they are valueless. Both in feudalism and in America, the lack of (valuable) property rights in land means that there is no source of surplus for investment. Modern economists recognize this as a description of the common property case, where all surplus is dissipated and there is an inefficient allocation of resources.

Wakefield's insights passed into the corpus of classical economics and are probably the origin of the idea, also associated with Merivale, that once empty lands are occupied, slavery will cease. Similar ideas appear in the German historical school and in the work of ethnographers, notably the Dutchman H. J. Nieboer. The modern statement is due to E. D. Domar, who came to the free land formulation from the side of Russian, not American or Australian, history.[26]

---

[24] Wakefield, p. 113.

[25] Karl Marx, *Capital: A Critique of Political Economy* (Chicago, 1906), chap. XXXIII, "The Modern Theory of Colonization," pp. 850–66. See also H. U. Pappe, "Wakefield and Marx," *Economic History Review*, 2nd Series, Vol. IV, No. 1 (1951), pp. 88–97.

[26] Evsey D. Domar, "The Causes of Slavery or Serfdom: A Hypothesis," *Journal of Economic History*, Vol. XXX, No. 1 (February 1970), pp. 18–32. Models of economic development with unlimited supplies of labor exist and have even won a Nobel

Domar presented a simple economic model of an economy with two factors of production, land and labor. He considered two cases: the first where land is limited, the second where land is unlimited. If land is fixed and additional units of labor are added, the resulting additions to output will eventually fall. The landowner will hire labor so long as the output produced by the last laborer hired is greater than the wage he commands. This output produced by the last laborer is less than the average output produced per laborer because of the operation of diminishing returns. Thus the landlord receives the proceeds (revenue) of the average product times the number of laborers, but he incurs as costs only the (lower) marginal product times the number of laborers. The surplus accrues as rent to the landlord.

In the case of unlimited land, as additional units of labor are added, there is no tendency toward diminishing returns. For every laborer there is a plot of land, and the first and last laborers produce the same product. The average product equals the marginal product. In this case, the landlord will find that after he has paid his laborers, there is nothing left over for him. Why would anyone go to work for anybody else if by so doing he earns less than he could on his own? If the landlord pays him what he would earn on his own, there is nothing left over for the rent.

The consequence of this simple model is that where land is free, there will never be a supply of hired labor. If anyone works for someone else, it is by coercion. Free land societies – where the assumptions hold – have either a population of owner-occupied farms or a landed aristocracy and slaves: Of the three elements of this simple agricultural society, Free Land, Free Labor, and a Landowning Aristocracy, only two but not all three will occur. This is the conclusion Domar draws. He does not presume to explain why slavery occurs: Whether slavery is profitable depends on costs and productivity; and whether slavery is introduced depends on the political decision of the state, and this decision, in turn, depends on a host of other factors. Domar is merely pointing to a set of conditions under certain assumptions with certain

Prize, but there is very little literature on the topic of unlimited supplies of land. The exceptions deal mostly in special cases. Cf. Robert E. Baldwin, "Patterns of Development in Newly Settled Regions," *Manchester School of Economic and Social Studies*, Vol. 22 (May 1954), pp. 161–79; Bent Hansen, "Colonial Economic Development with Unlimited Supplies of Land: A Ricardian Case," *Economic Development and Cultural Change*, Vol. 27, No. 4 (1979), pp. 611–27; Gerald K. Helleiner, "Typology in Development Theory: The Land Supplies Economy (Nigeria)," *Food Research Institute Studies* (1966). See also G. S. Callender, "The Early Transportation and Banking Enterprises of the States in Relation to the Growth of Corporations," *Quarterly Journal of Economics*, Vol. XVII, No. 3 (1902), pp. 111–62.

outcomes and asking us to consider why people will or will not work for other people.

It should go without saying that Domar's model is an abstraction, devised to capture central tendencies, and not a literal reproduction of reality. Land was not literally free. Land having differential fertility or locational characteristics will always command a rent. If the economy depends upon sizable inputs of capital, the model's simple conclusions do not follow. There certainly were positive rents and tenant farmers in colonial America, but the *essential* nature of the northern colonies was not that of a landed aristocracy and tenant farmers, and the *essential* nature of the southern and West Indian colonies was not that of a free white labor force.

The hypothesis has been around for a long time, Domar concludes; why not invite it in?

The first reason to invite it in is that it provides a framework for explaining the choice of social and economic organization that is neither deterministic, simplistic, nor unicausal. Criticisms of the free land approach have been based on substantial misunderstanding. Slavery is not *caused by* free land. Where land is free, slavery *may or may not* be more profitable than free labor. This depends on the costs and productivity of both kinds of labor and will vary at different times, in different places, and with respect to different crops. If slavery is more profitable, it *may or may not* be adopted; even if profitably established, it *may or may not* be abolished. These choices depend on human decisions shaped by political, social, and ideological as well as economic factors. If the assumptions of the model cease to hold, its usefulness is diminished. The advantage of the free land framework is that it points us to those factors that influence the choice of economic and social organization, and these factors, in turn, help explain why at certain times and in certain places such societies choose free or slave labor and what are the consequences of the choice. The free land framework does a better job of explaining the course, pace, and nature of British colonial history than the alternatives.

Grounding American exceptionalism in abundant land explains *simultaneously* Turner's frontier and Genovese's South, Jefferson's vision of yeoman agriculture and states' rights and Hamilton's of an industrial society and government intervention. To Jefferson, abundant land meant true democracy: It is the "immensity of land" that enables Americans to avoid the dependence on others that results in "subservience and venality, suffocates the germ of virtue, and prepares fit tools for the design of ambition." Alternatively, the "immensity of land" requires a tariff (or other intervention) to encourage industrialization and prevent the factor combination of cheap land and high wages from keeping America agricultural indefinitely. Wakefield put it succinctly: In the North the tariff, and in the South slavery, prevent America from becoming Jefferson's republic of independent yeomen, a republic that would be incapable of rapid economic development.[27]

Finally, the free land framework directs us to fruitful comparisons among other regions of the world in the same situation. We can understand the relation of the coureur de bois to the Brazilian *bandeirante*, between the American pioneer and the South African trekker, between the Argentine rancher and the Australian sheep farmer, between the American slave and the Australian convict, between the failed Swan River enterprise and the failed East Florida enterprise. The appearance in recent years of books comparing South African slavery with American slavery, the South African frontier with the American frontier, Russian serfdom with American slavery, and Brazilian racism with American racism make the same point: These comparisons are fruitful and enlightening because the free land framework is common to them all. Outcomes differ, but the comparisons are not between apples and oranges but rather between two kinds of apple tree that grow in different ways.

In sum, if we define as the central question of colonial history: "By what methods did Europeans solve the problem of exploiting overseas conquests in regions with abundant land?," we improve our understanding of the peopling and development of colonial British America (and of Latin America, South Africa, Canada, Australia, and New Zealand as well).

Consider briefly the alternative conceptual frameworks that have been offered for the colonial period.[28]

The literature on the economic history of early British America contains two distinct but poorly specified and even contradictory models concerning the relationship between the growth of population and the development of the economy. According to one model, population growth, by expanding the size of the domestic market, permitted specialization, the division of labor,

---

[27] Cf. Wakefield, *England and America*, in *Collected Works*, p. 496 n. "New Orleans is a great market because of slavery; Galena, because of the tariff." For a fuller interpretation of the relation between free land and American political and economic development in the postcolonial period, see the interesting paper by Peter Temin, "Free Land and Federalism: American Economic Exceptionalism," Working Paper No. 481, Department of Economics, Massachusetts Institute of Technology, February 1988.

[28] McCusker and Menard, p. 255. Their dismissal of the free land approach is found on p. 239.

and the capture of various scale economies in the distribution of goods and services and thus promoted development. On the other hand, a classic Malthusian argument is often invoked to describe a process in which population increase pressed against the local resource base and led to diminished yields, falling incomes, declining prospects, and growing inequality, tendencies only partially checked by movements to the frontier.

As McCusker and Menard point out, these interpretations cannot both be right; in fact, neither is helpful. We had indeed colonial development, but not in the way the first suggests and not entirely prevented by the process the second describes.

Consider next an older school of colonial history in the words of its distinguished proponent:[29]

The men who founded the colonies were Englishmen, the incentives that impelled them to migrate were English in their origin, and the forms of colonial life and government they set up were reproductions or modifications of institutions already established and conditions already prevailing in one way or another at home.

The men who founded the colonies were not all Englishmen; they were not all European; they were not even all men. The incentives of slaves were neither English nor exigent. The forms of colonial life were not modifications or reproductions of the landlord–tenant aristocratic manorial agricultural system so widespread in seventeenth- and eighteenth-century England – attempts to reproduce that tenure system failed – but consisted of either family farms or plantations, neither of which prevailed at home and one of which was unknown.

Only by viewing the peopling of America as a white Diaspora can we see the transatlantic flow of peoples merely as "an extension outward and an expansion in scale of domestic mobility in the lands of the immigrants' origins" and the form of transatlantic life just as "an exotic far western periphery, a marchland of the metropolitan European cultural system."[30] It will not rescue such conceptual frameworks to add a separate but equal account of a black Diaspora, for the effects of the two flows are not additive but interdependent.

Sustaining old myths requires the invisibility of slavery, and the invisibility of slavery inhibits the development of a better framework for colonial history. Consider next the thoughtful historiographical chapter by Greene and Pole on "Reconstructing British-American Colonial History," which introduces a volume of distinguished essays

---

[29] Andrews, p. v.
[30] Bernard Bailyn, *The Peopling of British North America* (New York, 1987), propositions 1 and 3.

on the colonial period. In this chapter, the word "slaves" appears just once, the word "slavery" not at all; the subject is not discussed.[31]

The foundation of a satisfactory framework for colonial history, say Greene and Pole, must be based on regional differences. They identify five (or seven) regions and consider several typologies: island versus continental colonies; southern versus northern colonies; settlement versus exploitation colonies; and farm versus plantation colonies (they prefer the last). If these regions are to be gathered into one comprehensive scheme, they must exhibit significant similarities. Greene and Pole suggest five: (1) each region began as a new society with a common problem of organizing social, political, and economic institutions; (2) each was tied to the Atlantic trading network; (3) all were multiracial and multiethnic; (4) all were characterized by exploitation of the environment and of the peoples living in them; (5) all bore a colonial relation to Great Britain.

The heart of the Greene and Pole approach can be conveyed by the following:[32]

> ... they were all cultural provinces of Britain whose legal and social systems, perceptual frameworks, and social and cultural imperatives were inevitably in large measure British in origin and whose inhabitants thereby shared a common identity as British peoples living in America. ... Arguably the most important similarity among the several regions of colonial British America, this common identity imposed upon British Americans in all regions a common set of expectations for their new societies, which they looked upon not merely as vehicles for their own sustenance and enrichment but also as places that would eventually be recognizable approximations of Albion itself. They thus came to the New World expecting, not to create something wholly new, but, insofar as possible, to recreate what they had left behind, albeit without some of its less desirable aspects. Their expectation, their hope, was that the simple societies with which they began would in time develop into complex, improved, and civilized societies as those terms were defined by their metropolitan inheritance.

All the regions in Greene and Pole's scheme, with the common characteristics just identified, are described as having gone through three phases: first, of social simplification of inherited forms; next, of social elaboration of these forms along demonstrably English lines

---

[31] Jack P. Greene and J. R. Pole (eds.), *Colonial British America: Essays in the New History of the Early Modern Era* (Baltimore, 1984). Greene and Pole's failure to deal with slavery is remarkable in view of the inclusion of several of the papers in their volume that deal with the subject, especially those of Richard B. Sheridan, Richard S. Dunn, and T. H. Breen.

[32] Ibid., p. 14.

(despite a certain creolization); and finally, of social replication of British society in America, not indeed always harmoniously achieved. Each region went through this developmental framework at different times and with varying results, driven by a tension between the functional imperatives of historical experience and the inherited imperatives of Old World culture.

Ignoring slavery presents serious problems for this story too. Certainly, all of the colonies faced the problem of organizing social, political, economic, and legal institutions: The crucial thing is that they organized them in two distinctly different ways. Whether we look at the forms of immigration, economic organization, social structure, political life, or legal codes, there is a fundamental difference between colonies with free labor and colonies with slave labor. The essential difference between mainland colonies and island colonies, between northern and southern colonies, between farms and plantations, between settlement colonies and colonies of exploitation is the difference between free and slave labor systems. There were very few free men on plantations, in the islands, or being exploited, compared with slaves. The system each region developed was not determined by its geographical characteristics, regionalism *qua* regionalism: The island societies began with farms and free labor and turned into societies with plantations and slaves; so did Georgia and South Carolina; parts of the Chesapeake changed in the opposite direction. Regionalism doesn't explain development.

Although the colonies had ties to the Atlantic trading system, the nature of their ties differed. Slave colonies sent by far the largest volume of commodities to Europe. Some colonies without slaves joined the Atlantic system by sending commodities to the slave colonies; other colonies without slaves hardly joined the Atlantic system at all; a few did succeed eventually in sending free-grown commodities across the Atlantic.

Of course, all colonists lived to some extent in multiracial and multiethnic environments, but it is naive to pretend that New Hampshire and Antigua are just two examples of this. The world the slaveholders made was not like Vermont or Connecticut, and there is no intelligent sense in which the Pennsylvania farmer and the Jamaican slave shared the same sort of exploitation. The plantation colonies were certainly not "recognizable approximations of Albion"; they were not even recognizable approximations of Rhode Island; and the world found out in 1861 (if it had failed to notice earlier) that the regions of colonial America had not undergone a common development pattern.

Historians – not just black historians – are entitled to ask whether the "perceptual frameworks, and social and cultural imperatives" of *everybody* in colonial America "were inevitably British in origin," and to ask for something better than a continuing homogenization of colonial history that ignores the social, political, economic, legal, and ideological differences between free and slave colonies.

In contrast, the free land framework directs attention to investigating why two streams of labor, voluntary and coerced, came to the colonies and resulted in two different (but interdependent) types of social and economic organization. An approach that skirts this problem violates the facts of history and ignores one of the central issues of the American past.

CHAPTER 2

The Old World background of slavery in the Americas

WILLIAM D. PHILLIPS, JR.

THE preconditions on the eastern side of the Atlantic helped shape the development of the transatlantic slave trade and slavery in the Americas. The Old World background features were numerous, and there are many facets that could be considered.[1] To deal with all of them would require more space and time than is available. Nevertheless, it is possible to address the most significant features. These include the decision to use imported slaves in the Americas, the role of disease in that decision, the distinctions between small-scale and large-scale slavery, the role of sugar, and the availability of black slaves.[2]

At the time of their initial contacts with the peoples of the Americas, both the Spaniards and the Portuguese hoped to make use of the factory (*feitoria, factoría*) system, in which they would establish links with an existing trading network and exchange their goods for those of the local peoples. This was the policy the Portuguese had successfully followed as they progressed down the west coast of Africa. However, such a strategy depended on having a number of conditions present. These include a sufficiently developed trading network among the indigenous peoples and the presence of goods and commodities that the

---

[1] Additional factors not examined in this chapter include the legal system, the attitudes toward manual labor and toward those who performed it, and the definitions of outsiders and the tasks appropriate for them.

[2] In the postconquest exploitation of the Americas, the Europeans might well have secured dependent, coerced labor for their new economic ventures even if they had not had over a thousand-year tradition of slavery. After all, the English colonists of North America developed slavery even though England had never adopted Roman law and had not had experience with slavery at home for a couple of centuries. Nevertheless, for most Europeans in the Americas, the long tradition of Mediterranean slavery, reinforced by the legal framework provided by Roman law, influenced the way in which the economic and social contexts would unfold in the Spanish and Portuguese colonial areas. For the Old World background and how it influenced the New World, see William D. Phillips, Jr., *Slavery from Roman Times to the Early Transatlantic Trade* (Minneapolis, 1985).

43

Europeans could acquire through exchange. Those conditions were present in Africa, but they were missing in the New World.

As the Spaniards explored and conquered the islands of the Caribbean and the American mainland, they found that they could not establish a commercial network of trading factories, because no preexisting trading networks were available. The conquerors and settlers had to create new economic and social systems to subdue the natives, to produce commercial crops that could be sold in Europe, and to mine the mineral wealth of the North and South American continents. All these enterprises required labor, but two major obstacles faced the Spanish colonists in their attempts to use native labor: royal regulations and depopulation.

Even though the Spaniards in the colonies sought to circumvent the laws, the Spanish crown enacted regulations designed to protect the Amerindians, who were claimed as subjects of the crown of Castile and therefore were not to be enslaved. By 1495, however, those natives captured in "just war" could be enslaved, and Spaniards were allowed to purchase captives held as slaves by other native groups. Nonetheless, the Spaniards at first conducted a thriving slave trade in native Americans throughout the Caribbean and the adjacent mainland. The Laws of Burgos in the early sixteenth century provided fair treatment for the Amerindians. In the reign of Carlos I, several laws limited the ability of the colonists to enslave natives or practice other forms of forced labor.[3]

The *encomienda* system, initially developed to provide for the Christianization of the natives, allowed the colonists to marshal labor. After a series of complaints from Spaniards in the Indies, the royal government began to curtail the settlers' authority over the indigenous population. First, native slavery was declared illegal in 1542, and in 1550 the system of *encomienda* labor was abolished. Passage of these

[3] On Amerindian slavery, see Silvio Zavala, *Los esclavos indios en Nueva España* (Mexico City, 1967); idem., "Los esclavos indios en Guatemala," *Historia Mexicana*, Vol. 19, No. 4 (1970), pp. 459–65; William L. Sherman, *Forced Native Labor in Sixteenth-Century Central America* (Lincoln, Neb., 1979); Peggy K. Liss, *Mexico under Spain, 1521–1556: Society and the Origins of Nationality* (Chicago and London, 1975); David L. Radell, "The Indian Slave Trade and Population of Nicaragua during the Sixteenth Century," in *The Native Population of the Americas in 1492* (Madison, Wisc., 1976), pp. 67–76; Marie Helmer, "Note sur les esclaves indiens au Pérou (XVIe siècle)," *Bulletin de la Faculté des Lettres de Strasbourg*, Vol. 43, No. 7 (1965), pp. 683–90; Marie Helmer, "Cubagua: l'île des perles," *Annales, E.S.C.*, 17, 4 (1962), pp. 751–60; Jacques Lafaye, "L'église et l'esclavage des Indiens de 1537 à 1708," *Bulletin de la Faculté des Lettres de Strasbourg*, Vol. 43, No. 7 (1965), pp. 191–203; Jean-Pierre Berthe, "Aspects de l'esclavage des Indiens en Novelle-Espagne pendant la première moitié du XVIe siècle," *Journal de la Société des Américanistes*, Vol. 54, No. 2 (1965), pp. 189–209.

laws did not end the previous practices overnight, but at midcentury the new *repartimiento* system came to be used, in which Spaniards who could demonstrate a need for labor would be provided with Amerindian workers from nearby communities on a rotational basis. The Spaniards were required to provide decent working conditions for the *repartimiento* laborers and to pay them a determined wage, but, again, practice diverged from legal doctrine. Because of abuses, the crown ended the *repartimiento* system except for mine labor. By the seventeenth century, labor in colonial Spanish America was generally based on the wage labor of native workers (*naboríos*), mestizos, and mulattos and on the slave labor of the blacks, even though coerced Amerindian labor continued illegally and could not be totally abolished.[4]

The colonists could circumvent royal regulations and delay their implementation, but they could do nothing to stop the decline of the Amerindian population. Because of their isolation from the rest of the world, the Americas were free of a number of diseases that were endemic elsewhere. When common diseases of the Old World entered the New, the deaths were massive. Modern estimates of the demographic decline vary widely. The preconquest Amerindian population has been placed anywhere from 13.3 million to 90–112 million; by 1650, according to the same estimates, it stood somewhere between 4.5 and 10 million.[5] The main killers were epidemic diseases, including influenza, smallpox, measles, malaria, plague, and perhaps even the common cold. Smallpox was probably the chief villain.[6]

[4] On *encomienda*, see Leslie Byrd Simpson, *The Encomienda in New Spain: The Beginnings of Spanish Mexico*, rev. ed. (Berkeley and Los Angeles, 1966); and François Chevalier, *Land and Society in Colonial Mexico: The Great Hacienda*, trans. Alvis Eustis (Berkeley and Los Angeles, 1970); Eugenio Fernández Méndez, *La encomienda y esclavitud de los indios de Puerto Rico, 1508–1550*, 5th ed. (Río Piedras, Puerto Rico, 1976).

[5] For a general synthesis of the scholarly opinion, see Nicholás Sánchez-Albornoz, *The Population of Latin America*, trans. W. A. R. Richardson (Berkeley, Los Angeles, and London, 1974), pp. 37–85; William M. Denevan, ed., *The Native Population of the Americas in 1492* (Madison, Wisc., 1976). For specific regions, see Charles Gibson, *The Aztecs under Spanish Rule* (Stanford, 1964), pp. 5–6, 136–47, 448–51, 460–2; Woodrow W. Borah and Sherburne F. Cook, *The Aboriginal Population of Central Mexico on the Eve of the Spanish Conquest* (Berkeley and Los Angeles, 1963), pp. 4, 88; William T. Sanders, "The Population of the Central Mexican Symbiotic Region, the Basin of Mexico, and the Teotihuacán Valley in the Sixteenth Century," in Devenan, pp. 85–150; Noble David Cook, *Demographic Collapse: Indian Peru, 1520–1620* (Cambridge, 1981), p. 94.

[6] The best available summary of these views is Alfred W. Crosby, Jr., *The Columbian Exchange: Biological and Cultural Consequences of 1492* (Westport, Ct., 1972). See also Percy M. Ashburn, *The Ranks of Death: A Medical History of the Conquest of America* (New York, 1947); Eric Wolf, *Sons of the Shaking Earth* (Chicago, 1959), pp. 195–7; and William H. McNeill, *Plagues and Peoples* (Garden City, N.Y., 1976), pp. 176–91.

Europe, Asia, and parts of Africa formed a common pool of numerous diseases. In those areas, smallpox was an ordinary disease of childhood. Although its victims were scarred by it, they usually recovered and acquired immunity from recurrences. When smallpox entered the New World, it affected an unexposed population that had built up no natural immunity. Smallpox was not alone, and other diseases struck in a many-pronged attack. Beyond this, the Spaniards imposed new political and economic structures that displaced many people from their traditional patterns of social organization and habits of work. The disruptions, and the insecurity that followed them, weakened the physiological and psychological ability of the uprooted to withstand disease.[7]

In the face of the rapidly declining Amerindian population and the equally rapidly expanding need for labor in the colonies, Spaniards in the Indies quickly began to report the high death rate and to question their reliance upon indigenous labor. Clerics denounced the exploitation of the Amerindians. Spanish colonists reported that they considered Amerindians to be unsuited for intensive labor and that blacks, who in their view had a much higher capacity for work, should replace them. A constant stream of letters from the Indies reached Spain bearing the message that one black could do the work of four to eight Amerindians.[8]

The Spanish, Portuguese, and English colonists in the New World all perceived that black slaves from Africa possessed numerous advantages. Although the colonists had only an incomplete understanding of all the variables involved, black labor did offer several advantages, especially in the early years. Many of the Africans, unlike many Amerindians, were accustomed to the labor discipline inherent in societies that practiced large-scale agriculture. Many blacks knew metal working, especially in iron, whereas the native Americans were unfamiliar with iron and used softer metals, primarily for decorative rather than productive purposes. Black slaves were not covered by the royal regulations on the exploitation of the native Americans. Epidemiologically, as well, there were advantages to the use of Africans. Africans came from a region that shared a pool of several diseases with the Europeans. Therefore, they were less susceptible to the European-borne diseases that were devastating the native

---

[7] Crosby, pp. 35–63.
[8] Colin A. Palmer, *Slaves of the White God: Blacks in Mexico, 1570–1650* (Cambridge, Mass, 1976), p. 8; Stuart B. Schwartz, "Indian Labor and New World Plantations: European Demands and Indian Responses in Northeastern Brazil," *American Historical Review*, Vol. 83, No. 1 (1978), pp. 76–7.

American population and to certain tropical diseases. For all these reasons, each of the first three colonial powers concluded that black slaves were an ideal choice for labor in the New World.[9] The decision that Africans were to be preferred to Amerindians as laborers ensured the development of the transatlantic slave trade.

In the first century and a half of its existence, Latin American slavery was complex, perhaps more complex than it was to become later. Although laws were the same for all slaves in the Spanish colonies, they were employed in two distinct systems: small-scale slavery for the domestics, artisans, and assistants of all sorts, and large-scale slavery for the gang slaves on the plantations and in the mines.[10] The first system followed the pattern practiced in the medieval Christian states of the Mediterranean; the second came from the more recent plantation slavery established in the Atlantic islands. In small-scale slavery, slaves were used in small numbers in homes, farms, and artisan establishments. In early Spanish America, many slaves were artisans and domestics. Other blacks in the early period were companions and auxiliaries of the conquerors and settlers. The number of Spanish settlers was tiny compared to the vast number of Amerindians, and many blacks served in a valuable intermediary role between the Spaniards and the native population.

The other variety of slavery, gang slavery, was also present from the beginning and was becoming more important by the early seventeenth century. By then, the sizable free population of mestizos and mulattos acted as intermediaries and domestics, having largely replaced the blacks in those roles. After the middle of the seventeenth century, the greatest, and almost exclusive, demand for black slaves was from the proprietors of large enterprises, such as plantations and mines. Gang slavery became the predominant form of slavery in Spanish America; the same pattern can be seen in Brazil and in the English colonies of the Caribbean and North America. The emphasis on gang slavery throughout the Americas during the last two centuries of slavery's existence there explains why conditions for slaves were so appalling in that period.

With the twofold division of small- and large-scale slavery firmly

[9] Frederick Bowser, *The African Slave in Colonial Peru, 1524–1650* (Stanford, 1974), pp. 110–24; also C. Duncan Rice, *The Rise and Decline of Black Slavery* (New York, 1975), pp. 25–6. For the medical history with a full bibliography, see Kenneth F. Kiple, *The Caribbean Slave: A Biological History* (Cambridge, 1984).

[10] The distinctiveness of the plantation system is stressed by Sidney W. Mintz, *Caribbean Transformations* (Chicago, 1974), pp. 43–130. See also Enrique Florescano (ed.), *Haciendas, latifundios y plantaciones en América latina* (Mexico City, 1975).

in mind as the main features of slavery in the Americas in the early colonial period, we can turn to an examination of the Old World preconditions. First, small-scale slavery, sometimes described as domestic slavery, was the longest-lasting variety of slavery in the Mediterranean world and the regions related to it. In the ancient period, slaves were found in the large households of the Roman elite and in more modest Roman homes. Slaves served as domestic servants for Muslims who could afford to purchase and maintain them. In medieval Europe, the use of slaves in agriculture virtually ceased, but there were always some domestic slaves, particularly in those places close to the main routes of long-distance commerce. Domestic slaves were present in sub-Saharan Africa. Much of the employment of domestic slaves must be described as unproductive labor, for slaves were usually assigned to noneconomic tasks; their employment often was totally independent of the normal mode of labor in the society. As servants, guards, and sexual partners, their primary function in many cases was to demonstrate the wealth and luxury enjoyed by their owners. Even with domestic slavery, however, there were exceptions and variations. In the preindustrial world, much, if not most, of the ordinary manufacturing of goods for common consumption was artisan production, taking place in workshops within the homes of the artisans. In these workshops a few domestic slaves could aid their artisan owners, and collectively their activity made a significant impact on production. In other words, domestic slaves, employed in this way, must be judged to have been productive. Slaves as domestic servants, artisans, or auxiliaries also had better material standards of living than gang slaves and greater prospects for manumission. Domestic slavery in Europe received an additional impetus after the Black Death of the mid-fourteenth century. In the aftermath of a demographic decline estimated at 25 to 40% of the total European population, the surviving workers could find better jobs than that of domestic. As a consequence, householders, especially in Italy, turned to slaves and indentured servants. Given the long-standing tradition of small-scale slavery, it is not surprising that domestic and artisan slaves were sent to the Americas, especially because they were already acculturated to European norms.[11]

Regarding large-scale slavery, the first important receptors of blacks slaves in the Americas were the sugar plantations. Here also the links between the eastern and western sides of the Atlantic were direct.

---

[11] For domestic slavery, see the references throughout Phillips, 1985. See also Jacques Heers, *Esclaves et domestiques au Moyen Age dans le monde méditerranéen* (Paris, 1981).

The form and functions of the sugar plantations were directly transplanted from the islands of the eastern Atlantic controlled by the Europeans. The sugar plantations that the Castilians and the Portuguese established on the Atlantic islands in the fifteenth century were prototypes of the New World enterprises that began in the sixteenth century.

In the Middle Ages, both Muslims and Christians used large establishments for the production of sugar. The Muslims spread sugar to all parts of the Mediterranean they controlled where it could be produced. Christian Europeans first found sugar plantations in Syria and Palestine when they conquered the region at the end of the eleventh century. When they lost the last of the crusader states at the end of the thirteenth century, they took the techniques of sugar cane cultivation and sugar refining to the Mediterranean islands they held, principally Cyprus, and to Sicily and the Iberian peninsula, where they rebuilt and expanded an industry previously established by the Muslims.[12] In the fifteenth century, the Castilians and the Portuguese took sugar to the Atlantic islands. Until then, the sugar plantations of both the Muslims and the Christians had relied predominantly on free labor. It was only in the Atlantic islands that the three elements that would become the norm in the Americas were joined: large land holdings, a crop to be sold in the growing markets of Europe, and nearly exclusive reliance on slave labor. It is worth repeating: The third element – wholesale reliance on slave labor – was new. The Atlantic islands thus serve as the link between Mediterranean sugar production and the plantation system in the Americas.[13]

---

[12] William D. Phillips, Jr., "Sugar Production and Trade in the Mediterranean at the Time of the Crusades," in V. P. Goss and C. V. Bornstein (eds.), *The Meeting of Two Worlds: Cultural Exchange between East and West during the Period of the Crusades*, (Kalamazoo, Mich., 1986), pp. 393–406; Sidney W. Mintz, *Sweetness and Power* (New York, 1985); Philip D. Curtin, *The Rise and Fall of the Plantation Complex: Essays in Atlantic History* (Cambridge, 1990); Eugene O. von Lippmann, *Geschichte des Zuckers, seiner Darstellung und Verwendung* (Leipzig, 1890); Noël Deerr, *The History of Sugar*, 2 vols. (London, 1949–50); J. H. Galloway, "The Mediterranean Sugar Industry," *Geographical Review*, Vol. 67 (1977), pp. 177–94; Carmelo Trasselli, "Produción y comercio del azúcar en Sicilia del XIII siglo al XIX," *Revista Bimestre Cubana*, Vol. 72 (1957), pp. 130–54; José Pérez Vidal, *La cultura de la caña de azúcar en el Levante español* (Madrid, 1973).

[13] It is commonly assumed that the close identity between sugar production and slave labor began in the Mediterranean region during the Middle Ages; the whole question needs reexamination. Even though slaves did work in the sugar fields on Cyprus, they were not the only laborers. Free peasants also worked in Cypriot sugar production. See David Jacoby, "Citoyens, sujets et protégés de Venise et de Gênes en Chypre du XIIIe au XVe siècle," *Byzantinische Forschungen*, Vol. 5 (1977), pp. 159–88; and Charles Verlinden, *The Beginnings of Modern Colonization: Eleven Essays with an Introduction*, trans. Yvonne Freccero (Ithaca, N.Y., and London, 1970), pp. 19, 96–7. Trasselli flatly states that only free workers were employed in Sicily (p. 135).

William D. Phillips, Jr.

Europeans first entered the uncharted portions of the Atlantic in the thirteenth and fourteenth centuries, landing in the Canaries and the Madeiras. Portuguese and Castilian ship captains initially visited the islands for easily obtainable items such as wood and the red dye "dragon's blood," the resin of the dragon tree. Some occasionally used the islands as pirate bases. Portuguese royal interest in the islands grew after 1417 because of the Castilian competition. John I of Portugal sent an expedition of some one hundred people, mostly from northern Portugal, to the principal islands of the Madeiras, Madeira and Porto Santo, and charged them to establish permanent settlements.[14]

The Madeiras were uninhabited and fertile, but careful and extensive preparation was needed before sugar or other crops would be successful. Forests had to be cleared by burning. Irrigation canals and terracing were necessary because rainfall was irregular and insufficient. By about 1450 Madeira began to produce profits based on grain production. The Portuguese first built a water-powered mill on Madeira in 1452. Thereafter, sugar production and other agricultural pursuits boosted the population of the islands. From some 800 in the mid-1450s it reached 2,000 by the 1460s, and by the early sixteenth century it stood at 15,000 to 18,000, including some 2,000 slaves.[15]

From the mid-fifteenth century, the Portuguese took slaves to work in the Madeiras: Moroccans and Berbers, black Africans, and native

[14] For the sugar background of the Atlantic islands, see Stuart B. Schwartz, *Sugar Plantations in the Formation of Brazilian Society* (Cambridge, 1985), pp. 3–15. For the general context of late medieval European expansion, see Felipe Fernández-Armesto, *Before Columbus: Exploration and Colonization from the Mediterranean to the Atlantic, 1229–1492* (Philadelphia, 1987); J. R. S. Phillips, *The Medieval Expansion of Europe* (Oxford and New York, 1988); Vitorino de Magalhães Godinho, *A economia dos descobrimentos henriquinos* (Lisbon, 1962), p. 165; Sidney M. Greenfield, "Madeira and the Beginnings of New World Sugar Cane Cultivation and Plantation Slavery: A Study in Institution Building," in Vera D. Rubin and Arthur Tuden (eds.), *Comparative Perspectives on Slavery in New World Plantation Societies* (Annals of the New York Academy of Sciences, Vol. 292) (New York, 1977), pp. 536–52; Sidney M. Greenfield, "Plantations, Sugar Cane and Slavery," *Historical Reflexions/Réflexions Historiques*, Vol. 6 (1979), pp. 85–119, especially pp. 98–9; Verlinden, p. 14.

[15] Greenfield, "Sugar Cane Cultivation in Madeira," p. 544; Deerr, Vol. 1, p. 100; Bailey W. Diffie and George D. Winius, *Foundations of the Portuguese Empire* (Minneapolis, 1977), pp. 306–7; Joel Serrão, "Le blé des îles atlantiques: Madère et Açores aux XVe et XVIe siècles," *Annales, E.S.C.*, Vol. 9 (1954), pp. 337–41. Greenfield, "Sugar Cane Cultivation in Madeira," pp. 543–4; Godinho, pp. 167–8; Greenfield, "Plantations," pp. 99–100, 102–3; Pierre Chaunu, "Le Maroc et l'Atlantique (1450–1550)," *Annales, E.S.C.*, Vol. 11 (1956), pp. 361–5; Antonio H. de Oliveira Marques, *History of Portugal*, 2 vols. (New York, 1972), Vol. 1, pp. 153–4; Verlinden, p. 216.

islanders from the Canaries. There was a limit on the number of slaves who could be profitably employed, because the Madeiran sugar plantations were relatively small in comparison to the later Caribbean and Brazilian plantations. As a consequence of the increasing population in Portugal itself in the sixteenth century, many free Portuguese laborers migrated to Madeira, depressing the market for slaves. The use of slaves soon began to decline, and there were even proposals to expel the Canary Islanders. In the fifteenth century, Madeira was a precursor of the future American colonial areas, but by the early sixteenth century its development had transformed it into a replica of metropolitan Portugal.[16]

The Portuguese established sugar production on other Atlantic islands, but none rivaled the early profits of Madeira. They introduced sugar into the Azores, without much success because of the unfavorable climate. In the Azores, grain and dyestuffs were always more important. Portuguese agriculture in the Cape Verde islands concentrated on cereals and fruits and was complemented by cattle raising. São Tomé, which became a crucial entrepôt for the transatlantic slave trade, experienced a sugar boom in the sixteenth century and can claim to be a prototype of the sugar islands of the Caribbean.[17]

The European settlers introduced sugar cane quite early in the Canaries, and sugar production reached a peak early in the sixteenth century. The Welsers, a German banking family, invested in sugar cane in Palma on Grand Canary. They owned four plantations at the height of their activity before withdrawing in 1520. Sugar was used as an alternative currency in these years, an indication of its importance in the economy. In 1526, near the peak of the Canarian sugar boom, there were twenty-nine mills in the islands compared to sixteen

[16] Godinho, pp. 167–8; Marques, Vol. 1, p. 238; Virginia Rau, "The Madeiran Sugar Cane Plantations," in Harold B. Johnson (ed.), *From Reconquest to Empire: The Iberian Background to Latin American History* (New York, 1970), pp. 75–7. For more detailed accounts of Madeiran sugar production, see Virginia Rau and Jorge Borges de Macedo, *O açúcar da Madeira nos fins do século XV: Problemas de produção e comercio* (Funchal, 1962); and Fernando Jasmins Pereira, *O açúcar madeirense de 1500 a 1537: Produção et preços* (Lisbon, 1969). On the proposal to expel the Canarians, see Lothar Siemens Hernández and Liliana Barreto de Siemens, "Los esclavos aborígenes canarios en la isla de Madera (1455–1505)," *Anuario de Estudios Atlánticos*, Vol. 20 (1974), pp. 111–43.

[17] Robert Garfield, "A History of São Tomé Island, 1470–1655" (Ph.D. dissertation, Northwestern University, 1971); Greenfield, "Plantations," pp. 108–16; Godinho, pp. 168, 176; Marques, Vol. 1, pp. 158, 239–40; Serrão, pp. 337–41; Deerr, Vol. 1, pp. 101–2, 260; Marian Malowist, "Les débuts des système de plantations dans la période des grandes découverts," *Africana Bulletin*, Vol. 10 (1969), pp. 9–30.

in Portuguese Madeira. The Canaries acted as a way station for Spanish sugar manufacturing, and sugar cane cuttings and sugar processing techniques were taken from the Canaries to the newly discovered Caribbean islands and installed there.[18]

Just as the Canaries served as a link in the history of sugar, actions there foreshadowed the events in the Americas regarding the relations between European and native peoples. Slaves were used both as laborers in the Canaries and as commodities for sale elsewhere. A short-lived phenomenon was the slavery of the natives of the Canary Islands. The first European captains who visited the Canaries, armed with Castilian crown patents, in the fourteenth and fifteenth centuries, found the islands inhabited by natives related to the Berbers of northwestern Africa. Because the peoples of the Canaries did not know metal work before the Europeans came, their culture has been classified as Neolithic. Primarily herders, only on Grand Canary had the natives developed an agricultural economy. They were organized politically into bands, and the Castilians made treaties with some of the bands and conquered others.[19]

In the initial phases of the conquest of the individual islands, the conquerors needed quick profits to pay for their expeditions, mainly financed on credit. The sale of slaves offered a quick and easy way to make the profits necessary to repay the loans. Many enslaved Canarians were taken and sold in Spain or in Portuguese Madeira; others remained in the islands and found themselves put to work by the Europeans. Household service was the most frequent use for Canarian slaves. In 1529–31 ordinances in Las Palmas prohibited non-Canarian slaves from being used in the home. The conditions they lived under resembled, not surprisingly, those of the slaves in late medieval Spain.[20]

---

[18] Felipe Fernández-Armesto, *The Canary Islands after the Conquest: The Making of a Colonial Society in the Early Sixteenth Century* (Oxford, 1982), pp. 80–1. For a recent interpretive account of this period of Canarian history, see Alfred W. Crosby, *Ecological Imperialism: The Biological Expansion of Europe, 900–1900* (Cambridge, 1986). On the Canarian sugar cane industry, see Guillermo Camacho y Pérez-Galdos, "El cultivo de la caña de azúcar y la industria azucarera en Gran Canaria (1510–1535)," *Anuario de Estudios Atlánticos*, Vol. 7 (1961), pp. 1–60; Vitorino de Magalhães Godinho, "A economia das Canarias nos séculos XIV e XV," *Revista de Historia*, Vol. 4 (1952), pp. 311–20.

[19] Manuela Marrero Rodríguez, *La esclavitud en Tenerife a raíz de la conquista* (La Laguna de Tenerife, 1966), pp. 17–18, 23–4, 26–7.

[20] Ibid., pp. 31–3, 54–5; Fernández-Armesto, *Canary Islands*, p. 37, n. 19; Antonio de la Torre y de Cerro, "Los canarios de Gomera vendidos como esclavos en 1489," *Anuario de Estudios Americanos*, Vol. 7 (1950), pp. 47–72; Vicenta Cortés Alonso, "Los cautivos canarios," en *Homenaje a Elías Serra Ràfols* (La Laguna, Canary Islands, Spain, 1970), pp. 137–48.

The conquerors and colonists often circumvented the laws in order to enslave the Canarians. It was legal to enslave Canarians who belonged to bands that resisted the Spanish incursion. It was not legal to enslave members of bands that had submitted voluntarily. Members of allied bands who later rebelled or refused to carry out the terms of their treaties could be enslaved as "captives of second war" (*de segunda guerra*). For those who were enslaved, ways to attain freedom were present. Canarians could use lawsuits to try to win their freedom. Nevertheless, manumission was the most easily available path to freedom. The inclination of the master was crucial, and most masters demanded payment before they would grant a slave freedom. Others demanded the promise of future payments or future labor service before manumission was granted.[21]

Native slaves in the Canaries had various ways to attain freedom. The process was called *ahorramiento*, and a freedman was designated as a *horro*. Under Castilian law, each slave controlled a *peculium*. Usually, however, the slave could not buy his freedom with money from the *peculium*, because de jure it belonged to the master. Nor could money be given directly to the slave, because any property he owned became part of his *peculium*. To achieve freedom, then, the slave needed the assistance of a third party. A frequent method of obtaining freedom was for relatives or other members of the slave's band to offer financial aid. Free Canarians constantly aided their enslaved compatriots to obtain freedom, and in numerous wills Canarians left money to executors charged with the redemption of Canarian slaves. The executor could purchase the slave outright, or he could purchase a black slave and exchange him or her for the Canarian. Such exchanges were more easily arranged for slaves who remained in the islands, because relatives could not easily determine the whereabouts of those who had been sold in European markets.[22]

The island population was relatively small to begin with, and its number was diminished by epidemic disease after the European incursion. Members of many bands could not be enslaved, at least legally, and those enslaved frequently attained manumission. Consequently, the natives of the Canaries did not make a substantial or long-lasting addition to the international slave trade. In the early years of the sixteenth century, the Canarian slave trade to Europe ceased

---

[21] Marrero Rodríguez, pp. 29, 34–5.
[22] Ibid., pp. 80–1, 84, 88, 96, 104; John Mercer, *The Canary Islanders: Their Prehistory, Conquest and Survival* (London, 1980), pp. 233–4; Fernández-Armesto, *Canary Islands*, 39–40.

as the islanders increasingly assimilated European culture and inter-married with the colonists. Native workers never filled the labor needs of the Canaries, and other sources of labor were necessary before the islands could be developed fully. So the Canaries witnessed the influx of other workers, including a number of free Castilian and Portuguese settlers. Wealthier settlers brought their own slaves with them from the peninsula. Portuguese slave traders brought in blacks from West Africa, and Castilian mariners raided the coast for North Africans, Berbers, and other slaves. Many of the Africans, especially the North Africans, were soon freed, and there was even voluntary immigration of Moors and Moriscos from Spain and North Africa. Following the first Spanish contact with the Americas, a few American Indians were sold in the Canaries, but the Spanish crown outlawed the slave trade in Indians.[23]

Black African, Muslim, and Morisco slaves came to constitute a significant component of the work force in the Canaries. The settlers in the Canaries acquired imported slaves in a variety of ways. Some, who had already spent time in Spain, accompanied their Spanish owners when they migrated to the Canaries. Others were purchased from Portuguese ships that stopped in the Canaries. Castilians engaged in armed forays mounted from the Canaries, and along the African coast north of Cape Bojador they acquired captives and cattle. At times, the raiders acquired black slaves directly. At other times, a more complicated process ensued. Most of the human booty from the raids consisted of Muslims. Some were enslaved, converted, and later freed. More often, the Muslim captives who were able to do so negotiated for their ransoms, and frequently they paid for their ransoms with variable numbers of black slaves. This became one of the most common means by which blacks entered the islands.[24]

From the Canaries, the Castilians also went directly to black Africa to obtain slaves. In the Cape Verde islands they could purchase African slaves from the Portuguese resident there. From the Canaries they also circumvented the Portuguese by going to Senegambia and the Upper Guinea coast to acquire slaves. This trade was illegal until the union of the Spanish and Portuguese crowns under Philip II. The expeditions to black Africa were always less frequent that the slav-

---

[23] Manuel Lobo Cabrera, *La esclavitud en las Canarias orientales en el siglo XVI: Negros, Moros, y Moriscos* (Gran Canaria, 1982); Marrero Rodríguez, pp. 45–53, 55, 102–3; Fernández-Armesto, *Canary Islands*, pp. 36–7, 173–4; Manuel Lobo Cabrera, "Esclavos indios en Canarias," *Revista de Indias*, Vol. 43, No. 172 (1983), pp. 515–33.

[24] Lobo Cabrera, *Esclavitud*, pp. 66–8; Antonio Rumeu de Armas, *España en el Africa Atlántica*, 2 vols. (Madrid, 1956) pp. 529–63; José-Enrique López de Coca Castañer, "Esclavos, alfaqueques y mercaderes en la frontera del Mar de Alborán (1490–1516)," *Hispania*, Vol. 38, No. 139 (1978), pp. 275–300.

ingraids to Barbary. Over the course of the sixteenth century, some twenty-five expeditions from Grand Canary Island went to black Africa, whereas fifty-nine went to Barbary. It has been estimated that from all sources, some 10,000 slaves were brought to Grand Canary during that century, and that slaves represented some 10 to 12% of the island's population.[25]

Most slaves whose sales left records in the notarial documents of Grand Canary during the sixteenth century were black. For most of the period, blacks made up from two-thirds to three-fourths of all slaves sold. Moriscos and mulattos were less numerous than blacks, each group representing some 12% of the total number of slaves. Grouped as "Indios" were all the slaves from Asia, Brazil, and Spanish America. Together the Indios accounted for less than 1% of the total sales.[26] The ratio of men to women reveals a male predominance: Men were 62%, whereas women were 38%. This imbalance, similar to that for the transatlantic trade, indicates that more of the slaves who were sold were destined for work outside the home.

The work of those slaves encompassed all aspects of the economy of the islands, and they were especially important in sugar cane production. Though slave labor had not been a major feature of sugar cane agriculture in the Mediterranean, it may have been used there on occasion. Slaves came to be used in greater numbers on the farms and in the mills of the Atlantic islands, but there too, free labor was often used as Portuguese and Spaniards migrated to the newly discovered islands. The connection between slavery and sugar, though, had been established. The groundwork was laid for the plantation system in the American colonial areas. In the Canaries the export of sugar remained important throughout the century, but increasingly its export was restricted to two major ports: Seville and Cádiz. The number of mills declined from some seventeen early in the sixteenth century to eleven or twelve by 1600. Slaves continued to be a majority in the work force of the sugar mills, although free Spaniards and Portuguese and freed slaves augmented the supply of labor. It seems that there were no real plantations in the Canaries on the model that would characterize the Spanish Americas. In Spanish America, one proprietor typically owned both land and mill, and both grew the cane and processed it. In the Canaries, small farmers and sharecroppers grew the cane and brought it to the mill for processing. The mill owner extracted a percentage of each farmer's sugar as the price for

---

[25] Lobo Cabrera, *Esclavitud*, pp. 101–30, 143–4.
[26] Lobo Cabrera, *Esclavitud*, pp. 155–6; idem., "Esclavos indios en Canarias," pp. 515–33.

processing. Slaves certainly worked in the mills and in the transport of sugar.[27] The importance of slave labor can be shown from the request of the citizens of Grand Canary to Philip II after he prohibited slaving raids to the mainland in 1572: "Because sugar mills and vineyards are the principal enterprises there, and because slaves to work and cultivate them are lacking, there is a daily decline."[28]

The reference to vineyards in the previous passage illustrates the fact that slaves worked in other forms of agriculture as well as in the sugar industry. They were herdsmen as well for the flocks of the islands. They also worked in artisan industries, often placed as apprentices to master artisans, who paid the slaves' owners a salary for their labor. They worked in lumbering and carpentry, in blacksmithing, and in the production of clothing and shoes. Wax was an important export crop, and there too slaves worked. In the first half of the sixteenth century, slaves also served as fishermen and sailors. By late in the century, some slaves from the Canaries worked as sailors on ships making the Indies run.[29]

The treatment of slaves in the Canaries in the sixteenth century mirrored that of other slaves in other times and places. Examples of good treatment afforded the slaves can be easily matched by counterexamples of harsh punishments meted out to them. Masters were supposed to govern the conduct of their slaves, but the masters could be punished if their treatment of slaves was too inhumane. Although the church and the civil authorities encouraged their conversion to Christianity and permitted them to marry, slaves who transgressed the laws were subject to strict penalties and brutal punishments. Regardless of how mildly or harshly they were treated, most slaves wanted out of slavery and sought freedom by all the means available to them.

One method was to flee. There are many examples of fugitive slaves in the Canaries, but probably very few attained freedom that way. On the islands they could not hope to evade capture for long, and sure safety lay only in reaching Africa. That, however, required a voyage. Stealing boats was not easy, and even if the fugitives secured a vessel, they had to know how to sail and navigate it. Of the many slaves in the Canaries, few achieved freedom by flight.

Most who obtained freedom did so through manumission. All the-

[27] Fernández-Armesto, *Canary Islands*, pp. 39, 79–86, 202; Lobo Cabrera, *Esclavitud*, pp. 232–7.
[28] Rumeu, p. 556.
[29] Unless otherwise noted, the discussion of slavery in the Canaries comes from Lobo Cabrera, *Esclavitud*.

methods of manumission available under Castilian law operated as well in the Canaries, but most freed slaves attained freedom by purchasing it, either by money or by services, which could be rendered before freedom was attained or contracted to be accomplished for a defined period after manumission.

Within the expanding Luso-Hispanic world of the sixteenth century, slavery in the Canaries came to occupy a minor role compared to slavery in the Americas. In the new colonies across the Atlantic, the vast areas of land and the expanded demand for labor created the beginning of the Atlantic slave trade. That the demand for labor could be met with black African slaves was due to the network of trade that the Portuguese had stitched together along the western coast of Africa.

As Spain and Portugal were settling the Atlantic islands, they also reconnoitered the western coast of Africa and, by the end of the century, the Portuguese found the eastern route to India and the rest of Asia. The Spaniards, especially the mariners of western Andalucía, rivaled the Portuguese for a time in voyages to Africa. In 1492 Columbus took the Castilian flag to the West Indies while searching for a western route to Asia. As these events were unfolding at the western end of the Mediterranean, an equally portentous series of changes was taking place at the eastern end of the inland sea. The Ottoman Turks completed their conquest of the Byzantine Empire by taking Constantinople in 1453. Thereafter they began an attempt to assert their sway over the Muslim lands of the Mediterranean.

All these changes had significant repercussions on the institution of slavery, especially the recruitment of slaves. The traditional areas of slave supply were no longer available to Europeans just at the time when the demand for more labor in Europe's new colonial areas began to rise. Europeans could not be enslaved. The Slavs and other eastern Europeans, so frequently enslaved in the early Middle Ages, had long been Christian and were no longer available as slaves. The Turks effectively barred European merchants from the Black Sea and the fertile slaving ground on its north shore. The Castilian conquest of the kingdom of Granada removed the last Muslim enclave on European soil and the last reservoir of potential Muslim slaves in Europe. Because of all these changes, few sources of slaves remained available to the Europeans.

There was still one vast reservoir of slaves that the Europeans could tap: black Africa south of the Sahara. Some black slaves trickled into Iberia from the trans-Saharan trade routes, but that slave trade was intended to supply the needs of Muslim markets. Only occasionally did such slaves reach the Iberian peninsula. Europeans gradually had become aware of the riches of sub-Saharan Africa, gold and slaves above all. They reached black Africa eventually because of their interest in Morocco and the African goods available there. Morocco and other parts of Africa farther to the south offered lures to the Iberians: grain in Morocco and gold in West Africa.[30]

Castilian seamen were interested in the Atlantic waters off the coast of Africa for fishing and trade, but the Castilian government, until the end of the fifteenth century, was too concerned with internal problems and the task of dealing with the Muslim kingdom of Granada to invest its resources in African exploration. Consequently, Portugal became the leader in Atlantic Africa.

A number of factors account for the early Iberian interest and success in Africa. One was simple geographic proximity. Another was the lack of interest exhibited by the other maritime powers of southern Europe, such as Aragón, Genoa, and Venice, whose leaders and merchants had no urge to investigate the Atlantic coastal regions.[31] More important was a series of technological advances in ship design and construction.

With the development of the caravel and similar types of ship in the fifteenth century, the Iberian mariners had vessels that could overcome the difficulties of Atlantic navigation. It was easy to sail down the African coast, because the winds blew predominantly from the northeast. Returning was far more difficult. Ship masters either had to tack slowly up the coast or swing far out into the Atlantic to catch southwesterlies to bring them home.[32] To deal with these problems, the Portuguese and the Spaniards had designed a new family of ships capable of coping with a wider range of wind conditions. The caravel developed from improvements in ship design in Portugal and Spain, whose shipwrights based some of their innovations on Islamic, Mediterranean, and North Atlantic precedents. The caravel with lateen rigging had triangular sails for sailing close to the

[30] Godinho, 1962; see also the relevant sections in Vitorino Magalhães Godino, *Os descobrimentos e a economia mundial*, 2nd. ed, 4 vols. (Lisbon, 1984).

[31] The Genoese, through their investments, influenced and profited from Spanish and Portuguese exploration and colonization. For the Genoese actions, see Jacques Heers, *Gênes au XVe siècle: Activité économique et problèmes sociaux* (Paris, 1961); and Fernández-Armesto, *Before Columbus*, pp. 96–120 and passim.

[32] Philip D. Curtin, in conversation, has often emphasized the importance of the Atlantic wind systems and the means by which they were overcome. See his published comments in *Disease and Imperialism Before the Nineteenth Century* (Minneapolis, 1990), pp. 3–6. See also, Alfred W. Crosby, *Ecological Imperialism: The Biological Expansion of Europe* (Cambridge, 1986), pp. 104–31.

wind, and the Spaniards developed the *carabela redonda*, a full-rigged vessel with a combination of lateen and square sails. Larger ships, called *naos* in Castilian and *naus* in Portuguese, began to incorporate features pioneered in the caravels, particularly the combination of lateen and square sails. By the 1430s, Europeans had vessels with a fairly large carrying capacity and much improved maneuverability. With the caravels and *naos*, Europeans for the first time had the oceans of the world truly open to them.[33]

The progress made in navigational instruments and charts in the late Middle Ages enabled Iberian pilots to find their way. In the Atlantic exploration, Iberian navigators had compasses to determine direction, astrolabes and quadrants to determine location, and means of estimating the speed of their vessels. Their portolano charts indicated geographical features and the compass directions between them. As voyagers reached previously unknown regions, the charts were expanded. By the second quarter of the fifteenth century, the new types of ships and improved navigational aids permitted the Castilians and the Portuguese to sail with a degree of confidence down the African coast and out into the Atlantic.[34]

Portugal was well placed to undertake Atlantic expansion, and the Portuguese possessed the necessary maritime and commercial expertise and experience. They had traditions of high seas fishing and maritime commerce to northwestern Europe. The Portuguese crown had close relations with the commercial groups. The monarchs supported trade, granted licenses for commerce, sponsored maritime insurance, and negotiated for capital with Italian merchants and bankers resident in Lisbon.[35]

The Portuguese also had a number of pressing motives for expansion. Like the rest of Europe, Portugal in the early fifteenth century was still suffering from the effects of the Black Death a half century before. Because a quarter to a third of the European population had

---

[33] Carla Rahn Phillips, "Sizes and Configurations of Spanish Ships in the Age of Discovery," *Proceedings* of the First San Salvador Conference "Columbus and his World," comp. by Donald T. Gerace (Fort Lauderdale, 1987), pp. 69–98; Richard W. Unger, *The Ship in the Medieval Economy, 600–1600* (New York and Montreal, 1980); J. H. Parry, *The Discovery of the Sea* (Berkeley and Los Angeles, 1981); Carlo M. Cipolla, *Guns, Sails, and Empires: Technological Innovation and the Early Phases of European Expansion, 1400–1700* (New York, 1965)

[34] E. G. R. Taylor, *The Haven-Finding Art* (London, 1965).

[35] Godinho; see also the general accounts in Charles R. Boxer, *The Portuguese Seaborne Empire, 1425–1825* (New York, 1969); Diffie and Winius; Marques; J. D. Fage, "Slavery and the Slave Trade in the Context of West African History," *Journal of African History*, Vol. 10 (1969), pp. 393–404; idem., "Slaves and Society in Western Africa, c. 1445–1700," *Journal of African History*, Vol. 21 (1980), pp. 289–310.

died in the first plague pandemic, labor was scarce and expensive. At the same time, the cities were draining peasants from the countryside. The nobles were under economic pressure. More goods were becoming available, and the nobles needed money to buy the luxuries they increasingly desired. The income of the nobles was based on ownership of land, but they had rented much of that land at fixed rates for long terms. The crown and the merchants needed more money as well, particularly gold, which came mainly from the gold regions of West Africa and reached the Mediterranean through the trans-Saharan caravan routes. But Muslims maintained a monopoly on those routes and consequently on gold. Portugal was also chronically short of grain, and purchases in foreign markets made more gold necessary. The fishing fleets of the coastal towns needed expanded fishing grounds. Portuguese sugar planters sought new lands to extend their activities. Slaves were increasingly in demand, both as investments and as cheap labor.[36]

Expansion into Africa could help solve all these problems. Morocco was the first Portuguese theater of operation, and the town of Ceuta was their first conquest in 1415. Control of Ceuta gave them a base in the Mediterranean and a trading position in North Africa. Morocco produced grain, including wheat and barley, and rich fishing grounds lay off the Moroccan coast. Moroccan textiles could be purchased and exported. Ceuta was one of the coastal termini of the caravan routes, offering gold and slaves. Nevertheless, the Portuguese did not secure everything they had hoped for, because the Muslims diverted much of Ceuta's Saharan trade to other Moroccan ports.[37] Nevertheless, with Ceuta the Portuguese had established a foothold in Africa from which they could continue their expansion farther to the south.

Throughout the fifteenth century, the Portuguese slowly moved southward along Africa's west coast. Between 1434, when the first Portuguese expedition passed Cape Bojador, and 1475, when they reached Benin, the Portuguese sailors explored thousands of miles of the African coast. At suitable locations they established fortified trading posts (*feitorias*) where they traded with the local rulers. The post and later fort at São Jorge da Mina was one of the most important.[38]

The slave trade expanded significantly. In the first decade, from about 1434 to 1443, the Portuguese often raided for slaves along

---

[36] Godinho, pp. 69–81; Philip D. Curtin, "The Lure of Bambuk Gold," *Journal of African History*, Vol. 14 (1973), pp. 623–31.

[37] Godinho, pp. 82–116. For the events of the conquest itself, see H. V. Livermore, "On the Conquest of Ceuta," *Luso-Brazilian Review*, Vol. 2 (1965), pp. 3–13.

[38] See, inter alia, John Vogt, *Portuguese Rule on the Gold Coast, 1469–1682* (Athens, GA, 1979).

the Saharan coast, but they soon came to realize that purchasing slaves was more acceptable to the local African rulers and that trade also made better economic sense. They brought goods from Europe and some from Morocco that could be exchanged in the African regions. The European products included horses, cloth, saddles and stirrups, saffron, lead, iron, steel, copper, brass, caps, hats, wines, and salt. In return they secured gold, especially at Mina, and a variety of exotic luxuries to be sold in Europe: slaves, animal skins, gum arabic, civet, cotton, malaguetta pepper, cobalt, parrots, and camels.[39] Of the slaves, some went to Europe, but before the sixteenth century, most went to the new European colonial areas in the Atlantic islands. When Spain reached the Americas and when the colonial demand for slave labor arose, the Portuguese could easily become the suppliers.

To recapitulate this discussion of the main background factors for black slavery in the Americas and for the transatlantic slave trade, we must recall the following pattern. Europeans introduced black slaves because the native Americans could not fill the demands for labor the Europeans were making. They could not do so because of the royal regulations, products of Roman law and monarchical tradition, and because of the demographic decline, a product of epidemic diseases unwittingly transmitted by the Europeans and of the social and economic disruptions. The black slaves taken to the Americas were assigned to domestic service or to gang labor, both of which had precedents in Europe. The small-scale version had existed in the Mediterranean since Roman times. The large-scale version, gang slavery, although it had existed in Roman times, had been mainly absent throughout the Middle Ages in both the Christian and the Muslim portions of the Mediterranean. Sugar cane plantations using slave labor and existing as prototypes of the Caribbean plantations were new features of the Castilian and Portuguese settlement in the Atlantic islands. Once the decision to use black slaves had been made, the Portuguese could fill the demand because of the trading network they had developed along Africa's western coast. If it had not been for the preconditions on the eastern side of the Atlantic, neither transatlantic slavery nor slavery in the Americas would have developed in quite the same way.

---

[39] See, inter alia, Vitorino de Magalhães Godinho, *L'économie de l'empire portugais au XVe et XVIe siècles* (Paris, 1969); Eugenia W. Herbert, *Red Gold of Africa: Copper in Precolonial History and Culture* (Madison, Wisc., 1983); Robin Law, *The Horse in West African History: The Role of the Horse in the Societies of Precolonial West Africa* (Oxford, 1980).

3

Slavery and lagging capitalism in the Spanish and Portuguese American empires, 1492–1713

FRANKLIN W. KNIGHT

THE long and complicated historical relationship between slavery and capitalism is both elusive and unclear. This is true both in its initial phase and in its later development. As elsewhere in Europe, the Iberians had employed slaves in various social and economic situations long before the manifestation of what may be properly termed the advent of capitalism. Indeed, slavery formed an integral part of the social and organizational structure of society from distant antiquity. Capitalism, on the other hand, represented a relatively modern innovation in European societies, dating probably no earlier than the seventeenth century – with some understandable lag time for the Spanish and Portuguese states.[1] Both slavery and capitalism, however, were essential characteristics of the new, dynamic imperialism that fueled the expansion of Europe after the fifteenth century. Although the connection between slavery and imperialistic capitalism may not have been either linear or direct, it is difficult to deny the catalytic function of the former for the latter. Expansion of slavery and the slave trade became an important instrument in the expansion of empire.

Portugal and Spain did not initiate their overseas empires merely

[1] Without becoming too involved in the endless dispute concerning the origins of capitalism in Europe, it may be important to indicate what I understand by capitalism and how it is employed in this chapter. I understand capitalism to be the coherent system of economic relations based on individual private property and private control of the means of production. Fundamental to this system is the pervasive *mentality* that the accumulation of profit for private purposes represents a worthwhile end in itself. See David Harvey, *The Urbanization of Capital: Studies in the History and Theory of Capitalist Urbanization* (Baltimore, 1985); and *Consciousness and the Urban Experience* (Baltimore, 1985)

to derive economic benefits from slavery and the slave trade. Slave trading was not foremost in their plans. Nevertheless, economic pursuits constituted an integral component of the early restless expansion of these two Iberian states across the Atlantic and into the Indian and Pacific oceans. The Portuguese explained their relentless overseas quest in terms of "Christians and Spices", meaning that their goal was as much the conversion of souls as the acquisition of wealth, and their first formal trading post – the first constructed by any European state overseas – was a slave trading factory on Arguim island established by Prince Henry of Portugal in 1448.[2] Overt missionary activity was notoriously inconspicuous until the Portuguese reached India.[3] It was more than half a century after they established their slave trading activity, and well after their arrival in India, that spices would temporarily supersede slaves among the commercial commodities of the Portuguese.[4] The early Spanish empire also combined equally the religious and economic motives of overseas expansion. In the words of the inimitable Bernal Díaz del Castillo, the intrepid soldier of Hernán Cortés, the Spanish went to the Americas "for the service of God and His Majesty, to give light to those who were in darkness, and to procure wealth, as all men desire."[5] This combination of acquisitive materialism and spiritual idealism was characteristic of the age.[6] The compatibility between the business of saving souls and the notion of acquiring material wealth formed a tradition extending back to the time of the crusades.[7]

In the earliest stages of the modern evolution of this international and intercontinental trade involving Europeans, slaves did not feature as one of the more important items. This should hardly be surprising. Slavery had virtually ceased to be a mode of production or an im

---

[2] See J. H. Parry, *Europe and a Wider World, 1415–1715* (London, 1949), pp. 29–43.

[3] This is not to deny the missionaries' efforts beyond the Muslim region north of the Sahara, but by their own admission, the activities were not zealously prosecuted. See C. R. Boxer, *Race Relations in the Portuguese Colonial Empire 1415–1825* (Oxford, 1963), pp. 6–9.

[4] Slaves are not frequently mentioned in the commercial activities noted by Martin Fernandez de Figueroa during the early years in India. See James B. McKenna, *A Spaniard in the Portuguese Indies: The Narrative of Martín Fernández de Figueroa* (Cambridge, (Mass., 1967).

[5] Bernal Díaz del Castillo, *The True History of the Conquest of Mexico*, translated from the Spanish by Maurice Keatinge, esq. London, 1800 (facsimile edition, La Jolla, Calif.: 1979), p. 502. Varying translations of this quotation appear elsewhere – for example, in John Parry, *The Age of Reconnaissance: Discovery, Exploration and Settlement, 1450–1650* (New York, 1963), p. 19.

[6] Gianni Granzotto, *Christopher Columbus: The Dream and the Obsession*, trans. Stephen Sartarelli (Garden City, N.Y., 1985).

[7] Steven Runciman, *A History of the Crusades*, 3 vols (Cambridge, 1951, rev. ed. 1987).

portant commercial commodity in Europe (although forms of serfdom prevailed). By contrast, slaves remained important trade items, and an important mode of production in most areas of Africa.[8] In the Mediterranean world's border disputes, certain social transgressions and religious rivalry produced victims who were sentenced to lifetime service in the galleys. Apart from the galleys, slaves comprised one segment of the category of unfree labor. This changed when the Europeans tried to break into the African and Muslim markets and found that slaves were valuable items of trade.

From the European perspective, colonial expansion involved the transportation of groups of settlers from the home country with the overt idea of re-creating a microcosm of the domestic model overseas. This certainly was the Portuguese model on the eastern Atlantic islands from the Cape Verdes to São Tomé, despite their relatively small domestic population.[9] In the elaborate agreement between Christopher Columbus, a professional explorer, and the monarchs of Castille there is no direct mention of slaves. The crucial part of the text relating to commerce, in characteristic legal language, states,

that of all merchandise, whether pearls, precious stones, gold, silver, spices, or other things of whatever kind, name or description they may be, which may be bought, bartered, found, acquired, or obtained within the bounds of the said Admiralty, Your Highnesses will, and decree that the said Don Cristobal Colon shall take and keep for himself one tenth part of the whole, after all expenses have been deducted so that of all that remains he may take the tenth part for himself and dispose of it as he pleases, the other nine parts to belong to Your Highnesses.[10]

It is tempting to think that the order of listing reflected the priority placed on such trade items by the Spanish court. But the available evidence does not warrant such an assumption. On the other hand, it seems certain that the lack of a general appreciation for the economic importance of slaves complicated the ability of the Spanish court to promote this branch of commerce aggressively in the early centuries of the transatlantic slave trade.[11]

---

[8] Paul Lovejoy, *Transformations in Slavery: A History of Slavery In Africa* (Cambridge, 1983), pp. 23–35.

[9] T. Bentley Duncan, *Atlantic Islands: Madeira, The Azores and the Cape Verdes in Seventeenth Century Commerce and Navigation* (Chicago, 1972); Felipe Fernández-Armesto, *The Canary Islands After Conquest: The Making of a Colonial Society in the Early Sixteenth Century* (Oxford, 1982); Demetrio Castro Alfin, *Historia de las Islas Canarias: De la prehistoria al descubrimiento* (Madrid, 1983).

[10] Quoted in Bjorn Landström, *Columbus* (New York, 1966), p. 44.

[11] This might indicate a relative underdevelopment of the slave mode of production in Iberia. It seems that the Spanish monarchs had difficulty distinguishing between

As they evolved during the fifteenth, sixteenth, seventeenth, and early eighteenth centuries, the Portuguese and Spanish empires depended greatly on an extensive legal and administrative system and a coherent set of economic relations between the center and the constantly changing periphery. Neither an empire – the unit of administrative authority – nor an economy – the basis of interdependent acquisition and management of wealth – could be established or maintained as complementary, watertight entities within any one community. The logic of total self-sufficiency simply did not work in practice. And the inadequacy was not confined to the Iberian powers. Mercantilism, constructed as a theory for imperial economic hegemony, floundered due to the changing and expanding needs of both center and periphery. The "economy world" (to employ the phrase of Fernand Braudel) of both the Portuguese and Spanish empires eventually evolved into an integral component of a much larger Atlantic economy world involving non-Iberians such as the English, French, Dutch, Danes, Swedes, and Italians, with the network of trade, commerce, and contacts spreading well beyond the geographical boundaries of the Atlantic Ocean or the American continent.[12]

What was the catalyst for this dynamic, ever-expanding commercial system? How did an international marketing system manage to operate smoothly and relatively efficiently in the absence of established and recognized institutions of capital such as banks and other clearing houses, accepted currencies, or standardized rates of exchange?

These questions are not easily answered, but any satisfactory answers depend on an examination of the role of a number of commodities including precious metals, luxury items such as spices, tobacco and sugar, and slaves, as well as the expansion within participating societies of the mentality of capitalism. The quest for profit was a driving force in the creation and continuation of markets. For states such as the Portuguese and Spanish, which were relatively resource poor for market engagement in the early modern age, the trade in slaves offered an unusual and novel opportunity to expand their commerce as well as to create new wealth.

Slavery offered two important advantages among the competitive preconditions of capitalism. In the first place, slaves were commod

---

slaves and vassals. Of course, the conquest of Mexico and Peru in the early sixteenth century and the resulting discovery of vast quantities of precious metals made the official consideration of increased wealth from agriculture and slave trading less important before the eighteenth century.

[12] Peggy K. Liss, *Atlantic Empires: The Network of Trade and Revolution, 1713–1826* (Baltimore, 1983).

ities of exchange as well as units of potential labor. As goods, they could be moved from market to market and sold or exchanged readily, thereby producing wealth. Excess slaves could, and were, incorporated into the society as additional labor and eventually, in some cases, as productive citizens.[13] In the second place, slavery provided the multifaceted linkages that promoted the rise of capitalism. The trade in slaves worked in concert with other trades and demanded a variety of exchange products on both sides of the market. In both the supplying African societies and the receiving American communities, the increasing commercial use of slaves accelerated the mechanisms of production and exchange, altering significantly the participating groups.[14]

Like any other market involving commodities of exchange, the slave market generally responded to the normal supply and demand characteristics of the marketplace. Nevertheless, social and political conditions within Africa, as well as political and economic conditions across the Atlantic, greatly influenced the operation and volume of the trade. When supply exceeded demand, prices tended to be depressed; conversely, excessive demand tended to increase prices. The Portuguese empire, with ready access to African supply points during the years of the transatlantic slave trade, invariably had a supply of cheaper slaves than the Spanish empire, which – apart from the period between 1580 and 1640, when both empires were united – lacked such facilities. But until well into the eighteenth century, prices were more nominal than real, since price was a function of barter rather than a straight exchange between commodity and cash. Moreover, many factors other than the market conditions at the point of exchange affected prices.[15] Since slavery represented one form of coerced labor organization, its viability depended on the degree to which its competitive systems remained feasible. Where alternate forms of labor were available and adequate for local needs, slavery involving Africans did not assume great significance. In the Americas, an active slave market indicated a high level of productive enterprises, usually

---

[13] See *Slavery in Africa. Historical and Anthropological Perspectives,* ed. by Suzanne Miers and Igor Kopytoff (Madison, Wisc., 1977), pp. 3–75.

[14] See, for example, Philip D. Curtin, *Economic Change in Precolonial Africa: Senegambia in the Era of the Slave Trade* (Madison, Wisc., 1975), pp. 6–58; Ray Kea, *Settlements, Trade, and Politics in the Seventeenth Century Gold Coast* (Baltimore, 1982), pp. 206–47; Paul Lovejoy, *Transformations in Slavery* (Cambridge, 1983), pp. 88–107.

[15] Philip D. Curtin, *The Atlantic Slave Trade: A Census* (Madison, Wisc., 1969); Herbert S. Klein, *African Slavery in Latin America and the Caribbean* (New York, 1986); Paul Lovejoy, "The Volume of the Atlantic Slave Trade: A Synthesis," *Journal of African History,* Vol. 23, No. 4 (1982), pp. 473–501.

in agriculture or mining, and significant changes in the local economy and society. The presence and availability of substantial numbers of indigenous Americans as alternate forms of servile labor weakened the demand for imported African slaves or bonded workers from Europe. This was an advantage that the Spanish had in some parts of the Americas – for example, in Mexico and Peru – but that the Portuguese lacked in their fledgling donatary colonies in Brazil.

In the early era of the slave trade, neither Portugal nor Spain possessed a domestic economy that by itself could provide adequate exchange commodities for the successful pursuit of African trade. Although market demands varied considerably across the continent, the principal foreign items required for profitable trade in Africa were salt, rice, cattle, glazed pottery (especially of the type brought by the Arabs from Persia and China), porcelain, glass beads, shells, iron bars, copper basins, brass ornaments, dried fish, cloth (especially Indian cloths), horses, tobacco, rum and other forms of alcohol, and sugar. Of these items, the Portuguese and Spanish could supply from domestic production only cattle, horses, pottery (especially from Talavera), and beads. In return, the Africans offered incense, ivory, tortoiseshell, rhinoceros horns, coconut oil, timber, grain, pig iron, gold, pepper, copper, indigo, amber, wax, hides, and beads. Most of these items reflected the long-established trade pattern with India and China, conducted through the overland caravan routes dominated by Jews and Arabs. Almost all could be sold in Europe, although not all could be sold profitably. For the Portuguese, the initial problem along the African coast involved the collection of information on the correspondence between items and markets, as well as the acquisition of local commodities that would reward the freight for the long sea voyage back to Europe. Successful trade was eventually a matter of trial and error. At the end of the fifteenth century, experience had already demonstrated that spices and precious metals were definitely profitable in Europe, adequately repaying the cost of the freight. In order to get these spices and precious metals, the Europeans had to supply transport services or locally desirable goods.

The initial Spanish experience in the New World was similar. Columbus, no doubt with some idea of the nature of Portuguese trade along the West African coast and with the firm conviction that he would reach China, had loaded drums, tambourines, glass beads, small bells, knitted caps (probably woolen), and samples of gold, silver, spices, pearls, and other jewels.[16] This collection of trade items

[16] Landström, pp. 49–50.

represented the notion of what the Spanish conceived as important
international trade items, as well as the relative scarcity of commodities of exchange that met their criteria for long-distance trade.
Throughout the Caribbean there was no ready market for the Spanish
products. As Columbus confided to his journal a few days after his
encounter with the original people of the Bahamas and Cuba, trade
prospects were slim:

> They afterwards swam out to the ship's boats in which we were sitting,
> bringing us parrots and balls of cotton thread and spears and many other
> things, which they exchanged with us for such objects as glass beads, hawks
> and bells. In fact, they very willingly traded everything they had. But they
> seemed to me a people very short of everything.[17]

For those who followed Columbus and went farther afield, things
were not much different on the mainland.[18] Normal trade was difficult, but plunder for the small amounts of ornamental precious metals
was rewarding enough to lead to the final conquest of the Aztec and
Incan empires. Among the "many other things" that the indigenous
Indians offered Columbus and his crew were tobacco, maize, cocoa,
and manioc (cassava), which would become important international
trade commodities much later. But the mechanics of the Atlantic market were not fully developed by the early sixteenth century – and,
what is more, to develop this market fully would require a massive
infusion of labor and basic reorganization of the local societies. Labor
constituted a form of capital investment.

As mentioned before, neither Spain nor Portugal produced a variety
of trade items that fit easily into the marketing system that they first
encountered in the world beyond Europe. As basically agricultural
societies, they were not especially geared to international trade (or to
the type of trade that seemed most profitable in the Americas and
Africa), though they both included elements of a flourishing, sometimes foreign, bourgeois class.[19] One example of this commercial in-
compatibility can be seen in the textile trade in Africa. The African

---

[17] *The Four Voyages of Columbus*, ed. and trans. J. M. Cohen (Baltimore, 1969), p. 55.
See also *The Log of Christopher Columbus*, trans. Robert H. Fuson (Camden, Me.,
1987), p. 76.

[18] Carl Orwin Sauer, *The Early Spanish Main* (Berkeley, 1966).

[19] It should be remembered that during the reign of Ferdinand and Isabella, latifundism
was rife in Spain. In Castille, according to John Elliott, some "2 per cent or 3 per
cent of the population owned 97 per cent of the soil of Castille, and that over half
of this 97 per cent belonged to a handful of great families." See J. H. Elliott, *Imperial
Spain 1469–1716* (New York, 1966), p. 111. On the foreign elements in Spanish trade,
see, for example, Ruth Pike, *Enterprise and Adventure: The Genoese in Seville and the
Opening of the New World* (Ithaca, N.Y., 1966).

market for textiles usually required woven cottons, not the woolen and silken fabrics that were common in the European markets. The Portuguese (and later the Dutch and English) brought these cotton fabrics from India for resale along the African coast. Only much later were the Europeans capable of producing comparable textiles. The indigenous Americans wove their own cloths and hammocks from locally grown cotton and, in some places, henequen.

The Portuguese, nevertheless, did manage to penetrate the African trade system slowly, beginning as transporters of commodities from one regional market to another and only gradually converting the nature of the market to their advantage.[20] To facilitate this conversion of the indigenous African market, the Portuguese had to do two things. In the first place, they had to create a plantation system on the tropical Atlantic islands of São Tomé and Fernando Po. This system allowed them to convert excess slaves derived from their coastal trade into servile laborers on the islands, producing principally sugar and alcohol. Most of the sugar was exported to Portugal, but some of the sugar and most of the alcohol became valuable items exchanged for slaves and gold with the mainland Africans. After 1500 these slaves were also shipped to Brazil and elsewhere in the Americas. In the second place, the Portuguese had to establish their hegemony (later lost to the Dutch) over the Arabs in the Indian Ocean trade, gaining access to Indian sources of spices and cotton textiles – commodities of high value in the European and African markets. The spices were shipped to Europe and the cotton textiles were incorporated into the African trade. In the Americas the Spanish were either unable or unwilling to enter and convert the local trading system. The commerce of the Americas in 1492 involved cotton cloths, cacao (which was also used as money in some places), quetzal feathers, onyx and jade, as well as wooden and stone knives.[21] Instead the Spanish created an entirely new system of trade, linking the Americas irrevocably to Spain (especially Seville and Cadiz) and the wider Atlantic pattern of commerce and emphasizing goods of value to Europeans.

Slavery formed the basis of this new commercial construct, and the American labor needs in large measure determined the volume of the trade in Africans and others to Iberia and the Iberian empires beyond Europe.[22] Indeed, the first forays of the English into the Iberian-

---

[20] C. R. Boxer, *Four Centuries of Portuguese Expansion, 1415–1825* (Berkeley, 1969), pp. 32–3; Philip D. Curtin, *Cross-Cultural Trade in World History* (Cambridge, 1984), pp. 57–9.

[21] Sauer, pp. 128–9.

[22] Pike, p. 40; Leslie B. Rout, *The African Experience in Spanish America, 1502 to the Present*

American world of the sixteenth century involved selling slaves as well as plundering Spanish treasure ships. The tradition of slavery had survived longer in Iberia than north of the Pyrenees. As early as the tenth century, slaves were employed – along with other types of coerced laborers – throughout the Mediterranean world. By the beginning of the sixteenth century, African slaves (recently purchased from the Portuguese) frequently worked in agriculture throughout southern Iberia, and in the Spanish port cities of Huelva, Cadiz, Sevilla, Málaga and Valencia, as porters, domestic servants, and laborers in the olive oil and soap factories. Though their use was extensive, slaves (within the category of bondsmen) did not constitute the major form of labor in Iberia, and their economic importance was somewhat obscured.[23] The Spanish monarchs, Ferdinand and Isabella, were reluctant to sanction the unmitigated sale of American Indian slaves in their mainland territories or in the Canary Islands, and as early as 1500 had prohibited the practice, although with some loopholes to allow a supply nearly adequate to the demand in their American possessions. They flatly rejected the offer of Columbus that the Indians of the Americas could be sold as slaves in Iberia.[24] But the demographic disaster among the indigenous populations during the first two centuries after the conquest forced the Castilian monarchs and the Council of the Indies to adopt measures to increase the importation and sale of African laborers in their overseas possessions.[25] Several thousand African slaves were shipped from Spain to the Indies between 1500 and 1518, but that measure was inadequate. Finally, in 1518, Charles I began to issue formal *asientos* (commercial licenses) to various individuals, who could then ship slaves directly from Africa to the Spanish Indies, free of customs duties paid in Spain. After 1713 these *asientos* became an English monopoly, and English slave traders dominated the transatlantic slave trade.

Day (New York, 1976), pp. 15–18; Vicenta Cortes, *La esclavitud en Valencia durante el reinado de los Reyes Católicos* (Valencia, 1964); Antonio Domínguez Ortiz, "La esclavitud en Castilla durante la edad moderna", *Estudios de Historia social de España*, 2 vols. (Madrid, 1952), Vol. 2, p. 380.

[23] Elliot, pp. 68–9.

[24] Landström, p. 121; Elliott, p. 68. Presumably the suggestion referred to the more warlike Carib Indians. Columbus also sent back Arawaks to be trained as translators. The majority of the Indians died before they arrived in Cadiz, and this might also have affected court opinion on their suitability as slaves in Iberia.

[25] See, Enriqueta Vila Vilar, *Hispanoamérica y el comercio de esclavos: Los asientos portugueses* (Seville, 1977); Colin A. Palmer, *Human Cargoes: The British Slave Trade to Spanish America, 1700–1739* (Urbana, Ill., 1981). The entire profile of the transatlantic slave trade may be reviewed in Curtin, *The Atlantic Slave Trade*, and an excellent summary of the various post–1969 revisions is offered by Lovejoy.

The adoption of the large-scale use of African slaves was a reluctant concession on the part of the Spanish authorities. Some of the reluctance to exploit fully the commercial advantages of slavery stemmed from the hallowed tradition of Hispanic law, especially the *Siete Partidas* of Alfonso X, King of Castile and Leon (1252–84). This was reinforced by a papal declaration in 1462 by Pope Pius II.[26] Iberian domestic slavery, however, was quite distinct from the later American practice. Both the *Siete Partidas* and the papal pronouncements referred to a type of slavery that was less capitalist, less phenotypically African than its development after the sixteenth century.[27] The steadfast refusal to permit the open enslavement of non-belligerent Indians in the Americas meant that non-Indian slaves had to be imported to supply needed labor and the *encomienda* – that ancient feudal Castillian system of *señorio* – had to be transformed in the Americas to serve as an instrument of local coercion.[28] The expansion of the Spanish slave trade to the Americas, therefore, served not only to provide ready labor where and when it was needed, but also to expand the capital base of both the metropolis and the colonies.

Wealth in the early modern world was closely identified with the possession of gold and silver.[29] If one purpose of the establishment of empire was the creation of wealth not only for individuals but also for the emergent nation-states, then the Iberians thought of only two ways to acquire it: by trade and by mining for precious metals. The Portuguese began with an emphasis on trade. That worked successfully along the West African coast and in India. But trading simply did not work well along the Brazilian coast, with its seminomadic, poorly organized, and relatively sparsely settled population of Tupi and Guarani Indians. When a central administration arrived with the Tomé de Sousa expedition of 1549, sounding the death knell to the modified feudal system of *sesmarias* (land grants), the general expectation was that Brazil would eventually become another slave-

---

[26] E. N. Van Kleffens, *Hispanic Law Until the End of the Middle Ages* (Edinburgh, 1968), pp. 199–200; John Esten Keller, *Alfonso X, El Sabio* (New York, 1967), pp. 111–33.

[27] Even the category of slaves was somewhat imprecise, and among the bondsmen in Iberia at the time were Spaniards, Jews, Moors, Canary Islanders, Arabs, Turks, and Russians, many of whom were condemned to the galleys. See Orlando Patterson, *Slavery and Social Death: A Comparative Study* (Cambridge, Mass., 1982), p. 44; Rout, p. 17; Herbert S. Klein, *African Slavery in Latin America and the Caribbean* (New York, 1986), pp. 21–43.

[28] Lesley Bird Simpson, *The Encomienda in New Spain* (Berkeley, 1950); S. Padilla, M. L. López Arellano, and A. González, *La Encomienda en Popayan: Tres Estudios* (Seville, 1977); Antonio Muro Orejon, *Las leyes nuevas* (Seville, 1961).

[29] See J. F. Richards, ed., *Precious Metals in the Later Medieval and Early Modern World* (Durham, N.C., 1982).

importing, sugar-producing colony like São Tomé. It quickly did, surpassing production elsewhere and creating a glut on the European sugar market. For their part, the Spanish, disappointed with the prospects of trade in the Americas, and lucky enough to find substantial deposits of gold and silver in Mexico and Peru, began to exploit the mines. Bullion was more profitable than spices. Both mining and sugar producing required enormous amounts of labor and a far more complex, interdependent economic system than the Spanish and Portuguese first realized.[30]

Once formalized, the European slave trade expanded rapidly. The volume of the trade at the various import points in the Atlantic islands and the Americas increased from less than 300,000 between 1451 and 1600 to nearly 1.5 million between 1601 and 1700.[31] The Spanish American colonies received about 27% of the total transatlantic trade before 1600, with Brazil getting 18%. For the entire seventeenth century, Spanish America received nearly 22% of the volume, with Brazil getting nearly 42%, reflecting the growing importance of the sugar revolution there. But the volume of the trade had expanded so much that the 22% that the Spanish Americas received during the seventeenth century almost equaled the number of the previous half-century.

Without African slaves and the transatlantic slave trade, the potential economic value of the Americas could never have been realized, since neither Portugal nor Spain had the reserves of labor needed to explore and develop their new possessions. Access to supplies of slaves made possible the "taming of the wilderness," construction of cities, pacification of the hostile frontiers, exploitation of the mines, and the establishment of haciendas, *fazendas*, and plantations. By enabling the development of a viable economy on the American frontier, slavery stimulated the accumulation of wealth and power in Spain and Portugal, as well as among the upper segments of American colonial society. The ownership of slaves even became one index of wealth and status.

Several sectors of the economy reflected the enormously increased trade. Shipping expanded, with thousands of slave ships crossing the Atlantic and specializing in the slave trade. To supply these ships, a wide range of goods had to be provided. According to Ray Kea, "one Dutch factor, referring to the late seventeenth century market de-

---

[30] James Lockhart and Stuart B. Schwartz, *Early Latin America: A History of Colonial Spanish America and Brazil* (Cambridge, 1983), pp. 181–252.

[31] Lovejoy, pp. 480–1.

mands, remarked that more than 150 different commodities were needed to conduct a proper trade at the Gold Coast ports" and that "textiles and metalware were in greatest demand."[32] No other type of trade could equal the broad-based economic stimulus of the slave trade. The requirements of successful intercontinental trade were often beyond the scope of a single European state. Countries that could not produce the necessary commodities and wanted to engage in the African trade simply had no other recourse than to purchase them. Portugal, with its access to India, Africa, and the Americas, had access to a variety of complementary markets. Spain, with its access to American-derived precious metals, was able to purchase commodities from any source – legally if it could and illegally if it had to. At the same time, American buyers of African slaves used their tropical staple products to finance their needs. Most of these tropical staples were sold in markets in Europe, giving rise to the misleading description that the slave trade was part of a "triangular trade" linking Europe, Africa, and the Americas. In reality, most trade was bilateral, although the trading system itself was enormously complex, involving Asian and Indian states as well as those of the Atlantic littoral. The slave trade was a lucrative enterprise that had extensive repercussions throughout the wider world of commerce in the period, affecting sectors of the economy and groups such as artisans and metalworkers that might seem peripheral to the trade itself.[33] For the local administrations of the precious metals–scarce Caribbean and circum-Caribbean regions, the slave trade provided a source of substantial public income, often ranking second only to the *situado*, or subsidy, sent from New Spain.[34]

By the beginning of the eighteenth century, the Atlantic marketing systems – in Africa, Europe, and the Americas – were already established. The mechanisms for obtaining and selling slaves were perfected, including the construction of ships specially designed for efficiently transporting slaves. During this century, the Europeans would transport and sell far more slaves than ever throughout the Americas.[35] But toward the end of the century, and especially after the French Revolution, the volume of the transatlantic slave trade began to decline and its proportional relationship to world trade pro

---

[32] Kea, p. 207.

[33] Pere Molas Ribalta, *La burguesía mercantil en la España del antiquo regimen* (Madrid, 1985).

[34] Levi Marrero, *Cuba: Economía y sociedad*, 14 vols. (Madrid, 1974–86), Vol. VIII, pp. 47–8.

[35] Lovejoy.

gressively fell. Slavery as a mode of production, and the slave trade as a mechanism for capital accumulation, yielded priority to other forms of commerce. Industrial capitalism took precedence over commercial capitalism. Ironically, this change coincided with the Spanish realization of the full economic potential of the slave trade and their attempts to exploit it more thoroughly.[36] Those dramatic changes of the eighteenth century lie outside the scope of this chapter. Industrial capitalism required new networks, new international measures of exchange, and a new order of commercial relations. Slavery created a commercial revolution that evolved until the arrival of the Industrial Revolution. Industrial capitalism, therefore, has part of its foundations in the existence of American slavery and the transatlantic slave trade.

---

[36] See *Reglamento y Aranceles reales para el comercio libre de España a Indias de 12 de Octubre de 1778* (Madrid, 1778; reprinted, Seville, 1979).

CHAPTER 4

The Dutch and the
making of the second
Atlantic system

P. C. EMMER

"In matters of commerce the trouble with the Dutch is giving too little and asking too much," a British foreign secretary once is supposed to have remarked.[1] Whatever the value of such political poetry, the contents of this rhyme apply very neatly to the Dutch expansion in the Atlantic. By giving little and asking much, the Dutch were forced to exploit the Atlantic in combination with many other nations. First, the Dutch turned to the Spanish and the Portuguese Atlantic empires and siphoned off part of their trade and produce. Later they turned to the British and the French and did the same. This role of intermediary gave the Dutch an important position in shaping the conditions in the Atlantic that went far beyond the economic importance of their own relatively modestly sized possessions.[2]

The impact of the Dutch can be fully appreciated only after contrasting the nature of the Portuguese and Spanish expansion in the Atlantic with that of the countries of northwestern Europe during the seventeenth and eighteenth centuries. The differences between the first and second Atlantic systems are discussed in part I of this chapter. The role of the Dutch in the creation of the second Atlantic system during the second and third quarters of the seventeenth century is outlined in part II. Part III provides a survey of the Dutch involvement in the slave trade and the use of slave labor in the Dutch colonial economy.

[1] Ascribed to George Canning, British foreign secretary and prime minister, 1770–1827.
[2] P. C. Emmer, "Suiker, goud en slaven; the Republiek in West-Afrika en West-Indië, 1674–1800," in E. van den Boogaart et al., *Overzee; Nederlandse koloniale geschiedenis, 1590–1975* (Haarlem, 1982), p. 164.

I

There were two Atlantic systems in the first phase of the expansion of Europe during the ancien regime. The first one was created by the Iberians and the second one by the Dutch, the British, and the French. The main differences between these two systems pertained to the location of their points of economic gravity, their demographic and racial composition, and their organization of trade and investment, as well as to the social fabric.[3]

The difference in economic geography between the two Atlantic systems was mainly limited to the Caribbean. The characteristics of the other geographical regions were present in both systems. The metropoles in Europe invested the initial capital for the conquest of the African and American possessions. In both systems Europe provided free and indentured settlers, the administrators, the military, and the navy.[4] The African sections in both systems provided bases for barter trade with a variety of African nations. Neither African section housed a European settlement or a European industry. The African regions of both systems were able to deliver the forced labor to the various American colonies.[5]

In the same general way, it seems possible to posit that the North and South American parts of the two systems played similar economic roles. The colonies in both North and South America provided an opportunity for European settlement. Both sets of New World colonies were able to develop an independent subsistence agriculture, and neither was in need of vital European imports. These colonies of settlement were all able to create their own trade links with other parts of the Atlantic system. In both there were certain regions that produced for export: the plantations of northeastern Brazil, of coastal

[3] The classic survey of these developments is Ralph Davis, *The Rise of the Atlantic Economies* (Ithaca, N.Y., 1973). The existence of two "systems" is forcibly argued by Immanuel Wallerstein, *The Modern World-System: Capitalist Agriculture and the Origins of the European World Economy in the Sixteenth Century* (New York, 1974), p. 199.

[4] The main difference between the emigration from Spain and Portugal, on one side, and the emigration from the United Kingdom, France, the Netherlands, Scandinavia, and Germany, on the other, was the absence of indentured servants among the Iberian emigrants; see B. H. Slicher van Bath, "The Absence of White Contract Labour in Spanish America during the Colonial Period," in P. C. Emmer (ed.), *Colonialism and Migration: Indentured Labour Before and After Slavery*, (Dordrecht, 1986), pp. 19–31.

[5] During the seventeenth century, many of the European strongholds in West Africa changed hands. During the eighteenth century, the European bases became less important to the increasing slave trade and the West African coast became even more internationalized, without rigidly delimited spheres of influence; see J. K. Fynn, *Asante and Its Neighbours, 1700–1807* (London, 1971), pp. 124–51.

Venezuela, and of "the South" in North America. However, these export-oriented regions retained their settlement character. The slave population never reached the 50% level, and the dominant population of Europeans, ex-Europeans, and inhabitants of mixed Amerindian and European descent increased by self-sustained demographic growth.[6]

The second Atlantic system, however, produced a new type of colony that did not exist elsewhere: the plantation islands, including the Guianas. In this type of colony, none of the imported ethnic groups was able to survive by itself for long. The chances of creating and expanding this type of plantation colony were not available in the Iberian Atlantic. They were possible only within the second Atlantic system, with its advanced capitalist economics. The second system allowed for far more economic specialization than was possible within the Spanish and Portuguese possessions in the New World.

In many ways, the organization of the Iberian expansion could be described as a halfhearted breakthrough to the new era of international capitalism. The orientation toward the market economy was severely curtailed in the first Atlantic system. The state, be it metropolitan or colonial, remained present in virtually every aspect of the Spanish and Portuguese economies. Transportation remained a constant problem in the South Atlantic; the Iberian shipping firms were never able to respond fully to the demands for transport, be it of people or of produce. Also, the Iberian capital markets – insofar as they existed – were unable to drive out non-Iberian investments in some of the most widely expanding sectors of their overseas world.[7] The Iberian manufacturers were not able to produce enough products or the kinds of products for which there existed a demand in Latin America, nor were they able to absorb fully the Latin American exports. These infrastructural drawbacks invited non-Iberians to participate in the first Atlantic system, but this foreign participation did not result in the development of an economy oriented towards the

---

[6] The ratios of whites and blacks for colonial North America are given in John J. McCusker and Russell R. Menard, *The Economy of British America* (Chapel Hill, N.C., 1985), pp. 136 and 172. For Brazil, see Stuart B. Schwarz, *Sugar Plantations in the Formation of Brazilian Society, Bahia, 1550–1835* (Cambridge, 1985), p. 338.

[7] The early Dutch involvement in the Brazilian sugar production is documented by E. Stols, *De Spaanse Brabanders of de handelsbetrekkingen der Zuidelijke Nederlanden met de Iberische Wereld, 1598–1648* (Brussel, 1971), by C. R. Boxer, *The Portuguese Seaborne Empire* (London, 1969), pp. 61–6, and by G. V. Scammell, *The World Encompassed: The First European Maritime Empires, c. 800–1650* (London, 1981), p. 250. For gaps in the monopoly system of Spanish America, see James Lang, *Conquest and Commerce: Spain and England in the Americas* (New York, 1975), pp. 55–60; Scammell, pp. 343, 344, 365, 367.

international market. International capital certainly penetrated certain regions of the Iberian Atlantic system, and it did create enclaves of capitalist development in Latin America. However, most of the Iberian colonies remained outside the influence of international investment and international demand. The slave trade is a case in point.

The importation of African slaves into Spanish America was dominated by the *asiento*, which gave exclusive trading rights to only one association of merchants. Certainly, these traders could belong to an international group of Atlantic traders, but that did not change the monopoly structure of the slave supply to Spanish America. It is also true that there were multiple possibilities for Spanish American slave owners in certain coastal regions to buy slaves on the international market. However, at any time, such illegal imports could be stopped and confiscated by the authorities. Thus the slave imports into Spanish America hardly enabled the producers of export products to develop a flexible response to changing market conditions, as was possible in the Caribbean.[8] Another argument to support this difference was Latin America's limited direct access to the international commodity markets in spite of constant smuggling operations.[9]

In view of these restrictions placed on the operation of the laws of demand and supply within the first Atlantic system, it is not surprising that the dominating agricultural production unit of that system was the hacienda or fazenda and not the plantation. The hacienda could not develop into a Caribbean-type plantation, where profits were maximized by bringing the factors of production into an optimum mix. The quantities of land, labor, and capital on a hacienda were relatively fixed; thus, profit maximizing was a different process in Latin America compared to the Caribbean and North America.[10]

In the second Atlantic system, the modern capitalist structure was much more dominating than in its Iberian counterpart. In many ways, one could even speak of a *"capitalisme sauvage."* In spite of the fact

[8] Even when the British South Sea Company was the *asentista*, the slave supply to Spanish America "was unpredictable at best." Colin A. Palmer, *Human Cargoes: The British Slave Trade to Spanish America, 1700–1709* (Urbana, Ill., 1981), p. 79.

[9] On the Spanish mercantile system, see Lyle N. McAlister, *Spain and Portugal in the New World, 1492–1700* (Oxford, 1984), pp. 373–5. On the limitations imposed on Brazil's access to the world market, see James Lang, *Portuguese Brazil, the King's Plantation* (New York, 1979), pp. 150–252.

[10] The debate on the feudal or capitalist character was started by Sidney W. Mintz and Eric R. Wolf, "Haciendas and Plantations in Middle America and the Antilles", *Social and Economic Studies*, Vol. VI, No. 3 (1957), pp. 380–412. The difference between a hacienda and a plantation can best be observed in a declining economy. In case of long-term losses a hacienda will always remain, whereas a plantation will be completely abandoned.

that the various European states of the second system also tried to dominate the flow of products and people, the result was different because private capitalism was too resistant, using the geography of the Caribbean and its international foundations, thus making it impossible to create anything like a Spanish or even Portuguese *"exclusif."* After the short-lived attempts at white settlement in the British and French Caribbean, an international group of European and North American plantation experts emerged, creating a unique, market-oriented set of cash crop – producing areas.

Both Cromwell and Colbert tried to curtail the international market of Caribbean demand and supply, but time and again their restrictions were contravened. Investment remained – relatively speaking – international in the Caribbean, and so did the supplies of foodstuffs and slaves. It is true that each of the countries with plantation colonies in the Caribbean had its own fleet of slavers, but it was impossible to prohibit these slavers from selling their human cargo at higher prices outside the plantation colonies of their own nationality. Also, within the Caribbean of the second Atlantic system, the development of capitalist export agriculture had severely limited the production of food crops for internal consumption. Thus many of the French, Dutch, and English Caribbean areas were dependent upon the North American mainland for food imports. In addition, the North Americans were contributing to the continued internationalization of the market for Caribbean produce by offering more money for the derivatives of half-refined cane juice than the distillers in the respective mother countries.[11]

The persistence of the international competitive markets within the second Atlantic system made the Caribbean the unique home of the capitalist plantation, strictly geared to the law of demand and supply. The world market decided on the amount of investment in the Caribbean plantations, and this, in turn, governed the increase or decrease of the (mainly servile) population. The changes in the acreage under cultivation were governed by the same market forces. Sometimes the uncultivated jungle areas were burned down in order to provide arable land, and at other times the same jungle was able to recover lost ground by overgrowing abandoned plantations.

Last, but not least, the demands of the market also shaped the social fabric of the second Caribbean. Nowhere else in the New World

[11] For the value of North American exports to the West Indies, see McCusker and Menard, p. 115, p. 130, p. 199. For the value of exports from the West Indies to North America, see p. 160.

– or, for that matter, anywhere else in Africa or Asia – were so many enslaved people subjugated to so few oppressors.

There is no need to revive the thesis that the first colonial powers, Spain and Portugal, were imbued with a Catholic "ethic" and that they displayed a more humane attitude toward enslaved Africans, whereas the colonists in the New World regions of the second Atlantic system – mainly Dutch and British – supposedly possessed much harsher attitudes toward slaves based on their Protestant capitalist ideology. Obviously, the French case speaks against such a thesis. The French belonged to the second Atlantic system, and their slave regimes were known to be as harsh as those of the Dutch and the British in spite of their Catholicism. Also, within British America itself, there were important differences in the treatment of slaves. In North America slaves were confronted with numerous controls imposed by their owners, who took an active interest in both the living conditions and the health care of their slaves, as well as in their conversion to Christianity. In the British Caribbean, on the other hand, the plantation managers had in general little or no interest in the living conditions of their slaves, or in their religion or social organization.[12]

Rather than being the outcome of different ideologies, it seems more likely that the social conditions in the French, British, Dutch, and Danish Caribbean were a result of the capitalist structure of the second Atlantic system. The main reason for the difference in race relations between the two Atlantic systems was the ratio between white and black. In the second system, that ratio clearly was a function of the demands of the world market.

In summing up the first section of this chapter – which by nature is rather speculative – it seems that most of the unique features of the second Atlantic system occurred in the Caribbean. No other region in the Atlantic was molded to the demands of the market to the same degree.

Why was it so difficult in the Caribbean to shy away from the demands of the market? In the previous pages, it has been pointed out that the market was the result of the international nature of investments, of the agricultural technology and its experts, and of shipping and trade in the Caribbean and between the Caribbean and other areas of the Atlantic.

The geographical location of the Caribbean colonies made it vir-

---

[12] The difference between the slave regimes in North America and the Caribbean is explained in Peter Kolchin, *Unfree Labor: American Slavery and Russian Serfdom* (Cambridge, Mass., 1987), p. 61.

tually impossible to impose a ban on cross-colonial and international trade. In addition, the frequent wars between the European metropoles allowed the Caribbean planter communities to shift allegiances or to threaten to do so. The Iberian colonies did not have similar opportunities for integrating themselves in the Atlantic world of international trade and production, except for some coastal regions.

The capitalist nature of the second Atlantic system's Caribbean must have been reinforced and perpetuated by the exclusive orientation toward production for export. There was no alternative; eighteenth- and nineteenth-century attempts to re-create settlement colonies in parts of Surinam, Jamaica, and French Guyana failed miserably. A counterpoint is provided by the Spanish Caribbean, where the settlement pattern continued to exist.

This inability to continue settlement colonization in the British and French Caribbean was revealed during the 1640s, and the Dutch played a crucial role in directing the British and French Caribbean toward sustained capitalist development.

II

The monopoly of the first Atlantic system lasted for more than a century after the voyages of Columbus. It was attacked by the British and the French, but these attacks were unsuccessful. More effective was the informal penetration of the Dutch of both the northern and the southern Netherlands. As early as 1520, two Dutch-sounding names appear as *asentistas* supplying slaves to Spanish America. It also is certain that at the end of the sixteenth century several Dutchmen took part in the creation of the Brazilian sugar industry, both as investors and as owners of sugar mills.[13]

The revolt of the Netherlands against Hapsburg Spain and the subsequent secession of the northern Netherlands had a slow but dramatic impact on the geopolitics of world trade. It became increasingly difficult for the Dutch merchant marine to limit itself to the role of European distributor, relying on the Iberian ports to obtain products imported from America, Africa, and Asia. In the last two decades of the sixteenth century, the Dutch merchants displayed a flurry of activities. The Dutch sailed around the Cape of Good Hope in order to establish their own trading links with Asia in defiance of those of the Portuguese; they again defied the Portuguese and established

---

[13] Elisabeth Donnan (ed.), *Documents Illustrative of the History of the Slave Trade to America* (Washington, 1930), Vol. I, pp. 16, 17, and Stols, 1971.

their own contacts with West Africa. And – perhaps more profitably
– they continued their efforts to siphon off some of the wealth of
Brazil and Spanish America, in spite of several Spanish measures
banning the Dutch from entering the Iberian colonial world, which,
after the Spanish occupation of Portugal in 1580, included everything
outside of Europe.[14]

At the beginning of the twelve years' truce with Spain (1609–21),
the Dutch had a well-established, informal trade empire both in the
Atlantic and in Asia without having invested in expensive ventures
against the Hapsburg crown or in creating settlements under their
own flag. The remarkable and very innovative Dutch East India Company had been founded with massive support from Dutch investors.
For the Atlantic trade, smaller local groups of merchants in the provinces of Holland and Zeeland had organized companies and cartels
trading with West Africa and North America and sailing to the salt
pans of Venezuela. Illegally, the Dutch transported half or perhaps
as much as two-thirds of the Brazilian sugar to Amsterdam.[15]

The truce with Spain between 1609 and 1621 diminished the velocity
of the Dutch expansion in the Atlantic: The Iberian ports again offered
an alternative to buying transatlantic produce. During the last years
of the truce, between 1619 and 1621, this situation changed when the
Dutch West India Company was created with a monopoly over all
trade in the Atlantic. In many ways, the structure of this company
was an almost perfect copy of its successful older forerunner, the
Dutch East India Company. In reality, however, the Dutch West India
Company turned out to be a completely different institution. First,
its very creation was opposed by many merchants trading in the
Atlantic, who were perfectly happy with the existing situation. The
opposition in commercial circles to the founding of the Dutch West
India Company resulted in a stalemate: The company could not sell
enough stock or collect enough other capital in order to start its op-

---

[14] E. Stols, "De Zuidelijke Nederlanden en de oprichting van de Oost- en Westindische
   Compagnie, *Bijdragen en Mededelingen betreffende de geschiedenis der Nederlanden*, Vol.
   88, No. 1 (1973), pp. 1–18.
[15] On the Dutch Asia Company, see F. S. Gaastra, "De VOC in Azië tot 1680," *Overzee*,
   pp. 20–2, and Niels Steensgaard, *Carracks, Caravans and Companies: The Structural
   Crisis in the European-Asian Trade in the Early 17th Century* (Copenhagen, 1972),
   pp. 151–3. On the early Dutch expansion into the Atlantic in *Overzee*, see E. v. d.
   Boogaart, "De Nederlandse expansie in het Atlantische gebied, 1590–1674," pp. 113–
   16. The important position of the Dutch in the trade to and from Brazil is confirmed
   by Lang, *Portuguese Brazil*, pp. 86, 87. On the Dutch salt trade, see Engel Sluiter,
   "Dutch–Spanish Rivalry in the Caribbean Area, 1594–1609," *Hispanic American Historical Review*, Vol. XXVIII (1948), pp. 165–96, and C. Ch. Goslinga, The *Dutch in the
   Caribbean and on the Wild Coast, 1580–1680* (Gainesville, Fla., 1971), pp. 119–23.

erations in full. Some of the Dutch state and city governments had to come to the financial rescue of the new company. Second, the company was not able to uphold its monopoly; over time it had to abandon it in virtually every branch of the Atlantic trade. During the first few years of the company's existence, the lucrative transatlantic salt trade had to be excluded, and before the first twenty-five years of the company's existence were over, the trade in almost all products had been opened up to private traders. In addition, Dutch merchants found several ways to trade legally in the Atlantic, avoiding the monopoly of the Dutch West India Company by founding and financing Atlantic companies in Sweden, Denmark, and Brandenburg.[16]

In spite of all these commercial drawbacks, the Dutch West India Company enabled the Dutch government to wage a constant war against the Spanish-Portuguese colonial empire by allowing the company to issue "letters of marque." In addition, the company received financial and naval support from the Dutch government in this war.[17]

The results of this "global war" between the Dutch and the Iberian countries were dramatic for every European nation with an Atlantic interest. By the conquest of the northeastern *capitanias* of Brazil, it seemed that the Dutch had succeeded in dismantling the Portuguese Atlantic empire. After the initial conquest, however, Dutch Brazil (or New Holland) remained the pivot of the Dutch Atlantic for only a very short period. The sugar industry stayed mainly in the hands of those Portuguese planters who had not fled. In order to provide those planters with slaves the Dutch could no longer rely on capturing Portuguese slavers, and the West India Company had to establish a regular, triangular slave trade. In order to do so, the company conquered strongholds on the African coast. Operating from Brazil, a Dutch fleet succeeded in taking Elmina on the Gold Coast and later Luanda in Angola, and between 1636 and 1644 the Dutch slave trade developed a capacity for transferring 2,500 slaves per year.[18]

On the surface, the Dutch seemed to have destroyed the first Atlantic system and to have started a new one. The reality, however, was quite different. Dutch Brazil could not be turned into a good

[16] P. C. Emmer, "The West India Company, 1621–1791: Dutch or Atlantic," in L. Blussé and F. Gaastra (eds.), *Companies and Trade: Essays on Overseas Trading Companies during the Ancien Régime* (The Hague, 1981), pp. 71–96.

[17] Goslinga, p. 94, and Franz Binder, "Die Zeeländische Kaperfahrt, 1654–1662," *Archief Zeeuws Genootschap der Wetenschappen*, (1976), p. 41.

[18] Ernst van den Boogaart and Pieter C. Emmer, "The Dutch Participation in the Atlantic Slave Trade, 1596–1650," in Henry A. Gemery and Jan S. Hogendorn (eds.), *The Uncommon Market: Essays in the Economic History of the Atlantic Slave Trade* (New York, 1979), pp. 353–71. The figure is derived from Table 14.5, p. 369.

location for the development of a reliable capitalist sugar industry. The cane growers and mill owners remained Portuguese, and their loyalty remained uncertain. The Portuguese enemy had to be held at bay at great expense both in Brazil and in Angola. The Dutch slave trade to Brazil was a financial disaster, since it was conducted mainly on credit and did not adjust itself to the limited purchasing power of the Portuguese planters. In short, the "Brazilian adventure" not only cost the Dutch West India Company all its capital, it also put the company solidly into debt from which it would never recover.[19]

The Dutch attack on the first Atlantic system did not destroy it, and by themselves the Dutch could not create a second one. Unfortunately, it seems impossible to give a direct answer to the question of why the Dutch were so reluctant to create a couple of settlements in the Caribbean in order to obtain a reliable area of cash crop production. It has been pointed out that the Dutch lacked the labor for such a settlement. Young, indentured, unmarried males, who peopled the early French and English Caribbean, had other employment opportunities in the Netherlands, notably serving in the Dutch East India Company as well as in the large trading and fishing fleets operating in European waters. On the other hand, it would have been possible for the Dutch or for the Dutch West India Company to employ foreign settlers, as had happened in the company's North American colony.[20]

Yet, in spite of the continued existence of an Iberian system in the South Atlantic and in spite of the absence of Dutch settlements in the Caribbean, the Dutch withdrawal from Brazil laid the foundations for the second Atlantic system by forcing the Dutch to offer their expertise in slave trading and transportation to the French and the British. First, the Iberian-Dutch "world war" left the Spanish with little energy to further defend the Caribbean, which anyway had become a marginal region in Spanish America, economically in decline with the exception of Cuba. The lack of Spanish defensive power enabled the British and the French finally to break through the Spanish defenses and to start colonizing the Caribbean. Second, in 1644 the Dutch were left with a relatively large supply system of African slaves but without a market

[19] Norbert H. Schneeloch, *Aktionäre der Westindischen Compagnie von 1674. Die Verschmeltzung der alten zu einer neuen Aktiengesellschaft* (Stuttgart, 1982), p. 22.
[20] Some Dutch attempts at settlement in the Caribbean were unsuccessful because of Spanish counterattacks. See Jonathan I. Israel, *The Dutch Republic and the Hispanic World, 1606–1661* (Oxford, 1982), pp. 133–4. On the demand for labor in the Dutch Navy and merchant marine, see J. R. Bruijn, "De personeelsbehoefte van de VOC overzee en aan boord, bezien in Aziatisch en Nederlands perspectief," *Bijdragen en Mededelingen van het Historisch Genootschap*, Vol. 91 (1976), pp. 218–48.

once Dutch slave imports into Brazil had been halted by the revolt of the Portuguese *moradores*. Third, the revolt in Dutch Brazil suddenly diminished the exportation of clay sugar to the Dutch refineries. Sugar prices in Europe increased.[21]

The Dutch tried to make up for the loss of their sugar-producing colony by continuing their previous policy of buying sugar from others. First, they turned to Portuguese São Tomé, then to Barbados, Guadaloupe, and Martinique. At the same time, they directed the supply of African slaves to São Tomé, to Curaçao, which functioned as a transit harbor for Venezuela, and to Barbados and the French Antilles.[22]

The story of the beginning of sugar cultivation on Barbados has been told many times. For the creation of the second Atlantic system, it seems of little relevance whether the downward movement of slave prices stimulated the rapid expansion of Barbadian sugar or whether the demand for slaves came in the wake of the first expansion of sugar cane cultivation. It is important to note, however, that during a crucial period in the history of Barbados the Dutch were able to bring down the prices of slaves, of imported victuals, of equipment, and of transportation by strengthening international competition.[23]

The importance of the supply side is further demonstrated by the fact that the Dutch needed buyers for their wares. First of all, the Spanish should be mentioned; they offered cash for the slaves who were delivered to Curaçao. Also, attention should be called to Dutch slave supplies to the planters of Martinique and Guadaloupe. Contemporary authors mention the arrival of 1,200 Dutchmen in the French Antilles from Dutch Brazil, mainly slaves with about 50 "*Hollandois naturels*." Contemporary authors also confirm that until 1664 the Dutch supplied most of the slaves to the French Antilles. For Barbados the cutoff period is considered to have been between the years 1660 and 1663, when the British slavers were able to offer more slaves, arresting further Dutch involvement in the trade to the British Caribbean.[24]

---

[21] William A. Green, "Supply versus Demand in the Barbadian Sugar Industry," *Journal of Interdisciplinary History*, Vol. XVIII, No. 3 (1988), p. 405, based on Robert Carlyle Batie, "Why Sugar? Economic Cycles and the Changing Staples on the English and French Antilles, 1624–1654," *Journal of Caribbean History*, Vol. VIII (1976), p. 30.

[22] Van den Boogaart and Emmer, pp. 371–5.

[23] Richard N. Bean and Robert P. Thomas, "The Adoption of Slave Labor in British America," in Gemery and Hogendorn, pp. 390–8. Hilary McD. Beckles and Andrew Downes, "The Economics of Transition to the Black Labor System in Barbados, 1630–1680," *Journal of Interdisciplinary History*, Vol. XVIII, No. 2 (1987), pp. 225–7.

[24] On the slave trade via Curaçao, see P. C. Emmer, "De slavenhandel van en naar

The growth of the second Atlantic system was largely due to this initial phase of free competition in the non-Spanish Caribbean between 1624 and 1665. The Dutch importance in the early slave trade to the British and French West Indies was based on the infrastructure that the Dutch West India Company had built up during its Brazilian years. The attempts to create a British monopoly company for the slave trade did not really succeed until 1672, with the founding of the Royal African Company. However, long before that year, private British slavers were perhaps as important as the Dutch. In the French Antilles, the Dutch dominance in the early slave trade was not seriously countered by French ships belonging either to companies or to private shipping firms. The French observer Du Tertre mentioned that the Dutch not only had larger and better-built ships than the French, but also that their crews were more experienced; they were less numerous and better paid than those on French ships. Also, the vital food imports from Europe became cheaper for the Caribbean planters. The prices of Dutch imports were lower than those from France; in the case of salted beef, the difference was as much as 50%![25]

After the initial phase of free trade within the Caribbean and between the Caribbean and Europe, the mercantilist policies tried to create a partioned Caribbean. Until the nineteenth century, the sugar-producing areas in the British Caribbean had exclusive access to the internal British home market, where consumers sometimes paid more for their sugar than elsewhere. For their Atlantic possessions the French also established – at least on paper – exclusive rights for their own merchants and ships, in spite of severe protests by their own colonists in the French West Indies. The Dutch did the same with their West Indian possessions. Was the second Atlantic system in danger of becoming similar to the first one?

There are several reasons, however, for the supposition that the economy of the non-Spanish Caribbean remained geared to market forces and that the area retained its unique, open economy. First,

Nieuw-Nederland," *Economisch- en Sociaal-Historisch Jaarboek*, Vol. 35 (1972), pp. 94–147. On the trade to the French Antilles, see Jacques Petit Jean Roget, *La société d'habitation à la Martinique; un demi siècle de formation, 1631–1685* (Lille and Paris, 1980), pp. 1435, 1154, 1160, 1178, 1232, 1233, 1282, 1436. For the British Caribbean, see Richard S. Dunn, *Sugar and Slaves, the Rise of the Planter Class in the English West Indies, 1624–1713* (New York, 1972), p. 80.

[25] On the early Dutch and British slave trade to the Caribbean, see Van den Boogaart and Emmer, p. 375. On the importance of British interlopers from the 1670s on, see David W. Galenson, *Traders, Planters and Slaves: Market Behavior in Early English America* (Cambridge, 1986), p. 17. On the earliest period of the slave trade to the British Caribbean, Galenson (p. 14) mentions both the Dutch and private British slavers but does not quantify their respective shares in the market.

there was the slave trade, which always remained competitive and to some extent international. The most important national slave trade to the Caribbean was that of Britain. At no time did the Royal African Company's monopoly dominate the trade; competition in the British slave trade remained important until the very end in supplying both British and non-British planters. The same applied to the French slave trade. The Dutch contributed to the international supply of slaves by directing part of their slave trade to the transit harbors of Curaçao and St. Eustatius. In addition, the British and Danish slave trades were larger than the demand for slaves in the Caribbean colonies under their own flags. Thus the slave ships of these nations also sold their human cargoes elsewhere in competition with national slave carriers.[26]

A second demonstration of the ongoing international character of the non-Spanish Caribbean concerns investments. Evidence from the Amsterdam capital market as well as from the Dutch Guyanas indicates that the Dutch remained interested in financing foreign plantations during the eighteenth century, mainly in Tobago, Grenada, Dominica, St. Vincent, Barbados, and the Danish Caribbean. The British also expanded beyond their formal empire: Many plantation owners in the Dutch Guyanas were British, in Demarara perhaps even more than half.[27]

A third indication of the market orientation of the non-Spanish Caribbean is the international distribution of its produce. Here the Dutch again continued to play a role, which they had assumed at the beginning of their penetration into the Caribbean. During the frequent wars of the eighteenth century, the French West Indies shipped part

---

[26] On the internal competition among British slavers, see James A. Rawley, *The Trans-Atlantic Slave Trade: A History* (New York and London, 1981), pp. 153–64. For the British slave trade to non-British America, see Robert Louis Stein, *The French Slave Trade in the Eighteenth Century: An Old Regime Business* (Madison, Wisc., 1979), p. 26. The British slave trade to the Dutch colonies became important after the Anglo-Dutch War ending in 1784; see W. S. Unger, "Bijdragen tot de geschiedenis van de Nederlandse slavenhandel," *Economisch-Historisch Jaarboek*, Vol. XXVI (1952–4), pp. 164–6. On the Dutch transito-slave trade via Curaçao and St. Eustatius, see Johannes Postma, "The Dutch Slave Trade: A Quantitative Assessment," in Walter E. Minchinton et al., *La traite des noirs par l'Atlantique; nouvelles approches* (Paris, 1976), p. 242. On the international aspects of the Danish slave trade, see Sv. E. Green-Pedersen, "The History of the Danish Negro Slave Trade, 1733–1807: An Interim Survey Relating in Particular to Its Volume, Structure, Profitability and Abolition," in *La traite*, p. 209.

[27] On Dutch investments in the non-Dutch Caribbean, see J. P. van de Voort, "Dutch Capital in the West Indies during the Eighteenth Century," *The Low Countries' History Yearbook/Acta Historiae Neerlandicae*, Vol. XIV (1981), p. 93. On Dutch investments in the French slave trade, see Stein, p. 149.

of its coffee and sugar to Europe via St. Eustatius. In peacetime, the Dutch imported French Antillean sugar from France. There are indications that until 1750 most of the distribution of French sugar in Europe outside of France was done by the Dutch. In addition, the British exported part of their West Indian sugar to the continent.[28]

A fourth indication of the international character of the non-Spanish West Indies was the constant presence of large numbers of North American ships. By offering foodstuffs and horses and by buying molasses, the "Yankee traders" constituted an important barrier to the monopolistic tendencies of the metropole.[29]

To sum up this section: There is ample evidence to suggest that the Dutch were instrumental in the creation of a new, non-Spanish Caribbean geared to the exportation of tropical cash crops. The loss of Brazil forced the Dutch to develop international trading contacts, resulting in fierce competition in the Caribbean and forcing down the prices of transportation, commodities, and slaves.

To some extent, the international market was lost due to the application of mercantilism after the exciting and very international first phase of the non-Spanish Caribbean had come to an end. However, in many branches of the economy of the non-Spanish Caribbean, international competitiveness was maintained; the supply of slaves, and the imports as well as the distribution of Caribbean produce, remained at least partly international.

The whip of international demand and supply was perhaps best felt in the small Dutch Atlantic, because its trade and production did not enjoy any protection at home. This explains why the Dutch Atlantic slave trade yielded relatively low profits, and why investments in the production of slave-grown sugar and coffee in Surinam sometimes inflicted considerable losses on its financiers.

III

The Dutch expansion overseas had a different orientation than that of the other European countries. The main Dutch effort overseas was concentrated in Asia, where the Dutch East India Company overshad-

---

[28] On the Dutch involvement in the trade from the French Antilles, see J. P. van de Voort, *De Westindische plantages van 1720 tot 1795; financiën en handel* (Eindhoven, 1973), pp. 134–52; this is confirmed by Stein, p. 118. On the British and French reexports (20.7 and 62.6%, respectively), see Richard B. Sheridan, *Sugar and Slavery: An Economic History of the British West Indies, 1623–1775* (Barbados, 1974), p. 25.

[29] Sheridan, pp. 352–7. McCusker and Menard, p. 160, indicate that the exports from the West Indies to North America amounted to about one-seventh of the total exports.

owed its other European competitors. The trade figures speak for themselves. Toward the end of the eighteenth century, the annual turnover of the Dutch trade within Europe was estimated at 200 million guilders per year, of the Dutch trade with Asia at 35 million guilders, and of the Dutch trade in the Atlantic at 28 million guilders. Furthermore, it seems probable that roughly 25% of these turnover figures can be attributed to service payments (shipping, stowage, salaries, commission payments, and profits). This would mean that about 12% of the Dutch GNP, estimated at 600 million guilders, was generated by overseas trade. Only 0.5% of the Dutch GNP was derived from services and profits in that part of the Atlantic trade that had any connection with slavery or the slave trade (estimated at about half of the Dutch trade in the Atlantic).[30]

Does this mean that the major share of the Dutch national income derived from overseas trade came from activities not connected with slavery? The answer must be negative, because slavery played a modest but important role in every aspect of the Dutch worldwide long-distance trade, including the trade to Asia.

In spite of the limited research in this field, recent publications indicate that slavery was widespread in the Dutch East Indies. As many as 4,000 slaves were brought yearly from south Sulawesi to the capital city of Batavia. Per year, a total of 7,000 slaves entered the slavery system of Southeast Asia. The role of those slaves was, however, different from the one in the New World. Generally, slaves were not used to produce agricultural export produce. A case in point were the Spice Islands, where slaves sometimes made up 20 percent of the

---

[30] For the breakdown of the Dutch overseas trade figures, see I. J. Brugmans, "De Oost-Indische Compagnie en de Welvaart in de Republiek," I. J. Brugmans, *Welvaart en Historie; Tien Studies* ('s Gravenhage, 1950), pp. 28–37. On the national income figure, see Th. P. M. de Jong, "Sociale veranderingen in de neergaande Republiek," *Economisch- en Sociaal-Historisch Jaarboek*, Vol. XXXV (1972), p. 3. The 25% profit and factor payments are calculated from J. G. van Dillen, "Memorie betreffende de Kolonie Suriname," *Economisch-Historisch Jaarboek*, Vol. XXIV (1950), pp. 163–7. The turnover of the Dutch trade in the Atlantic linked in any way to slavery did not exceed 14 million guilders per year, even at the height of the slave trade and of sugar production in Surinam. See Emmer, "Suiker, goud en slaven," p. 154. The importance of the maritime sector in the Dutch economy is also reflected in the labor markets of Holland and Zeeland. In total there were about 60,000 jobs in both the navy and the merchant marine during the eighteenth century. If we assume that the average length of employment was ten years (in the Dutch East India Company it was not even five years), about half the yearly growth of employable men in the nonagrarian sector (estimated at 12,500 yearly) would be absorbed by the maritime sector. J. R. Bruijn and J. Lucassen, eds., *Op de schepen der Oost-Indische Compagnie; vijf artikelen van J. de Hullu, ingeleid, bewerkt en voorzien van een studie over de werkgelegenheid bij de VOC* (Groningen, 1980), p. 26.

population. They were mainly used as domestics rather than as agricultural laborers. They staffed the houses of the Dutch merchant community in Asia, and they manned the docks in Batavia and thus handled the Dutch (and Chinese) ships, which were so important in producing the Asian trade profits for the metropoles.[31]

A similar observation can be made for the Dutch possession at the southern tip of Africa: the Cape of Good Hope. After the mid-seventeenth century, this colony was the only Dutch colony of white settlement. In addition to the Europeans, slaves were imported into the Cape Colony from a wide range of catchment areas in the Indian Ocean: the Indonesian archipelago, India, Sri Lanka, Madagascar, and Mauritius, as well as from the East African mainland. In 1793 there were 14,747 slaves in the colony compared to 13,830 Europeans. Most of the slaves had been imported, since the Cape slaves did not reproduce themselves, unlike the European segment of the colony's population.[32] The importance of slavery in the economy of the Cape Colony was certainly not as fundamental as in most of the Caribbean plantation colonies. However, slaves provided much of the labor for the large cattle, wine, and grain farms in South Africa. About one-third of the Cape's produce was exported via the ships of the Dutch East India Company on their way to or from Asia. The Capetown docks were manned by slaves. Thus it could be argued that the Dutch Asian trade could not have reached its actual volume without slave labor.[33]

In turning to the Atlantic, the economic importance of slavery in New Netherland – the short-lived Dutch colony in North America – was similar to that in the Middle Colonies under British colonial rule. Some of the slaves in New Netherland had come directly from Africa; the majority, however, were brought to the colony via Curaçao. In total slaves made up 5% of the population of New Netherland, estimated at 9,000 in 1664.[34]

---

[31] H. Sutherland, "Slavery and the Slave Trade in South Sulawesi," in Anthony Reid (ed.), *Slavery, Bondage and Dependency in Southeast Asia* (St. Lucia, London, and New York, 1983), pp. 263–86, and Anthony Reid, "Introduction, Slavery and Bondage in South-East Asian History," ibid., p. 19. For the situation on Amboina, see G. J. Knaap, *Kruidnagelen en Christenen; de Verenigde Oost-Indische Compagnie en de bevolking van Ambon, 1656–1696* (Dordrecht, 1987), pp. 128–37.

[32] Nigel Worden, *Slavery in Dutch South Africa* (Cambridge, 1985), p. 53.

[33] On the Cape economy, see P. C. van Duin and Robert Ross, *The Economy of the Cape Colony in the Eighteenth Century* (Leiden, 1987). The main export products of the Cape Colony were wheat (p. 27), meat (p. 69), and wine (p. 55).

[34] Emmer, "De Slavenhandel," pp. 94–147. A shorter survey in English in Oliver A. Rink, *Holland on the Hudson: An Economic and Social History of Dutch New York* (Ithaca, N.Y., 1986), pp. 163–4.

The second area in the Dutch Atlantic, where slavery again played only a very minor role, was situated along the Gold Coast in West Afria. Like the British, the French, and the Danes, the Dutch possessed a string of strongholds along the coast, which housed, at most, about 100 to 200 European personnel and about 600 slaves. The slaves were used for various purposes, but not for the production of export produce. However, during the seventeenth and eighteenth centuries, these forts were vital in the shipping of gold and slaves. The importance of these trading stations decreased over time, when the slave trade moved to other parts of the African coast.[35]

The third area, where slavery played a relatively modest role, was situated in the Dutch Antilles: Curaçao, Aruba, Bonaire, St. Maarten, St. Eustatius, and Saba. The number of slaves on Curaçao came to about 7,000; slaves made up about half of the population of this island. The second largest group of inhabitants were the free people of color, totaling about 4,500. The whites numbered 2,500. The economy of the islands was mainly geared to the transit trade. There were few plantations producing for export, mainly situated on St. Eustatius. Salt was exported from Aruba and St. Maarten. The slaves in the Dutch Antilles worked these salt pans, and they also produced food for the ships and slaves in transit. It has been estimated that 33,000 slaves passed through Curaçao during the seventeenth century and 34,000 during the eighteenth century. The main destination of these slaves was Spanish America, as has already been mentioned. Curaçao was also used as a transit harbor for ships arriving from Venezuela with export products, mainly hides and cocoa. In the transit trade, St. Eustatius gained a position similar to that of Curaçao during several decades of the eighteenth century. It has been estimated that 20,000 slaves passed through that island, mainly destined for the French Caribbean. In addition, St. Eustatius became an important transit harbor for produce during the period of the American War of Independence.[36]

[35] Johannes Postma, "The Origins of African Slaves: the Dutch Activities on the Guinea Coast, 1675–1795" in Stanley L. Engerman and Eugene D. Genovese (eds.), *Race and Slavery in the Western Hemisphere; Quantitative Studies* (Princeton, N.J., 1975), pp. 33–49.

[36] W. E. Renkema, *Het Curaçaose plantagebedrijf in de negentiende eeuw* (Zutphen, 1981), p. 336. H. Hoetink, "Surinam and Curaçao," in W. Cohen and Jack P. Greene (eds.), *Neither Slave Nor Free: The Freedmen of African Descent in the Slave Societies of the New World* (Baltimore and London, 1972), pp. 59–83; Harry Hoetink, "Race Relations in Curaçao and Surinam", in Laura Foner and Eugene D. Genovese (eds.), *Slavery in the New World; A Reader in Comparative History* (Englewood Cliffs, N.J., 1969), pp. 178–88. The figures of the transit slave trade are derived from Postma, "The Origins of African Slaves," Table 7 (p. 49), and Postma, "The Dutch Slave Trade," Tables VII

The fourth area among the Atlantic possessions of the Dutch was the Guianas. The largest of these areas was called Surinam (with 50,000 slaves in 1770), and there were three smaller neighboring colonies situated to the west: Essequibo, Demerary, and Berbice, with about 8,000 slaves each. In all of these colonies, slavery was the basis of the economy: The slave-worked plantations in the Dutch Guianas fully resembled the plantations in the British and French Caribbean.[37] Little is known about the financial development of the Guianas during their first eighty years as Dutch colonies. Whatever their productive capacities, it seems safe to assume that the major portion of the sugar imported into the Netherlands always came from foreign producers. The Dutch interest in their sugar colonies increased after 1750, when the French started to distribute their French Antillean sugar themselves. Between 1750 and 1770 a group of Amsterdam investors tried to expand sugar production in the Dutch Guianas by investing more than 60 million guilders.[38] The outcome of this speculative wave of investments was disastrous. The influx of money from Holland into the Dutch Guianas did increase the importation of slaves, but it did not sufficiently increase the income derived from the sale of cash crops. Having absorbed these large investments, most Surinam plantations were faced with high debt-servicing costs. In fact, it can be calculated that the colony developed a considerable deficit in its balance of payments.[39]

The explanations for this dramatic development have not all been discovered. Contemporaries mentioned that the plantation loans had allowed the planters to buy too many slaves for nonproductive purposes. Also, far too much credit had been given to the Surinam planters, because the influx of money from the Netherlands had inflated the prices of the plantations in Surinam, and this, in turn, had enabled the planters to get even higher mortgages, since they used their plantations as collateral. The massive influx of money after 1750 did increase the value of the Surinam exports but not sufficiently to pay the interest on the loans, let alone their repayment.[40]

and VIII (p. 242). On the transit trade from Curaçao to Venezuela, see Eugenio Pinero, "The Cacao Economy of the Eighteenth Century Province of Caracas and the Spanish Cacao Market," *Hispanic American Historical Review*, Vol. 68 (1988), pp. 76–97, and Van de Voort, *De Westindische plantages*, pp. 56–60.

[37] Figures on slave populations are given in Cornelis Ch. Goslinga, *The Dutch in the Caribbean and in the Guianas, 1680–1791* (Assen, 1985), pp. 341, 456, 457.

[38] Van der Voort, *De Westindische plantages*, p. 102.

[39] See Appendix, taken from Emmer, "Suiker, goud en slaven," p. 157.

[40] Van de Voort, "Dutch capital," p. 102. The value of Surinam exports appears in Emmer, "Suiker, goud en slaven," p. 154.

Surinam's negative trade balance also explains why the Dutch slave trade declined at the end of the eighteenth century. By then the Dutch had long since lost their position as international slave suppliers. The transit trade via Curaçao and St. Eustatius had been lost. In the course of the eighteenth century, the Dutch slave trade had become increasingly dependent on the demand for slaves in the Dutch Guianas. As a result of the large investments in that region, the Dutch slave trade reached its numerical zenith during the decade 1760–9, transporting more than 7,000 slaves per year. By the same token, the Dutch slave trade suffered immediately once further investments were stopped due to the sudden decline in the market value of the West Indian plantation loans. After the French occupation of the Netherlands between 1795 and 1813, the resumption of the slave trade was disallowed.[41]

The relative indifference to the abolition of the slave trade in the Netherlands seems to indicate that the country's largest slave-worked colony mattered little to Dutch industry and trade. No concerted action against abolition was taken by the owners of the many Amsterdam sugar refineries. Their supply of raw sugar came from a wide variety of plantation colonies, and the possible loss of or reduction in shipments from the Dutch Guianas seemed not to have been of much importance to this industry. Nevertheless, the production of guns and powder used as barter in the trade to Africa must have had some importance to this branch of the Dutch manufacturing industry, especially in time of peace when other sales declined. The Dutch East India Company must have also been affected by the decline of the Dutch trade to Africa, since some of its imports of Indian textiles were used as barter there. Cowries from the Maldives, imported by the Dutch East India Company from Ceylon, ceased to have Dutch buyers. Unfortunately, there are no data on the composition and total value of the products used as barter in the Dutch trade on the African coast. There exists no information as to what extent some of these goods were specially manufactured in the Netherlands for that purpose.[42]

In reviewing the declining interest of the Dutch metropolitan econ

[41] On the Dutch slave trade, see Postma, "The Origins of African Slaves," p. 49, and Postma, "The Dutch Slave Trade," p. 242. On the transit trade via Curaçao to the Spanish Main, see Palmer, pp. 59 and 98. On the abolition of the Dutch slave trade, see P. C. Emmer, *Engeland, Nederland, Afrika en de slavenhandel in de negentiende eeuw* (Leiden, 1974).

[42] On the composition of a cargo or of barter products destined for the slave trade on the African coast, see Unger, pp. 27–34. On cowries, see Jan Hogendorn and Marion Johnson, *The Shell Money of the Slave Trade* (Cambridge, 1986), pp. 39, 40, 91.

omy in its Atlantic possessions, it is necessary to explain why the Dutch were so keen on retaining at least some of their West Indian colonies. First of all, the many financiers of the plantation mortgages wanted their money back. Before 1800 only 15 to 25 percent of the principal had been paid back. The many investors feared that the planters in Surinam would stop paying at all as soon as they became part of a different colonial empire. This actually occurred during the fourth Anglo-Dutch War of 1780–4. During that war the Surinam planters purchased slaves from British slavers, paying with the coffee and sugar belonging to their creditors in Amsterdam. In addition, the trade with North America in victuals, horses, and molasses had increased, again using the proceeds of the plantations as payment. It was with this experience in mind that after the end of the war in 1784 the Amsterdam investors tried to link Surinam more closely to their city. They suggested a revival of the Dutch slave trade by offering a subsidy to slave traders in order to drive out foreigners from trading with the Dutch Guianas.[43]

A second reason for retaining the Atlantic possessions was the export trade to Amsterdam. This city received about 90% of all Surinam produce shipped to Europe. Contemporary estimates assume that Amsterdam alone would earn about 3 million guilders a year in freight charges and in profits from the sale of European products in Surinam. The 70 ships from Surinam constituted only about 5% of all ships coming into Amsterdam during the second half of the 18th century. However, they were Dutch ships, which were increasingly driven off the seas in other trades.[44]

After the ending of the Napoleonic Wars several parts of the Dutch empire, where slavery dominated the labour supply, became permanently British: the Cape Colony and Berbice, Demerary and Essequibo. The incorporation into the British empire stimulated the rapid growth of their respective slave economies. The slave economies of the Dutch Antilles and Surinam on the other hand stagnated or

---

[43] Van de Voort, *De Westindische plantages*, pp. 205–13; Evidence for a decline in exports to the Netherlands and an increase in imports from North America can be found in P. C. Emmer, "Het Atlantische gebied," in F. J. A. Broeze, J. R. Bruijn, and F. S. Gaastra (eds.), *Maritieme Geschiedenis der Nederlanden* (Bussum, 1979), Vol. III, p. 300.

[44] Unfortunately, there are only contemporary figures on the importance of the Surinam trade for Amsterdam. Van de Voort, *De Westindische plantages*, mentions a yearly sum of 2 million guilders as income derived from insurance, transportation, and sale of the Surinam products. Goslinga, *The Dutch in the Caribbean and in the Guianas*, p. 323, mentions the same figure and adds 1 million more for profits made on the export of European goods to Surinam. The data on Amsterdam shipping in general are from J. V. Th. Knoppers, "De vaart in Europa," in *Maritieme Geschiedenis*, Vol. III, p. 233.

even declined during the first decades of the 19th century.[45] It had become obvious, that the Netherlands no longer were able nor willing to invest in new slave frontiers. The dynamics of 19th century colonial slavery had outgrown the stagnating Dutch economy.

CONCLUSION

The Dutch role in the Atlantic was important in that the Dutch were instrumental in combining the production technology of the first Atlantic system with the capitalism of the second Atlantic system. As a result, the major production areas of tropical cash crops shifted from Brazil to the Caribbean and to the southern regions of North America.

Slavery was the only source of labor in both Atlantic systems, making up for the insufficient supply of both European migratory labor and labor available in the New World as offered by Amerindians and by settlers of European descent. The supply of African labor was relatively elastic, and that elasticity was one of the key elements in the distinctive orientation of the second Atlantic system toward the international market.

After the first fifty years, the international competitive elements within the second Atlantic system were reduced. The system was in danger of separating into several national systems. Again, the Dutch played an important role in keeping the second Atlantic system as international and as market-oriented as possible. At home, the Dutch provided an international market for the purchase of goods destined for the African barter trade. They provided slaves to non-Dutch territories via their Antillean transit harbors. These harbors also functioned as international assembling points of Caribbean produce to be shipped to Europe.

The international importance of the Dutch in the creation and operation of the Atlantic economy sharply contrasted with the modest Dutch share in the production of Atlantic cash crops, as well as with the negative returns on Dutch plantation investments.

---

[45] For Berbice, Essequibo, and Demerary, see P. M. Netscher, *Geschiedenis van de Koloniën Essequibo, Demerary en Berbice van de vestiging der Nederlanders aldaar tot op onzen tijd* (Den Haag, 1888), pp. 300, 301, and Seymour Drescher, *Econocide: British Slavery in the Era of Abolition* (Pittsburgh, 1977), pp. 95–7.

Appendix. *Surinam's trade balance/balance of payments, 1766–76, on average per year*

	Debit	Credit	Balance
1. Trade with the republic			
a. Exports of cash crops		6,525,091	
b. Imports of European goods	1,337,513		
c. Service charges (auctions, transportation, insurance)	2,001,401		
Balance			+ 3,186,177
2. Trade with North America			
a. Exports (molasses, dram, firewood)		90,096	
b. Imports (foodstuffs, cattle, building materials)	282,333		
			− 192,237
3. Trade with Africa Average imports of 4,000 blacks per year at 325 guilders each	1,300,000		
			− 1,300,000
Positive balance of trade			+ 1,693,000
Payment of taxes and mortgages		2,600,000	
Negative balance of payments			− 903,000

CHAPTER 5

Precolonial western Africa and the Atlantic economy

DAVID ELTIS

SCHOLARS researching the origins and development of the Atlantic economy tend to be more interested in the contribution of precolonial Africa to the Atlantic economy than in the importance of that economy to Africa. The vital role occupied by Africa in the development of the Americas is beyond question, yet that contribution cannot be understood fully without an awareness of the significance of transatlantic trade to Africans. Most scholars with an "Atlantic" orientation would probably argue that transatlantic trade ties affected Africa as profoundly as they affected the Americas, though in obviously different ways. The shift in the 1970s toward a new focus on that part of the historical African economy producing for domestic consumption, as represented by Curtin's work on Senegambia and Peukert's on Dahomey, seems to have halted.[1] Recently, both detailed regional studies and continentwide syntheses have returned to an older concern with the effects on Africa of the slave trade, its abolition, and the subsequent rapid increase in transatlantic produce exports.[2]

Research for this chapter was aided by a grant from the Social Sciences and Humanities Research Council of Canada. The chapter benefitted from the comments of Stanley L. Engerman and numerous participants in the conference sessions. Sections of the chapter draw on David Eltis and Lawrence C. Jennings, "Trade Between Western Africa and the Atlantic World in the Pre-Colonial Era," *American Historical Review*, Vol. 93 (1988), pp. 936–59.

[1] Philip D. Curtin. *Economic Change in Precolonial Africa: Senegambia in the Era of the Slave Trade*, 2 vols. (Madison, Wis., 1975); Werner Peukert, *Der Atlantische Sklavenhandel von Dahomey, 1740–1797* (Wiesbaden, 1978).

[2] There is clearly no consensus on the role of external forces on the precolonial African economy. Two recent studies that give more weight to production for domestic consumption than most are Patrick Manning's work on Dahomey, *Slavery, Colonialism and Economic Growth in Dahomey, 1640–1960* (Cambridge, 1982), and Ralph Austen's synthesis, *African Economic History: Internal Development and External Dependency* (London, 1987). Yet Manning sees the century of rapid growth in the Dahomean economy between 1840 and 1930 as stemming from agricultural exports, just as slave trade exports in the two preceding centuries "slowed the growth of domestic product" (pp. 49, see also 281–3). For Austen, likewise, integration of the African economy

This more recent concern with external trade is firmly rooted in the quantitative work of the last two decades. Few scholars have failed to take advantage of numerous new estimates of volume and prices in both the slave and commodity trades. But despite this interest, most researchers have not aggregated the different data sources to arrive at estimates for particular African regions (as opposed to countries in Europe and the Americas). More important, they have not given center stage to the implications of these new data for the importance of the overseas economy to Africans. The African historiography contains no counterpart to the Brenner debate on the origins of European development or, to move to a different ideological milieu, the exchange over Douglass North's model of export-led growth in North America. Except for the issue of the demographic impact of the slave trade on Africa, where ironically the data are weak, recent economic historians have assumed a strong impact from the external sector rather than attempted to assess how great that impact was. The mechanism through which the Atlantic affected Africa has received rather more attention than the strength of that effect. But even here the plausibility of competing hypotheses has tended to rest on qualitative evidence.

A quick review of these hypotheses from an economist's standpoint might go as follows. For the traffic in people, the older literature often depicted slaves as having been stolen from Africa. At the very least, Europeans sold merchandise to Africans for extortionate prices. This can be represented as very unfavorable terms of trade for Africans. A second and more recent view is the opposite of the first. According to it, the influx of trade goods at low prices was so great that domestic production was seriously impaired and an African dependency on foreign producers developed. In a sense, leaving aside for the moment the issue of private versus social costs, the first argument suggests that the slave traders paid too little, whereas the second suggests that they paid too much. The third broad interpretation focuses on the social dislocation that the slave trade caused within Africa. From this standpoint, the slave trade was responsible for spreading the institution of slavery, encouraging social stratification in African societies, and altering relations between African states. For economists, a variant of this view is that the negative externalities (or social costs not

into the world economy was important enough that "Atlantic Africa, with the fullest exposure to European commerce, experienced the most impressive economic growth of any pre-colonial region on the continent" (pp. 268–9).

covered by slave prices) of selling an African into the Atlantic traffic
were considerable. These would include the disruptions of slave raiding and the effects of population decline or slower population growth.

The first two of these broad interpretations, as well as the broader
issue of the relative importance of domestic and external sectors
within the economies of most West African societies, are, in fact,
amenable to quantitative evaluation. New data on prices, volumes,
and the composition of trade between Africa and the Atlantic world
make possible the reconstitution of decadal "snapshots" of aggregate
trading activity from an African perspective over nearly two centuries
of the prepartition era. These new aggregations, used in conjunction
with backward population projections and inferences about African
living standards, permit some new insights on the scale and nature
of the impact of the Atlantic world on western Africa.

We turn first to the data. It is now possible to estimate the value
of total trade between the Atlantic world and western Africa from
Senegambia to Angola for five widely separated decades between the
seventeenth and nineteenth centuries. They are the 1680s, the 1730s,
the 1780s, the 1820s, and the 1860s. Southeast Africa, whence came
nearly one-fifth of all transatlantic slaves in the 1820s, is omitted from
this analysis. For four of these decades, estimates of the regional and
compositional distributions are also possible – in the latter case, on
the basis of physical volumes as well as values. These new aggregations are something less than the last word on the subject. The
total value estimates for the slave trade, at least, are largely the product of the prices and quantities of slaves carried across the Atlantic.
With both slaves and merchandise there is a thorny valuation problem
in that goods and slaves entering and leaving Africa were counted
when they left from or arrived in Europe (or the Americas) rather
than Africa. No adjustment has been made for this, so that the merchandise included here is largely as it appears in the historical record.
Thus African exports are valued c.i.f. Europe and the Americas rather
than f.o.b. Africa, and African imports are counted f.o.b. Europe/the
Americas rather than c.i.f. Africa. This makes the estimates rather
different from those for other regions. However, the total trade figures
(exports and imports combined) should not be much affected by
whether the count was made in Africa or in Europe and the Americas.[3]

---

[3] Whenever imports and exports, valued c.i.f. and f.o.b., respectively, are added together, shipping costs for only one branch of trade are included in the resulting
aggregate. The situation is no different from the procedure followed here, except
that it is the shipping costs of African exports, rather African imports, that are

Thus the aggregate trade data are useful for assessing Africa's role in the Atlantic economy.

Table 1 presents aggregate estimates for all five decades spanning the rise and decline of the Atlantic slave trade.[4] The values in this table are all in current prices, though as movements in the British price level, at least, between these particular decades were not dramatic, conversion to real values would not change the picture very much. Prices of produce and people in the African trade per se, however, followed a path different from the general price level. The first column shows that the slave trade expanded rapidly and more or less continuously in the century from the 1680s. Indeed, this secular trend probably dates from the mid-seventeenth century. It is now generally accepted that the 1780s was the peak decade in terms of the value of the transatlantic traffic and probably too in the volume of slave departures. But though the growth in value was rapid, its composition shifted. Down to the 1730s, expansion was based on a doubling of both the number and the price of Africans sold into the traffic. In the next half-century slave prices doubled again, but the volume of slaves increased by only 50%. In the next forty years a nice symmetry emerges, in the nominal trends at least, in that both the price and quantity of slaves in Africa had fallen back by the 1820s to approximately the levels of the 1730s. The fact that the value of combined imports and exports in the slave trade was 50% higher in the 1820s than ninety years earlier was due entirely to increases in the price of slaves in the Americas.

Five pairs of observations are scarcely enough to support a price

---

included. Unless the cost of carrying exports to Africa differed greatly from the cost of shipping African imports, the combined import/export figure should not be much affected by which aggregation procedure is employed.

[4] The estimates developed here differ from those in David Eltis, "Trade Between Western Africa and the Atlantic World before 1870: Estimates of Trends in Value, Composition and Direction," *Research in Economic History*, Vol. 12 (1989), pp. 197–239, in two respects. First, prices of slaves in the Bight of Biafra for the 1780s have been set at £13.3 instead of the £22.1 assumed for the rest of West Africa. Second, estimates for the 1730s are developed. These comprise essentially the sum of two total revenue (price × quantity) calculations for the slave trade – one for each side of the Atlantic – together with an allowance for the nonslave trade of 15% of all trade. This allowance is based on the following considerations. Commodity trade with Senegambia in the 1730s made up one-third of all Senegambian Atlantic trade in these years (Curtin, Vol. 2, p. 98). Produce imports into Britain from Africa ranged from 10% to 25% of the value of British exports to Africa in these years [David Richardson, "Slave Prices in West Africa: A Tentative Annual Series, 1698–1807," *Bulletin of Economic Research* (forthcoming)]. Allowing for c.i.f. adjustments, this implies a ratio of produce to total trade of less than 10%. Most other national traders would likely have been closer to the British figure than the Senegambian ratio.

Table 1. *Estimated value of total trade (imports and exports combined)*
between Africa and the Atlantic world in selected decades, 1680s–1860s
(millions of current pounds sterling)

	Value of slave trade	Value of commodity trade	Value of total trade
1681–90	4.5	3.7	8.2
1731–40	18.0	3.2	21.1
1781–90	43.9	3.5	47.4
1821–30	27.2	10.7	37.9
1861–70	4.9	88.3	93.1

Sources: Rows 1, 3, 4, 5: David Eltis, "Trade Between Western Africa and the Atlantic World before 1870: Estimates of Trends in Value, Composition and Direction," *Research in Economic History*, Vol. 12 (1989), pp. 197–239. Row 2: constructed from David Richardson, "The Eighteenth Century British Slave Trade: Estimates of Its Volume and Coastal Distribution in Africa," *Research in Economic History*, Vol. 12 (1989), pp. 151–95; Joseph C. Miller, "Slave Prices in the Portuguese Southern Atlantic, 1600–1830," in Paul Lovejoy (ed.), *Africans in Bondage: Studies in Slavery and the Slave Trade* (Madison, Wis. 1986), pp. 43–78; Johannes Postma, *The Dutch in the Atlantic Slave Trade, 1600–1815* (Cambridge, 1990), pp. 110, 118; Robert Louis Stein, *The French Slave Trade in the Eighteenth Century* (Madison, Wis., 1979), pp. 207–11; Jay Coughtry, *The Notorious Triangle* (Philadelphia, 1981), pp. 241-3; Jean Mettas and Serge Daget, *Répertoire des espéditions négrières françaises au XVIIIe siècle*, 2 vols. (Paris, 1978–84); Patrick Manning, "The Slave Trade in the Bight of Benin, 1640–1890," in Henry A. Gemery and Jan S. Hogendorn (eds.), *The Uncommon Market: Essays in the Economic History of the Atlantic Slave Trade* (New York, 1979), pp. 107–41; Herbert S. Klein, *The Middle Passage* (Princeton, N.J., 1978), p. 27.

elasticity of supply elasticity, but at least we know that for this period, which straddles the apogee of the plantation system in the Americas as well as partial suppression of the traffic, the major disturbances in the market for slaves on the African coast as a whole came from the demand side. We can have some confidence that it is the supply function that we are observing here. The present estimates thus do support LeVeen's finding of an elastic response,[5] but it would appear that the supply of slaves was much less price elastic at higher than at lower volumes of slave exports.

The commodity column reveals different trends. Despite the decline in gold exports, the value of commodity trade probably changed little in the eighteenth century – partly because of a sharp rise in gold prices after 1760. The rapid increase in commodity trade, as is well known, dates from the early nineteenth century. Except for gum, the

[5] E. Phillip LeVeen, *British Slave Trade Suppression Policies, 1821–1865* (New York, 1977), pp. 139–51.

price increases associated with this expansion were rather modest.[6] In the case of palm oil, British imports more than quintupled from the early 1820s to the late 1840s, although the price in Britain increased little. This would suggest, inter alia, that the vent-for-surplus model, which some have used to explain Africa's response to the Atlantic economy, might be more appropriate for the traffic in produce than for the slave trade.[7] On the import side, on the other hand, the cost of manufactured goods, particularly textiles, fell dramatically after 1800.[8] The produce of the Americas, also an important component of African imports, generally rose in price in the eighteenth century, but this trend was reversed after 1815. Thus, from 1800 down, the fall in prices of African imports was considerably greater than the rise in prices for African exports.

The total trade series of Table 1, which combines the slave and commodity trades, indicates two cycles of growth in Africa's Atlantic trade. The first, based on the slave trade, and the second, on commodities supplied to an industrializing Europe, were interrupted by a marked decline corresponding to the partial closing of markets for slaves in the Americas. Given the trends in prices of African exports and imports discussed previously, however, there can be little doubt that the volume of total trade increased much more rapidly after 1780 than before, and much more rapidly than the current value totals for the 1780s, 1820s, and 1860s suggest. The volume of goods imported into Africa in the 1820s was certainly no less than it had been in the 1780s. The volume of British exports to Africa increased ten times between 1817–20 and 1846–9, and there was a fivefold increase in the volume of British imports.[9] If the British data are any guide, it follows

---

[6] For slave prices see Joseph C. Miller, "Slave Prices in the Portuguese Southern Atlantic, 1600–1830," in Paul Lovejoy (ed.), *Africans in Bondage: Studies in Slavery and the Slave Trade* (Madison, Wis. 1986), pp. 43–78; Johannes Postma, *The Dutch in the Atlantic Slave Trade* (Cambridge, 1990), pp. 265–9; Richard N. Bean, *The British Trans-Atlantic Slave Trade, 1650–1775* (New York, 1975), pp. 139–40; LeVeen, pp. 114–15; David Eltis, "Prices of Slaves in the African Slave Trade After 1810" (unpublished paper, 1984). For commodity prices see Curtin, Vol. 2, pp. 86–112; A. J. H. Latham, "Price Fluctuations in the Early Palm Oil Trade," *Journal of African History*, Vol. 19 (1978), pp. 213–18.

[7] Henry A. Gemery and Jan S. Hogendorn, "The Atlantic Slave Trade: A Tentative Economic Model," *Journal of African History*, Vol. 15 (1974), pp. 223–46. But see the criticism of this in Stefano Fenoaltea, "Europe in the African Mirror: The Slave Trade and the Rise of Feudalism" (unpublished paper, 1988).

[8] Albert H. Imlah, *Economic Elements in the Pax Britannica* (Cambridge, Mass., 1958), pp. 208–15; Curtin, Vol. II, p. 110; LeVeen, *British Slave Trade Suppression Policies*, pp. 118–19.

[9] Calculated from official values in the ledgers in Customs 4 and 8, Public Record Office. The official value series effectively indicates trends in physical volumes.

that trade volumes between Africa and the Atlantic world may well have increased five times between the 1820s and 1860s rather than more than doubling, as suggested by the current value figures. What also follows from the previous discussion is that except for a short reversal during the Napoleonic wars, the terms of trade moved steadily in favor of Africa from the end of the seventeenth century. Probably no other major area trading with Europe in the two centuries before 1870 experienced as continuous and massive a shift. Thus an average slave or a hundredweight of ivory sold on the African coast in the 1860s could command fifteen times the textiles and six or seven times the muskets of their counterparts in the 1680s.[10]

These figures are dramatic, though the scale of the trade expansion and the apparently much greater price elasticity of supply that existed for produce than for slaves probably conform to what most scholars would expect. However, these findings are likely to mislead if we concern ourselves purely with African Atlantic trade. A broader perspective suggests two less obvious and more controversial themes. First, despite the rapid growth of the trade in African produce after 1800, it was only in the slave trade era that African Atlantic trade kept pace with the growth of world trade. Second, despite the relative strength of the slave trade, the economy of western Africa remained little affected by trade with the Atlantic in the period covered here – measured at least with the statistics currently available to us.

The first of these two propositions can be dealt with quickly. Between the 1680s and the 1780s, the growth rate in the volume of African trade with the Atlantic was probably about the same as that between Britain and the Americas.[11] This is hardly surprising in view of the interconnection of the slave and plantation produce trades. But the important point to note is that English trade with both Africa and the Americas increased much faster in these years

---

[10] David Eltis and Lawrence C. Jennings, "Trade Between Western Africa and the Atlantic World in the Pre-Colonial Era," *American Historical Review*, Vol. 93 (1988), pp. 942–3.

[11] It is assumed here that trade between England and Wales and Africa may be taken as a proxy for trade between the whole of the Atlantic world and Africa. Between 1701–5 and 1786–90, exports and reexports from England and Wales to the continental colonies that became the United States increased eightfold. This is very similar to the rate of increase in English exports and reexports to Africa in the same years [calculated from Elizabeth B. Schumpeter, *English Overseas Trade Statistics, 1697–1808* (London, 1960), p. 17. Schumpeter's data are in official values]. The years 1786–90 were perhaps the peak quinquennium for slave departures from Africa during the whole period of the slave trade.

than did English trade with the rest of the world.[12] A different picture emerges after the 1780s, however. In that decade the Atlantic slave trade peaked in volume, and once this peak had passed, African trade with the Atlantic fell behind in relative terms. Between 1800 and 1860, world trade increased nearly fivefold measured in current values and perhaps tenfold in quantity.[13] Whether we look at current values or physical volumes, the changes in African trade between the 1780s and the 1860s look less impressive by comparison. The traffic in slaves continued to be of major importance in the nineteenth century, but once it stopped expanding in the 1780s, the growth of commodity trade was not enough to sustain Africa's relative position in world trade. In this sense, Africa differed from other less developed regions, most of which participated fully in the nineteenth-century expansion of world trade.[14] Indeed, it is probable that Africa's share of world trade continued to shrink into the twentieth century and has never approached the levels attained when the slave trade was at its height.[15]

Yet the question of the importance of overseas trade to Africa cannot be addressed without reference to the African domestic economy. There are four ways of approaching this crucial issue in the premodern African context. One is to examine the types of goods imported into and exported from western Africa. Products with a pronounced antisocial impact could have had an effect beyond what the data might at first suggest. The second is to estimate the approximate physical quantities of major products imported on a per capita basis. The third is to compare the levels of per capita trade in Africa with those of Africa's main trading partners. The fourth is to sample the evidence on African domestic product in light of the trade figures discussed previously. Three of these approaches require some reference to population estimates of Africa. Patrick Manning has developed estimates for those parts of sub-Saharan Africa that were affected by the slave trade. On the whole, they posit a severe demographic impact by the

---

[12] John J. McCusker and Russell R. Menard, *The Economy of British North America, 1607–1789* (Chapel Hill, N.C., 1985), p. 40.

[13] Imlah, p. 189; John R. Hanson, *Trade in Transition: Exports from the Third World, 1840–1900* (New York, 1980), p. 14.

[14] Hanson, pp. 13–31. Hanson, however, includes Africa in his generally favorable assessment of the economic performance of less developed countries.

[15] Ralph Austen has raised the intriguing possibility that trans-Saharan gold exports gave Africa an even larger role in the world economy in medieval times than it had in the slave trade era (pp. 36–7). The assumptions on medieval trade and gold exports on which this position is based seem improbable, but in the absence of data we cannot reject this possibility out of hand.

slave trade, though the series used here actually lies midway between the upper and lower limits of the range of estimates that Manning develops. Specifically, a population of 20.6 million is projected for 1860, 20.3 for 1820, 22.5 for 1780, and 23.0 for 1680.[16] A lower assessment of the demographic impact of the slave trade would generate larger populations than these and smaller per capita trade figures than appear subsequently.

The first of the preceding approaches examining the composition of trade with Africa is outlined elsewhere.[17] On the export side, the rise and fall of the slave trade is summarized in Table 1, and little need be added to the debate on the socially disruptive impact of that trade. We should at least note that there is no consensus on the extent of that disruption. On the produce component of exports, it has been argued that the produce exports that superseded the slave trade actually maintained rates of enslavement (and therefore the extent of social disruption) at levels that existed prior to suppression of the traffic. However, the prices of slaves declined sharply in Africa subsequent to suppression, which suggests that domestic demand did not fully take the place of declining demand from overseas markets.[18]

On the import side, Table 2 presents estimates of the types of goods imported into Africa for four widely separated decades. Although capital goods appear to have been scarce, and although the disruptive impact of firearms, alcohol, and perhaps tobacco needs to be acknowledged, there is actually little in Table 2 to separate out Africa from other importers of the pre- and early industrializing worlds.

[16] Using the names and boundaries of 1931, western Africa comprises Senegal, Gambia, Mauritania, Guine, Guinea, Sierra Leone, Liberia, the Ivory Coast, the Gold Coast and British Togo, French Togo, Dahomey, western Nigeria, eastern Nigeria, French Cameroon, Gabon, the Congo, Oubangui-Chari (portion), Equateur (portion), Angola, Kasai, and Katanga (personal communication from Patrick Manning). Clearly, parts of the savanna and other areas excluded here did trade with the Atlantic, though the volume cannot have been significant. The most recent of Manning's demographic studies that employs this concept of western Africa is "The Impact of Slave Exports on the Population of the Western Coast of Africa," in Serge Daget (ed.), *Communications au colloque international sur la traite des noirs* (Paris, 1989). See the broader geographical limits used in John D. Fage, "Slavery and the Slave Trade in the Context of West African History," *Journal of African History*, Vol. 10 (1969), pp. 393–404; "The Effect of the Export Slave Trade on African Populations," in R. P. Moss and R. J. A. R. Rathbone (eds.), *The Population Factor in African Studies* (London, 1975), pp. 15–23.

[17] Eltis, "Trade Between Western Africa and the Atlantic World."

[18] Paul Lovejoy, *Transformations in Slavery: A History of Slavery in Africa* (Cambridge, 1983), pp. 8–12, 269–82; David Eltis, *Economic Growth and the Ending of the Transatlantic Slave Trade* (New York, 1987), pp. 226–7.

Table 2. Estimated relative distribution of imports into western Africa, 1680s, 1780s, 1820s, and 1860s

	Textiles	Alcohol	Tobacco	Misc. manufactures	Iron	Food	Guns and gunpowder	Raw[a]mats	Unassigned
1680s	0.500	0.125	0.025	0.125	0.050	0.050	0.075	0.050	0
1780s	0.564	0.097	0.081	0.105	0.035	0.018	0.086	0.017	0
1820s	0.394	0.116	0.070	0.090	0.018	0.086	0.146	0.026	0
1860s	0.316	0.120	0.117	0.048	0.012	0.085	0.077	0.046	0.173

[a]Includes cowries.
Source: Eltis, "Trade between Western Africa and the Atlantic World before 1870."

Consumer goods may be divided into those that satisfy the basic requirements of nutrition, clothing, and shelter and those that satisfy psychological needs. In the preindustrial context the latter included sugar, tobacco, and alcohol, along with a host of purely decorative items, some textiles, and most luxury goods.[19] Such "psychic" goods formed no greater share of African imports than of the imports of most other parts of the world. It is likely, in fact, that luxurious textiles and other expensive gifts made up a considerably smaller share of Africa's overseas imports than elsewhere. If the composition of trade magnified the impact of the Atlantic on Africa, it was more likely because of the nature of African exports than imports. The evidence of the composition of trade on the issue of Atlantic impact is thus mixed, with much hinging on the contentious questions of what proportion of the captives were the product of war and the demographic implications of the trade.

The physical quantities of four products imported into sub-Saharan Africa over the two centuries preceding partition may be inferred from the customs data used earlier. These, combined with Manning's population estimates, yield crude per capita import figures that form the second of the four approaches to assessing the domestic importance of overseas trade. The four products are textiles, guns, alcohol, and tobacco, which together accounted for well over half of all imports. We begin with textiles. During each year of the 1860s the British and French exported on average about 45 million yards of cotton textiles to Africa. A rough allowance for exports by other nations, and a further adjustment for textiles other than cottons – a very small category at this time – suggests that about 57 million yards of imported textiles of all kinds were traded annually in the decade 1861–70.[20] Using the preceding population estimate, this amounts to nearly three yards per person; and as a two-yard "wrapper" is sufficient to clothe one person, it would seem that overseas imports supplied up to half (depending on one's estimates of per capita consumption) of the re

---

[19] For the high income elasticities of textiles in West Africa, see Johnson, "Technology, Competition, and African Crafts," in Clive Dewey and A. G. Hopkins (eds.), *The Imperial Impact: Studies in the Economic History of Africa and India* (London, 1978), p. 266.

[20] PP, 1866, LXVIII, pp. 252, 260, 322, 394–6; 1871, part 2, LXIII, pp. 228, 236, 300, 370–2, give the cotton yardage exported from Britain. French values are available from France, L'Administration des douanes, *Tableau decennal du commerce de la France avec ses colonies et la puissance étrangères, 1857 à 1876* (Paris, 1868, 1878), and declared values per yard from the British data are used to estimate French quantities. The proportion of all textile exports accounted for by these two nations is calculated from Eltis, "African Trade with the Atlantic World." Five percent is allowed for noncotton textiles.

gion's textile consumption. The point to note, however, is that per capita textile imports were far below what they were shortly to become. In Dahomey between 1890 and 1914, imported cloth provided no less than fifteen yards per person each year, and there was still a vibrant domestic industry in existence, exporting some of its output to Brazil.[21] Total consumption no doubt increased between the 1860s and 1900s, but the large gains by imports over these years seem beyond doubt.

Nevertheless, the volume of imports in the 1860s was much higher than in earlier decades. For the 1820s a similar procedure yields an estimate of 6.0 million yards per year and a per capita consumption of 0.3 yard.[22] For the 1780s the equivalent figures are 9.5 million yards in total and 0.4 yard per person.[23] A similar calculation for the 1680s is not possible, but reference to the aggregate trade figures given earlier indicates that only a small proportion of Africans could have been wearing imported cloth. It might be concluded that imported cloths reached a wider African market in the eighteenth century but began to impinge on the domestic textile industry only as the slave trade was replaced by the traffic in commodities in the mid-nineteenth century. This increase in imported textile use was a function of the dramatic decline in the price of English fabrics in the nineteenth century, but the domestic industry remained competitive.

The population estimates permit a new perspective on gun imports. Per capita gun imports were likely greater in the 1860s than in any of the major slave-exporting decades. Combined values of African imports of guns and gunpowder are estimated here at £0.008 per person for each year in the 1780s, or one gun per 118 persons; £0.009 in the 1820s, or one gun per 145 persons; and £0.016 in the 1860s, or one gun per 103 persons, all values measured f.o.b. in the source countries.[24] One further relative perspective might be considered.

---

[21] Manning, p. 124.

[22] The yardage of British cottons is taken from the Customs 8 ledgers, P.R.O., but this series is also in Newbury, "Credit in Early Nineteenth Century West African Trade," *Journal of African History*, Vol. 13 (1972), p. 83. Exports from Britain (as opposed to British-made goods) accounted for about one-quarter of all cotton textiles taken to Africa (most British textiles at this time reached the coast via slave traders sailing from the Americas), and an allowance of 20% has been made for noncottons as well as for cottons already made up into clothing.

[23] Calculated from Johnson, "Commodities, Customs and the Computer," *History in Africa*, Vol. 11 (1984), pp. 359–66, and from Eltis, "Trade between Western Africa and the Atlantic World."

[24] Arms imports calculated from Eltis, "Trade Between Western Africa and the Atlantic

Census data for the United States make possible a transatlantic comparison of guns and gunpowder. In 1820 a lower bound estimate of the value of these items produced in the United States implies a ratio of £0.013, larger than the African ratio for the 1820s though somewhat below the 1860 figure.[25] By 1860 in the United States, however, Americans were producing £0.037 arms per person, more than double the contemporary African import ratio.[26] As net exports of guns and gunpowder from the United States were very small before the Civil War, and domestic production of armaments in Africa was negligible at this time, we can conclude that more guns and gunpowder were used in the United States, and probably by other societies in the Americas, than in that part of Africa affected by the slave trade. Similar comparisons are not possible for the eighteenth century, but the 1780s African ratio of £0.008 worth of guns and gunpowder per person in Africa was lower than any of the previously given nineteenth-century ratios. The discussion suggests that those claiming a major impact from arms have to build their arguments on some basis other than just the volume of imports. The supply of arms obviously facilitated slave raids, and guns may have been concentrated geographically, so that local effects may have been considerable. If this was the case, then it is also clear that over large geographic areas their impact must have been small.

The other two imported products examined here were less important. Tobacco, in semiprocessed form, averaged 12.8 million pounds per year in the 1860s, or about half a pound per person – not a large amount by modern standards. It was, nevertheless, more than double the per capita consumption of the 1820s or the 1780s, though exact comparisons are complicated by the switch from roll to leaf tobacco.[27]

World." The value figures are in current prices, but conversion to real values would not affect the conclusion.

[25] Calculated from *Digest of Accounts of Manufacturing Establishments in the United States* (Washington, D.C., 1823). Data are not consolidated, being listed in the census abstract by county. In addition, complete information on annual production is not always supplied. In most cases, inference on the basis of other statistics that are listed is possible. Population figures taken from *Historical Statistics of the United States* (Washington, D.C., 1976).

[26] U.S. Bureau of the Census, *Manufactures of the United States in 1860 Compiled from the Original Returns of the Eighth Census* (Washington, D.C., 1865), pp. 736–7. Valuation of the product under the census survey was probably not greatly different from the customs' valuation. For those who fear that approaching secession might have inflated U.S. arms output in 1860, it should be noted that per capita output in 1850 was £0.023 [calculated from *Abstract of the Statistics of Manufactures According to the Returns of the Seventh Census* (Washington, D.C., 1858), pp. 58, 96], about where we might expect it to be, assuming a linear trend from 1820.

[27] British exports in the 1860s were 2.5 million pounds per year and accounted for just

Alcoholic beverages averaged 0.75 million gallons in the 1780s, 1.0 million gallons in the 1820s, and 6.1 million gallons in the 1860s, again on a per year basis. The annual per capita consumption is calculated at 0.033, 0.05, and 0.3 gallon for the 1780s, 1820s, and 1860s, respectively.[28] For the 1680s, consumption of both products by Africans must have been infinitesimally small. Again, perspective is provided by consumption ratios for the late nineteenth and early twentieth centuries. In this period, Dahomey was importing four or five times the amount of both tobacco and alcohol per person that western Africa had imported in the 1860s.[29] The scale of precolonial imports of these products signals something less than a revolution in consumer behavior – even in the 1860s. Just as clearly, however, rapid growth did occur in the mid-nineteenth century. These figures suggest that merchandise distributed from the Atlantic was of small importance relative to what it was shortly to become. Furthermore, if elite groups took a disproportionate share of these goods, many, perhaps most, living within reach of the Atlantic would have had little experience of imports.

The third approach to assessing the significance of overseas trade to the sub-Saharan Africa economy involves a simple comparison of per capita trade values. Table 3 presents data for several of Africa's trading partners around the Atlantic basin. Western Africa must have had the lowest ratio of any large trading area fringing the Atlantic. Indeed, in view of the earlier comments on population estimates, the African ratio must be regarded as an upperbound figure, with the actual ratio more likely smaller than that shown here.[30] Moreover,

under one-fifth of all tobacco exports to Africa. In the 1820s, British exports were 0.286 million pounds per year and about 7% of total exports (for sources see Eltis and Jennings, n. 56 and n. 57).

[28] British exports were 1.25 million gallons a year and 20% of total exports of spirits in the 1860s; 1.1 million and 12% in the 1820s; and 0.28 million and 21% in the 1780s. For sources see ibid., n. 57, and private communication from Marion Johnson. The rapid growth of per capita textile imports relative to imports of other goods in the mid-nineteenth century echoed productivity improvements in the British textile industry. Between 1780 and 1860, total factor productivity in the cotton industry grew four times faster than productivity in the economy as a whole and nearly 50% faster than average productivity in six leading industrializing sectors [D. N. McCloskey, "The Industrial Revolution, 1780–1860: A Survey," in Roderick Floud and Donald McCloskey (eds.), *The Economic History of Britain since 1700* (Cambridge, 1981), p. 114].

[29] In Dahomey in the early twentieth century, tobacco imports averaged 1 kilo per year per person, well before the mushrooming of cigarette sales. Imported alcohol ranged from 4 to 7 liters for each person per year (Manning, pp. 122, 127).

[30] For a discussion of this issue see Eltis, *Economic Growth*, chap. 5. John R. Hanson, using the population of all sub-Saharan Africa as a base, has calculated an 1860 per capita export ratio of only £0.1, compared to £1.2 for the whole of South America (p. 21).

Table 3. *Annual average per capita trade in selected regions of the Atlantic basin for the 1780s, 1820s, 1860s (half the sum of exports, reexports, and imports in nominal current values – pounds sterling divided by the population of the region)*

	1784–6	1824–6	1864–6
British West Indies	5.7[a]	7.7[b]	4.9[c]
Britain[d]	2.3	4.1	8.7
United States[e]	1.4[f]	2.0	2.4
Brazil	—	1.1	1.7
Western Africa[g]	0.1	0.1	0.2

Notes:
[a] Population base is for 1780.
[b] Population base is for 1830.
[c] Population base is for 1871; values are for exports and reexports only.
[d] United Kingdom in the 1860s. Population base is for census years.
[e] Imports are multiplied by 1.5 to approximate c.i.f. values.
[f] 1790.
[g] For a definition, see footnote 16.

Sources:
Row 1: Calculated from Ralph Davis, *The Industrial Revolution and British Overseas Trade* (Leicester, 1979), pp. 91, 94, 98, 111, 119; John J. McCusker, "The Rum Trade and the Balance of Payments of the Thirteen Continental Colonies, 1650–1775" (Ph.D. dissertation, University of Pittsburgh, 1970), pp. 692–701, 703; B. W. Higman, *Slave Populations of the British Caribbean, 1807–1834* (Baltimore, 1984), p. 77; G. W. Roberts, "Movements in Population and the Labour Force," in G. E. Cumper (ed.), *The Economy of the West Indies* (Kingston, Jamaica, 1960), p. 30; Alan H. Adamson, *Sugar Without Slaves: The Political Economy of British Guiana, 1838–1904* (New Haven, Conn., 1972), p. 215; PP, 1884, XLVII, *Report of the Royal Commission . . . into . . . the Public Revenues, Expenditures, Debts, and Liabilities of the Islands of Jamaica, Grenada, St. Vincent, Tobago, and St. Lucia, and the Leeward Islands*, pp. 252, 461, 655.
 Row 2: Calculated from Davis, p. 86; B. R. Mitchell and P. Deane, *Abstract of British Historical Statistics* (Cambridge, 1962), pp. 5, 8, 283.
 Row 3: Calculated from U.S. Bureau of the Census, *Historical Statistics of the United States* (Washington, D.C., 1976), pp. 8, 884, 886.
 Row 4: Calculated from Stanley J. Stein, *Vassouras: A Brazilian Coffee County, 1850–1900* (Princeton, N.J., 1958), p. 294; Instituto Brasileiro de Geografia e Estatística, *Anuário Estatístico do Brasil: Ano V 1939/40* (Rio de Janeiro, 1940), p. 1358.
 Row 5: Calculated from Table 1; Patrick Manning, "The Impact of Slave Exports on the Population of the Western Coast of Africa, 1700–1850," in Serge Daget (ed.), *Actes du Colloque International sur la Traite Noirs, Nantes, 1985*, 3 vols. (Paris, 1989).

despite the much larger ratios for Brazil and the United States, the former had a large subsistence economy, and for neither country did international trade contribute anything but a minor share to national income compared to domestic economic activities. The slave-based sectors of these economies were, of course, highly export oriented, but in both countries, as in western Africa, the nonexport sectors were far more important.[31] Perhaps the Americas could supply more of the produce that an industrializing North Atlantic required, but it is equally the case that European goods could make far fewer inroads into Africa than they could in the Americas. African textiles, metal goods, and merchandise satisfying psychic wants were simply more competitive in the face of European competition than their counterparts in the Americas.

The fourth approach to assessing the importance of the Atlantic to the African domestic economy is to look at export income relative to possible ranges of African domestic income. Evidence concerning African income levels in the precolonial era is thin but not nonexistent. There can be little doubt that early-nineteenth-century nutritional intakes, and probably living standards, as the twentieth century would conceive the term, were lower in Africa than in the Americas.[32] Yet there also seems little doubt that per capita income was high in Africa relative to most parts of the world outside the Americas and that, at the very least, assessments that place Africa at the bottom of the preindustrial continental income tables need to be revised.[33]

This last statement can be supported in three ways. First, land/labor ratios in Africa were high. Africa was under- rather than overpopulated. Moreover, as Boserup has pointed out, the technology used by Africans ensured a high marginal physical product.[34] The question of why Africans were forcibly removed from one area of high marginal physical product (Africa) to another (the Americas) is an intriguing one when we consider the large transatlantic transpor-

---

[31] For the United States see Claudia D. Goldin and Frank D. Lewis, "The Role of Exports in American Economic Growth during the Napoleonic Wars, 1793 to 1807," *Explorations in Economic History*, Vol. 17 (1980), pp. 6–25; and the discussion in Stanley L. Engerman and Robert E. Gallman, "U.S. Economic Growth, 1783–1860," *Research in Economic History*, Vol. 8 (1983), pp. 25–9. For Brazil see Nathaniel H. Leff, *Underdevelopment and Development in Brazil*, 2 vols. (London, 1982). For similar arguments in the British case see the essays in Floud and McCloskey.

[32] For anthropometric evidence of this, see B. W. Higman, "Growth in Afro-Caribbean Slave Populations," *American Journal of Physical Anthropology*, Vol. 50 (1979), pp. 373–86; David Eltis, "Nutritional Trends in Africa and the Americas: Heights of Africans, 1819–1839," *Journal of Interdisciplinary History*, Vol. 12 (1982), pp. 453–75. See also Kenneth F. Kiple, *The Caribbean Slave: A Biological History* (Cambridge, 1984), pp. 23–31.

[33] See, for example, the low estimates of Paul Bairoch, "The Main Trends in National Income Disparities since the Industrial Revolution," in Paul Bairoch and Maurice Levy-Leboyer (eds.), *Disparities in Economic Development since the Industrial Revolution* (New York, 1981), pp. 12–15.

[34] Ester Boserup, *The Conditions of Agricultural Growth: The Economics of Agricultural Change under Population Pressure* (Chicago, 1965); and *Population and Technological Change* (Chicago, 1985), pp. 144–57.

tation costs. The explanation no doubt has something to do with the epidemiological environment and African military pressures that prevented the establishment of European plantations in Africa before the late nineteenth century.[35] Second, of the approximately 911,000 intercontinental indentured migrants who came to the Americas after the end of slavery, only 57,900, or 6%, came from Africa.[36] To the flow of laborers to other recruiting regions such as Malaya, Fiji, Australia, and, more surprisingly, Natal and the Mascarene Islands, Africans contributed nothing.[37] The great bulk of the indentured laborers recruited between 1826 and 1939 came from Asia, and in particular India – areas with much lower land/labor ratios, and presumably per capita incomes, than Africa.

Empirical evidence forms the third indicator of relatively high African income. Slave merchants in the late eighteenth century would allow £0.01 a day (or £3.8 a year) per slave for provisions on the middle passage, and in the 1820s and 1830s the British government paid 3 pence a day (or £4.6 a year) per slave for the outdoor relief of tens of thousands of Africans liberated at Sierra Leone by the British navy.[38] This is broadly consistent with Curtin's tabulation of wages paid to laptots and unskilled Senegambians of £11.9 in current values for the first half of the nineteenth century (or a per capita figure for the lowest income groups of perhaps £5, depending on the labor force participation rate used).[39] Partly because of the slave trade, food costs were no doubt higher in coastal areas than in the rest of Africa, and

---

[35] For a full discussion of this paradox and a rather different resolution to that suggested here, see Fenoaltea.

[36] Calculated from Stanley L. Engerman, "Servants to Slaves to Servants: Contract Labour and European Expansion," in P. C. Emmer (ed.), *Colonialism and Migration; Indentured Labour before and after Slavery* (Dordrecht, 1986), p. 272. I have excluded the *engages* taken by the French from Africa to the West Indies, since this traffic is more properly categorized as a slave trade. For fuller information on the African indentured flow, see Monica Shuler, "The Recruitment of African Indentured Labour for European Colonies in the Nineteenth Century"; ibid, *"Alas, Alas, Kongo"* (Baltimore, 1980); and Johnson U. J. Asiegbu, *Slavery and the Politics of Liberation, 1787–1861* (London, 1969).

[37] Engerman.

[38] LeVeen, *British Slave Trade Suppression Policies*, p. 164; PP, 1830, X, p. 539. See Captain Theophilus Conneau, *A Slaver's Logbook or 20 Years Residence in Africa* (Englewood Cliffs, N.J., 1977), p. 78. Henry A. Gemery and Jan S. Hogendorn assess minimum physical subsistence income in eighteenth-century West Africa as £0.8 to £1.25 per year ["The Economic Costs of West African Participation in the Atlantic Slave Trade: A Preliminary Sampling for the Eighteenth Century," in Gemery and Hogendorn, eds., *The Uncommon Market: Essays in the Economic History of the Atlantic Slave Trade* (New York, 1979), pp. 148–54]. This appears well below what the average African, certainly West African, could expect to consume – even in a famine year.

[39] Curtin, Vol. 2, pp. 82–3.

the representativeness of these data for Africa as a whole might be questioned. On the other hand, it was precisely in these areas, rather than in the interior, that the decision on whether or not to sell a slave into the African trade was taken – and it is this that concerns us here.

It is doubtful if the figures given here incorporate fully allowances for surpluses for intra-African trade[40] and services, which even in a premodern economy could be one-third of domestic product. Per capita income of over £5 per year is plausible. Thus per capita overseas trade estimates of £0.1 to £0.2 amount to just 1 to 2% of African domestic product, considerably less than Manning argues for Dahomey.[41] That the relatively high per capita income indicated by this discussion was not of recent origin is suggested by fragmentary evidence from early-sixteenth-century Senegambia, where slaves reputedly could provide for their own subsistence with only one-seventh of their labor time.[42] Post–early-nineteenth-century trends may well have reduced incomes, however, as increasing contact with the Atlantic world or perhaps the massive population increase of the last century depressed incomes. Perhaps the culture-bound perspectives of the abolitionists when they looked at "underemployed" Africans stemmed from the scale of the "surplus" income that Africans chose to consume in the form of leisure.[43]

As already noted, there remains the possibility that the income generated by overseas commerce was concentrated either geographically or among classes in such a way as to guarantee it an impact beyond what the aggregate figures here would suggest as likely. There is also the very real possibility that the social costs of the slave trade were of a different order of magnitude to the essentially private returns estimated here. These are issues largely beyond the scope of the present chapter. It is, however, possible to make a tentative dis-

---

[40] Colin W. Newbury, "Trade and Authority in West Africa from 1850 to 1880," in L. H. Gann and P. Duignan (eds.), *The History and Politics of Colonialism, 1870–1914* (Cambridge, 1969), p. 67.

[41] Manning, pp. 5, 333. As noted subsequently, it seems reasonable that Atlantic trade would be many times more important to Dahomey than to western Africa as a whole. It should be noted that the ratios presented here are calculated in current prices, whereas Manning's ratios for Dahomey are in constant pounds (1913 = 100); there are also differences in the valuation of foreign trade. Adjustment for these factors would not change the broad picture.

[42] Th. Monod, A. Texeira de Mota, and R. Mauny, *Description de la Cote Occidentale d'Afrique (Senegal au Cap de Monte, Archipels) par Valentim Fernandes (1506–1510)* (Bissau: Cento de Estudios da Guine Portuguesa, 1951), pp. 10–11, cited in Fenoaltea.

[43] Anthony J. Barker, *The African Link: British Attitudes to the Negro in the Era of the Atlantic Slave Trade* (London, 1978), pp. 110–12; James McQueen, *A Geographical Survey of Africa* (London, 1840), p. xci.

Table 4. *Estimated value of trade (exports and imports combined) between western Africa and the Atlantic world: African region by selected decades, 1730s to 1860s (millions of current pounds sterling)*

	1731–40	1781–90	1821–30	1861–70
Senegambia	1.92	2.19	5.32	21.25
Sierra Leone and Windward Coast	0.40	6.13	3.06	11.23
Ivory and Gold Coasts	3.09	4.37	1.27	13.37
Bight of Benin	5.08	10.05	7.82	19.45
Bight of Biafra	1.93	10.68	11.25	14.53
West-central Africa	8.73	13.96	9.22	13.32
Total	21.15	47.39	37.94	93.14

Sources: see text.

tribution of trade from the 1730s to the 1860s. This is based on two types of sources. First, regional breakdowns for the major national slave traders in the eighteenth and nineteenth centuries are now available,[44] and the trade in produce is assumed to have had the same distribution as the slave trade for the 1730s and 1780s. Second, for the nineteenth-century produce trade, rough geographical distributions are possible from British, French, and U.S. customs data – if these are combined with knowledge of the major types of produce traded, as well as the occasional estimate of strategically placed consular officials.[45]

Table 4 presents the results of these assessments. The well-known wide geographic dispersion of African trade is the most obvious feature of the table. With the exception of west-central Africa in the 1730s, no region ever accounted for as much as one-third of total western African Atlantic trade – and west-central Africa, it might be

[44] See the sources cited for Table 1.
[45] British and French customs data are organized into national colonial groupings, with the remainder of the African coast simply termed "West Coast of Africa." However, in the British case, palm oil products, and in the French case, gum and peanuts, tended to predominate. With the help of comments from officials, it is possible to infer the regional outline of this trade [see in particular PRO, B. Campbell to Malmesbury, Feb. 2, 1858 (enc.), FO 84/1061; and Adm. to Malmesbury, Oct. 15, 1858 (enc.), FO 84/1070. See also the sources cited in Eltis, *Economic Growth*, p. 362, n. 66, and the discussion in p. 386, n. 16]. For the much smaller U.S. trade, heavy reliance is placed on George E. Brooks, *Yankee Traders, Old Coasters and African Middlemen* (Boston, 1970), together with some guesswork.

noted, is easily the biggest in terms of coastline, hinterland and perhaps, too, population, of all the regions represented here. Table 4 also shows that the Bight of Benin and the Gold Coast, regions with a high profile in the historiography, were not the highest revenue earners, and that only two areas – the Bight of Biafra and Senegambia – weathered suppression of the slave trade without a drop in trade revenues. The Bight of Biafra had consistently the greatest trade contact with the Atlantic – probably from the 1740s. This was also the region with the highest population density of those shown in Table 4. Per capita calculations of regional trade might be stretching the data too far. But the order of magnitude of the figures in Table 4 suggests that in no region could the revenue per person of ocean-going trade have been significant. To put the same point differently, African populations would have had to have been extremely small for Atlantic trade to have been important – so small, in fact, that transatlantic traffic on the scale and duration of the latest estimates of the slave trade would have been impossible.

This assessment requires at least two qualifications. First, ocean-going trade was only one of the long-distance trading outlets. For some west African and west-central African societies, trans-Saharan and Indian Ocean trade provided an alternative outlet, and for most Africans the long-distance intra – sub-Saharan African traffic had at least potential importance. Thus, for example, the large drop in Gold Coast revenues between the 1780s and the 1820s may be more apparent than real. The Asante state developed a strong land-based trade in cola nuts in the early nineteenth century, the scale of which is beyond assessment but which might have more than offset the decline in revenues from the Atlantic.[46] The second qualification is that revenues within a region may have been severely skewed in favor of one or more states. It is highly likely that two-thirds or more of all slaves entering the Atlantic traffic left from no more than a dozen ports. The "coasting" trade was mainly an Upper Guinea phenomenon, induced probably by the lack of a major river between the Senegal and the Volta. Communities within or adjacent to the estuaries of the Senegal, Niger, and Zaire rivers, as well as those located at strategic points on the lagoon systems of the Slave and Loango coasts, obviously depended heavily on trade with the Atlantic. The pleading for the return of the slave trade in the early nineteenth century on the part of the Loango Mafouks was a result of this de-

---

[46] Paul E. Lovejoy, *The Caravans of Kola: The Hausa Kola Trade 1700–1900* (Zaria, 1980), pp. 11–27.

pendence.[47] The greatest geographic concentration of trade within any region during the precolonial decades surveyed here was probably in the nineteenth-century Niger Delta communities. Brass, New Calabar, Old Calabar, and Bonny together must have received close to £0.5 million pounds worth of merchandise a year in the 1820s and probably over £0.5 million in the 1860s (in current values).[48] But these were essentially trading rather than producing states, and the further away from these points the analysis is carried, the more dispersed would be the impact of the Atlantic. There is surely no realistic estimate of population and/or income for the region stretching from the Niger Delta east to the Cameroon mountains and north to Hausaland, which would make £0.5 million of goods per year significant.

The hinterlands of other regions were less densely populated than this, but trading entrepots were also generally more widely scattered than in the Bight of Biafra, and few regions had annual Atlantic trade as high as £0.5 million before the 1860s. In the Bight of Benin, the eighteenth-century slave trade did tend to be more geographically concentrated than the later produce traffic. Whydah, the main outlet for Dahomey, dominated Atlantic trade in the Bight of Benin in the 1730s and 1780s, and probably during the years in between. Indeed, although the Bight of Benin permanently lost its position as the major Atlantic trading region of Africa after the 1730s, the popular impression of Dahomey as the African state most involved in Atlantic trade is probably supported by this analysis. If there is a possible exception to the generally small quantitative impact of the Atlantic on western Africa argued for in the present chapter, Dahomey would come closest to qualifying. At the very least, the Manning and Peukert ratios of trade to domestic income should be regarded as upperbound estimates for any large African state, but the evidence here suggests that Peukert's estimate of 2.5% of Dahomean income comprising exports is closer to the historical reality than Manning's estimate of 15%.[49] For the region as a whole, the 1820s was a transitional decade in the sense that the slave trade was probably still accounting for 95% or more of total Atlantic trade in the region, but that trade was more dispersed than ever before. Lagos was now shipping more slaves than Whydah as Yorubaland was pulled more fully into the slave trade vortex, and the widely separated embarkation points of Bada-

---

[47] Phyllis Martin, *The External Trade of the Loango Coast, 1576–1870* (Oxford, 1972), p. 139.
[48] Calculated by taking half of the figure for total trade in column 3 of Table 3 and dividing by 10 to derive an annual figure. These four communities must have accounted for at least 75% of all ocean-going trade in the Bight of Biafra.
[49] Manning, *Slavery, Colonialism and Economic Growth*, p. 44.

gry, the Popos (Little and Grand), and Porto Novo were also of greater relative importance. But the 150% increase in the value of trade from the 1820s to the 1860s was accompanied by the virtual demise of the slave trade. Palm oil exports, now far greater in value than the slave trade had ever been, were distributed evenly over trading points along the littoral.

We can now return to the broad historiographical themes discussed at the beginning of this chapter. Clearly, the slave trade engulfed Africa's Atlantic commerce in the eighteenth century and in much of the nineteenth too. But it is equally clear that any plausible numerical assessment indicates a similarly massive dominance of the domestic sector over the external *within* most African societies. This assessment obviously ignores the social costs of the external slave trade, but to this we will return. At the very least, the ratio of overseas trade to domestic economic activity was far lower for the majority of Africans than for the typical inhabitant of Europe or the Americas.

As for the three possible mechanisms in the historiography through which Atlantic trade might have manifested itself in Africa, severely unfavorable terms of trade, creation of a dependency, or heavy negative externalities, only the third is not called into question by the data assembled here. The first, positing strongly negative terms of trade for Africa, is highly unlikely. As the Royal African Company's records testify, significant volumes of merchandise were exchanged for slaves in the 1680s, and for most of the nearly two succeeding centuries the terms of trade shifted in favor of Africa. The second, positing a volume of merchandise imports high enough to create an African dependency on overseas producers, seems equally unlikely. The value of Atlantic trade relative to possible African income and population levels, and relative, too, to what it was to become in the early twentieth century, makes a dependency effect before 1870 improbable. We are left with the negative externalities or socially dislocative effects of the slave trade. The data developed here shed little light on this approach, except to imply that the disruption did not undermine the predominance of domestic economic activity. It would seem, nevertheless, to be the most promising route to evaluating the effect of the slave trade on Africa.

Some might see the later part of this analysis as tending to minimize the significance of the transatlantic slave trade, at least as far as Africa is concerned. This would be unfortunate. It is highly likely that what the British extracted from their North American mainland colonies represented a tiny fraction of North American income, and that the drain from India to Britain in the late eighteenth century was an insignificant share of Indian domestic product.[50] But these facts in no way reduced the significance of British imperialism to contemporaries, nor will it reduce it for modern historians of the United States and India. The same point may be made about the present analysis of the forced removal of Africans from Africa. The intention here is merely to focus the search for the effects of the slave trade on Africa and to nudge scholars into giving more attention to trends within Africa in understanding precolonial African history. Like the peoples of the Americas, and more than most populations in the nineteenth-century world, Africans were feeding, clothing, and sheltering themselves, as well as developing the full panoply of a multifaceted cultural existence, without overseas economic exchange.

The opening sentence to the published proceedings of a recent symposium on Africa's long distance trade reads "[T]he period 1800–1914 was one of deep structural change in economic organization in many parts of Africa" and goes on to link this with growing external trade.[51] The evidence examined here suggests that this is misleading for the years before 1870 – at least as far as the Atlantic is concerned. Except for some coastal regions, it is hard to believe that any significant domestic industry was threatened by overseas imports until well past midcentury.[52] Nor, with the exception of new food crops and possibly firearms – easily the largest precolonial capital good imports – is it easy to see a large impact from any imported technology. West Africans had iron, sophisticated textiles, a range of indigenous metalwares, and, outside the tsetse zone, draught animals. Despite a prolonged shift in the terms of trade in favor of Africa, European products could not penetrate the African market until the second half of the nineteenth century. The same products made greater inroads into other parts of the Atlantic world at much earlier dates. George Brooks has commented that Africans were remarkably self-sufficient in 1800 after three centuries of Atlantic trade.[53] The same may be said of 1870.

[50] See the literature in McCusker and Menard, pp. 354–8, and, on Indian national income and balance of payments, Dharma Kuma (ed.), *The Cambridge Economic History of India*, 2 vols. (Cambridge, 1983), Vol. 2, pp. 376–8, 869–72.

[51] G. Liesegang, H. Pasch, and A. Jones, eds., *Figuring African Trade: Proceedings of the Symposium on the Quantification and Structure of the Import and Export and Long Distance Trade in Africa, 1900–1913* (Berlin, 1986), p. 2.

[52] For a discussion of the regional impact of imported cloth, see Johnson, "Technology, Competition, and African Crafts," pp. 262–5.

[53] Brooks, pp. 10–11.

CHAPTER 6

A marginal institution on the margin of the Atlantic system: The Portuguese southern Atlantic slave trade in the eighteenth century

JOSEPH C. MILLER

SLAVING's economic contribution to the Atlantic system has proven a slippery beast, simultaneously of sensible significance[1] but difficult to measure.[2] Examination of the economics of slave trading on the scale of an "Atlantic system," often mixed with the function of slavery in America, a closely related but analytically distinct economic sector, has until very recently focused narrowly on its direct contribution to the most dramatic and portentous development in the eighteenth- and nineteenth-century Atlantic economy: Britain's transition to in-

---

[1] Eric Williams, *Capitalism and Slavery* (Chapel Hill, N.C., 1944).

[2] Roger T. Anstey, "*Capitalism and Slavery* – A Critique," and John Hargreaves, "Synopsis of a Critique of Eric Williams' *Capitalism and Slavery*," both in Centre of African Studies (University of Edinburgh), *The Transatlantic Slave Trade from West Africa* (Edinburgh, 1965), pp. 13–29 and 30–2, with discussion, pp. 33–43; also C. Duncan Rice, "Critique of the Eric Williams Thesis: The Anti-Slavery Interest and the Sugar Duties, 1841–1853," in ibid., pp. 44–60; Roger T. Anstey, "Capitalism and Slavery: A Critique," *Economic History Review*, Vol. 21, No. 2 (1968), pp. 307–20; Stanley L. Engerman, "The Slave Trade and British Capital Formation in the Eighteenth Century: A Comment on the Williams Thesis," *Business History Review*, Vol. 46, No. 4 (1972), pp. 430–43; Stanley L. Engerman, "Comments on Richardson and Boulle and the 'Williams Thesis'," *Revue française d'histoire d'outre-mer*, Vol. 62, 1–2, Nos. 226–7 (1975), pp. 331–6; Walter Minchinton, "The Economic Relations between Metropolitan Countries and the Caribbean: Some Problems," in Vera Rubin and Arthur Tuden (eds.), *Comparative Perspectives on Slavery in New World Plantation Societies*, Annals of the New York Academy of Sciences, Vol. 292 (New York, 1977), pp. 567–80. For a recent summary, see Seymour Drescher, "Eric Williams: British Capitalism and British Slavery," *History and Theory*, Vol. 26, No. 2 (1987), pp. 180–96.

dustrial capitalism.[3] Now, however, Barbara Solow and Stanley Engerman have productively both broadened the range of economic effects relating slavery and slave trading to European growth and expanded the focus beyond the boundaries of separate imperial systems to explore the entire Atlantic system as an integrated economic unit extending from the banks of the Zambezi, Plate, and Mississippi – if not also the Indus – to the Bank of England.[4] A paradoxical leitmotif that emerges from this recent work, if not a dominant theme, is that the economic significance of slavery and the slave trade lies not in their centrality to the course of British or European economic growth,

[3] With vigorous debate among British economic historians from internal perspectives; see P. J. Cain and A. G. Hopkins, "The Political Economy of British Expansion Overseas, 1750–1914," *Economic History Review*, Vol. 33, No. 4 (1980), pp. 463–90; and the references in David Richardson, "The Slave Trade, Sugar, and British Economic Growth, 1748–1776," *Journal of Interdisciplinary History*, Vol. 17, No. 4 (1987), pp. 739–70. Also see the recent discussions conceived in terms of the profitability of the British African trade: Joseph E. Inikori, "Market Structure and the Profits of the British African Trade in the Late Eighteenth Century," *Journal of Economic History*, Vol. 41, No. 4 (1981), pp. 745–76; B. L. Anderson and David Richardson, "Market Structure and Profits of the British African Trade in the Late Eighteenth Century: A Comment," *Journal of Economic History*, Vol. 43, No. 3 (1983), pp. 713–21; Joseph E. Inikori, "Market Structure and the Profits of the British African Trade in the Late Eighteenth Century: A Rejoinder," *Journal of Economic History*, Vol. 43, No. 3 (1983), pp. 723–8; B. L. Anderson and David Richardson, "Market Structure and the Profits of the British African Trade in the Late Eighteenth Century: A Rejoinder Rebutted," *Journal of Economic History*, Vol. 45, No. 3 (1985), pp. 705–7; William Darity, Jr., "The Numbers Game and the Profitability of the British Trade in Slaves," *Journal of Economic History*, Vol. 45, No. 3 (1985), pp. 693–703; Joseph E. Inikori, "Market Structure and Profits: A Further Rejoinder," *Journal of Economic History*, Vol. 45, No. 3 (1985), pp. 708–11; in addition to an older debate on the profitability of West Indies sugar. Recent debate on the profitability of Caribbean slavery, mostly in relation to British abolitionism, has derived from Seymour Drescher, *Econocide: British Slavery in the Era of Abolition* (Pittsburgh, 1977); see also Selwyn H. H. Carrington, "'Econocide' – Myth or Reality? – The Question of West Indian Decline, 1783–1806," *Boletín de estudios latinoamericanos y del Caribe*, No. 36 (1986), pp. 13–38, with response by Drescher, pp. 49–65, and Carrington, "Postscriptum," pp. 66–7. Even Pierre Boulle's innovative conceptualizations of the problem as it related to Nantes were conceived primarily in reference to British industrial growth, i.e., why a French slave trade with a volume similar to that of the British had not produced comparable industrialization in France; see "Slave Trade, Commercial Organization and Industrial Growth in Eighteenth-Century Nantes," *Revue française d'histoire d'outre-mer*, Vol. 59, 1, No. 214 (1972), pp. 70–112, and "Marchandises de traite et développement industriel dans la France et l'Angleterre du XVIIIᵉ siècle," *Revue française d'histoire d'outre-mer*, Vol. 62, 1–2, Nos. 226–7 (1975), pp. 309–30.

[4] Barbara L. Solow and Stanley L. Engerman (eds.), *British Capitalism and Caribbean Slavery: The Legacy of Eric Williams* (New York, 1987), with the economic history papers also appearing in "Caribbean Slavery and British Capitalism," special issue of *Journal of Interdisciplinary History*, Vol. 17, No. 4 (1987).

where others have sought it and that they demonstrably lacked,[5] but precisely in their marginality to the main currents of economic growth and development around the Atlantic.

Slaving was marginal to the Atlantic economy in structural terms, in a sense not so much inconsistent with formal analysis of a fully market economy as one highlighting the institutional aspects of a mercantilist system fraught with monopoly, privilege, and other imperfections. As it was an integrated economic market, growth occurred throughout the system, and the groups competing within it each found niches in which they enjoyed comparative advantages. Specialization of economic function increased as the scale expanded and the parts worked out their complementarities, with financial resources – central banking, efficient currencies, and credit, allocated responsively to more productive and profitable sectors – and, eventually, fossil fuel–powered technology and higher productivity becoming concentrated in a northern Atlantic core with the capital to stimulate, direct, and draw monetary profits from the other sectors. As the large economies with their gold and silver reserves concentrated as monetary reserves, rather than, say, on gilded altars, Britain, northern Europe, and the United States became central to the system, and Portugal, Brazil, and Africa became marginal.

Slavery and the slave trade operated at the margins of this growing system in the sense that they exhibited fewer of the economic institutions typical of the core, principally costly technology and hard currency assets – that is, capital – and in fact facilitated its concentration there. Beyond lack of specie, the economic characteristics of the slaving margins of the Atlantic system also included lower productivity, higher risks, lower costs of entry, and slower rates of growth that – in the end – resulted in sharply lower levels of wealth. Profits throughout the system might approximate the same level, but the slavers on the margin took their gains in consumption goods and more slaves rather than in the specie and productive technology that accumulated at the center.

Remote and increasingly backward Portugal and its empire present an opportunity to examine the slave trade as a marginal, but critical, element in the development of the Atlantic system in the eighteenth century. Despite the drama of intrepid Lusitanian exploration in the fifteenth and sixteenth centuries, Portugal had always been at the fringes of European and world economic development. Located on

---

[5] Despite the emphasis placed on export-led economic growth in the nineteenth century in David Eltis, *Economic Growth and the Ending of the Transatlantic Slave Trade* (New York, 1987).

the southwestern periphery of the Iberian peninsula and facing a vast, empty Atlantic, Lisbon played no significant part in the fourteenth- and fifteenth-century intensification of Mediterranean trading centered in Italy and its spice trade with the Levant and gold trade with Africa.[6] It was precisely because of Portugal's exclusion from these main lines of Mediterranean commerce that its kings sent ships south to brave the hazards of Africa's Atlantic coast and to seek the sub-Saharan sources of Africa's gold and, ultimately, a maritime route to Indian Ocean spice markets that would circumvent the Italians and the Muslims to the east.

By the eighteenth century, Portugal had become one of Europe's great slaving nations, but it had moved no closer to the center of European economic growth, by then displaced northward from the Mediterranean to the English Channel. Booms in sugar and gold from Portugal's richest colony, Brazil, had consumed slaves in massive quantities, more than 40% of the total Atlantic trade in the seventeenth century and still nearly one-third of the much greater numbers carried in the eighteenth.[7] If slavery and the slave trade made a significant direct contribution to economic growth, Portugal surely would not have found itself more marginal than ever to the accelerating pace of development around the Atlantic, economically stagnant, lacking internal transport systems, unable to feed its own population, and becoming more and more dependent on manufactures imported from northern European trading partners, particularly the British. But precisely because the slave trade stands out so prominently in the Portuguese context, its general function in sustaining weak and uncompetitive economic sectors appears clearly there in ways not always visible amid all the other elements of the larger and more complex economy of Britain.

The Portuguese southern Atlantic trade in question drew slaves primarily from the Angolan coast, south of the mouth of the Zaire River as far as the Kunene, and there principally from two embarkation points: the colonial capital of Luanda, larger and dating from the 1570s, and Benguela, founded in the 1610s but growing slowly as a source of slaves to a scale comparable to that of Luanda only late in the eighteenth century.[8] Angolan slaves headed mostly for Brazil's

---

[6] John Day, "The Great Bullion Famine of the Fifteenth Century," *Past and Present*, Vol. 79 (1978), pp. 3–54.

[7] Philip D. Curtin, *The Atlantic Slave Trade: A Census* (Madison, Wis., 1969), pp. 119, 216, and Paul E. Lovejoy, "The Volume of the Atlantic Slave Trade: A Synthesis," *Journal of African History*, Vol. 23, No. 4 (1982), p. 483.

[8] Joseph C. Miller, *Way of Death: Merchant Capitalism and the Angolan Slave Trade, 1730–1830* (Madison, Wis., 1988).

northeastern sugar captaincies of Pernambuco and Bahia in the seventeenth century, but in the eighteenth century they went in greater and greater proportions south to Rio de Janeiro and to the mining districts of Minas Gerais, just inland. The resulting shortage in the supply of slaves for the sugar plantations of Brazil's northeast was filled by substantial numbers of captives from West African shores east of the Volta River and on toward the location of modern Lagos, an area known to the Portuguese as the "Mina Coast" but to the British familiar as the "Slave Coast," beginning about the 1680s.[9] Much smaller numbers of captive Africans embarked from Portugal's two small trading towns on the Upper Guinea coast, Bissau and Cacheu, mostly destined for Brazil's far northern captaincies, Maranhão and Pará, in the middle and later eighteenth century.[10] In addition, from time to time in the eighteenth century and in growing numbers from about 1800 on, Brazilians obtained slaves from Portugal's southeastern African possessions in Mozambique.[11]

LISBON SLAVING INTERESTS ON THE SIDELINES OF THE EMPIRE

If Portuguese mariners generally operated on the fringes of the European economy, the Lisbon interests among them who engaged in trading slaves repeatedly entered slaving from positions marginal even to their own domestic and imperial economies. Their African commerce never approached the value of Portugal's commodity trade with the remainder of Europe, or with its trading posts in the Indian

[9] Pierre Verger, *Flux et reflux de la traite des nègres entre le golfe de Bénin et Bahia de Todos os Santos du XVIIe au XIXe siècle* (Paris, 1968), translated (by Evelyn Crawford) as *Trade Relations Between the Bight of Benin and Bahia from the 17th to the 19th Century* (Ibadan, 1976) and (by Tasso Gadzanis) as *Fluxo e refluxo do tráfico de escravos entre o Golfo do Benin e a Bahia de Todos os Santos dos séculos XVII a XIX* (São Paulo, 1987).

[10] Jean Mettas, "La traite portugaise en Haute Guinée, 1758–1797: problèmes et méthodes," *Journal of African History*, Vol. 16, No. 3 (1975), pp. 343–63.

[11] Eltis, pp. 177–9, 250–2, for the volume; what little is known about this trade from the Mozambican end may be found in António Carreira, *O tráfico português de escravos na costa oriental africana nos começos do século XIX (estudo de um caso)* (Lisbon, 1979) (Centro de Estudos de Antropologia Cultural, Estudos de Antropologia Cultural, no. 12). Also see José Capela, "The 'Mujojos' Slave Trade in Moçambique 1830–1902" (unpublished paper, Workshop on the Long-Distance Trade in Slaves Across the Indian Ocean and the Red Sea in the 19th Century, School of Oriental and African Studies, London, December 1987); José Capela and Eduardo Medeiros. *O tráfico de escravos de Moçambique para as ilhas do Índico 1720–1902* (Maputo, Mozambique, 1987), and José Capela, "O tráfico da escravatura na relações Moçambique-Brasil" (unpublished paper, Escravidão – Congresso Internacional, São Paulo, Brazil, 7–11 June 1988).

Ocean or with the colony of Brazil, the jewel in the imperial crown from the 1570s on. Even within the more limited sphere of slave-dependent Brazil's imports and exports, its trade in African labor probably ran less than 10% of imports at most periods and hardly ever more than 20%.[12] Nonetheless, slaving from the very beginning of Portugal's adventures in the Atlantic repeatedly became a target of opportunity for merchants in Lisbon unable to compete with the leading groups of merchants in the city.

During the sixteenth century, when the crown and Lisbon's grandest overseas merchants thrived on African gold and Asian pepper, the buying, selling, and owning of slaves in Portugal's empire fell to foreign interests and to traders and planters without access to the main sources of wealth of the time: specie and spices. Even Portugal's early center of slave-grown sugar on the island of Madeira was an enterprise not of Lisbon investors but rather of the Genoese.[13] The slave-worked plantations on tiny equatorial São Tomé in the Gulf of Guinea, the world's leading producer of sugar for fifty years or so later in the century, grew from an early colony of impoverished exiles into an island of mulatto planters descended from poor Portuguese settler-traders and noblewomen from the Kongo kingdom on the adjacent mainland.[14] Although Portuguese aristocrats collected taxes on their enterprise and Italians bought their sugars, ownership and supply of the slaves in the Gulf of Guinea remained in the hands of local interests. Slaving off the Upper Guinea coast, serving Madeira, the Cape Verde Islands, and peninsular Portugal itself, remained primarily an occupation of colonial settlers.[15] To the extent that merchants from the metropole involved themselves at all in this early trade in slaves, they tended to come from New Christian circles then coming under heavy pressure from the Inquisition at home and seeking respite from persecution in flight to the remote corners of the

---

[12] Miller, *Way of Death*, pp. 452–6.

[13] Themselves secondary participants in an Italian-Mediterranean commercial sphere dominated by the Venetians. Sidney M. Greenfield, "Plantations, Sugar Cane, and Slavery," *Historical Reflections/Réflexions historiques*, Vol. 6, No. 1 (1979), p. 112; Stuart B. Schwartz, *Sugar Plantations in the Formation of Brazilian Society* (New York, 1985), pp. 9–10.

[14] René Pélissier, *Le naufrage des caravelles: études sur la fin de l'empire portugais (1961–1975)* (Montamets, France, 1979), pp. 215–16; John K. Thornton, "Early Kongo – Portuguese Relations: A New Interpretation," *History in Africa*, Vol. 8 (1981), pp. 191–2; Isabel Castro Henriques, "Ser escravo em S. Tomé no século XVI: uma outra leitura de um mesmo quotidiano," *Revista internacional de estudos africanos*, Vols. 6–7 (1987), pp. 167–78.

[15] A. C. de C. M. Saunders, *A Social History of Black Slaves and Freedmen in Portugal, 1441–1555* (London, 1982).

empire or to Protestant northern Europe.[16] Portugal's sixteenth-century slave trade – and the ownership of slaves themselves – thus originated as a refuge for Jews, gypsies, exiles, and others excluded from more attractive currents of its Asian and African commerce.

Established Lisbon merchants participated in slaving primarily indirectly, through an interest in its finance and administration. In Spain's *asiento* contracts, awarding well-heeled investors the right to introduce slaves into its American colonies, they perceived a highly attractive opportunity to reap returns in gold and silver, the primary objectives of the bullionist merchants of the era. Lisbon interests dominated those contracts in the sixteenth century and during the sixty years of the Dual Monarchy from 1580 to 1640, when Hapsburg kings in Madrid ruled Portugal as well as Spain. However, they restricted themselves to the financial and diplomatic aspects of these complex affairs; licensed lesser interests to engage in the dirty and risky business of buying, transporting, and selling slaves; repeatedly failed to promote slaving itself sufficiently to deliver the numbers of *piezas* they had promised; and prospered from smuggling goods and specie aboard the slave ships. Thus, only Spain's dazzlingly lucrative American minerals lured prominent Lisbon interests to associate themselves with the slave trade, and even there they held themselves as aloof as possible from slaving itself.

Even as Portugal's northeastern Brazilian captaincies of Pernambuco and Bahia emerged as prosperous plantation colonies in the 1570s, able to supply slave-grown sugar on a scale far surpassing that of Madeira and São Tomé, Lisbon began to harvest the bitter fruits of its consistent failure to establish a firm financial interest in the primary products of its own Atlantic empire. In part for want of capital sufficient to undertake the expensive, long-term investments required by sugar, they had limited themselves to a short-term search for specie, in Africa and in Spain's New World colonies, and had left sugar on the Atlantic islands to the Genoese and to the colonists of São Tomé. With even greater demand for capital from Brazil's much more extensive plantations, the necessary financial resources came from the Netherlands, in part through commercial contacts established by Portuguese New Christian families with branches in northern Europe as well as in Brazil. Even the largest Lisbon merchants

---

[16] José Gonçalves Salvador, *Os Cristãos-novos e o comércio no Atlântico meridional (com enfoque nas capitanias do sul 1530–1680)* (São Paulo, 1978); idem, *Os magnatas do tráfico negreiro (séculos XVI e XVII)* (São Paulo, 1981).

found themselves edged to the periphery of the Brazilian sugar trade that came to form the heart of Portugal's early-seventeenth-century empire.

It was as a second-best alternative to Brazil's booming sugar industry, and after African gold and Asian spices had both failed, early in the seventeenth century, that Angola's slaves finally attracted Lisbon's attention, in part because of firming prices for African labor[17] but also because Dutch control of the shipments of sugar making their way back to Europe left them no real alternative.[18] The details of slaving at Luanda then are too little known to identify the precise Lisbon initiatives taken, but during that period Lisbon excluded the early donatary proprietors from further involvement in the colony's affairs, began to bring the first generation of settlers and missionaries there under administrative control, and attempted to regularize the colony's slave exports.[19] It is unlikely that Lisbon made significant inroads on the colonials' slaving at that time, as metropolitan attention concentrated in the 1620s on resisting the Dutch West India Company's attacks on Portugal's colonies in Brazil and Africa and then in the 1630s on breaking free of Spanish overrule.

Restoration of Portuguese autonomy in 1640 under the new royal house of Bragança brought political independence but in the longer term pushed many Lisbon merchants still farther out to the remote edges of their own southern Atlantic empire. Portugal had long depended on England as an ally and guarantor in the arena of continental European politics, and the weak monarchy restored at Lisbon in the middle and later seventeenth century depended heavily on its English sponsor. A dynastic union between the Portuguese princess Catherine and King Charles II sealed this alliance in 1662 and brought the English substantial commercial privileges in Portugal as part of the bargain. Though Portugal was already sensing not only its diplomatic weakness but also its economic decline relative to the northern

---

[17] Joseph C. Miller, "Slave Prices in the Portuguese Southern Atlantic, c. 1600–1830," in Paul E. Lovejoy (ed.), *Africans in Bondage: Studies in Slavery and the Slave Trade* (Madison, Wis., 1986), pp. 43–77; ibid., "Quantities and Currencies: Bargaining for Slaves on the Fringes of the World Capitalist Economy" (unpublished paper, Escravidão – Congresso Internacional, São Paulo, Brazil, 7–11 June 1988).

[18] Cornelius Ch. Goslinga, *The Dutch in the Caribbean and on the Wild Coast, 1580–1680* (Gainesville, 1971), and *The Dutch in the Caribbean and in the Guianas 1680–1791* (Dover, N. H., 1985).

[19] See the papers of Governor Fernão de Sousa (1626–30) in Beatrix Heintze, *Fontes para a história de Angola do século XVII*, 2 vols. (Wiesbaden, 1985, 1988).

Europeans, it had no choice but to open its domestic and colonial markets to its powerful champion.[20] The famous Methuen Treaty of 1702 confirmed the failure of a long effort at Lisbon to stimulate domestic industry by conceding the entire Portuguese woolen market to England in return for preferential treatment of wines from Portugal there.

For Portuguese merchants, the English woolen trade was both good news and bad news. Lisbon trading houses contracted to represent English importers in Portugal acquired the backing of the wealthiest exporters in Europe as brokers of a profitable reexport of English goods to their richest colonial market, the slave and colonist populations of Brazil. For other houses not so prosperous or so advantageously affiliated, the Anglo-Portuguese connection meant exclusion from the most lucrative market still open to them among the Atlantic and continental economies increasingly closed by mercantilist restrictions and where they could hardly compete with the English, Dutch, and French. The losers in the contest for economic advantage at Lisbon accordingly turned again to the trade of Angola, almost entirely in slaves, as a consolation prize.

In Angola, Lisbon traders ran up against formidable opposition to their plans from the old colonial settlers, not wealthy rivals like the English and their Portuguese factors but nonetheless successors to the slavers established earlier at São Tomé and acclimated residents almost impossible to dislodge from control of Luanda's shipments of slaves to Bahia and Pernambuco. They slaved in close association with Brazilian governors in the colony. Luanda had fallen to the Dutch West India Company in 1641 but had been restored to Portuguese authority by an expedition from Rio de Janeiro at a moment in 1648 when Lisbon remained too weakened by its struggle to consolidate its break from Spain to take firm steps in the faraway southern Atlantic. For the entire last half of the seventeenth century, these powerful Brazilian governors, many of them linked to planter families in Pernambuco, ruled Angola almost as a personal fiefdom and held a firm grip on its exports of slaves. They exploited the surrounding African populations in a highly militaristic style, raiding widely for slaves in alliance with entrenched Angolan settler interests – here termed "Luso-Africans" for their joint Portuguese and African descent – and intricately intermarried with the African gentry who furnished captives to them and were no less committed than the

---

[20] Carl A. Hanson, *Economy and Society in Baroque Portugal, 1668–1703* (Minneapolis, 1981).

governors to war as a means of securing slaves. Portugal's southern Atlantic slaving in that early phase functioned largely independently of metropolitan interests and thus lay structurally on the edges of an Atlantic system defined in terms of commercial initiatives emanating from the centers of finance and credit in Europe, England, and the Netherlands, through Portugal.

In the late seventeenth century, Lisbon interests losing ground abroad took the first feeble steps in what became a lengthy series of efforts to break up this transatlantic alliance of colonial slave raiders and planters. Brazilian sugar, though the most promising trade left to Portugal, had fallen on hard times in the second half of the seventeenth century. Bahia and Pernambuco planters competed on the European market only with difficulty against the new and more efficient English plantations in Barbados and then in Jamaica. Mercantilist policies excluded their sugars from the major continental European and English markets. Lisbon then issued strict, though futile, instructions to its governors forbidding key elements of their strategy of violence in the 1660s and 1670s, but these efforts at control slackened off in the last two decades of the century for want of resources to enforce them.

The losers at Lisbon intensified their campaign to employ Angola and its slaves as a back door to the wealth of America when the stakes in the larger contest over Brazil's commercial potential increased sharply around 1700. Discovery of gold in the mountains of Minas Gerais in south-central Brazil in 1695 opened up entirely new visions of colonial wealth, and by the turn of the eighteenth century, thousands of Portuguese prospectors were rushing to the mining district and drawing tens of thousands of African slaves after them.[21] Clearly, the preferred economic strategy from the point of view of a merchant in Lisbon was to buy the glittering yield of the mines with provisions – Portuguese food products and alcohol, as well as English woolens – and equipment sent direct to Minas Gerais either through Bahia or through Rio de Janeiro, the seaport nearest the gold fields. Lisbon's Anglo-Portuguese factors, already with established connections in Brazil and capable of mobilizing the capital necessary to supply this vast and rapidly growing new market, quickly secured it for themselves.

The Lisbon interests thus excluded from the mother lode of Por

---

[21] A. J. R. Russell-Wood, "Colonial Brazil: The Gold Cycle, c. 1690–1750," in Leslie Bethell (ed.), *Cambridge History of Latin America* (Cambridge, 1984), Vol. 2, pp. 547–600.

tugal's early-eighteenth-century empire seized on the desperate need
for several thousand slaves on the placers and in the pits and shafts
of Minas Gerais each year as the core of a strategy of using slaves
from Angola to gain access to the American gold for themselves.
Lisbon prohibited Angolan governors from engaging in slaving in
1703 and, through a series of other strategies,[22] gradually opened the
door to metropolitan merchants by the 1730s. The intended benefi-
ciaries appear to have been the old Asia traders, who had lost the
spice trade to the Dutch but who controlled supplies of Indian and
Chinese cotton textiles that, in Brazil, competed with English woolens
but were utterly basic to the purchase of slaves in west-central Africa.[23]
They introduced these Asian goods through Luanda with further
government assistance in the form of legal privileges conveyed in a
royal tax-farming contract on duties levied on the slaves exported
there. They sold these goods on terms of credit so generous by Angolan standards – however modest their resources may have been in
relation to those of the great merchants who engrossed the gold trade
of Brazil – that they substituted credit for conquest as the key to slaving
in Angola, secured a strangehold on the financing of the colony's
commerce by the 1730s, and with that gained slaves to sell in Rio de
Janeiro for gold. By the 1740s they ruled supreme at Luanda, evidently
having found in southern Atlantic slaving the returns needed to sal-
vage a colonial commerce, to Asia as well as America, threatened by
Britain's growing prominence in Portugal's empire. Though slaving
thus produced a roundabout success in this contest for Brazilian specie, it diverted the slavers' attention from domestic production of
manufactures competitive with those of the British to a mercantile
strategy that enriched the Asians who wove the cottons and the Africans who sold labor.

The looming presence of British merchants, and the example of
accelerating industrial growth in Britain, motivated another, more
forward-looking group of threatened metropolitan interests to attempt

---

[22] Miller, *Way of Death*, pp. 546–51.
[23] See Joseph C. Miller, "Capitalism and Slaving: The Financial and Commercial Organization of the Angolan Slave Trade, According to the Accounts of António Coelho
Guerreiro (1684–1692)," *International Journal of African Historical Studies*, Vol. 17, No.
1 (1984), pp. 1–56, for a detailed list of imports as of 1684–92, and "Imports at Luanda,
Angola: 1785–1823," in Gerhard Liesegang, Helma Pasch, and Adam Jones (eds.),
*Figuring African Trade: Proceedings of the Symposium on the Quantification and Structure
of the Import and Export and Long Distance Trade of Africa in the 19th Century (c. 1800–
1913)* (St. Augustin, January 3–6, 1983) (Berlin, 1986) (Kölner Beiträge zur Afrikan-
istik, 11), pp. 165–246, in general. See Phyllis M. Martin, *The External Trade of the
Loango Coast 1576–1870* (Oxford, 1972), for the coasts north of the Zaire.

to seize Angolan slaving as a means of revitalizing the faltering Portuguese economy in the 1750s. Would-be textile and munitions manufacturers and others unable to compete against British products or imported Asian cottons in Brazil sought to open a protected market in Angola behind the forceful policies of the dynamic and authoritarian prime minister of king D. José I, Sebastião José Carvalho de Mello (at first Count of Oeiras, later Marquis of Pombal). At Luanda, two strong governors, António de Vasconcelos (1758–64) and Francisco Inocêncio de Sousa Coutinho (1764–72), subjected the colony's Luso-African suppliers of slaves to stricter repayment of the debts they had accumulated over the years of metropolitan sales of goods on credit and tried to exclude the superior imports of British and French slavers active along adjacent coasts from Angola's commercial hinterland.

With the ground thus prepared, Pombal's protégés arrived about 1760 with monopoly trading privileges granted to two chartered trading companies, the Companhia Geral de Pernambuco e Paraíba (Pernambuco Company) and the Companhia Geral do Maranhão e Pará (Maranhão Company). The underlying weakness of the Pernambuco and Maranhão companies was transparent. In Angola they competed with the old slave-duty contract holders, who controlled too great a portion of the colony's commercial assets to expel at once without destroying the entire slave trade. Their contract was finally terminated formally only in 1769. The transatlantic geography of the privileges granted under their charters revealed their economic marginality as well. Their monopolies over the African end of the trade covered only the parts of the coast theoretically off-limits to wealthier foreign merchants, and in Brazil they were confined to captaincies from Pernambuco north not dominated by agents of the British. None of Pombal's Angola initiatives attained much success, and the companies foundered by the 1770s on the perennial problem of uncollectable debts in both Africa and Brazil. Lisbon interests willing to resort to Angolan slaving had grown too weak relative to the waxing commercial strength of the northern Europeans to compete with British and French products even on the sidelines of the empire.

The 1770s and 1780s saw Lisbon all but acknowledge its inability to influence commerce in Angola and Brazil. In Brazil, the gold boom had run its course, but agriculture entered into an end-of-the-century renaissance that Portugal, in cooperation with colonial interests, attempted to channel through metropolitan intermediaries.[24] In Angola,

---

[24] Dauril Alden, "Late Colonial Brazil, 1750–1808: Demographic, Economic, and Polit-

the government concentrated its efforts on limiting foreign goods in its intended trading preserve at the coast, both by driving away foreign slavers and by introducing closer customs inspections of illegal – presumably British – merchandise entering Luanda aboard Brazilian slavers, the dominant carriers in the trade by that time, who brought it in from Rio de Janeiro. The only faint Lisbon initiative visible in the 1790s was an attempt to buy slaves for an emerging cotton-exporting sector in Maranhão and Pará, in remote northern Brazil, far from the center of British strength at Rio in the south.

Lisbon reentered Angolan slaving only after 1810, but this time it was the Portuguese merchants allied to the British who had fallen far enough behind that they turned to Angolan slaves as a strategy to avoid the next phase of Britain's steadily increasing dominance of the rich Brazilian sectors of Portugal's colonial trade. Napoleon had invaded Portugal in 1807, and the British, solicitous of the welfare of a monarchy so long allied and so open to the products of a domestic textile industry then on the verge of replacing the Indians as suppliers of cottons to Europe, Africa, and America, removed the Lisbon court and its Anglo-Portuguese merchant supporters to the safety of Rio de Janeiro in 1808. They received generous compensation in an 1810 treaty of commerce and alliance that opened the Brazilian market – and through Brazil, also the trade of Angola – to British goods, free of restrictions.[25] That put British shippers in direct control of southern Brazil's imports and its agricultural exports to Europe and left the old Anglo-Portuguese group to broker distribution within Brazil and to exploit Rio's non-European commerce, that is, with Africa.

The Lisbon merchants in exile at Rio became the dominant slavers at Luanda during the last two decades of the legal trade until 1830. Metropolitan merchants and manufacturers of cotton textiles and gunpowder left behind in Portugal also worked the Angolan market, mostly through Pernambuco, where they encountered few British agents, had old contacts of their own, and could supply African labor to cotton plantations in the Brazilian far north that briefly became important suppliers of fiber to Britain through Lisbon. Lisbon merchants thus retreated to the risky, dirty, and increasingly disreputable business of Angolan slaving in the last years of the legal trade, often with financial support from British importers, after Britain had pro-

ical Aspects," in Bethell, Vol. 2, pp. 601–60; Kenneth R. Maxwell, *Conflicts and Conspiracies: Portugal and Brazil 1750–1808* (New York, 1973).

[25] Alan K. Manchester, *British Preëminence in Brazil: Its Rise and Decline: A Study in European Expansion* (Chapel Hill, N.C., 1933).

hibited its own national traders from further participation in the trade in African labor.

Portugal's southern Atlantic slave trade thus repeatedly served Lisbon interests pushed to the sidelines of the empire to compensate for their weakness relative to the merchants – increasingly British – dominant at each era of Portuguese economic history. In the earliest years, when wealth came from the spices of Asia, the gold of Africa, and the silver of Spain's colonies in America, and when Italian merchants financed Portuguese sugar, New Christians and other peripheral interests did well by making Portugal the leading slaving nation of the sixteenth century. Well enough, in fact, that branches of them displaced to the Low Countries underwrote and brokered the new wealth in Brazilian sugar early in the seventeenth century, to the exclusion of Old Christian traders of Lisbon, thereby relegated to slaving but by no means uncompensated so long as Spanish American markets remained open to them and the price of Brazilian sugar – and slaves – remained high. But the 1640 break with Spain and the growing competition from Caribbean sugar left fewer prospects to Lisbon's traders, who turned to Angolan slaves as competition rose in the Indian Ocean and as English woolens flooded Brazil. They achieved a certain local success by the 1740s, though mostly as tax farmers manipulating currencies and the financial aspects of the trade at the expense of colonials left to engage in the direct handling of the slaves. Lisbon's distaste for owning slaves at this stage expressed their own awareness of the marginality of the business relative to the attractions of Brazilian gold.

The Pombal generation of domestic industrialists and traders turned to the slave trade of the southern Atlantic to escape British and French competition in the 1750s and, with gold production in Minas Gerais dwindling and Brazilian agriculture in a midcentury trough, were willing to buy and sell the slaves they carried to northeastern Brazil. They succeeded only against the holders of the slave-duty contract, and that mostly by dint of massive government intervention on their behalf, not by their economic strength or skills. By the 1770s, Lisbon had turned to the agricultural resources of Brazil, leaving Angola's trade in slaves once again to Brazilians, who traded to Africa with their own sugar cane brandies and, increasingly, with goods smuggled by British interests rather than merchandise from Portugal. Rio-based merchants of metropolitan origin returned to slaving for the last time after 1810, no longer as competitors of the British but rather as their agents. Just as old ships often gained a shabby extension of their useful lives by carrying slaves across the southern Atlantic, An gola's slave trade restored the fortunes of a succession of commercial interests on the defensive in Lisbon. But in no case did this happen more than temporarily – except for the Jewish pioneers of the sixteenth century, whose collaboration with the Dutch gave them advantageous access to Brazilian sugars, but only as foreigners – as Portugal and its empire drifted steadily past the darkened hulks of these once-influential merchantmen into the economic straits of nineteenth-century British industrial capitalism.

The Portuguese had thus become more and more specialized as slavers, while foreign suppliers and financiers and Brazilian planters led the economic growth within their empire. Slaving obviously produced profits, as the long series of marginal groups drawn into it frequently built strong positions out of its returns, if only in Angola. However, it marginalized the slavers by drawing them into extractive, destructive, and commercial sectors that lay increasingly on the fringes of an Atlantic system built on more highly capitalized foundations. The slavers' economic prominence in Angola, but less so in Brazil and hardly at all in Lisbon, provided a clear geographical expression of slaving's structural marginality to an Atlantic economy centered on northern European finance and production.

SLAVE TRADING ON THE PERIPHERIES OF BRAZIL'S COLONIAL ECONOMY

If informal British influence in Portugal pressured Lisbon's waning commercial interests to the southern Atlantic periphery of the empire, the tight constraints of colonial rule in Brazil made Angola's slave trade all the more necessary to independent American merchants there. The relevant economic watershed divided metropolitan creditors and their resident agents, whether Anglo-Portuguese, importers of Asian cottons, or domestic manufacturers, from American debtors, planters, and colonial traders in a large local provisioning network excluded from direct participation in the currency economy of the empire. The substantial borrowing requirements of sugar and mining, enlarged by a capitalized labor force of slaves, high currency prices for imports, prohibitions against import-substitution industries in Brazil, high implicit interest rates for the credit extended, and Brazil's uncompetitiveness in cash-earning world sugar markets, made the colony a persistent debtor to Portugal in the eighteenth century. These factors produced shortages of specie so severe that large portions of the colony remained peripheral to the cash economy of the Atlantic system, and even its commercial sectors operated on the basis of commodity currencies and merchant notes of indebtedness.[26] Brazil's colonial economy, in short, functioned very much according to Portugal's intention of concentrating specie and commodities salable for cash in the metropole, leaving planters perennially owing future harvests for slaves and equipment, and forcing local merchants to trade on working capital borrowed in the form of imports purchased from firms based in Portugal and resentful of competition from direct agents – the infamous *comissários volantes* – the same suppliers then sent out to undercut them.

Colonial merchants and planters thus owing cash debts to Portugal found a partial means of covering these deficits in slaving. They devised African trades that used low-value by-products of their export agriculture to acquire the labor they needed, thus lessening the amount of currency they would otherwise owe to metropolitan slavers willing to sell new Africans only for specie, bills of exchange payable in metropolitan currency, or commodities worth currency in Europe. This strategy of exploiting the noncash sectors of the African and American economies had originated in the militarism of the Pernambucan governors in Angola from the 1650s until the end of the seventeenth century, as they conducted their slave raids with African mercenaries compensated in booty and with the partial support of government arms supplied by Lisbon.[27] These wars thus required very little cash to mount but produced slaves salable in Brazil for currency credits or substituting for labor they would otherwise have had to buy from their metropolitan competitors for cash or its equivalent.

The well-known eighteenth-century Bahian tobacco and slave trade to the Mina Coast of West Africa rested on an exchange involving similarly low cash opportunity costs and comparably lessening the struggling northeastern Brazilian sugar sector's debt to Europe. Bahia exported primarily sugar and tobacco to Portugal.[28] But the process of boiling the cane syrup down to the muscovado sugar shipped to Lisbon left molasses and other residues that could be distilled into cane brandies of very high alcohol content, predecessors of modern Brazil's famed *cachaça* known in the African trade as *gerebitas*. In addition, Bahian tobacco fields could be made to yield a third picking of strong, coarse leaf unacceptable in the refined markets of Europe. The Bahians found insatiable African markets for these low-value by-

[26] Mircea Buescu, *300 anos de inflação* (Rio de Janeiro: APEC, 1973); Schwartz, chap. 8.
[27] John K. Thornton, "The Art of War in Angola, 1575–1680," *Comparative Studies in Society and History*, Vol. 20, No. 2 (1988), pp. 360–78.
[28] Schwartz.

products of their main export crops, soaking rolls of the third-grade tobacco in molasses and selling them for slaves on West Africa's Mina Coast.[29] Their *gerebitas* they employed in Angola to undercut much more expensive Portuguese brandies and less potent metropolitan and Madeiran wines.[30]

These Brazilian *gerebitas*, particularly those of Rio de Janeiro's relatively uncompetitive sugar industry early in the eighteenth century, became staples of Angolan slaving, accounting for almost 20% of imports by value and for nearly the entire incoming cargo aboard the Brazilian ships that carried most of the Angola slaves across the southern Atlantic.[31] Thus, Brazil's southernmost port, at least in its sugar industry's earlier, difficult years, appears to have sold *gerebitas* in Angola to compensate not only for colonial debt and Brazil's general uncompetitiveness in world commodity markets but also for its remoteness, relative to Bahia and Pernambuco, from the limited European markets for Portuguese sugars. Slaves bought with inexpensive *gerebita* thus lessened the cash indebtedness of marginal Brazilian slave owners and merchants, unable to offer British woolens, Asian textiles, or other manufactures on comparably advantageous terms, until the end of the legal trade.

Brazilians, for all their advantage in inexpensive American commodities in high demand in Africa, still remained among the weaker economic and political interests in the Portuguese southern Atlantic as merchant capital from Lisbon shifted the trade's basis toward commercial credit. They therefore retreated to its geographical fringes to preserve even their secondary position in slaving, itself the marginal component of the empire. Bahian merchant interests transferred their slaving from Angola to the Mina Coast in the 1680s partly out of frustration at the power of Pernambucan governors at Luanda, as well as in reaction to their inability to trade peacefully in the midst of their continual violence, consequent epidemics, African flight from the war zones, and incipient depopulation in and around the colonial territories. In doing so, they extended a Dutch and English trading region centered on the Gold Coast to the east, thus avoiding, once again, more established competitors and opening up African regions not yet intensely committed to selling slaves. With the gold rush of the early 1700s, Rio traders, marginalized by the miners' preference for Mina slaves available through Bahia, followed Lisbon's Asia mer-

---

[29] Verger.
[30] For price differentials in the 1680s, see Miller, "Capitalism and Slaving."
[31] Miller, "Imports at Luanda."

chants to Angola in search of slaves, whom they hoped to sell to gain a share of the riches available in Minas Gerais.

At Luanda, however, these Rio slavers ran up against not only the Pernambucan governors but also the metropolitan tax contractors. Those who stayed to trade at the colonial capital sold *gerebita* and accepted subordinate positions in the export market as transporters of slaves belonging to the contract holders and the Angola Luso-Africans. More aggressive Rio traders seeking slaves to buy and sell on their own accounts found them at Benguela, Angola's smaller, remote, mortiferous southern port. There they developed an independent trade to Rio, less dependent on credit and complex financial arrangements, and set off a wave of warfare in the populous highlands to the east in the 1720s and 1730s. After jurisdictional conflicts with the tax contractors were resolved in favor of the Rio traders, they developed Benguela's slave trade to a level nearly equal to that of Luanda by the 1780s and 1790s, decades in which searing drought in west-central Africa provoked wars and created refugees and captives available for purchase without heavy commercial investments in trade goods that poor Brazilians could not afford.[32] Benguela, as a refuge for Rio traders excluded from Luanda by the strong metropolitan governors and Lisbon merchants, contractors, Pombaline chartered companies, and others there, once again illustrated the spread of slaving through retreat by the weak to the geographical margins of the Atlantic economy.

In the 1780s and 1790s, Rio merchants not only brought Benguela to its peak exports of slaves but also moved into the void left at Luanda itself by Portugal's virtual withdrawal from Angolan slaving. Though they thus temporarily commanded southern Angolan slaving, these gains came at a time when Lisbon was excluding them from Brazil's revived trade back to Europe in sugar, cotton, and coffee. Removal of the Portuguese court and metropolitan merchants to Rio in 1808 and the Anglo-Portuguese traders' resurgence in Angolan slaving after the British entered the Brazilian market in 1810 once again drove the colonials away from the sources of slaves they had developed at Luanda. As a consequence, Rio traders sought out riskier and more remote sources of slaves in order to retain any niche at all in an early-nineteenth-century slave trade falling under growing British abolitionist pressure.

[32] For statistics, see Herbert S. Klein, *The Middle Passage: Comparative Studies in the Atlantic Slave Trade* (Princeton, N.J., 1978), esp. pp. 27, 255–6; for the drought, see Joseph C. Miller, "The Significance of Drought, Disease, and Famine in the Agriculturally Marginal Zones of West-Central Africa," *Journal of African History*, Vol. 23, No. 1 (1982), pp. 17–61.

Rio traders thus led the way in diverting Mozambique's slave exports from Indian Ocean markets into the long and deadly passage across the Atlantic. They also, along with Pernambuco merchants, momentarily strengthened by the booming cotton exports of the north, replaced the British and French formerly dominant along the Loango Coast north of the mouth of the Zaire River. Bahians, confined to the Mina Coast by their dependence on tobacco for buying slaves and insufficiently prosperous to compete in the southern hemisphere with other Brazilian slavers, particularly those from the rapidly growing capital of the Portuguese monarchy and of British finance at Rio, stuck it out in the illegal trade north of the equator, even at the risk of seizure by British antislavery naval patrols. The forced retreat of colonial slavers to the riskier, more remote, and even dangerous sources of African labor in the early nineteenth century thus helps to explain their persistent defiance of the British West Africa Squadron when Luanda and other ports remained legally available to them.

Other familiar elements in the structure of Brazilian slaving, Bahia's tobacco trade on the Mina Coast and Rio's prominence as a destination for growing southeastern African exports of slaves after 1800[33] thus combine with the importance of *gerebita* in Angolan slaving, Benguela's growth as a source of slaves, and other aspects of Portugal's African trade in the southern Atlantic to illustrate slaving's function as a retreat for colonial planters and merchants so debilitated by Portuguese mercantilism – and eventually British capitalism – that they could find no other method of supporting their pervasive indebtedness. As Portugal moved toward the periphery of the Atlantic economy through increased specialization in slaving, its Brazilian subjects found themselves driven out to its irregular and dubiously legal fringes by Lisbon merchants themselves in retreat from growing British power and wealth.

AFRICAN SLAVING FROM THE PERIPHERY OF THE ATLANTIC ECONOMY[34]

Africa as a whole, and particularly west-central Africa, stood even further from the commercial and industrial growth at the core of the

---

[33] Klein, pp. 51–72; Joseph C. Miller, "Sources and Knowledge of the Slave Trade in the Southern Atlantic" (unpublished paper presented at the Western Branch meeting of the American Historical Association, La Jolla, California, 1976).

[34] Peripheral in the sense of an integrated network of exchange and investment developed in this chapter, and in Solow and Engerman, "Introduction" to *British Capitalism and Caribbean Slavery*; not the position assigned Africa in Wallerstein's

Atlantic economy than did the Portuguese and Brazilian merchants engaged in slaving. Its economies possessed large, and in west-central Africa comprehensively, nonexchange sectors at the moment Christian merchants appeared with trade goods and commercial credit from the Atlantic. Africa also had a technology based mostly on the strength of the human hand and back and a profound lack of financial resources to expand commerce or to invest in costly material technology. Wealthy Africans held their assets instead in the form of human dependents: subjects, clients, wives, junior kin, pawns, and slaves.[35] Africa thus embodied to an extreme degree slaving's apparent association with economic marginality, in the specific sense of its function of supporting groups lacking the financial strength to establish a viable position in the more capital-intensive, fastest-growing, and most cash-profitable sectors of the Atlantic economy. It therefore comes as no surprise that Africa's less commercialized regions borrowed – as receivers of the trade goods that Lisbon merchants sank, on credit, into the Angolan backlands – in order to develop economic contacts abroad and that they resorted to slaving when they lacked other means of paying off what they owed.

Throughout west-central Africa's growing involvement with Atlantic commerce, established authorities, the men in control of labor and hence of productive power, tended to open trade with Europeans not in slaves but rather in commodities – ivory, raffia textiles, dyewoods, copper, wax, and cattle. They consolidated these early commercial relations at very low initial opportunity costs or investments in production, tending to sell off accumulated surpluses of commodities like ivory, disposing of the by-products of productive activities oriented to the domestic economy, or applying labor time unutilized during slack periods in the agricultural calendar. Those who gained wealth and power from selling commodities produced through these low-investment strategies built commercial networks and political systems with overhead costs requiring greater surpluses to support than they could have drawn from the people under their control by other means. Since they seldom possessed sufficient authority to intensify production for export significantly, increased volumes of exchanges tended to deplete their stocks of these by-products or to absorb the time available to produce them. Faced with declining supplies of commodities for export and unable to invest in increasing production of

world-systems theory [Immanuel Wallerstein, *The Modern World System*, 3 vols. to date (New York, 1974, 1980, 1989)].
[35] A perspective sketched more fully in *Way of Death*, chap. 2.

them, they covered their institutional overhead costs by continuing to import, delaying deliveries on what they owed, and thus living off debt to European traders, who – however modestly financed by North Atlantic standards – disposed of commercial capital on a scale all but unimaginable in the nascent exchange sectors of west-central African economies.

Even without rising volumes of trade, herds of elephants retreated to the interior, imported textiles lowered the scarcity value of domestic palm cloths, European demand for African dyewoods or wax failed to grow, or copper exports threatened to deplete reserves of the continent's principal monetary and prestige metal. Exporters then faced both debt to the foreign merchants and dependence on trade with them to preserve the shaky prominence they had achieved, a structural position not unlike that of the colonials in Brazil. In that circumstance, Africans resorted to slaving – though selling rather than buying – to defend political or economic gains they could not otherwise preserve.[36]

In Angola – an ecologically fragile region with commercial institutions rudimentary even by African standards – the early commodity strategy appeared at the coast only as a feeble stream of ivory, dyewoods, and wax exported amid a rapid and overwhelming resort to slaving. The preference for commodities was clearer in other African regions less marginal to the Atlantic system, with more developed commercial systems and greater productive capacity, and commodity trade lasted longer there.[37] The clearest example comes from eastern

[36] See the argument applied to the Lake Chad–Fezzan–Libya trade, concentrated narrowly on slaves, that thrived in the nineteenth century. The central Sudan lacked the gold and grain at the heart of desert-side trade in the western Sudan and the relatively low-cost river transport of the Nilotic Sudan to the east; see, e.g., Ralph Austen, "The Mediterranean Islamic Slave Trade Out of Africa: Towards a Census" (unpublished paper, Workshop on the Long-Distance Trade in Slaves Across the Sahara and the Black Sea in the 19th Century, The Rockefeller Foundation Bellagio Study and Conference Center, Villa Serbelloni, Italy, December 1988), p. 8. For the credit involved, see Abdullahi Mahadi, "The Aftermath of the Jihad in the Central Sudan as a Major Factor in the Volume of the Trans-Saharan Slave Trade in the 19th Century" (unpublished paper, Bellagio Conference, December 1988).

[37] Other examples would include the low proportion of slaves in exports from the intensely commercial desert-side economy of Senegambia [Philip D. Curtin, *Economic Change in Pre-Colonial Africa: Senegambia in the Era of the Slave Trade* (Madison, Wis., 1975)], from the gold-producing Akan area [Richard Bean, "A Note on the Relative Importance of Slaves and Gold in West African Exports," *Journal of African History*, Vol. 15, No. 3 (1974), pp. 351–56], or, in adjacent parts of west-central Africa, from the trading economy of the Zaire river basin [Martin, *External Trade of the Loango Coast*, and Jan Vansina, "The Peoples of the Forest," in David Birmingham and Phyllis Martin (eds.), *History of Central Africa* (London, 1983), Vol. 1, pp. 75–117].

Africa, where the profits of a hundred years or more of systematic ivory hunting allowed hunters to build specialized, well-equipped ivory hunting systems in the eighteenth century that they could no longer maintain once they had depleted the herds of elephant near the coast. As they pursued vanishing supplies of tusks farther and farther into the interior, and as Indian Ocean demand for slaves grew after about 1750, the hunters found it expedient to cover their rising transport costs and to sustain the polities and economic institutions they had created by converting their hunting capabilities to seizing humans.[38] On the Atlantic side of Africa, the large quantities of goods Europeans were willing to pay for African labor, compared to the low valuation they placed on most commodity exports, critically facilitated the early and profound turn to slaving, but the limited capital, marginal commercial institutions, and restricted productive capacity of the African economies also left Africans unable to compete with Europe on the capitalist terms of the Atlantic system in ways that paralleled the marginality of the Portuguese and Brazilians and thus similarly forced them to make use of slaves to participate in it at all.

Just as economically and politically weak Brazilians found slaving relief from the pressures of Portuguese mercantilism in buying slaves, so also did selling slaves in Africa frequently represent a defensive maneuver by parties threatened on the local scene with eclipse. Bush traders in Portuguese Angola often accepted the trade goods Lisbon offered on credit to recover from previous economic failures in Brazil or Portugal, were gypsies or Jews driven out of Portugal by the criminal courts or by the Inquisition, or had come to Angola as political exiles with no choice but to head for the backlands in search of slaves. Beyond the borders of the colony, marginalized African groups took up slaving when other alternatives failed. The earliest systematic sales of slaves in the 1510s came from monarchs of a Kongo kingdom arguably peripheral to the main lines of political consolidation on the opposite, northern, bank of the lower Zaire River, and they seized the captives they sold to merchants from Portugal in raids on still more marginal borderlands. Kings in name more than in their limited

---

[38] Edward A. Alpers, *Ivory and Slaves in East Central Africa: Changing Patterns of International Trade to the Later Nineteenth Century* (London, 1975), and François Renault, "Structures de la traite des esclaves en Afrique Centrale" (unpublished paper, Workshop on the Long-Distance Trade in Slaves Across the Indian Ocean and the Red Sea in the Nineteenth Century, School of Oriental and African Studies, London, December 1987), translated as "The Structures of the Slave Trade in Central Africa in the 19th Century," *Slavery and Abolition*, Vol. 9, No. 3 (1988), pp. 146–65.

ability to dominate their subjects, they also strengthened their domestic position relative to powerful regional competitors within the
polity by resorting to slaving.[39]

The Kwanza River mouth developed as a second – and eventually
the major – source of slaves in Angola through a congruence of Eur-
African and African interests marginalized by Kongo's sales of slaves
to Portuguese merchants. The obscure planters of São Tomé in the
mid-sixteenth century found cheaper captives there, sold by an African warlord in the remote interior, the Ngola a Kiluanje, whose title
became the name of the colony later Portuguese conquerors carved
out of his lands, bent on shoring up his defenses against Kongo border
raids into his lands. The wars of the Ngola a Kiluanje, exacerbated
by two decades or more of drought in the 1590s and 1600s, drove
roaming bandits, the Imbangala or "Jaga," out of settled agricultural
villages and into the arms of early Portuguese military governors,
who welcomed them as mercenaries in their wars of conquest and
pillage during the 1610s and 1620s.[40] With drought and disruption,
Luanda's slave exports thus leaped after 1610 to their mature
seventeenth-century levels, in the vicinity of 10,000 slaves per year,
on the strength of captives sold by the next generation of local people
driven to desperation by the wave of dislocations thus set in motion.
Successful Imbangala war leaders repeated the pattern of slaving by
the dispossessed by establishing new states bordering lands controlled by the Portuguese, at first raiding their marcher territories for
captives and then brokering sales of slaves sent west from later, still
more remote supply areas in a wave of violence peripheral to the
growing Atlantic system that spread inland until the end of the trade
in the nineteenth century.

These scattered instances exemplify both the marginality of slave
selling – though not of slavery itself – in Africa and the degree to
which Africans consolidated political systems and created new commercial institutions, at least in substantial part, by borrowing trade
goods from the Atlantic. Commercial credit was critical, as people
without followers of the sort forced to resort to slaving in Africa could
not have got their start without it, nor would established African

[39] The reference is to the Tio; Jan Vansina, *The Tio Kingdom of the Middle Congo 1880–
1892* (London, 1973). On Kongo, I expand on the argument made by Anne Hilton,
The Kingdom of Kongo (Oxford, 1985), with acknowledgment of the rather different
approach in John K. Thornton, *The Kingdom of Kongo: Civil War and Transition, 1641–
1718* (Madison, Wis., 1983).

[40] For the Imbangala, see Joseph C. Miller, *Kings and Kinsmen: Early Mbundu States in
Angola* (Oxford, 1976), and reinterpreted to stress the ecological factor in "Significance
of Drought, Disease, and Famine."

commodity exporters vulnerable to depleting resources have survived in its absence. Their precarious successes brought Africa well within the orbit of the Atlantic system, though at its margins, and made African slaving states and networks, like slavery itself in the New World, assets – albeit very risky ones – in which merchants unable to buy directly into American silver and gold, profitable sugar and other valuable agricultural commodities, tobacco monopolies, or other more secure forms of wealth found export markets, investment opportunities, and the productive slave labor that sustained the more marginal contributors to European economic growth from all around the Atlantic system.

THE FINANCIAL CONTRIBUTIONS OF SLAVING AND THE SLAVE TRADE

The fundamental importance of European credit in financing commercial, and related political, growth on the American and African margins of the Atlantic system highlights the general marginality of slavery and the slave trade to sources of expansion in the seventeenth- and eighteenth-century economy in banking and credit. Slavery and the trade in slaves were consequences, as much as causes, of the rapid economic growth. Expanding abilities to finance growth, to offer trade goods on credit in Africa and to sell slaves in America months and years in advance of payment in Europe, greater monetarization, and larger home and reexport markets for slave-grown commodities opened up an Atlantic-wide shortage of labor that firmed the level of wages on the side of the European cash sector and drew Africans in as slaves on the noncash fringes of the system. The slaves, both traded and put to work, permitted newer and faster-growing economic sectors of the sort continuously created in economies undergoing rapid growth, as well as poorer and obsolescent sectors like the Portuguese empire, to participate in the changes underway. Structural change by definition tends to occur at the fringes of established institutions, and it was precisely there – rather than in older or dominant industries – that overseas trade, including slavery and the slave trade, made a difference.

Slaving and slavery were critical because they allowed groups lacking the efficient monetary forms of wealth central to merchant capitalism – specie, currency, or currency credits – to get a start or, in the case of Portugal, to hold out long after they had ceased to perform efficiently in the center ring. European capitalism had itself taken shape on an earlier margin, as merchants and then bankers expanded the small commercial sectors of the late medieval European economy, in some part then itself a Mediterranean periphery of much wealthier and more sophisticated trading economies in southwestern Asia and the Indian Ocean.[41] Christian and European Jewish merchants, unable to penetrate the ecclesiastical, warrior, and landed aristocracies at home, found little opportunity to reinvest the profits they made in anything but more trade, and especially in opening markets abroad.

Succeeding overseas, they converted their peripheral sector of the Asian commercial system to a new Atlantic capitalist center of their own and set about building up stocks of the precious metals that financed their trade. Growth in such a system depended on enlarging the currency base from which bankers could multiply investment capital through institutions of credit. But trade with Asia's still more monetized markets drained specie, and financing growth itself absorbed another portion of Europe's scarce monetary stocks, so that the critical means of expanding the commercial sector of the European economy became the purchase and production of specie – the gold trade of western Africa, Spanish American silver, Brazilian gold – or other forms of commerce not requiring investments of scarce cash. The trade to Africa fit the latter requirement well, despite its risks, because Africa did not monetize silver or gold and would accept European goods, not cash, for gold dust itself, commodities, or – eventually – labor salable for money. Africans in fact often prized goods of derisory monetary value in Europe and, where necessary, monetized them to lubricate exchanges in the expanding commercial sectors of their own economies. Africa's limited ability to expand production and the Atlantic labor deficit turned the early gold and commodities trade so highly advantageous to specie-hungry Europeans to slaves. The advantage was not only that slaves produced sugar, precious metals, tobacco, and cotton worth cash in Europe but also that they were mobile assets obtainable for goods cheap in terms of Atlantic (and Mediterranean, and Indian Ocean) currencies.

The abstract shortage of financial capital available to the growing commercial sector of an expanding European economy manifested itself, inevitably, at its margins, among traders and producers short of cash but trying to compete nonetheless in the dynamic exchange sphere. The African market's advantage was relatively greater for them than for cash-rich bankers, or for merchants established in staple

---

[41] A parallel developed in other, more formal, ways by Stefano Fenoaltea, "Europe in the African Mirror: The Slave Trade and the Rise of Feudalism" (unpublished paper, 1988).

commodities like salt or herring or grain in Europe, or for spinners and weavers of flax or wool. Hence, fifteenth-century Portuguese and Genoese went to Africa to divert its gold from the Arabs and Venetians, but the marginal traders who followed in their footsteps became the slavers and stayed on into the sixteenth century and later, after wealthier interests had abandoned Africa to seek shares of Spain's American silver. Africa's slaves gave these weaker competitors the means to sell wine, inexpensive woolens, shells, and other goods of little value elsewhere in Europe or Asia for American specie otherwise bought up by manufacturers of metalwares and better textiles. The seventeenth- and eighteenth-century sequence of losers in Lisbon and Brazil, all taking their residual stocks to Africa for distribution by exiles and renegades to African upstarts, continued the pattern evident since the start. Their marginality was economic, in the sense that they worked with little currency in a system based on specie, as well as social in their lack of respectability.

Slavery in America functioned analogously as an investment remunerative in terms of cash but requiring relatively little commercial wealth to commence and finance. A salient characteristic of merchant capitalism – indeed, perhaps its defining feature, if not a tautology – is that traders themselves do not invest in processes of production. Under the conditions of rapid growth and attendant shortages of financial capital present from the beginning in the Atlantic, overseas merchants – almost axiomatically strapped for funds – found it cheaper and more efficient to invest in opening new markets than to commit the much larger sums that would have been necessary to create new systems of production. The first ventures into production, in what would eventually become industrial capitalism, fell to established interests, better able to afford them, of varying specific strengths in Europe. Slaves were inexpensive in cash terms, but they represented a collateralized productive asset that would even support credit as a means of purchasing them. Hence the debt ubiquitous throughout the history of Angola's slave trade and Brazil's slave plantation sectors.

Brazilian slavery as a labor system, as well as in its commercial aspects, presented similar advantages in low cash maintenance costs. To the considerable extent that Brazilian plantations grew their own food or purchased it through direct exchange of services or American commodities with local provisioning sectors where specie did not circulate, they required only modest commitments of cash, within the reach even of men at the edge of bankruptcy, to produce sugar or other commodities worth cash. The greater the leverage thus attained

on the cash invested, through credit, self-supporting slave populations, illiquid investments in land and buildings, and livestock, the
more rapidly they could expand. Reproduction among slaves to the
limited extent that it occurred, further lessened their need for cash
to buy additional labor. The Bahians' and Cariocas' extremely low-
cost methods of buying slaves in Africa with otherwise worthless by-
products of sugar and tobacco must have been even more efficient in
these terms than breeding, given the negative demographic growth
rates of the slaves taken to Brazil and the large numbers of slaves
brought to Brazil through these means. Most important of all, slaves
required no costly expenditure of cash paid out as wages on a daily
or weekly basis, months or years in advance of sale of their product
for the currency necessary to fund such payments. From the perspective of the currency definition of the Atlantic system, slavery was
a method of borrowing, or extracting, the costs of production from
the worker, whereas wages were an expensive method of remuner-
ating labor affordable only by the wealthiest and most cash-rich European sectors of the economy. With unpaid slave labor from Africa,
the credit arrangements and commercial notes – bills of exchange –
characteristic of the slave trade turned small, even negligible, original
cash investments in surplus goods for the Africa market in Europe
into American labor systems highly productive of commodities worth
sufficiently near their weight in gold to repay the risks and delays
involved.

In the monetary terms pertinent to explaining how a commercial
capitalist system spread throughout the Atlantic with such extraordinary rapidity from the sixteenth through the eighteenth centuries,
slavery and the slave trade thus functioned as a cash-efficient method
of financing the expanding, productive asset base under European
control. As a sector yielding significant cash returns but requiring low
cash investment and maintenance expenditures, it functioned in
a manner similar to peasant economies on the fringes of Asian or
modern world capitalist systems. The defining feature of a peasant
productive sector is its displacement of housing, food, and other
significant labor costs into a domestic economy not involving exchange or expending cash. Peasants can thereby survive, and even
experience a net gain in cash holdings, while selling their product
into the cash economy at prices that return far less than their full
(imputed) costs of production or even subsistence. Family farm labor
systems, and even the unremunerated contributions of women in
modern households, represent more attenuated manifestations of the
same principle of financing economic growth by drawing labor from

beyond the limited currency resources of a monetizing economy. All operate by drawing labor, time, and effort in from beyond its margins. So also did slave trading, both for west-central Africans and in Portugal, and slavery in Brazil in the ways sketched.

BROADER IMPLICATIONS

On only a preliminary review of patterns of slaving nearer the monetarized center of the Atlantic system, similar themes of marginality – though subtle ones seldom clamoring for attention because of their very insignificance in relation to the more prominent economic sectors surrounding them – appear to lend general significance to the cash-saving function of Portugal's slaving on the fringes of the Atlantic system and the Brazilians' retreat to the periphery of empire. In the Netherlands, early-seventeenth-century Amsterdam's wealthy merchants enjoyed too strong a position in continental commerce, and then in the advantageous Asian trade they seized through their Dutch East India Company, to bother with the hazards of stealing slaves from the Portuguese (and during the Dual Monarchy, from the Spaniards) in the Atlantic. There it was rather the smaller interests of Zeeland in the south that captured Portugal's fort on the Gold Coast, held Luanda, and eventually occupied the sugar-producing captaincies in Brazil.[42] In England, it was not the dominant agricultural interests, or the woolens merchants and manufacturers with secure markets on the continent and, later, in Spanish and Portuguese colonies, or the London banks leading the financial revolution in Britain that forged the way out to Africa. Rather, outport merchants in Bristol and Liverpool evidently found their prospects in these fast-evolving domestic and European sectors so poor that they found relative advantage in the Atlantic, despite the risks.[43] One need not deny the geographical advantages in Atlantic trade that these ports on England's western coast also enjoyed to fit them as well into the larger

---

[42] Goslinga, *Dutch in the Caribbean and on the Wild Coast*. See also Johannes Menne Postma, *The Dutch in the Atlantic Slave Trade 1600–1815* (New York, 1990), esp. pp. 36, 127, 131ff.

[43] Which is not to deny London's role in the trade, though generally as financier rather than as venturer to Africa; the Portuguese parallel lies in the wealthier Lisbon merchants' preference for the financial aspects of the Spanish *asiento*, brokering the British woolens trade to Brazil and – even in Angola – the function of selling goods rather than buying slaves. For London, see James A. Rawley, *The Transatlantic Slave Trade: A History* (New York, 1981), chap. 10, pp. 219–46; also his "Humphry Morice: Foremost London Slave Merchant of his Time," in Serge Daget (ed.), *De la traite à l'esclavage* (Actes du Colloque international sur la traite des Noirs, Nantes 1985) (Paris/Nantes, 1988), Vol. 1, pp. 269–81.

scheme of slaving initiatives coming from the edges of Europe's economies.

In France, the same tendency would help to explain the similarly minor slaving activities of major ports like Rouen or Bordeaux, respectively centers of trade in the English Channel and to the Antilles, compared to Nantes and a dozen otherwise – and significantly – unremarkable Atlantic and Breton towns with no particular superiority in location.[44] In British North America, Boston, New York, and Philadelphia, the major Middle Atlantic and New England ports, never approached small Rhode Island towns in their commitment to slaving.[45] Rhode Islanders bought West Indian molasses, distilled it into strong rum salable for slaves in Africa, returned to the West Indies with their captives, and sold them there for sterling credits to offset persistent sterling deficits with Britain. Their strategy exactly paralleled that of Bahian and Rio de Janeiro planters, trapped in a similar debtor position relative to Portugal, and also buying slaves with by-products of American agriculture. The uniformly peripheral economic position of the major slaving ports of the European and American participants in the trade suggests that the Portuguese were not the only slavers who went to Africa out of weakness rather than strength.

Recent reinterpretations of British economic growth, export trade, and imperialism bring out the marginality, combined with the critical significance, of domestic interests in slaving and slavery. For Cain and Hopkins, who review the *longue durée* of British imperial expansion, the overseas impulse, from the middle of the eighteenth century until World War I, was repeatedly initiated by groups losing at home.[46] The value-for-money efficiency of slaving and slavery made Africa and the sugar economy of the West Indies merely extreme cases of a general phenomenon long familiar in political, if not economic, terms: Foreign wars have saved many a weakened political leader in domestic trouble throughout world history. Looking at the critical period in British industrial development from 1748 to 1776, David Richardson suggests that a declining woolen industry revived its fortunes by selling to Portuguese and Spaniards, who used British textiles to buy

---

[44] A convenient English-language survey of the French trade is Robert Stein, *The French Slave Trade in the Eighteenth Century: An Old Regime Business* (Madison, Wis., 1979).

[45] Jay Coughtry, *The Notorious Triangle: Rhode Island and the African Slave Trade, 1700–1807* (Philadelphia, 1981); Elaine F. Crane, "'The First Wheel of Commerce': Newport, Rhode Island the Slave Trade, 1760–1776," *Slavery and Abolition*, Vol. 1, No. 2 (1980), pp. 178–98.

[46] Cain and Hopkins.

slaves in Africa and to clothe them in America, that Britain's own colonies in the West Indies provided protected markets necessary to sustain weak "infant" metals fabricators and weaving factories, and that it was these still-peripheral economic sectors – whose export volume he distinguishes carefully amid aggregate figures dominated by other, larger industries – that made the greatest gains from exporting at the crucial early stage in their development.[47] Pierre Boulle makes essentially the same case for Nantes: One significant contribution of slaving to industrial development there was the African trade's ability to dispose of the crude products of early experiments with mass production and mechanization.[48] Robert Stein hints at a related advantage for French merchants on the brink of trouble in emphasizing their tendency to use Africa as an outlet for excess inventories and to mount ventures with minimal expenditures of cash.[49]

In the British and French centers of Atlantic economic growth, resort to low-cash-investment slaving in Africa, or slave markets in the Americas, sustained marginal new industries through early inefficient phases of technical experimentation, high start-up costs, and political weakness and positioned them, in Britain at least, to grow toward later dominance by moving into the domestic, intra-European, and North American markets that alone possessed sufficient size and wealth to sustain the complex transformations visible in retrospect as an "industrial revolution." In contrast, for Portugal and its empire, as well as elsewhere on the peripheries of the Atlantic economy, declining and threatened economic interests resorted to slavery and the slave trade as means of delaying impending collapse. Slaving there entrenched old inefficiencies and removed Portugal further and further from the growth and structural changes gathering momentum elsewhere. The American colonies engaged in slaving, reliant on European credit and drained of specie, thrived on a noncash labor system that brought local prosperity, but their very success concentrated gold, silver, and credit across the Atlantic and consolidated their positions on the margin of a system centered in Europe. Slaving and slavery thus contributed to functional specialization within a capitalist Atlantic system defined more and more in terms of cash. Africa sim-

---

[47] Richardson, "Slave Trade, Sugar, and British Economic Growth." Joseph E. Inikori, "Slavery and the Revolution in Cotton Textile Production in England;" *Social Science History*, Vol. 13, No. 4 (1989), pp. 343–79, gives an institutional history of the cotton industry, providing specific details to the same effect.

[48] Boulle, "Slave Trade".

[49] Stein, pp. 17, 22, 64–6ff, 154ff.

ilarly invested its wealth in slaves and trade goods – from the Europeans' perspective, since many were also currencies in the Africans' view – and thus allowed the complementary concentration of the fundamental assets of capitalism, silver and gold, in Europe, and especially in London. With the financial innovations of the City based on the Brazilian gold in its vaults, capital became available to finance nonslave forms of economic growth in Britain and throughout the northern Atlantic.

Slavery and the slave trade, as cash-conserving methods of underwriting growth, thus contributed to apparently contrary features of the Atlantic system, all of them aspects of regional economic specialization that moved Britain toward wage labor and industrialization but left Portugal, the colonies, and Africa in currency debt to Europe. Slaves coming from Africa and laboring in the colonies were far from the only factors involved in this vast and complex process, of course, but their marginality to it is precisely the point.

CHAPTER 7

The apprenticeship of colonization

LUIZ FELIPE DE ALENCASTRO

In the sixteenth century, Iberian colonists went across three continents, dealt with exotic communities, and tried in several ways to ensure control over natives and exploit conquered territories. Sometimes, however, these practices were antagonistic either to the national mercantile network or to the metropolitan state apparatus. Before the Century of Discoveries came to an end, metropolitan powers resumed European expansion in order to colonize their own colonists.

"Among remote people they built the new kingdom they so much exalted," Camões wrote in the "Lusíadas." But how did the overseas "new kingdom" relate to the European "old kingdom?"

Although slavery and coerced labor allowed domination of conquered populations, they did not always entail successful colonial exploitation. These relations of production did not ensure the transformation of surplus labor wrested overseas into trade connected to metropolitan networks. Colonial surplus might be consumed by colonists or traded outside areas under the control of metropolitan powers. Therefore, the establishment of slavery and coerced labor was not a sufficient condition to implement dependent economies in overseas territories occupied by Portugal and Spain.

Moreover, even though the economic surplus of overseas territories was incorporated into the metropolitan network, Iberian expansion did not necessarily lead to the reinforcement of monarchic authority. New power relations emerged inside metropolitan states and conquered territories as mercantile zones expanded and merchants improved their political influence, complicating the ruling of European territorial monarchies.

Researcher at the Centro Brasileiro de Análise e Planejamento, (CEBRAP) and Professor at the Instituto de Economia, Universidade Estadual de Campinas (UNICAMP), São Paulo, Brazil.

Three distinct problems combined, thus, to trouble the colonial order: (1) the consolidation of royal authority over the colonist; (2) the inclusion of production from conquered areas in Atlantic trades; and (3) the confrontation between authorities, colonists, and clergy over the control of natives. In Peru, Angola, Goa, Mozambique, and Brazil, as well as in other places, colonization went astray from the very start.

THE COLONISTS' OPTIONS

In Peru and most of Spanish America, conflicts pitting colonists against clergy and crown derived from the fight to control the natives. Between 1542 and 1543 Charles V proclaimed the "New Laws," acknowledging a certain sovereignty over the Amerindians. These laws abolished concessions of Indians granted to the conquerors and gradually turned all natives to dependence on the crown, to whom they would pay tribute. Such measures invalidated former concessions that had given colonists the opportunity to initiate, at their own cost, the first stages of the conquest.[1] Insurrections then broke out in Peru.

Searching for reasons for the mutiny led by Hernandéz Girón, the fiscal (attorney) of the Audiencia (High Court) in Lima summarized in 1550 the rebels' point of view: "They started saying that they realized your Majesty's wish was to have the whole of Peru to himself, and that being so, Peru could not forbear becoming sovereign and governing on its own, freely, as Venice did."[2] Yet troops loyal to the crown, mobilized and led by the clergy, triumphed over reluctant colonists. A compromise was reached by the two sides. The *conquistadores* kept the Indians but resigned themselves to the taxation imposed on the *encomiendas*. The crown precluded the emergence of hereditary fiefs and succeeded in establishing its authority over the conquered lands and peoples, as well as over future conquests.[3]

But the essential development occurred in rather different circumstances. By the mid-1540s, Peruvian silver mines began to send their metal into European markets, reorienting both intercolonial trade and colonial society.[4]

---

[1] Marcel Bataillon, *Etudes sur Bartolomé de Las Casas* (Paris, 1965).

[2] Alain Milhou, "*Sufficientia* – Les notions d'autosuffisance et de dépendance dans la pensée politique espagnole au XVIe s.: De la Castille des comuneros au Perou Colonial," in *Mélanges de la Casa de Velazquez*, (Paris, 1981), tome XVII pp. 106–45, 132.

[3] Bataillon, pp. 291–308; idem., "La rébellion pizarriste, enfantement de l'Amérique Espagnole," *Diogène*, Vol. 43 (1963), pp. 47–63.

[4] Huguette Chaunu and Pierre Chaunu, *Séville et l'Atlantique 1504–1650*, 12 vols. (Paris, 1955–9), 8 Vol. Vol. VIII, tome 2, part 1, pp. 255–352.

The situation in Angola bore some resemblance to the preceding case, except that there the crown also fought against the regular clergy, that is, the Jesuits. In 1571 that colony was given to Paulo Dias Novais grandson of Bartolomeu Dias, discoverer of Angola, in the form of a hereditary possession, according to the method already tried in the African island of São Tomé and in Brazil. Troubled with high expenses, Novais granted to the conquerors – some of his captains and the Jesuits – concessions of natives and lands.[5] These new feudatories, called *amos*, managed Angolan native chiefs (the *sobas*) and collected taxes from the Ambudu population. Most of the time these taxes were paid in the form of slaves, whom *amos* would soon export them to America.

Finding that Angola had no silver mines, as was initially supposed, and that the slave trade had turned out to be an important activity in the area, the crown resumed control over the colony: The hereditary possession was abolished, and a general-governor – an immediate entrustee of royal authority – was nominated by Lisbon.[6] Disappointed, the colonists and Jesuits revolted against Francisco de Almeida, who had been installed as general-governor in 1592 and, following royal orders, decreased the *amos'* power. Some months after his arrival at Luanda, Francisco de Almeida, excommunicated by the Jesuits and jailed by the colonists, was forced to sail to Brazil.[7] In 1605 the Jesuit Fernam Guerreiro justified the priests' attitudes in Angola: "There will be no better way of attracting and keeping them [the Ambudu] than by making them the priest's 'sobas'." However, he recognized that this opinion did not please the king, inasmuch as "some people at the Court were beginning to say that it was not convenient for the 'sobas' to acknowledge any other authority but that one of her Majesty; so that the 'sobas' should be put away from priests and captains."[8]

In 1607 the institution of the *amos* was abolished, and vassal native

[5] Carlos Couto, "Documentos para a história da sucessão de Paulo Dias Novais na doação da capitania de Angola," *Estudos Históricos*, Vol. 15 (1976), pp. 133–85; Pe. Antonio Brásio, *Monumenta Missionária Africana (MMA)*, Africa Occidental, first series, 15 vols. (Lisbon, 1953–88), Vol. III, pp. 36–51, Vol. IV, pp. 276–7; Ralph Delgado, *História de Angola*, 4 vols. (Banco de Angola, n.d.), Vol. I, pp. 258–62.

[6] Beatrix Heintze, "Die portugiesische Besiedlungs-und Wirtschaftspolitik in Angola 1570–1607," *Aufsätze zur portugiesischen Kulturgeschichte*, Vol. 17 (1981–2), pp. 200–19; idem., "Luso-African Feudalism in Angola? The Vassal Treaties of the 16th to the 18th Century," *Revista Portuguesa de História (RPH)*, Vol. XVIII, (1980), pp. 111–31.

[7] *MMA*, Vol. III, p. 476, und Vol. IV, pp. 53, 554; Delgado, Vol. I, pp. 372–7.

[8] Pe. Fernam Guerreiro, *Relação Anual das coisas que fizeram os Padres da Companhia de Jesus nas suas Missões*, 4 vols., 3 tomes (Evora, 1603–1611; Coimbra, 1930–42), tome I, p. 395; *MMA*, Vol. IV, pp. 442–52.

chiefs were placed under the control of the crown.[9] Though quarrels still went on between governors and captains who intended to restore the *amos'* privileges, the action of the crown and of metropolitan merchants put Angola in the Atlantic trading system. In 1594 the first *asiento* gave the Portuguese a monopoly in providing Spanish America with slaves. Up to 1623, Portuguese merchants who owned the *asiento* were also contractors in Angola, managing the purchase of slaves in Luanda.[10] It is, indeed, the slave trade that connected Angola with the world market.

Unlike the events in Africa and America, Portuguese colonization produced a rather softened impact in the Indian Ocean. European conquerors tried to arrogate markets previously controlled by Arabs and Gujerati merchants. Lisbon intended to direct this trade toward the metropolitan network along the route of the Cape of Good Hope.[11] This policy created clashes between royal authority and Portuguese settled in India.

In Goa these colonists, called *casados* (married men) – as opposed to the group formed by Portuguese soldiers called *solteiros* (single men) – were wholesalers who carried out most of the important commercial business at seaports along trade routes to China and Japan. Represented by Goa's House Senate, the *casados* imposed the rule that no Jews, Indians, or Hindus converted to Catholicism were to be allowed to associate with Portuguese officials or military personnel trading at Asian seaports.[12]

The *casados* then get from Portugal's crown limitations on the activity of Lisbon's trade agents who had business with India. Facing also the *fidalgos* – the Portuguese military aristocracy holding the crown's authority in India – the *casados* tried to control the whole brokerage of European trade in Asia. Apparently the crown took no advantage in that situation, for in 1587 it gave the indigo monopoly – the main economic activity in Goa – to a group of Lisbon merchants.[13]

---

[9] "Regimento do governador Manuel Pereira Forjaz de 26 março 1607," *MMA*, Vol. V, pp. 264–79.

[10] Enriqueta Vila Vilar, *Hispano-America y El Comercio de Esclavos – Los Asientos Portugueses* (Seville, 1977), p. 27, n. 15.

[11] Ralph A. Austen, "From the Atlantic to the Indian Ocean: European Abolition, the African Slave Trade, and Asian Economic Structures," in D. Eltis and J. Walvin (eds.), *The Abolition of the Atlantic Slave Trade* (Madison, Wis., 1981), pp. 117–40, 118, 126; Vitorino Magalhães Godinho, *Os Descobrimentos e a Economia Mundial*, 4 vols. (Lisbon, 1981–3), Vol. I, pp. 183–208, and Vol. II, pp. 183–223.

[12] C. R. Boxer, *Portuguese Society in the Tropics – The Municipal Councils of Goa, Macao, Bahia and Luanda 1510–1800* (Madison, Wis., 1950), pp. 12–41.

[13] M. N. Pearson, "The People and Politics of Portuguese India during the Sixteenth

Revolts then broke out among the *casados* in Goa. Rebellions keep on disturbing the colony every time the crown increased tributes or tried to attract commerce involved in bilateral trade with Asia and the Persian Gulf, to the benefit of local traders – Portuguese, Persians, and Indians – but to the disadvantage of metropolitan merchants and Royal Treasure.[14] A study of those rebellions concludes: "Many of these incidents show a considerable lack of patriotism on the part of "casados" of Portuguese India; they usually place their trade above their loyalty to the Crown".[15]

It was in Goa that Diogo do Couto wrote, in 1593, his masterpiece *"O Soldado Prático"*, a key book of Lusitanian historical skepticism, pointing out frauds practiced by colonial officials who crossed cities and seas, plundering natives and robbing merchants. According to Diogo do Couto, "Nowhere else is the King [of Portugal] less obeyed than in India."[16] But as Magalhães Godinho explains: "Whatever were military and naval means gathered, and however righteous the official's honesty, the Portuguese could not afford substituting all Moors and Gentiles in interregional circuits. . . . Between the beginning and the middle the sixteenth century, Portuguese State of East Indies was set up; the Portuguese, very numerous, settled in many towns and thrust themselves into interregional trade circuits. From that time the Luso-oriental economic complex was opposed to the interests of Lisbon and of the route of the Cape."[17] That situation illustrated one of the colonial impasses mentioned earlier: The colonists' trade evaded the metropolitan networks.

In Mozambique the fragility of Lusitanian colonial intervention in the Indian Ocean was even more transparent. In its first stage, the Monomotapa pre-European empire was permeated by Portuguese conquerors who took over native feudatories' powers in domains (*prazos*) of the Zambezi valley. The first Europeans owning *prazos* (the *prazeiros*) were confirmed in their posts by the Monomotapa emperor himself.[18] *Prazeiros* got from their vassals – natives of the Tonga people

and Early Seventeenth Centuries," in D. Alden and W. Dean (eds.), *Essays Concerning the Socioeconomic History of Brazil and Portuguese India* (Gainesville, Fla., 1977), pp. 1–25, 16, 17; C. R. Boxer, *A India Portuguesa em meados de seculo XVII* (Lisbon, 1982), pp. 26–31.

[14] K. S. Mathew, "India Merchants and the Portuguese Trade on the Malabar Coast during the Sixteenth Century," in T. R. de Souza (ed.), *Indo-Portuguese History, Old Issues, New Question* (New Delhi, 1985), pp. 1–12; Guerreiro, tome 2, pp. 389, 390.

[15] Pearson, p. 23.

[16] Diogo do Couto, *O Soldado Prático* (1593) (Lisbon, 1954), pp. 30, 54.

[17] Magalhães Godinho, Vol. III, pp. 81–134, esp. pp. 133, 134; see also A. Farinha De Carvalho, *Diogo do Couto, o Soldado Prático e a India* (Lisbon, 1979), pp. 95–103.

[18] Thomas D. Boston, "On the Transition to Feudalism in Mozambique," *Journal of*

– rent in ivory or maize or in labor (*mussôco*). The *prazeiros* themselves paid the Portuguese crown a tax in powdered gold. Where there was no Portuguese sovereignty, the colonists paid – only to the native authority – a tribute in cloths (*fatiota*). Those were the "lands in *fatiota*," located in the province of Tete.[19]

Gradually absorbed by the native society and institutions, the colonists tended to Africanize, or to "kaffirize," as a Portuguese author has pointed out.[20]

Leaving untouched native conditions of production, the Portuguese were unable to change the regional trade. The external exchanges remained directed toward the North and the East, with Omani Arabs controlling the slave trade to the Persian Gulf, the main market in the area.[21] The first Portuguese customs tariff to collect taxes on slaves was set in Mozambique in 1756, two and a half centuries after similar tariffs had come into operation in Portuguese West Africa. Except for some extra deliveries, Brazil would regularly receive East African slaves only from the second decade of the nineteenth century on. The emerging intercolonial division of labor had already designated the other side of Africa – mainly Angola – as the preferred market for the Luso-Brazilian slave ships.

In fact, the importance of Mozambique rested on its strategic situation between India and Europe. Portuguese fleets remained for several months at the Mozambican harbors waiting for the maritime monsoons to cease.[22] Having failed to achieve economic control over the area, Lisbon tightened its political authority over the Mozambique colonists.

African Studies (JAS), Vol. 8, No. 4 (1981–2), pp. 182–8; A. Lobato, *Colonização Senhorial da Zambézia e outros estudos* (Lisbon, 1962), pp. 80, 81.

[19] Fritz Hoppe, *A Africa Oriental Portuguesa no tempo do Marques de Pombal* (Lisbon, 1970), p. 40; A. Lobato, *Evolução Administrativa e Econômica de Mocambique 1752–1763* (Lisbon, 1957), p. 231; M. D. D. Newitt, *Portuguese Settlement on the Zambezi: Exploration, Land Tenure, and Colonial Rule in East Africa* (London and New York, 1973), pp. 181, 182; "Viagem que fez o Padre Ant. Gomes, da Companhia de Jesus, ao Imperio de Manomotapa; e assistencia que fez nas ditas terras de alguns anos (1648)," in *Studia*, No. 3 (Janeiro 1959), pp. 155–242, 239.

[20] Lobato, *Evolução*, p. 153; M. D. D. Newitt, "The Early History of the Marawi," *Journal of African History (JAH)*, Vol. 23 (1982), pp. 145–62.

[21] See Sebastião Xavier Botelho, *Memórias Estatísticas sobre os domínios portuguezes Africa Oriental* (Lisbon, 1835); E. Alpers, *Ivory and Slaves in East Central Africa* (London, 1975); Cyril A. Hromnik, "Canarins in the Rios de Cuama 1501–1576," *JAS*, Vol. 6, No. 1 (1979), pp. 27–37; Austen, pp. 117–26; Hubert Gerbeau, "La traite esclavagiste dans l'Océan Indien," in UNESCO, ed., *La traite négrière du XVe au XIXe siècle* (Paris, 1979), pp. 194–217.

[22] W. G. L. Randles, *L'Empire du Monomotapa du XVe au XIXe siècle*, (Paris and La Haye, 1975), pp. 41–8; Justus Strandes, *The Portuguese Period in East Africa*, 3rd ed. (Nairobi, Dar es Salaam, and Kampala, 1968), p. 153.

From 1625 on, the domains of Zambezi were no longer hereditary possessions. Changed into *"prazos* of the crown," they were issued – under an emphyteusis contract – to petitioners for a period of three generations. The concession could either be renewed for the same family or granted to other petitioners. Concentration of *prazos* in the hands of one grantee alone was, however, very common, as the crown preferred to let the law lapse than leaving *prazos* uninhabited – "Not to break off the continuity of its control over the natives" – as Fritz Hopppe explains.[23]

The emphyteusis contract, linking the crown with the *prazeiro* marked the originality of Portuguese policy in the region.[24] Contrary to entire Lusitanian legislation – which excluded women from concessions' heritage as well as from estates bestowed by the crown – this contract determined that *prazos* were inherited in feminine lineage, when the heiress married a colonist born in Portugal – a *reinol* – or a *reinol's* son.[25] The *prazeiro* was therefore subjected to metropolitan sovereignty by a double temporary contract: the contract of three generations (the emphyteusis) established by the crown with his wife's family, and the contract of one generation, which he took over by marrying the legal proprietor of the crown's *prazo*. By forcing each heiress to marry a *reinol*, the crown hoped to restrain the colony's self-sufficiency and the overwhelming ascension of mulattos who took possession of the *prazos*.[26] This system gave birth to odd situations where by old women proprietors of *prazos* (the *donas*) were as much at strife as royal princesses: Many *donas* became successively widows and married suitors wishing to become proprietors.[27] In fact, *prazeiros'* powers rested more on compromises with natives than on the legal status acknowledged by Lisbon.

Among fifty-five *prazos* found in 1750 in the province of Tete, five

---

[23] Hoppe, p. 46.

[24] On *prazos* see M. D. D. Newitt, "The Portuguese on the Zambezi: an Historical Interpretation of the Prazo," *JAH*, Vol. X (1969), pp. 67–85; Allen F. Isaacman, *Mozambique, the Africanisation of a European Institution: The Zambezi Prazos 1705–1902* (Madison, Wis., 1972), esp. Appendix B, pp. 172ff; Botelho, pp. 264–271.

[25] See *Lei Mental* in Joel Serrão et al., *Dicionário de História a de Portugal*, 4 vols. *(DHP)* (Lisbon, 1963–71), Vol. III, pp. 29, 30; A. Lobato, *A Evolução*, pp. 216–18; Newitt, *Portuguese Settlement*, pp. 97–102.

[26] A. Lobato and G. Papagno gave a different explanation of the *prazos'* feminine inheritance. For Lobato, this law was created to help widows and orphans coming from Portugal (*Colonização*, p. 103 *sq.*); for Papagno the law was also made to stimulate migration from Portugal to Mozambique; see Giuseppe Papagno, *Colonialismo e feudalismo; la questione dei prazos da Coroa nel Mozambico fine del secolo XIX* (Torino, 1972), p. 39.

[27] Newitt, *"Portuguese Settlement,"* pp. 87, 88, 145.

had a title of concession and twenty-five had no title at all. The other twenty-five *prazos* were either merely confirmed by local authorities or had doubtful property warrants.[28] Notwithstanding continuous raids launched against the natives, Portugal long delayed the imposition of sovereignty over the area. Following a practice previously adopted by Arab merchants, Portuguese governors and general-captains bestowed a gift on the Monomotapa – as a symbolical bond of vassalage – at the moment they took their posts in Mozambique. When this tribute – called *curva* and generally consisting of a certain amount of cloths – was not paid, trouble developed in the colony. In 1807, when three centuries of Portuguese presence would lead one to suppose that this custom was lost, the governor of one of Zambezi's provinces decided not to pay the *curva*, provoking a guerrilla revolt that ended only in 1826, when the Portuguese finally offered the tribute to the Monomotapa emperor.[29]

In 1752 Mozambique was separated from the State of India, on which it was administratively dependent, to become an autonomous colony in the Portuguese empire. Authorities tried to control the *prazos* in 1760, but the fragility of the links of these domains with metropolitan networks caused continuous rebellions among the *prazeiros*.[30] The *prazos* were disconnected from the pre-Portuguese social system in the first quarter of the nineteenth century when the Brazilian slave trade pulled Mozambique trade into the Atlantic stream.[31]

Colonial conquest, as we said at the outset, did not guarantee successful economic exploitation by the metropolis. The overseas surplus did not reach the metropolis when it was directly consumed by colonists, as happened in Mozambique, or when it was taken by trade running out of the Portuguese economic and fiscal networks, as was the case in Goa. The colonists' permanence in a territory did not guarantee the colonial exploitation of this territory. Political domination was not necessarily a synonym for colonial exploitation.

In Brazil, measures were taken accordingly in 1534 to consolidate the occupation and valorization of the territory, responding to French invasion at home as well as to the decline of Portuguese trade in Asia.

---

[28] Lobato, *Evolução*, pp. 228–33.

[29] "Viagem," *Studia, op. cit.*, p. 172, n. 31; Oliveira Boleo, "Vicissitudes históricas da política de exploração mineira no Império de Monomotapa," *Studia*, No. 32 (June 1971), pp. 167–209, 207.

[30] J. J. Lopes De Lima and F. Bordalo, *Ensaios sobre a Statística das possessões portuguezas*, 5 vols. (Lisbon, 1844–62), Vol. IV, p. 245; Lobato, *Evolução*, pp. 219, 220.

[31] Papagno, pp. 141–74.

The colony was divided into fifteen hereditary captaincies yielded to twelve grantees. The crown offered several privileges to attract candidates to the position of donatary captain. Nevertheless, six of the first twelve donataries either never went to Brazil or came back at once to Portugal; two were killed; two others gave up their rights; and only two thrived: Duarte Coelho in Pernambuco and, somehow, as we will see later, Pero do Campo Tourinho in Porto Seguro. The *capitania* of São Vicente prospered for a certain time, though its donee had never visited it. In 1549 a general-government was established, impelling a movement of centralization designed to reduce donees' privileges.[32]

Circumstances peculiar to Pernambuco allowed local donataries to resist general-governors' attempts to assume their prerogatives.[33] In all other places, however, a central government authority was set up. In 1549 the economy based on Indian labor and exploitation of brazilwood started to change into an economy of agricultural production based on sugar mills and African slave labor. The colony's linkage with the Atlantic trade was deliberately emphasized by royal legislation restricting employment of Amerindian slave labor and stimulating African slave trade, as well as by measures restraining internal trade among Brazilian captaincies.[34]

This summary illustrates the antagonisms arising when the metropolis no longer confines itself to mere exercise of domination (*dominium*) but also asserts its rights over lands to be conquered and its guardianship of conquered peoples. The conflict between Iberian powers and their subjects had different effects on overseas territory. In Peru, the rise of the mining economy put an end to the colonists' move toward autonomy and stimulated integration of Spanish America markets into European trade. In Angola, maritime exchanges – triggered by the slave trade – gave Portugal additional means of control over the colony. In Mozambique, where Portuguese trade took its place in a pre-European mercantile network, colonists became kaffirized and fulfilled roles in the traditional trade network of the native society. Finally, in Goa, where exchanges with Arab and Indian merchants as well with the Far East provided profitable choices, trade

---

[32] J. Capistrano De Abreu, *O Descobrimento do Brasil*, 2nd ed. (Rio de Janeiro, 1976), pp. 75–8; Harold B. Johnson, "The Portuguese Settlement of Brazil 1500–1580," in Leslie Bethell (ed.), *The Cambridge History of Latin America (CHLA)*, 5 vols. (Cambridge, London, and New York, 1986), Vol. I, pp. 263–7.

[33] Francis A. Dutra, "Centralization vs. Donatorial Privilege: Pernambuco, 1602–1630," in D. Alden (ed.), *Colonial Roots of Modern Brazil* (London, 1973), pp. 19–60.

[34] "Regimento de Tomé de Souza (1548)," *Revista do Instituto Histórico e Geográfico Brasileiro*, Vol. LXI (1898), pp. 39–75.

with the Portuguese gave way to more attractive opportunities outside metropolitan control.

THE METROPOLIS'S OPTIONS

It is well known that private investment in the first stages of Lusitanian colonization was not exclusively Portuguese. Except for some royal monopolies, Catholic foreigners, settled or not in Portugal, could get privileges similar to those of national Catholics for trade with Portuguese colonies. Moreover, if they employed a Portuguese crew, those foreigners were also allowed to use their own ships in this commerce.[35]

The *exclusivo colonial*, that is, the national trade monopoly over colonies, was imposed only after 1580. Through its association with the Spanish monarchy, the Portuguese crown became so involved in European conflicts that it ended by ruining its overseas domains.[36] Lisbon started, therefore, to restrain the activities of traders from other countries. After 1591, to avoid heresies – but also because it was "against all reason and good sense" that foreign merchants would be allowed to damage "the trade of the kingdom" – foreigners were forbidden to go to overseas territories. In 1605 a prohibition vetoed all foreign transactions in Portuguese domains. Aliens settled in Brazil had to go back to the kingdom within a year.[37]

Hence, a sharp move occurred in Portuguese colonial policy on the eve of the Century of Discoveries. Initially the crown granted powers both to its subjects owning capital and also to Catholic foreigners trading with its overseas markets. Some decades later, the monarchy moved back and impelled a movement of "metropolitan restoration" abroad, delimiting the autonomy of the main actors of colonial conquest. On the one hand, a national monopoly (the *exclusivo*) was established over colonial trade. On the other hand, new laws submitted colonists to general-governors entrusted with ample powers and charged to remind *urbi et orbi* the *purpose of colonization*, that is,

---

[35] Bailey W. Diffie, "The Legal Privileges of the Foreigners in Portugal and Sixteenth-Century Brazil," in H. H. Keith and S. F. Edwards (eds.), *Conflict and Continuity in Brazilian Society* (Columbia, S.C., 1969), pp. 1–19; Susan C. Schneider, "Commentary," ibid., pp. 20–3; Johnson, pp. 262–4; Magalhães Godinho, Vol. III, pp. 190–214.

[36] Stuart B. Schwartz, "Luso-Spanish Relations in Hapsburg Brazil, 1580–1640," *The Americas (TheA)*, Vol. XXV, No. 1 (1968), pp. 33–48, 45–8.

[37] *MMA*, Vol. I, p. 414; Vol. III, pp. 192–6; Vol. IV, pp. 62–6.

the colonial policy.[38] The crown had to learn how to make all colonial rivers flow toward the metropolitan sea. The colonists had to understand that the apprenticeship of colonization was mainly the apprenticeship of the market, which was, first and foremost, the metropolitan market. Only then could colonial domination and colonial exploitation coincide and correlate with each other.

Having decided to be the only bestower of lands and the only controller of natives to be conquered, the imperial power appeared also as the organizer of productive labor, the conveyor of social privileges, and the gendarme of religious orthodoxy.[39]

Like the Spanish monarchy, the Portuguese crown exerted direct control over secular clergy, thanks to the *jus patronatus* (the *padroado*), a set of privileges popes granted to Iberian monarchs between 1452 and 1514. According to these texts, the Iberian religious hierarchy could undertake its functions only after royal approval. The crown supported the secular clergy financially and could forbid the proclamation of pontifical edicts and briefs.[40] Framed by the *padroado*, the secular clergy and episcopate became chains of metropolitan power, especially in Brazil and Africa. In the context of migrations and cultural transfers, where accusations of heresy spread easily, exclusion from the ecclesiastic community brought harsh consequences. Hence excommunication became an efficient tool against colonists rebelling against metropolitan policy. Sometimes excommunication was pronounced *lato sensu*, that is, on a large scale, clearly to implement the royal monopoly. Responding to a request from the governor of Cape Verde Islands, the local bishop excommunicated in 1613 "all those who had robbed or defrauded any of Your Majesty's goods."[41] It is clear that religious orthodoxy had its share in the process of coloni

---

[38] See Caio Prado, Jr., *Formação do Brasil Contemporaneo* (São Paulo, 1971), pp. 19, 31; conceptual and historical implications of Prado's thesis on the "purpose of colonization" are discussed by Fernando A. Novais, "Caio Prado Jr. na historiografia brasileira," in R. Moraes et al. (eds.), *Inteligencia Brasileira* (São Paulo, 1986), pp. 68–9; idem., *Portugal e Brasil na Crise do Antigo Sistema Colonial 1777–1808* (São Paulo, 1979); see José Roberto de Amaral Lapa et al., *Modos de produção e Realidade Brasileira* (Petropolis, RJ, 1980).

[39] J. Lúcio de Azevedo, *História dos Cristãos Novos Portugueses*, 2nd ed. (Lisbon, 1975); Arnold Wiznitzer, *Os Judeus no Brasil Colonial* (São Paulo, 1966); Anita Novinsky, *Cristãos Novos na Bahia* (São Paulo, 1967); Maria Luiza Tucci Carneiro, *Preconceito Racial no Brasil Colonia – Os Cristãos Novos* (São Paulo, 1983).

[40] Bull of Sixto IV, "Clara devotionis," 21 August 1472 and bull of Alexandre VI, "Cum sicut nobis," 23 August 1499, in João Martins da Silva Marques, ed., *Descobrimentos Portugueses, Documentos para a sua historia (DP)*, 3 vols. (Lisbon, 1971), Vol. III (1461–1500), pp. 119, 120, 549, 550.

[41] *MMA*, Vol. IV, p. 502.

zation of colonists. The situation of Jesuits, Franciscans, Carmelites, and Benedictines – the regular clergy who engaged in missionary tasks in Brazil – must be examined in other perspectives. In their holistic strategy of evangelizing the Amerindians, the Jesuits came into conflict with the colonists and bishops but also set themselves against the crown. It is also necessary to point out the specific role of missions. As C. R. Boxer observes, since important military posts were nonexistent in the colonies before the second half of eighteenth century, it was mostly the clergy's task to keep the conquered populations loyal to the Iberian crown.[42]

The action of the Inquisition is more complex. In the metropolis, the Holy Office often appeared as a weapon of the aristocracy against the mercantile bourgeoisie. Also, when metropolitan merchants or the crown faced foreign competition, denunciations of Judaism abounded. Against all evidence, the captain of Santiago (Cape Verde) informed the court in 1544 that "Guinea [was] lost" to Portugal, since the land was already "crowded" with New Christians engaged in smuggling.[43] Accused of usury and heresy, important merchants were arrested in Brazil and put on trial by the Holy Office in Lisbon.[44] Between 1580 and 1640, when Portugal was associated with the Spanish crown, there was a new move of the inquisitorial power: The Holy Office's metropolitan agents decided to play the card of Madrid policies and attack Portuguese nationalistic movements. The same thing happened in Peru, where Spanish traders manipulated the Inquisition and decimated Portuguese merchants.[45] Unbelievers were permanently unsafe in the tropics, for the crown alternated repressive fury and usurpation with the desire to profit from the economic activity of the New Christians. Legislation concerning emigration reflected this contradictions. A law of 1587 forbade New Christians and their families to leave the kingdom. In 1601 this law was revoked, and they were allowed to move to the colonies. A warrant of 1612 abrogated the previous law, reestablishing the prohibitory order of 1587.[46] New

---

[42] Pe. Serafim Leite, *História da Companhia de Jesus no Brasil 1549–1760 (HCJB)*, 10 vols. (Lisbon and Rio de Janeiro, 1938–50), Vol. VI, p. 552; Boxer, *A Igreja, e a Expansão Ibérica* (Lisbon, 1978), pp. 98–100.

[43] See Armando Castro, *Doutrinas econômicas em Portugal, séculos XVI a XVIII* (Lisbon, 1978), pp. 79, 80; see also a more balanced analysis in Frederic Mauro, "La Bourgeoisie Portugaise au XVIIe siècle," in Foundation Gulbenkian, *Etudes Economiques sur l'Expansion Portugaise* (Paris, 1970), pp. 15–36; and David Grant Smith, "Old Christian Merchants and the Foundation of the Brazil Company, 1649," *HAHR*, Vol. 54 (1974), pp. 233–59.

[44] *MMA.*, Vol. II, p. 372.

[45] Wiznitzer, pp. 18, 19.

[46] Vitorino Magalhães Godinho, "Restauração," in J. Serrão et al., *DHP*, Vol. III,

liberations followed new prohibitions. Even though the number of executed individuals from Brazil stayed at around 20 and the number of convicts did not exceed 500 – a sum that current research may increase – the fear infused by the Inquisition struck many more men and women overseas.[47]

In Angola, the Inquisition interfered only after 1626. Permanent residence of New Christians was allowed if they were confined to the role of merchant.[48] However, missionaries' correspondence recorded several examples of indirect action of the inquisitorial hand.[49] Let us follow the priest Pero Tavares in his journey across the Angola back country in 1631. Arriving at a hamlet, he found an idol and was ready to destroy it. The local *soba* ran for help to an ally, a Portuguese colonist, asking him to save the idol that was "physician and remedy" for the natives. Entangled in a quarrel with the colonist amid a dangerous tumult arising in the hamlet, Tavares acted quickly:

I feared incidents and, thus, brought the matter to an end in a few words; I clearly told the man – for I knew he belonged to "the nation" [Jew, New Christian] – that he should no longer discuss such an affair, as I would inform the governor and the bishop of everything since these matters were to be undertaken by the Holy Office. Those were my last words . . . the poor Hebrew was almost struck dumb; then, self-composed, he said to me: Father of my soul, the one who said it is no longer here. Your Reverence may thus burn the idol.[50]

This apparently trivial incident shows the insidious efficacy of the pressures exerted by priests in Brazil and Angola, even though the fires of the Inquisition did not burn in those territories. A historical trait of Portuguese authoritarianism stands out here. Without thoroughly banishing the Jews, as Spain had done, or declaring open war on religious dissenters, as the French monarchy did against Protestants, Portugal punished, plundered, and usurped the rights of its crypto-Jewish mercantile bourgeoisie. The denial of civil rights to an economically powerful community was established as a political prin

---

pp. 609–28; José Veiga Torres, "Uma longa guerra social: Os ritmos da repressão inquisitorial em Portugal," *Revista de História Económica e Social (RHES)* (Lisbon, 1978), Vol. 1, pp. 55–68; Harry E. Cross, "Commerce and Orthodoxy: A Spanish Response to Portuguese Commercial Penetration in the Viceroyalty of Peru, 1580–1640," *TheA.*, Vol. XXXV, No. 2 (1978), pp. 151–67.

[47] Novinsky, pp. 141–62; Tucci Carneiro, pp. 195–205; *MMA*, Vol. IV, pp. 15–17, 477–9; Tucci Carneiro, pp. 68–84.

[48] *MMA*, Vol. IV, p. 473; Delgado, Vol. II, pp. 129, 130.

[49] Lúcio De Azevedo, p. 232; *MMA*, Vol. VIII, p. 68.

[50] *MMA*, Vol. VIII, pp. 78, 79 passim.

ciple. This revenge of the aristocracy on the bourgeoisie dramatically marked the evolution of the Brazilian and Portuguese societies.

Through the indirect action of the Inquisition or the political zeal of the clergy, the church thus acted in a double way. On the one hand, it helped to consolidate the *dominium*, for in some regions it set up the occupation of the territory. On the other hand, it reinforced the *imperium* insofar as it led to a relation of submissiveness between the imperial people and the metropolis.

This brief view of the contrasting situations arising with the Discoveries makes clear the double drift that occurred some decades after the beginning of colonization.

Parallel to the political centralization carried on to the disadvantage of the colonists, a national trade monopoly was settled to restrain the activities of foreign Catholic merchants. At this time, the colonies' links with the Iberian metropolis depended more on knots tied by royal officials and clergy than on links provided by world-market exchanges. Only after the mining production in Spanish America and the connection of slave trade with Brazil would the dynamics of the Atlantic system come to involve Iberian possessions in Africa and America.

Spanish metropolitan control rested weakly on the colonial process of production and strongly on the commercialization of colonial goods. Spanish colonial goods – precious metals – were stocked and carried by a fleet system channeled through three American seaports and Seville, the only communication points allowed between Spain and America. Given the fact that the slave trade did not fit in with such restrictions, Madrid was compelled to establish *asientos*, subcontracting to Genoese and Portuguese the slave trade to Spanish America. In Portuguese America, the colonial process was rather different. The nature of tropical goods made it difficult to have, between Brazil and Portugal, a trade system similar to that of Spanish America. Rigid centralization, and long waits in buying, storing, and carrying goods, which characterized Spanish trade, were inadequate arrangements for the perishable quality and the price fluctuations of Brazilian agricultural products, as well as for the growing activity of Portugal's secondary ports.[51] In fact, the introduction of Africans and the prohibition of Indian enslavement allowed Portugal to control operations taking place upstream and downstream in Brazilian colonial production; colonists depended upon the metropolis to export their products but also to import their factors of production, that is, the African

[51] Schneider, pp. 21, 22.

slaves. Such phenomena fundamentally framed Portuguese colonization in South Atlantic.

Intermetropolitan wars in the second half of the seventeenth century led Lisbon to organize trade fleets between Brazil and Portugal – a system that would be kept during the first half of the eighteenth century to carry Brazilian gold to Lisbon. But that system was less severe than the one in Spanish America. Discredited by colonists and merchants, Brazil's organized fleets were extinguished in 1765.[52]

The slave trade, which formed the basis of colonial production, was a decisive instrument in the achievement of the Portuguese colonial system in the Atlantic. Gradually this trade transcended the economic field and became integrated into the metropolitan political apparatus. The two issues presented in the preceding pages thus gain their whole meaning: The exercise of imperial power in overseas territories and the set of exchanges between metropolis and colonies were equated in the sphere of slave traffic.

Nevertheless, by allowing the colonization of colonists, that is, their inclusion in the metropolitan network, the slave system's dynamics contradictorily transformed the colonial system. After the seventeenth and eighteenth centuries, this colonial pattern was breached as Luso-Brazilian interests – distinct from metropolitan interests – stratified on both sides of the Atlantic: in African slave trade ports as well as in Brazilian slavery areas. Consequently, the notion of a "colonial pact" loses, in the Brazilian case, part of the significance generally attached to it. In fact, the slave trade was not just the traffic in slaves: It involved more complex aspects than those derived from the single operation of purchasing, selling, and transporting Africans from one side of the Atlantic to the other.

THE AIMS OF THE PORTUGUESE SLAVE TRADE

Exploring the international essence of the mercantile capital already accumulated in Europe, the Portuguese crown precociously laid the bases of an imperial market area.[53] But Portugal had neither the means

---

[52] M. A. Soares De Azevedo, "Armadas do Brasil," *DHP*, Vol. 1, pp. 186–8; Arthur Cézar Ferreira Reis, "O Comércio Colonial e as Companhias privilegiadas," in Sérgio Buarque De Holanda, ed., *História Geral da Civilisação Brasileira*, tome I, Vol. 2 (São Paulo, 1960), pp. 316–18; Virgílio Noya Pinto, *O Ouro brasileiro e o comércio anglo-portugues* (São Paulo, 1979), pp. 133–84.

[53] Pe. Antonio Brasio, "Do último Cruzado ao Padroado Régio," *Studia* January (1959), pp. 125–53; see also Antonio José Saraiva, "Le Père Antonio Vieira, S. J. et l'esclavage des Noirs au XVIIe s.," *Annales E.C.S.*, Vol. 22 (1967), pp. 1289–1309; Magalhães Godinho, *Os Descobrimentos*, Vol. I.

nor the power to unify or keep this transcontinental space. Surpassed by their European rivals, Portugal lost, mainly in Asia, control over trade zones, peoples, and territories to nations better equipped for this sort of imperial dominion. Nevertheless, the Portuguese crown established in the South Atlantic a production economy that was more efficiently exploited than the circulation economy of its former Asian empire.[54] Facing the nonexistence of a regular surplus to be incorporated in maritime trade, the crown, supported by private capital, stimulated in South America the production of export goods through African slavery, thus giving rise to a more advanced system of colonial exploitation. The superiority of the Portuguese colonial process soon became evident: Benefitting from the Lusitanian example, other European maritime nations created in the seventeenth and eighteenth centuries similar systems in the Caribbean and Africa.

In such a context, what were the initial aims of the Portuguese slave trade? Papal edicts between 1455 and 1481 extinguished excommunication punishing Portuguese who bought slaves and gold from Muslims. The plea of an edict from 1481 justified this liberation by explaining that the purpose of this trade was "to diminish the infidels' power and not to increase it." In the political-military field, the treaty of Alcaçovas, signed by Portugal and Spain in 1479, put an end to the Succession War in Castile and transferred the Canary Islands to Castilan sovereignty, but also recognized the Portuguese king as the only lord of Madeira, the Azores, the Fez Kingdom (Morocco), and the Cape Verde islands, as well as of the lands "discovered and . . . the ones to be discovered" in Guinea, that is, in black Africa.[55] Insofar as the legitimacy of Lusitanian conquest and trade in Africa was acknowledged by Spain and the pope, Lisbon was able to hold commercial and territorial guarantees that would make it play, for four centuries, a decisive role in the great slave business.

In the first place, the slave traffic constituted a segment of the vast commercial network connecting Portugal to Asia. In its relations with Asia, Lisbon had to pay for its imports with shipments of gold (to the Ottoman empire), silver (to the Far East), and copper (to India),

---

[54] In the 1550s, French smuggling had already provoked a fall in brazilwood prices at Antwerp and a diminution of Portuguese profits in the Brazilian trade; see Johnson, pp. 258, 259.

[55] Bulls of Sixte IV, "Aeterni Regis Clementia", 21 June 1481; Nicolau V, "Romanus Pontifex," 8 January 1455; Calixto III, "Inter coetera," 13 March 1456; also articles 27 and 28 of the Alcáçovas Treaty, signed 4 September, 1479, in *DP*, Vol. III pp. 222–38, 232; See also bull "Sedes Apostolica" of Julio II, 4 July 1505; idem., "Breve Desideras," *MMA*, Vol. II, pp. 21–3, 27–8; *DP*, Vol. III, pp. 181–209, 206.

metals of which Portugal had little supply.[56] The first Portuguese expeditions in Africa searched for mines and native markets where those metals were traded. To get gold, the Portuguese, taking slaves farther in the East, at Benin, bartered and carried those slaves to the fort they built at São Jorge da Mina in 1482, as well as to other seaports of the Gold Coast, thus starting a maritime slave traffic in the area.[57] In a famous text, *Esmeraldo de situ orbis*, Duarte Pacheco Pereira described such operations in 1508. Slaves were sold to native merchants who brought gold to the fort, though they had no "asses or mules" to carry back inland the goods bartered with Europeans.[58]

In the second place, the slave trade constituted an income source to the royal treasury. Despite protests from the court of Lisbon and Portuguese slave owners, King Afonso V supported slave traders, refusing to forbid in 1472 the reselling abroad of slaves previously brought to Portugal.[59] In the Portuguese slave trade, the national demand for slaves – whether metropolitan or colonial – was only part of the total demand. Slaves from Portuguese Africa continued to be exported abroad. This strategy was consecrated by Luso-Spanish *asientos* between 1594 and 1640. After the Restoration of 1640 and the opening of hostilities between Portugal and Spain, the Portuguese crown made haste in separating war from trade, proclaiming the warrant of June 2, 1641, which allowed its vassals to sell Africans to Spaniards in America so long as one-third of the slaves were reserved for Brazilian markets. In 1647 that warrant was ratified, but the reserve of one-third of the slaves for Brazil was abolished. In 1651, the Ultramarine Council set up the official policy: Ships coming directly from Spanish America should have preference in Angola, because they brought silver for the purchase of slaves and paid high customs taxes. Those going directly from Spain to Angola should not be received, for they brought goods instead of gold, thus rivaling Portuguese commerce. In addition, "if all ships were admitted, slaves who

---

[56] Magalhães Godinho, *Os Descobrimentos*, Vol. I, pp. 219–73; Vol. II, pp. 36–49, 134–41.

[57] J. B. Ballong-Wen-Mewuda, "Le Commerce Portugais des esclaves entre la côte de l'actuel Nigéria et celle du Ghana Moderne aux XVeme et XVIeme siècles," in Université de Nantes, *Colloque International sur la Traite des Noirs (CITN)*, 3 vols. (Nantes, 1985); Ivor Wilks, "Waranga, Akan and the Portuguese in the Fifteenth and Sixteenth Centuries – I. The Matter of Bitu," *JAH*, Vol. 23, No. 3 (1982), pp. 333–49.

[58] Duarte Pacheco Pereira, *Esmeraldo de situ orbis* (1508) (Lisbon, 1975), pp. 115, 119.

[59] J. Lúcio De Azevedo, *Epocas de Portugal Econômico (1928)* (Porto, 1978), p. 74; A. C. de C. M. Saunders, *A Social History of Black Slaves and Freedmen in Portugal 1441–1555* (London and New York, 1982), p. 34.

are necessary to Brazilians' sugar mills might lack."[60] A certain priority was thus given to the Brazilian market, but it was not until 1751 that a new warrant stopped the export of Africans to foreign colonies, thus recognizing the exclusive Luso-Brazilian claim on the Luso-African supply of slaves.

In the third place, the slave trade constituted the productive vector of sugar plantations in the Atlantic Islands. There is a key text that allows us to understand the *moment* when the comparative advantages of the slave system over free labor in Atlantic sugar plantations were verified and turned into economic policy. This text is the royal law sent in 1562 to the farmers (*lavradores*) of Madeira:

Concerning the great expenses in sugar sales faced by owners at their farms and sugar plantations in the Island of Madeira, with laborers and men brought in salary and journal; and as some of those owners, afraid they may not cope [with] such expenses, many times give up cultivating the soil and end up by not getting as much sugar as they would *if they had their own slaves* constantly working to care and service of their farms; as it is thus necessary – so the mentioned farms can always be of good use and never damaged, and so they will not happen to decrease for need of the mentioned [slave] laborers, once such a fact makes the owners of those farms have heavy losses, and also because in my incomes too, there is waste on that account – as it is thus necessary, and as I do want to look after that ... I am pleased to give them place and permission to equip a ship [yearly] in the mentioned island of Madeira ... to go barter for slaves in the Rivers of Guinea ... according to each owner's needs of slaves.[61] (Italics added)

This passage has a clear meaning: Given metropolitan experience with the slave system, it is possible to foresee in 1562 that royal income and plantations' productivity would increase as soon as the free laborers of Madeira were supplanted by slaves from Guinea. Thus proceeding, the king of Portugal permanently marked the horizon of the Atlantic economy.

Considering the international composition of mercantile capital accumulated in Europe, the slave and sugar businesses associated Genoese, Florentines, Germans, Spaniards, and Portuguese in rather itinerant activities. Indeed, Portuguese dealing with slaves and sugar

---

[60] Marcos Carneiro De Mendonça, *O Marquez de Pombal e o Brasil* (São Paulo, 1960), pp. 89–90; *MMA*, Vol. X, pp. 28, 29; Vol. XI, p. 67.
[61] "Alvarás" of 16 October 1562 and 30 October 1562; *MMA*, second series, Vol. II, pp. 491–8; see Virginia Rau, "The Madeiran Sugar Cane Plantations," in H. B. Johnson, Jr. (ed.), *From Reconquest to Empire: The Iberian Background to Latin American History* (New York, 1970), pp. 71–84.

exploited other American zones before definitely entering Brazil. At Hispaniola there were thirty sugar mills in 1550, set up and managed since 1535 by "more than two hundred Portuguese sugar technicians [*oficiais de açucares*]." Besides that, there were on the island many Portuguese tillers, masons, carpenters, and blacksmiths, generally from the Canary Islands. At the height of activity, in the years 1560–70, there were between 12,000 and 20,000 black slaves on the island, most of them provided by Portuguese slave ships. Thanks to Genoese capitalists and Portuguese craftsmen, slave traders, and sugar technicians, Hispaniola was then able to produce more sugar and possess more Africans than Brazil itself. However, that sugar industry stagnated when the fleets' itinerary and the pattern of Spanish economic geography were thoroughly reorganized under the impact of silver mines' activity on the continent.[62] In the last quarter of the sixteenth century, Brazil became an attractive market for slave traders. Around 1575, only 10,000 Africans had gone to Brazil, whereas Spanish America – where regular introductions of Africans had been going on since 1525 – had received around 37,500 slaves. The Atlantic islands had already imported 123,600 slaves. Up to 1600, Portuguese traded most of the 125,000 Africans deported to America, but Brazilian ports got just 40 percent of that amount.[63] Nevertheless, by 1580, Brazilian sugar achieved first place in the Portuguese empire. Brazilian sugar mills produced around 5,100 tons a year, whereas Madeira and São. Tomé, now declining, produced 590 and 300 tons, respectively.[64] Initially based on Indian slavery, the development of the Brazilian sugar culture became tributary to African labor and slave trade. That change occurred in response to a series of circumstances to be carefully examined.

THE SLAVE TRADE AS AN INSTRUMENT OF COLONIAL POLICY

The crown's action is clearly visible at the root of the productive process established in Brazil. The building of sugar mills, stimulated by fiscal measures assigned at a royal warrant (*alvará*) of July 23, 1554,

---

[62] Alain Milhou, "Los Intentos de Repoblacion de la Isla Espanola por Colonias de Labradores (1518–1603) – Razones de un Fracaso," in Université de Bordeaux, ed., *Actas del Quinto Congreso internacional de Hispanistas* (Bordeaux, 1977), Vol. II, pp. 643–54; Chanu and Chaunu, tome VI-2, Tables 240–7, pp. 496–502.

[63] J. D. Fage, *A History of West Africa* (Cambridge and New York, 1969), pp. 63–5.

[64] F. Mauro, *Le Portugal et l'Atlantique au XVIIe siécle 1570–1670* (Paris, 1960), pp. 183–200; idem., *Le XVIe s. européen – aspects économiques*, 3rd ed. (Paris, 1981), p. 155.

was completed by a warrant of March 29, 1559, allowing each mill owner to import 120 slaves from São Tomé (actually from the Congo, Angola, Gabon, and Nigeria), paying only one-third of the taxes.[65] Such measures attracted to Brazilian plantations a segment of the slave trade formerly directed to the Caribbean. Gradually, in successive stages – most of the time regular and generally expected – the slave trade with Brazil tied Portuguese enclaves in western Africa to the Atlantic trade. Far from being contradictory, the events occurring on the American and African coasts clarified each other through a series of reciprocal effects.

The introduction of Africans to American plantations progressively synchronized various stages of the colonial system. This consolidation of the structure historically determined by mercantile capitalism was activated at several levels:

1. The metropolis was invested with preeminent power, since control of the slave trade permitted it to control the reproduction of the slaves' productive cycle. For three centuries economic complementarity tied Africa to Brazil, making remote the possibility of diverging, and moreover competitive, development among Portuguese colonies on both sides of the South Atlantic.

Actually, the relevance of colonial exploitation in West and Central Africa to exploitation undertaken in South America was clearly perceived by Lisbon only in the seventeenth century. André Alvares de Almada, a mulatto from Cape Verde, finished his "Tratado Breve" (1594) by listing the advantages of Senegambia compared with Brazil: "Populated, it [Senegambia] would have a greater trade than Brazil, for in Brazil there is no more than sugar, brazilwood and cotton; in this land there is cotton and brazilwood, besides ivory, wax, gold, amber, malagueta pepper; many sugar mills can be built, and there is iron, lots of woods for the mills, and slaves to work at them."[66] In Angola colonists had land and slaves in rural properties similar to those in Brazil.[67] Also, the metropolis regularly sent instructions stating that sugar cane and cotton should be cultivated in Angolan lands. In 1655 the municipal chamber of Luanda made Lisbon authorities face the new colonial order, showing them that such a task ran up

[65] Instituto do Açucar e do Alcool, ed., *Documentos para a História do Açucar*, 3 vols. (Rio de Janeiro, 1954–63), Vol. I, pp. 11–113.

[66] André Alvares De Almada, "Tratado Breve dos Rios de Guiné do Cabo Verde" (1594), *MMA*, Vol. III, pp. 230–377, 376; see also "Carta de Bartolomeu Velho ao Rei" (1606), *MMA*, Vol. IV, pp. 114–25.

[67] *MMA*, Vol. IX, pp. 26ff; Beatrix Heintze, "Traite de 'Pièces' en Angola: ce que nos sources passent sous silence," *CITN*, Vol. II, pp. 1–21.

against problems concerning sugar (shortage of firewood and low quality of the sugar) and, mainly, the trade dominant in the Atlantic routes. Given the prevailing flows of trade, sugar and cotton cultivated in Angola would go first to Brazil, and only afterward would be sent to Portugal. Burdened with freight costs, these Angolan products could not compete with Brazilian tropical products.[68]

At this point, the cards to be played at the game in the South Atlantic were already on the table: Angola would not export sugar, and the sugar mills of São Tomé would gradually extinguish their furnaces.[69] Portuguese colonization in South Atlantic would be complementary, not competitive: Brazil would produce sugar, tobacco, cotton, and coffee, and Africa would provide slaves. The plan to create another Brazil in Angola would take shape again only in the second half of the nineteenth century, when Brazil escaped from Portuguese control and after the slave trade to America was extinguished.

2. Confrontation pitting the Jesuits against both the royal administration and the colonists was provisionally avoided. Employment of African slaves made evangelization easier, relieving the Amerindians from coerced labor imposed by planters and authorities charged with providing public works.

The first serious clash between a donatory captain and the metropolitan apparatus happened in the captaincy of Porto Seguro and concerned the administration of Indian labor. After colliding with Vicar Bernardo de Aurejeac, Donatary Pero do Campo Tourinho was arrested and sent to the Inquisition Court in Lisbon. The interrogatory, made in 1550, described the accusations against the defendant:

Asked whether he had said that in his captaincy no holiday was to be kept – nor lady-Day, the Apostles' Day or All Saints' Day – so much so that he had ordered his [Indian] servants to work on those days, he answered no, and said that he rather told them to keep and celebrate; and that he just sometimes reprimanded the French vicar [Aurejeac] for he wanted Saint William's, Saint Martin's, Saint George's and other Saints' Days to be kept as well, which were not ordered to be kept by Saint Mother Church and either by prelates in their constitutions, because the land was new and it was necessary to work to populate it. . . .[70]

This conflict between colonists' mercantile productivity and evangelization would be lessened by the slave trade. Two of the most

[68] Delgado, Vol. III, pp. 168–70; "Consulta do Conselho Ultramarino," 21 June 1655, *MMA*, Vol. XI, pp. 490, 491.
[69] Mauro, pp. 190–2.
[70] J. Capistrano De Abreu, "Atribulações de um Donatário," in *Caminhos Antigos e Povoamento do Brasil* (Rio de Janeiro, 1930), pp. 37–50.

important protectors of the Indians, the Dominican Bartolomé de Las Casas in the sixteenth century and the Jesuit Antonio Vieira in the seventeenth century, suggested to metropolitan authorities implementation of the African slave trade to free Indians from the servitude they were reduced to by the colonists.[71] Jesuits would quarrel with the colonists in areas where the slave trade had not penetrated and where Indian coerced labor prevailed. Insofar as their temporal power increased, the Jesuits would come into conflict with the authorities. That contest lasted until the crisis of the 1750s, when the Society of Jesus was driven from Portugal and the colonies. This conflict demonstrates the political nonviability of American colonial enclaves based on Indian coerced labor and placed outside metropolitan control.

3. The crown and the colonial administration found new income sources in the slave trade. This income came from export duties in African seaports, from entrance fees in Brazilian seaports, and from donations, subsidies, preferential duties, excise taxes, and other taxes included in the slaves' price. The civil administration was not the only one to benefit from such tributes: There was also the tax paid to the clergy for obligatory baptism of each slave in seaports. Around 1630 a slave went to Brazil burdened by tributes corresponding to 20 percent of his price and to Spanish America with taxes corresponding to 66 percent of his price in Angola.[72] After 1714, overland transportation of slaves to Brazilian mining regions was also taxed; and in 1809 a 5 percent tax was levied on the purchase and sale of slaves throughout the Brazilian territory. Portugal derived other advantages from its quasi-monopoly over the slave trade up to the first half of the seventeenth century. Thanks to this African trade, Portugal was able to enter Peru and the Caribbean, penetrating the Spanish silver monopoly, obtaining gold, and speculating on other American products such as the Venezuelan cocoa exported to Mexico.[73]

[71] Marcel Bataillon observes that when Las Casas proposed the African slave trade to Hispaniola (1516), the justice or injustice of that trade was not yet discussed in Europe; see Bataillon, pp. 91–4. In any case, this argument is inapplicable to Antonio Vieira, since his famous letter to Pará's municipal chamber recommending the employment of Angolan slaves in Pará and Maranhão was written in 1661, when abuses of African enslavement were widely known and discussed; see "Carta a Camara do Pará, 12 Feb. 1661," in J. L. de Azevedo, (ed.), *Cartas do Padre Antonio Vieira*, 3 vols. (Lisbon, 1925), Vol. I, p. 581.

[72] See De Azevedo, p. 71; D. de Abreu E. Brito, *Um Inquérito à vida administrativa e econômica de Angola e do Brasil 1591*, prefácio de A. de Albuquerque Felner (Coimbra, 1931), p. 30; *MMA*, first series, Vol. VIII, pp. 243, 394; B. Heintze, "The Angolan Vassal Tributes of the 17th Century," *RHES*, No. 6 (1980), pp. 57–78, p. 63 n. 14.

[73] Magalhães-Godinho, *Os Descobrimentos*, Vol. II, pp. 60–5, 98–9; Robert J. Ferry, "En-

4. Portuguese merchants in Brazil combined the advantages of oligopsony (in the purchase of sugar) with those of oligopoly (in the sale of slaves). Sustained by traders and royal officials living in Angola, the Gold Coast, and Senegambia, these merchants facilitated the sale of African slaves – by giving credit to planters – in order to control the commercialization of agricultural products.

Lack of money in the colony and intensification of Atlantic exchanges permitted the credit to take direct forms. In Brazil, sugar was exchanged for African slaves.[74] In Luanda and other African ports, barter goods were given to intermediaries on the condition of being exchanged for slaves. A Portuguese text from 1594 illustrates this: "The same way in Europe currency is gold and coined silver, and the same way in Brazil it is the sugar, in Angola and other neighborly courts the currency is the slave."[75] Of course, planters kept on exporting brazilwood during the low-sugar season.[76] And on the other side of the ocean, slave exports did not exclude trades of other African products. Up to the second half of the nineteenth century, Brazil would import African textiles from Senegambia and Niger.[77]

5. Exchanges between the metropolis and Brazil increased. The trade with Africa enlarged the demand and increased the permeability of the Brazilian colonial economy: The slave trade became a privileged instrument in showing the way to colonial complementarities of production. As the potential gains of properties served as a guarantee for the purchase of new factors of production (slaves), the economic surplus was productively invested. Soon the colonial system developed a mechanism able to stimulate regular development of production. At the same time, the transfer of income from the productive sector to the mercantile sector – a crucial factor of colonial exploitation – was assured.

Equipment for sugar mills and consumer goods was bought in the metropolis by colonists. Research has shown that luxury products were a minor item in foreign purchases of the colony's seigniorial class.[78] However, ostentatiously employed in households or in land

comienda, African Slavery, and Agriculture in Seventeenth-Century Caracas," *HAHR*, Vol. 61, No. 4 (1981), pp. 609–36.

[74] De Abreu E Brito, pp. 71, 72.

[75] Quoted by W. G. L. Randles, *L'Ancien royaume du Congo, des origines à la fin du XIXe s.* (Paris and La Haye, 1978), p. 176.

[76] Mauro, pp. 118ff.

[77] Robin Law, "Trade and Politics Behind the Slave Coast: The Lagoon Traffic and the Rise of Lagos 1500–1800," *JAH*, Vol. 24 (1983), pp. 321–48.

[78] Pe. Fernão Cardim, *Tratado da terra e qente do Brasil* (1585) (São Paulo, 1978), pp. 201, 202; on sugar mills' accounts see S. B. Schwartz, *Sugar Plantations in the Formation of*

lords' social presentation, the slave also became a luxury product. One of the main characteristics of Brazilian traditional society was the habit of considering the number of domestic servants as a sign of wealth. Obviously, the "qualification" of slaves did not change their economic and juridical essence. Whatever his functions, his condition, or his complexion, the slave went on being a factor of production and a negotiable asset. Thus, he could also be "disqualified," reintegrated in field labor, or sold, according to his master's convenience. Thus the ostentatious attitudes of the dominant class also intensified the demand for slaves. In 1845, when the free population in Rio de Janeiro was already permeated by ways and customs spread by industrial and bourgeois Europe, Martins Pena, a playwright, showed in one of his plays a gift a gentleman brought, in a big basket, to his fiancée: a slave, "around seven or eight years old, dressed in blue breeches and a red cap," to be the girl's servant.[79]

6. Access to credit and the anticipated purchase of slaves favored colonial planters as well. Considering the magnitude of the investment in the slave trade and the size of the African market, the supply of African slaves became more regular and flexible than that of Amerindian slaves. In addition, the capture, the march toward the ports, and the successive barters to which slaves were submitted in Africa, as well as the crossing of the Atlantic, worked in a selective way. In this sequence of exchanges and traumas, the unfit or physically weak individuals were eliminated and the survivors underwent an intense dissocialization. In his "Tratado da Terra do Brasil" (1570), Pero de Magalhães Gandavo wrote: "One of the reasons that keeps Brazil from growing even more are rebellions and daily escapes of [Indians] slaves; if those Indians were not so fugitive and inconstant, Brazil's wealth would be unique . . . there are also [in Brazil] many slaves from Guinea, who are more constant than Indians and who never escape [once] they have no place to go."[80] It was also known that, in contrast to Indians, whose mortality was high due to their vulnerability to microbial, bacterial, and viral shock that the discoveries brought to America, Africans had already been victimized and partially immunized by the same epidemic diseases that had hit the Europeans.[81]

Brazilian Society – Bahia 1550–1835 (Cambridge, London, and New York, 1985), pp. 212–18.

[79] Martins Penna, "Os dois ou o ingles maquinista," in *Comédias* (Rio de Janeiro and Paris, n.d.), cena 9, pp. 130, 131.

[80] Pero de Magalhães Gandavo, *Tratado da Terra do Brasil* (1570), introduction by Capistrano De Abreu (Rio de Janeiro, 1911), pp. 38, 39.

[81] Alfred W. Crosby, Jr., *The Columbian Exchange: Biological and Cultural Consequences of 1492* (Westport, Conn., 1972), pp. 3–34.

The introductions of Africans would soon provoke epidemic outbreaks among American Indians, compelling planters to acquire greater numbers of slaves from African populations already immunized against contagious diseases, especially smallpox. Brandão, a skilled merchant and eyewitness to the damage caused by smallpox in Brazil between 1616 and 1617, stated that the epidemic made "lots of rich men become poor." Following the time of Brandão, smallpox was lethal among Indians, blacks from Senegambia, and whites and mestizos born in Brazil, but affected few slaves from Allada and the Congo. Such observations, recorded by Brandão, were surely known to many Brazilian colonists. All those reasons combined to make the exploitation of Africans in Brazil easier.

Nevertheless in the first quarter of the seventeenth century that resort to non-American labor became irreversible in Brazil.[82] Since then, the xenophagy of plantations – that is their appetite for incorporating laborers from outside productive areas – appears to have been the result of internal demand and of slave traders' pressures on the supply level. From the beginning of the eighteenth century, colonial authorities also maintained the African slave trade's predominance in order to prevent competition among different Brazilian productive zones inside the territorial labor market.[83]

DEMAND FOR AND SUPPLY OF SLAVES: WHAT WAS THE "PRIMUM MOBILE"?

The introduction of Africans in Brazil is generally explained by the insufficiency of the Indian population or by cultural and somatic factors making Indians unfit for slave labor. Historical tradition bequeathed by the romantic writers of the nineteenth century imputed the failure of Indian slavery to the rebelliousness of the Ameridians. Thus, Africans and, more generally, blacks seemed more fit for slavery. Gilberto Freyre partially contested such a thesis, revaluing the Africans and showing Indians as "backward" and "lazy."[84] Hence, he did not question the idea that the transition from Indian slavery

---

[82] Goulart, pp. 99, 100. Stuart B. Schwartz, "Indian Labor and New World Plantations: European Demands and Indian Response in the Northwestern Brazil," *American Historical Review*, Vol. 83, No. 3, (1978), pp. 43–79; idem., *Sugar Plantations*, pp. 51–72.

[83] L. F. de Alencastro, "L'Empire du Bresil," in M. Duverger et al., eds., *Le Concept d'empire* (Paris, 1980), pp. 301–9.

[84] Gilberto Freyre, *Casa Grande e Senzala*, 25th ed. (Rio de Janeiro, 1987), chaps. II and V.

to African slavery was imposed by an Indian labor shortage. It is surely right that the colonists had been complaining since the seventeenth century of a "shortage of arms," but it is also true that they complained – more surprisingly – of a "shortage of lands."[85] Actually, we are dealing with an economy growing under the pressure of European demand. In such a context, land and labor are not independent factors but, rather, variables that are the result of forces ruling commercial capitalism. Insufficient recognition of this essential trait of colonization has given rise to confusion in Brazilian historiography. Whether intentional or not, the effects induced by the slave trade ensured accumulation peculiar to commercial capitalism, as well as to the Portuguese colonial system. More than any other, the slave trade was an administered trade. As has been suggested, metropolitan control over the reproduction of colonial production – or, better, the political establishment of the colonial economic system – had a fundamental importance in creating this process. It is also clear that trade in African slaves had already reached a large scale and had been strongly integrated with the Atlantic system *before* it was connected to Brazilian agriculture. Submitted for three centuries to the European power controlling a large part of the African slave market, Brazil became the colony receiving the majority of slaves carried to the New World. A lost link in Brazil's history, the African connection means that the slave trade is not a secondary effect of slavery but the reverse. This system led also to a differentiation between Brazilian slavery and its American counterparts; finally, it imposes an Atlantic interpretation on the formation of Brazilian nation.

[85] Ernesto Ennes, *Os Palmares – Subsídios para a sua historia* (Lisbon, 1938), p. 135.

CHAPTER 8

Exports and the growth of the British economy from the Glorious Revolution to the Peace of Amiens

P. K. O'BRIEN AND S. L. ENGERMAN

I think I need not tell them that *they live* by TRADE: That their Commerce has rais'd them from what *they were*, to what *they are*; and may, if cultivated and improv'd, raise them yet farther to what *they never were*;...[1]

It is obvious that the present strength and pre-eminence of this country is owing to the extent of its resources arising from its commerce and its naval power which are inseparably connected.[2]

I

V ERY-long-term trends in the growth and structure of English foreign trade cannot be quantified with any precision. Nevertheless, developments over the centuries before the Industrial Revolution are fairly clear. First, there occurred a protracted but unmistakable shift in the composition of English exports away from primary produce (principally raw wool, but including hides, skins, tin, and lead) toward a concentration on woollen textiles. That shift had already proceeded a long way by the mid-fifteenth century, when about two-thirds of the value of English exports took the form of woollen cloth. Sales of woollens outside the realm multiplied by a factor of three over the following century and by the opening years of Elizabeth's reign ac-

[1] Daniel Defoe, *An Humble Proposal to the People of England, For the Encrease of their Trade, and Encouragement of their Manufactures* (London, 1729), p. 1.
[2] H. Dundas, *Memorandum for the Consideration of His Majesty's Ministers*, 31 March 1800.

counted for 80% of the nation's total exports (which amounted, at that time, to roughly £750,000).[3]

Elizabeth's tiny kingdom enjoyed a comparative advantage in the manufacture of woollen cloth, which was exported undyed and unfinished, principally in the form of the internationally renowned broadcloth, but supplemented increasingly by cheaper and lighter fabrics such as "kerseys." England's advantages had developed in the context of European trade and were based on favorable geographical endowments (lush grass) for the production of wool and a long historical buildup of skills in the manufacture as well as the marketing of cloth. Over time control of the kingdom's trade passed from foreigners (Italians, Hansards, Flemmings) to London merchants, who by the 1550s had organized the sale of over 70% of woollen cloth exported through the metropolis.[4]

If we are bold enough to *guess* that average annual incomes in the 1560s stood midway between the wages of a builder's laborer and a craftsman in southern England (i.e., around £10 a year) and that the participation rate for a population of 2,985,000 people was 60%, then gross national income in current prices might have been £18 million. This implies that exports could have accounted for around 4% of national income in the reign of Elizabeth I.[5]

But expressing the value of the output produced within any sector of economic activity as a percentage of national income seems almost calculated to create an impression of insignificance. Economic development continues to be highly correlated with structural change, which means that the long-run growth of per capita incomes is accompanied by the diversification of national output and the allocation of labor away from primary production and toward industry and services. Recent estimates, which suggest that some 27% of Queen Elizabeth's subjects depended on the production of industrial commodities and services for their incomes, indicate just how far structural change had proceeded by the third quarter of the sixteenth century.[6]

---

[3] Data related to foreign trade before the eighteenth century have been collected from the overviews by D. C. Coleman, *The Economy of England, 1450–1750* (Oxford, 1977), pp. 48–68 and 131–50; C. G. A. Clay, *Economic Expansion and Social Change: England 1500–1700*, Vol. II: *Industry, Trade and Government* (Cambridge, 1984), pp. 103–202; and L. A. Clarkson, *The Pre-Industrial Economy in England, 1500–1750* (New York, 1972), particularly pp. 123–34.

[4] G. D. Ramsay, *The English Woollen Industry, 1500–1750* (London, 1982).

[5] E. H. Phelps Brown and Sheila V. Hopkins, "Seven Centuries of Building Wages," in E. M. Carus-Wilson (ed.), *Essays in Economic History*, 3 vols. (London, 1954–62), Vol. II, pp. 168–78; and E. A. Wrigley and R. S. Schofield, *The Population History of England, 1541–1871: A Reconstruction* (Cambridge, Mass., 1981).

[6] E. Anthony Wrigley, "Urban Growth and Agricultural Change: England and the

Table 1. *Estimates of English commodity exports, 1560s–1700*

Years circa	Commodity exports (£ million in current prices)	Textile price index (Phelps Brown and Hopkins)	Export volume
1560s	0.75	220	100
1640s	2.30	285	237
1660s	3.00	305	289
1700	4.40	295	438

Source: Column 1: D. C. Coleman, *The Economy of England, 1450–1750* (Oxford, 1977), pp. 61, 133; Column 2: C. G. A. Clay, *Economic Expansion and Social Change: England 1500–1700*, Vol. I: *People, Land and Towns* (Cambridge, 1984), p. 49, derived from annual estimates in Henry Phelps Brown and Sheila V. Hopkins, *A Perspective of Wages and Prices* (London, 1981), pp. 44–59. The index base is 1451–75 = 100. The last entry is for the 1690s.

By making plausible assumptions and reasonable inferences, we can take that reasoning further and estimate that two-fifths of that productive minority of the work force (disengaged from agriculture) sold the manufactures and services produced by their labor, capital, and enterprise in foreign markets. Most (perhaps up to 60%) of the Tudor kingdom's nonagricultural population continued to depend for their livelihood on domestic markets and on intersectoral trade between industry and agriculture (town and country), but involvement with international commerce was already on a considerable scale.[7]

Although the seventeenth century is a statistical dark age, there are estimates for the values of English commodity exports for 1640, the 1660s, and 1699–1701. On the eve of the Civil War, England's domestic commodity exports amounted to £2.3 million, rising to £3.0 million for 1663–9 and going up to £4.4 million by the turn of the eighteenth century. An index of export volumes is presented in Table 1.

Continent in the Early Modern Period," *Journal of Interdisciplinary History*, Vol. XV (1985), pp. 683–728.

[7] This calculation is based on English exports valued at £750,000. We estimated that 50% consisted of raw materials, either embodied in manufactured goods or sold in their primary form. At the start of the eighteenth century, 38% of the gross value of woollen output consisted of raw wool; see Phyllis Deane and W. A. Cole, *British Economic Growth, 1688–1959* (Cambridge, 1962), p. 196. In the sixteenth century, domestic processing constituted a lower ratio of gross output. At grain prices prevailing in the 1560s, this was equivalent to 469,000 quarters of grain. See Clay. Colin Clark argues in *Population Growth and Land Use* (London, 1967), p. 139, that functional subsistence could be procured for 300 kilograms of grain equivalent per annum. Thus receipts from exports would allow 335,000 people (or 42% of the nonagricultural population) to obtain a livelihood by using their labor skills, capital, and enterprise in production for foreign markets.

Despite the "crises" of the late sixteenth and seventeenth centuries, the volume of domestic exports may have risen over four times between 1560 and 1700. At a guess, their shares of national income could have been around 4% in the reign of Elizabeth and 5 to 6% in the reign of Charles II, rising to 8 to 9% at the end of William's reign.[8]

At average grain prices prevailing toward the very end of the seventeenth century (36 shillings a quarter for wheat), total receipts from commodity exports were *sufficient* to procure subsistence for roughly one-third of the English population. By that time, the value added to raw materials transported, processed, and manufactured for export (and available as rent, interest, profits, and wages for all those engaged in export trades) was sufficient to procure a reasonable standard of living for over one-half of the kingdom's nonagricultural population. This ratio implies that the share of the work force engaged in industry and services and dependent on foreign markets for their livelihood had increased by roughly one-quarter since Elizabethan times. In 1700 exports did not dominate the nonagricultural economy, but sales overseas had become more important. Adjustment to a complete (and sudden) closure of foreign markets might have been very difficult and painful for those families whose livelihood was disconnected from the development of domestic agriculture.[9]

England already possessed the raw materials, manufacturing know-how, and commercial expertise to compete successfully in European textile trades in Tudor times. Over the century and a half after 1550, English craftsmen and merchants built upon their traditional advantages in several ways. For example, they captured markets from European rivals (Italians and Dutchmen) by successfully competing on the basis of lower wage costs. That was accomplished by shifting industry away from guild-controlled urban centers to the countryside to take advantage of cheaper labor.[10] In addition, the woollen industry diversified production toward lighter, more finished cloths and successfully invaded new markets, particularly in Mediterranean and southern Europe. Old draperies (i.e., heavy cloths such as broadcloth, Spanish cloth, and northern dozens) had been sold mainly in northern

---

[8] For estimates (and guesses) of national income see Patrick K. O'Brien, "The Political Economy of British Taxation, 1660–1815," *Economic History Review*, Vol. XLI (1988), pp. 1–32.

[9] This calculation, and the methods we used to estimate that the net value added from exporting was sufficient to procure subsistence for 53% of the nonagricultural work force and their dependants, is outlined in footnote 7. We assumed that by 1700 30% of gross export receipts represented the value of agricultural raw materials embodied in exports.

[10] Ramsay.

Europe. New draperies (bays, serges, says, and stuffs) were suitable for warmer climes and more fashionable to wear. By the early seventeenth century, 22% of the woollen cloth exported consisted of new draperies; in 1640 that proportion has risen to 47% and by 1700 to 58%.[11]

Alterations in the commodity composition of exports became visible toward the end of the century. Manufactured goods, apart from woollens, such as hats and stockings, appear in the lists. By the 1670s, grain emerged as a major export. When William III took over the English throne, primary produce (principally wheat, but also fish, lead, tin, and coal) accounted for around 20% of total exports.[12]

Geographical shifts in the sources of the nation's imports and destinations for its exports (which became marked features of English trade over the eighteenth century) were discernible from the Restoration onward, if not before. Between 1660 and 1700, imports of tobacco, sugar, dyestuffs, rice, and spices from the New World poured into London, and English exports across the ocean leaped forward. An Atlantic economy constructed by capital and enterprise from several European nations (Spain, Portugal, Holland, France, and England) had taken more than 150 years of faltering progress to establish.[13] Although England came late to that great endeavor, at the end of the seventeenth century, the country stood poised economically and militarily to reap the largest gains from commerce with the Americas.[14] By that time English enterprise and capital had established viable colonies and, more significantly, plantations along the Atlantic seaboard and on islands in the Caribbean.[15] English merchants handled the lion's share of intercontinental trade between Asia, Europe, and the Americas. English shippers dominated the business of transporting slaves from Africa to the New World. Without the enforced and cheap labor of Africans, the rate of growth of transnational commerce between 1660 and the abolition of the slave

---

[11] N. B. Harte and K. G. Ponting (eds.), *Textile History and Economic History: Essays in Honour of Miss Julia de Lacy Mann* (Manchester, 1973). See also the books by Coleman, Clay, and Clarkson cited in footnote 3.

[12] David Ormrod, *English Grain Exports and the Structure of Agrarian Capitalism, 1700–1760* (Hull, 1985).

[13] Ralph Davis, *The Rise of the Atlantic Economies* (London, 1973).

[14] Immanuel Wallerstein, *The Modern World-System*, 3 Vols. (New York, 1974–89), Vols. I and II; and Kenneth R. Andrews, *Trade, Plunder, and Settlement: Maritime Enterprise and the Genesis of the British Empire, 1480–1630* (Cambridge, 1984).

[15] Wallerstein, *The Modern World-System*, Vol. III; and Ian K. Steele, *The English Atlantic, 1675–1740: An Exploration of Communication and Community* (Oxford, 1986).

trade in 1808 would have been far slower.[16] That adolescent phase in the expansion of the Atlantic economy dominated by England rested ultimately upon the exploitation of slave labor in the New World. It is difficult to envisage an alternative path of development that might have carried both international and British trade to the level attained by the early nineteenth century.[17]

Nevertheless, it is important to observe that when William III took the English throne, discernible tendencies toward the Americanization of the nation's trade had not proceeded far, and England's base position in international commerce and its comparative advantages had been established through intra-European and not oceanic trade.[18] As late at 1700, Europe still purchased 85% of England's domestic exports and 83% of its reexports. At that juncture in English commercial history markets of the future, the Americas, purchased only 12% of domestic exports and 16% of reexports. Imports, especially strategic imports, came overwhelmingly (68%) from the continent. England remained an integral part of the European economy, trading a limited range of manufactures (principally woollens) for other European industrial products (30% of imports), for raw materials for its textile industries (35% of imports), and for alcoholic beverages, tobacco, and tropical groceries, which came increasingly from across oceans.[19] All this was to change radically over the next century.

II

There is no need to review difficulties with the basic data for foreign trade, but fortunately, Crouzet has established trends and long cycles for the growth of domestic exports for the years from 1697 to 1802. His figures suggest that for this period as a whole the mean annual rate of growth in the volume of English exports was 1.5% per annum, which could be compared with our estimated rate of just over 1% per

---

[16] Barbara L. Solow, "Capitalism and Slavery in the Exceedingly Long Run," *Journal of Interdisciplinary History*, Vol. XVII (1987), pp. 711–37. Also in Barbara L. Solow and Stanley L. Engerman (eds.), *British Capitalism and Caribbean Slavery: The Legacy of Eric Williams* (Cambridge, 1987), pp. 51–77.

[17] Solow and Engerman (eds.); and W. Darity, "Mercantilism, Slavery, and the Industrial Revolution," in Paul Zarembka (ed.), *Research in Political Economy* (Greenwich, Conn., 1982), Vol. 5, pp. 1–21.

[18] G. D. Ramsay, *English Overseas Trade During the Centuries of Emergence: Studies in Some Modern Origins of the English-Speaking World* (London, 1957).

[19] Deane and Cole; and W. E. Minchinton (ed.), *The Growth of English Overseas Trade in the Seventeenth and Eighteenth Centuries* (London, 1969).

Table 2. *The growth of domestic
exports, 1697–1802, for England
and Wales*

1697–1714	2.8% per annum
1714–44	0.9
1744–60	3.0
1760–83	−1.4
1783–1802	5.9

Source: François Crouzet, "Toward an Export Economy: British Exports during the Industrial Revolution," *Explorations in Economic History*, Vol. 17 (1980), pp. 51, 61.

annum from the 1560s to 1700.[20] The growth curve for exports is now conventionally divided into two cycles of fast growth, one of slow growth, with a period of stagnation from 1760 to 1783 and a "long boom" from 1781–3 to 1800–2. Crouzet's periodization (which follows that of Deane and Cole) is shown in Table 2.

The cycle of stagnation overlaps with the Seven Years War and the long struggle between Britain and its thirteen colonies. It also came at a time when European markets, especially for woollens, became difficult to penetrate.[21] Forces behind the long boom from 1783 to 1802 (which witnessed rates of growth unsurpassed in the long history of British foreign trade) include the rebound of trade after the American War of Independence and dislocations caused by war among rival European economies from 1793 to 1802, as well as the more familiar impact of technical progress in cotton textiles.[22] But factors promoting long cycles in the sales of British goods beyond its borders are best exposed by an examination of particular markets and particular commodities.

At the end of the seventeenth century Britain's exports were dom-

---

[20] François Crouzet, "Toward an Export Economy: British Exports during the Industrial Revolution," *Explorations in Economic History*, Vol. 17 (1980), pp. 48–93. There can be nothing definitive about the selection of turning points for the growth of domestic exports. An alternative periodization (again using official values as proxies for volumes) is: 1744–50, 7.2% per annum; 1750–60, 1.5%; 1760–71, −0.2%; 1771–5, −1.8%. Stagnation emerges during the Seven Years War and apparently persists right down to 1781–3. For shorter cycles and fluctuations, see T. S. Ashton, *Economic Fluctuations in England, 1700–1800* (Oxford, 1959).

[21] Ralph Davis, "English Foreign Trade, 1700–1774," in Minchinton (ed.), *The Growth of English Overseas Trade*, pp. 99–120.

[22] The period is brilliantly surveyed in the introduction to François Crouzet, *L'Economie britannique et le Blocus Continental* (Paris, 1987).

Table 3. *The composition of manufactured exports*
(measured in official values)

	1699–1701	1752–4	1800
Woollens	85.0%	61.9%	28.5%
Linens	—	3.3	3.3
Silks	2.2	2.5	1.2
Cottons, etc.	0.6	1.3	24.1
Metals	3.2	9.2	12.4
Rest	9.0	21.7	30.5

Source: Columns 1 and 2: Ralph Davis, "English Foreign Trade, 1700–1774," in W. E. Minchinton (ed.), *The Growth of English Overseas Trade in the Seventeenth and Eighteenth Centuries* (London, 1969), p. 120; Column 3: B. R. Mitchell, with the collaboration of Phyllis Deane, *Abstract of British Historical Statistics* (Cambridge, 1962), pp. 281, 295 (all domestic exports).

inated by manufactures, principally woollens. That dominance weakened slightly over the long cycle from 1697 to 1760, when foodstuffs (particularly grain) and raw materials rose to account for nearly one-quarter of total exports by midcentury.[23] But population growth and rising productivity in manufacturing pushed the proportion of primary exports back down to 12% by 1802. Unfortunately, revenue from the sale of invisibles cannot be estimated, but receipts from shipping, banking, insurance, and distributive services sold to foreigners probably expanded more rapidly than any other sector of exports from 1697 to 1802.

Within commodity exports there are also observable shifts away from woollens to other textiles and diversification into ferrous and nonferrous metals and metalwares. These tendencies are visible in the rates of growth for the export of linens, silks, and, above all, for cottons compared to woollens, but are more readily (but not entirely accurately) encapsulated in breakdowns of total official values of manufactured exports (see Table 3).

Cotton yarn and cloth exports grew at the extraordinary rate of 12.3% a year from 1783 to 1814, compared with 1.8% for woollens, 2.2% for linens, and 2.3% for ferrous metals. By the end of the wars with France they accounted for about one-half of total British exports of manufactured goods.

Looking at eighteenth-century exports in terms of two very long

[23] Ormrod; and Ralph Davis, *The Industrial Revolution and British Overseas Trade* (Leicester, 1979).

swings of expansion interspersed by stagnation from 1760 to 1783, it appears that the long wave of modest growth in exports (from 1697 to 1760) was "balanced" in the sense that it was broadly based on a diversity of textiles, metals, and other manufactures, whereas the second and more spectacular upswing in exports from 1783 to the Peace of Amiens was to a very considerable extent carried forward and upward by cotton textiles. Indeed, no less than 56% of the *increment* to total export receipts in current prices from 1784–6 to 1804–6 emanated from the sale of cotton yarn and cloth outside the kingdom.[24]

Explanations for the rapid rise of cotton manufactures in England and Scotland are familiar. No doubt primacy should continue to be accorded to the diffusion of machinery, which lowered the price of yarn to a fraction of its cost before 1783. But the price and cost data required to weight and compare the contributions of machinery and factory organization with those of manifold other factors behind the growth of cotton are not available. The industry certainly benefitted from falling costs of raw materials and transportation; from changes in tastes and perceptions that led to the substitution of cotton cloth for linens, silk, and, particularly, woollens in a variety of uses; and from upswings in international incomes and demand.[25] Furthermore, the French Revolution, followed by a global war, provided Britain (the hegemonic naval power of the period) with an opportunity to capture and retain an "inordinate" share of the world markets in the new fabric.[26]

The eighteenth century witnessed the Americanization of British trade in the sense that rising proportions of exports consisted of sales to the Americas (North and South, including the Caribbean), and increasing proportions of imports of food and raw materials also emanated from across the Atlantic. Britain ceased to be simply part of a traditional European trading network with growing interests in American and Asian markets and became the center of an Atlantic economy (see Table 4).

Table 4 makes this point, but the continued importance of European markets down to and after the American War of Independence should

---

[24] Crouzet, "Toward an Export Economy."

[25] S. D. Chapman, *The Cotton Industry in the Industrial Revolution* (London, 1972); and Michael M. Edwards, *The Growth of the British Cotton Trade, 1780–1815* (Manchester, 1967).

[26] Patrick Karl O'Brien, "The Impact of the Revolutionary and Napoleonic Wars, 1793–1815, on the Long-Run Growth of the British Economy," *Review*, Vol. XII (1989), pp. 335–95.

Table 4. *The destination of English exports*
(measured in official values)

Years	Europe	Americas	Rest of world
1663–9	90.5%	8.0%	1.5%
1700–1	85.3	10.3	4.4
1750–1	77.0	15.6	7.4
1772–3	49.2	37.3	13.5
1797–8	30.1	57.4	12.5
1818–20[a]	46.7	43.5	9.8

[a] At current prices.
Source: Row 1: Ralph Davis, "English Foreign Trade, 1660–1700," in W. E. Minchinton (ed.), *The Growth of English Overseas Trade in the Seventeenth and Eighteenth Centuries* (London, 1969), p. 97; Rows 2–5: Phyllis Deane and W. A. Cole, *British Economic Growth, 1688–1959* (Cambridge, 1962), p. 87; Row 6: B. R. Mitchell, with the collaboration of Phyllis Deane, *Abstract of British Historical Statistics* (Cambridge, 1962), p. 313.

also be noted. Nevertheless, the share of the *increment* to British exports from 1700–1 to 1772–3 that was sold on European markets comes to a mere 4 to 5%, measured in official values. In other words, something like 95% of the addition to the volume of commodity exports over that period were sold on imperial markets (the bulk to North America and the West Indies), which underlines the significance of sea power, imperial connections, slavery, and mercantilist regulation for the sale of British manufactures overseas.

Compared to the first long swing of modest expansion from 1697 to 1760, when consumers across the Atlantic absorbed nearly all of the increment to British manufactured exports sold overseas, European markets evidently became more important again during the boom from 1783 to 1802. For that extraordinary upswing, estimates can be made in current prices. These figures suggest that Europeans purchased roughly one-third of the addition to British exports from 1784–6 to 1804–6 and Americans about 60%. Was it factors connected with the French Revolution and its contingent wars or technical superiority that allowed British industry to regain markets in Europe from 1783 to 1802?[27] After the war (1814–73), exports to Europe grew more rapidly than they did to America and the Caribbean.[28] The

[27] François Crouzet, "The Impact of the French Wars on the British Economy," in H. T. Dickinson (ed.), *Britain and the French Revolution, 1789–1815* (London, 1989), pp. 189–209.
[28] Crouzet, "Toward an Export Economy."

Table 5. *Exports and GNP*

Year	Ratio of exports to GNP (at current prices)	Increase in exports as a proportion of increase in GNP
1700	8.4%	
		30.4%
1760	14.6	
		5.1
1780	9.4	
		21.0
1801	15.7	

Source: N. F. R. Crafts, *British Economic Growth during the Industrial Revolution* (Oxford, 1985), p. 131.

Americanization of Britain's trade, which had proceeded rapidly over the eighteenth century, peaked during the long wars with revolutionary France.

III

Let us begin the discussion of the significance of exports for the growth of the British economy with some taxonomic exercises. We first relate cycles in domestic exports to national output, industrial production, and nonagricultural employment (see Tables 5 and 6).

Table 5 makes the obvious point that foreign consumers purchased a minor share of national production, but two phases occurred when overseas markets absorbed nearly one-third (1697–1760) and over one-fifth (1783–1802) of the *increment* to national output. As usual, for a country of any size, the bulk of the output was sold within the national boundaries.

The significance of exports is derogated by using national income as the sole point of reference. Foreign trade needs to be considered in the context of a dynamic general equilibrium model that considers the contribution of exports (and other sources of changes in demand) to the cycles of growth achieved by the British economy from 1697 to 1802.[29] Clearly, the contribution was negligible for almost one-quarter of a century after 1760. This period, which includes a major colonial war, has emerged in recent interpretations of the Industrial

[29] R. Findlay, "The 'Triangular Trade' and the Atlantic Economy of the Eighteenth Century: A Simple General-Equilibrium Model," *Universidade Nova de Lisboa, Faculdada De Economia*, Working Paper 124 (1989).

Table 6. *Exports and industrial output*

Year	Gross industrial output (in current prices) (£ million)	Exports (£ million)	Ratio of exports to gross industrial output	Increase in exports as a proportion of increase in gross industrial output
1700	£15.6	£3.8	24.4%	56.3%
1760	23.6	8.3	35.2	2.5
1780	39.9	8.7	21.8	46.2
1801	82.5	28.4	34.4	

Source: N. F. R. Crafts, *British Economic Growth during the Industrial Revolution* (Oxford, 1985), p. 132.

Revolution as a phase when the growth of per capita output slumped to virtual stagnation.[30]

Many regard industry (not agriculture or services) as the leading sector in economic progress over the eighteenth century, and since exports were dominated by manufactured commodities, the role of trade is, perhaps, more illuminatingly considered in relation to industrial production.

Over the century as a whole, Cole and Crafts agree that something like 40% of the addition to industrial output took the form of manufactured exports.[31] Exports were particularly important for three industries – cotton, wool, and iron – which in 1801 sold 62, 35, and 24%, respectively, of their gross outputs abroad. High, but unmeasurable, proportions of shipping, banking, and insurance services were also sold outside the national market. Proportions for other industries (except for shipbuilding and perhaps coal) were probably less than one-tenth. Nevertheless, the weight of these export industries in total industrial output ranges from 40 to 45% over the century. And cotton, woollens, and metallurgy have long been regarded as the most dynamic and innovative industries in the Industrial Revolution.

As a point of comparison with the earlier exercises for 1560 and

---

[30] See *Explorations in Economic History*, Vol. 24 (July 1987), a special issue on the Industrial Revolution; and Joel Mokyr (ed.), *The Economics of the Industrial Revolution* (London, 1985).

[31] N. F. R. Crafts, *British Economic Growth during the Industrial Revolution* (Oxford, 1985); and W. A. Cole, "Factors in Demand, 1700–80," in Roderick Floud and Donald McCloskey (eds.), *The Economic History of Britain Since 1700*, Vol. I, 1700–1860 (Cambridge, 1981), pp. 36–65.

1700, the share of the nonagricultural population in 1801 who could potentially have been sustained by net receipts from exports can be estimated. The arithmetic for this exercise consists essentially of converting the income from exports (net of raw material inputs) that accrued to nonagricultural workers and their families into grain equivalents at the current prices prevailing for wheat at the turn of the nineteenth century. For 1801, if all net export revenues had been spent on grain, that expenditure would have supported around half of the nonagricultural population.[32] Between 1700 and 1801 the nonagricultural population of England and Wales increased by 3.14 million people.[33] Over the century, the growth of domestic exports provided enough net revenue (in the form of wages, interest, and profits) to sustain about 70% of the previously mentioned increment at reasonable levels of subsistence.

These essentially taxonomic exercises in quantification help illustrate the importance of exports for the development of the British economy over the eighteenth century. They reinforce traditional and contemporary perceptions that the revolution in industry and the growth of employment outside agriculture continued to depend, in large measure, as they had done since Tudor times, on the sales of manufactured goods (particularly textiles) beyond the borders of the kingdom. The extent of English dependence, first on European and, after 1700, on American markets was not overwhelming. Yet politicians and mercantilists of the day claimed that exports remained highly important for the nation's economic prosperity and security.[34] Lord Haversham emphasized the point for their lordships in 1707:

Your Fleet, and your Trade, have so near a relation, and such mutual influence upon each other, they cannot well be separated: your trade is the mother and nurse of your seamen; your seamen are the life of your fleet, and your fleet is the security and protection of your trade, and both together are the wealth, strength, security and glory of Britain.[35]

Foreign markets had, moreover, been seized, created, and protected by relatively high levels of investment in naval power. Indeed, there was scant recognition in articulated political perceptions or in mercantilist thought that foreign trade rested upon impersonal market

---

[32] See footnote 7 for the methods and assumptions behind this calculation.
[33] Wrigley.
[34] Leonard Gomes, *Foreign Trade and the National Economy: Mercantilist and Classical Perspectives* (London, 1987).
[35] *The Parliamentary History of England*, Vol. 5, 1702–1714 (London, 1810), p. 598; and Robert Livingston Schuyler, *The Fall of the Old Colonial System* (New York, 1945).

forces. Markets had to be captured. Trade was rarely created and more often was diverted from rival merchants. In Coleman's study of the political debate on the Anglo-French Treaty of 1713, "the nation's total commerce" is seen "as an aggregation of separate, national quasi-political 'trades' all participating in a conflict over an international cake of a more or less fixed size."[36] Except under duress, as the outcome of colonial rebellion or as part of bilateral negotiations, Britain's imperial markets were never opened to rival European powers for something like seven decades after radical suggestions for free trade were first published in *The Wealth of Nations*.

IV

Export volumes increased by a factor of 4.6 over the eighteenth century. Their share, expressed as a proportion of national income, probably doubled from 1700 to 1800, and the ratio of sales overseas to gross industrial output went from around 20% to 35% over the same century. Although their contribution to the reallocation of labor from agriculture to industry and services cannot be estimated accurately, demographic arithmetic suggests that it was possibly substantial. But exercises in social accounting are limited in that they fail to describe the possible range of spinoffs from exports and other sources of demand that also helped push the British economy forward to the status of the First Industrial Nation. Unfortunately, externalities cannot be easily measured, but the benign connections between foreign commerce and British industrialization were well described and recognized at the time.[37] For example, the savings and skills of merchants acquired in overseas trade found their way into industrial enterprises. Perhaps more frequently, merchants became bankers and lent their support and funds indirectly to manufacturing or to the creation of transportation and other forms of social overhead capital upon which industrial expansion in their regions depended. Lobbies from the mercantile community in London exerted what was, by European standards, rather strong influence on the strategic, fiscal, and eco-

---

[36] Cited in Gomes, p. 82; see also D. C. Coleman (ed.), *Revisions in Mercantilism* (London, 1969).

[37] See, for example, John Millar, *An Historical View of the English Government from the Settlement of the Saxons in Britain to the Revolution in 1688* (London, 1812); and Klaus E. Knorr, *British Colonial Theories, 1570–1850* (Toronto, 1944). For an excellent modern analysis, see Jacob M. Price, "What Did Merchants Do?: Reflections on British Overseas Trade, 1660–1790," *Journal of Economic History*, Vol. XLIX (1989), pp. 267–84.

nomic policies pursued by England's aristocratic governments.[38] Merchants' horizons were distant, their knowledge international, and their ambitions global in scope. They demonstrated and diffused advanced industrial techniques and commercial practices to other sectors of the economy. They created and widened markets for British manufactured goods both at home and abroad.

Exports of British textiles and metalwares "fed back" to demand for wool, flax, iron, and coal. They augmented demand for the services of internal transport, ships, insurance companies, and other financial intermediaries. Export revenues gave rise to increasing possibilities for importing foodstuffs and raw materials (coffee, tea, sugar, spices, tobacco, wine, spirits, silk, timber, cotton fibers, dyestuffs, and natural oils) that could not be produced in Britain except at prohibitive costs. Tropical groceries (referred to by Malthus and Mill as "incentive goods") stimulated the work and investment required to buy such highly desirable and energy-giving foodstuffs.[39] Imported raw materials created the base for processing foodstuffs and tobacco and for the manufacture of cotton cloth and silks. Finally, imports provided the British state with an accessible and elastic source of taxation allocated in large part to expand and defend the empire. Mercantilist thought recognized that "money is the sinews of war. . . . One cannot make war without men, maintain them without pay, find pay without taxes, levy taxes without trade."[40]

Export industries (such as cotton, woollens, iron, and shipbuilding) were among the more advanced sectors of manufacturing and demonstrated what might be achieved by the rest of the economy. Firms engaged in foreign trade could achieve internal economies of scale; and, what was possibly more important, the larger export industries, such as Lancashire cottons, Yorkshire woollens, and Birmingham metalwares, generated external economies connected with conglomeration and specialization within regions.[41]

Finally, claims can be made for the benign effects that flowed through changes in money supplies and interest rates, emanating from a favorable balance of payments. Specie flows continued to be

[38] Patrick Crowhurst, *The Defence of British Trade, 1689–1815* (Folkestone, 1977); and John Brewer, *The Sinews of Power: War, Money, and the English State, 1688–1783* (London, 1988).

[39] Ralph A. Austen and Woodruff D. Smith, "Private Tooth Decay as Public Economic Virtue: The Slave–Sugar Triangle, Consumerism, and European Industrialization," *Social Science History*, Vol. 14 (1990), pp. 95–115.

[40] See the comments of Montchrétien, cited in Gomes, p. 62.

[41] P. Hudson (ed.), *Regions and Industries: A Perspective on the Industrial Revolution in Britain* (Cambridge, 1989).

the focus of intelligent commentaries on foreign commerce through-out the long eighteenth century.[42] Nowadays these preoccupations of mercantilists with slowly expanding or contracting monetary reserves are less often dismissed as a simple-minded confusion of gold and silver with real wealth. Mercantilists certainly failed to appreciate the nature and theoretical ramifications of specie flows across national borders. Their concerns, entirely explicable, were not, however, with the invisible and not exactly verifiable properties of a self-equilibrating international monetary system, but rather with the immediate and possibly serious deflationary impact on the English economy flowing from an adverse balance of trade. What they perceived and wrote about were associations between trade balances, money supplies, output, and employment.[43] They did not expect automatic adjustment mechanisms to work any more effectively and quickly than they do today. Meanwhile, and for the times and circumstances they lived through, English mercantilists recommended policies designed to procure export surpluses and inflows of monetary reserves to support an expanding economy and an aggressive polity on its way to achieving hegemony at sea.[44]

Specie flows and other spinoffs from exports to the rest of the economy are not difficult to exemplify. They make the point that estimated ratios of exports to national income and to industrial output may not encapsulate the full range of complex connections between trade and growth. Unfortunately, such ratios, expressed either at points of time or incrementally, even when supplemented with some discussion of the full range of both the real and monetary linkages between foreign trade and domestic production, cannot resolve the basic question concerning the significance of exports for the growth of the British economy from 1688 to 1802. That problem has formed a lively topic for discussion among historians of the First Industrial Revolution for several decades and will remain in the realm of point and counterpoint unless and until general equilibrium models of the international economy and Britain's place within it are specified and empirically tested for the eighteenth century.[45]

---

[42] Terence Hutchison, *Before Adam Smith: The Emergence of Political Economy, 1662–1776* (Oxford, 1988).

[43] Rudolph C. Blitz, "Mercantilist Policies and the Pattern of World Trade, 1500–1750," *Journal of Economic History*, Vol. XXVII (1967), pp. 39–55.

[44] Charles Wilson, "Treasure and Trade Balances: The Mercantilist Problem," *Economic History Review*, Vol. II (1949), pp. 152–61.

[45] Unfortunately, the quantitative impact of trade in Findlay's model (as in all other models for this period) is untested, making these issues difficult to resolve satisfactorily in their historical context. See Findlay, "The 'Triangular Trade'," and an earlier

V

At intermediate and more realistic levels of historical debate there seem to be two general issues. First, were exports a leading sector (an "engine of growth") or, alternatively, were sales overseas merely a response to the growing efficiency of British industry and agriculture, rooted in technical progress, superior commercial and industrial organization, and entrepreneurial vigor? Second, what exactly were the gains from exporting compared to alternative possibilities for economic growth from 1688 to 1802? The first question is involved with the nature and strength of external and internal forces behind the growth of exports; the second is concerned with counterfactual scenarios for growth and with the marginal gains from pursuing a strategy (or responding to opportunities) of selling an ever-increasing share of industrial production outside the kingdom.

Since most (perhaps up to 85%) of the *increment* to exports sold overseas from 1697 to 1802 was absorbed by colonial or neocolonial markets (such as India and the United States after 1783), there is a sense in which additional sales of British manufacturers beyond the frontiers of the metropolis over the eighteenth century might be represented as dependent upon governmental investment in state power and imperial rule. Thus high and rising levels of military expenditure were designed and maintained to secure an exclusive right to trade with Britain's territories overseas and to protect hazardous trades such as in African slaves.[46] Generations of "mercantilist" politicians believed that without such strong involvement, the rights to trade enjoyed by England's businessmen and public corporations in Asia and the Americas would have been appropriated by rival European powers (Spain, Holland, and, above all, France).[47] As Defoe observed:

'Tis for this, that these Nations keep up such a Military Force; such Fleets and such Armies to protect their Trade, to keep all the Back-doors open.... Trading nations are obliged to defend their Commerce.... If the Doors of our Commerce are shut, we must open them....[48]

Opportunities for domestic industry to escape from the confines of its home and traditional European markets after 1688 can be perceived

paper, R. Findlay, "Trade and Growth in the Industrial Revolution," in Charles P. Kindleberger and Guido di Tella (eds.), *Economics in the Long View: Essays in Honor of W. W. Rostow*, 3 vols. (London, 1982), Vol. 1, pp. 178–88.

[46] Brewer; Crowhurst.

[47] Knorr; and Jacob Viner, *Studies in the Theory of International Trade* (London, 1937).

[48] Cited by Gomes, p. 81; see also Richard Pares, "The Economic Factors in the History of the Empire," *Economic History Review*, Vol. VII (1937), pp. 119–44.

as opportunities created and maintained by investment in military power. This geopolitical perception of exports becomes blurred but nevertheless remains valid after the Treaty of Paris, when the Royal Navy "tacitly protected" the king's former American colonies from potential aggression from other European predators. Even the reentry of British industry into European markets during the export boom from 1783 to 1802 owed something to military power and political influence.[49]

The power of the state could underpin, but not guarantee, any particular pace and pattern of trade. That evolved over the eighteenth century on the basis of different resource endowments available to the metropolis and its possessions overseas and, after 1783, in relation to internal developments in Europe. Furthermore, economic development within the empire was regulated in order to ensure its complementarity with capital and skills located in the metropolitan economy. Competition between them was actively discouraged. In other words, trade based upon initial resource endowments was to be held, by regulation, constant through time. Recent cliometric research has suggested, however, that mercantilist constraints were flexibly administered and easily evaded or, at the least, imposed relatively low costs upon the colonies. They did not engender any significant misallocation of resources during the eighteenth century. The strategies for investment, employment, and trade actually pursued within the regulations of the empire did not lead to any pronounced loss of potentially realizable output.[50]

What is more difficult to estimate is the degree to which the growth of trade between Britain and its empire from 1688 to 1802 can be attributed to those economic forces at work within the home economy that were communicated overseas and that then elicited a positive response and generated higher levels of trade. Obviously, in the early stages of opening up territory beyond its borders, the level and growth of exports from Britain to the empire depended almost entirely upon inflows of capital and labor from the metropolis, as well as upon the willingness of British consumers to buy colonial merchandise. This suggestion takes for granted the now well-documented colonial pref-

[49] O'Brien "Impact of the Revolutionary and Napoleonic Wars"; and Crouzet, *L'Economie brittannique*. Note that this military power required the use of British resources.

[50] Robert Paul Thomas, "A Quantitative Approach to the Study of the Effects of British Imperial Policy on Colonial Welfare: Some Preliminary Findings," *Journal of Economic History*, Vol. XXV (1965), pp. 615–38; Peter D. McClelland, "The Cost to America of British Imperial Policy," *American Economic Review*, Vol. LIX (1969), pp. 370–81; and Gary M. Walton "The New Economic History and the Burdens of the Navigation Acts," *Economic History Review*, Vol. XXIV (1971), pp. 533–42.

erence for trade, truck, and barter compared to a supposedly more idyllic lifestyle of self-sufficient independence.[51]

At later stages of their history, population growth, investment, and improvements in productivity within colonial economies in the Americas, as well as their expanding exports to non-British markets, rendered them not only less dependent on the metropolis for labor supplies, investible funds, technology, and markets but also sufficiently autonomous to mature into an independent source of demand for domestic exports from the mother country. Where, when, and to what extent that occurred varied from market to market.

Only one of several relevant political and economic interconnections between Britain and its overseas customers in the eighteenth century has, however, attracted serious attention from historians: the relationship between exports and imports. Deane and Cole first advanced the hypothesis that after 1688 variations in the rate of growth of British exports could be systematically linked to variations in retained imports. They hypothesized that the capacity of countries and especially colonies (trading within an imperial network) to buy British manufactures continued to depend on sales of tropical groceries and raw materials in metropolitan markets. Within their model, the growth of domestic exports is perceived to respond with an appropriate lag to the growth of incomes in Britain and a high British propensity to import from the colonies. Thus the efficacy of exports as an engine of growth over the eighteenth century was in large part powered by investment and productivity growth within the home economy itself.[52]

There is no need to deny force to this relationship, but tests, correlating long swings in the gross barter terms of trade (which is an index of changes in the volume of domestic exports divided by an index of the volume of domestic imports) with long cycles in the growth of exports show that the suggested connection was weak and even "perverse." In their examination of potential links between imports and exports over shorter cycles, Hatton et al. used causality regressions and found "no evidence that variations in British retained imports systematically preceded variations in exports and indeed, when no special allowance is made for the effects of war the evidence

---

[51] T. H. Breen, "An Empire of Goods: The Anglicization of Colonial America, 1690–1776," *Journal of British Studies*, Vol. 25 (1986), pp. 476–99; and Carole Shammas, "How Self-Sufficient Was Early America?," *Journal of Interdisciplinary History*, Vol. XIII (1982), pp. 247–72.

[52] Deane and Cole; and W. A. Cole, "Eighteenth-Century Economic Growth Revisited," *Explorations in Economic History*, Vol. 10 (1973), pp. 327–48.

points in the opposite direction." They concluded that "exports cannot be regarded as a purely passive element in eighteenth century trade."[53]

Obviously, these correlations relate to exports and imports as a whole and do not apply to particular markets or particular commodities. The capacity and propensity of plantation economies in the Caribbean to buy British manufactures obviously depended on sales of sugar and other tropical groceries in the metropolitan market.[54] For the thirteen colonies and the independent United States (which were far larger markets for British manufactures), the posited connection was decidedly weaker and diminished as American dependence on exports decreased over the eighteenth century.[55] Population growth in most of the thirteen colonies had become autonomous long before the end of the seventeenth century. And recent quantitative analyses suggest that inflows of investible funds from Britain ceased to be important for capital formation and income growth after 1700.[56] Americans depended less and less on the British market in order to earn the sterling required to purchase British manufactures. They ran trade surpluses with the West Indies and with southern Europe. They supplied the goods and services required to support British military and administrative expenditures on the mainland.[57] As a last resort, they could readily fund deficits on current account by using lines of credit available at low interest rates in London.[58]

The posited link between American goods sold in metropolitan markets and British exports to the Americas became increasingly tenuous as time went on. North American exports of commodities and services to Europe and the West Indies, and autonomous increases in population and in the real per capita incomes of Americans, must have shifted demand curves for British manufactures to the right.[59]

---

[53] T. J. Hatton, John S. Lyons, and S. E. Satchell, "Eighteenth-Century British Trade: Homespun or Empire Made?," *Explorations in Economic History*, Vol. 20 (1983), pp. 163–82.

[54] David Richardson, "The Slave Trade, Sugar, and British Economic Growth, 1748–1776," in Solow and Engerman (eds.), pp. 103–33.

[55] The significance of different markets in the Americas has been estimated by Stanley L. Engerman, "Notes on the Patterns of Economic Growth in the British North American Colonies in the Seventeenth, Eighteenth and Nineteenth Centuries," in Paul Bairoch and Maurice Lévy-Leboyer (eds.), *Disparities in Economic Development since the Industrial Revolution* (London, 1981), pp. 46–57.

[56] James F. Shepherd and Gary M. Walton, *Shipping, Maritime Trade, and the Economic Development of Colonial North America* (Cambridge, 1972).

[57] John J. McCusker and Russell R. Menard, *The Economy of British America, 1607–1789* (Chapel Hill, N.C., 1985).

[58] Jacob M. Price, *Capital and Credit in British Overseas Trade: The View from the Chesapeake, 1700–1776* (Cambridge, Mass., 1980).

[59] Ronald Hoffman, John J. McCusker, Russell R. Menard, and Peter J. Albert (eds.),

Similar, although less pronounced, shifts may well have occurred in the Spanish and Portuguese empires in South America when bullion shipments to Europe picked up in the eighteenth century.[60] Only West Indian expenditures on British manufactures remained mainly dependent on sales of sugar to Britain.[61] If there had been only limited autonomous increases in the demand for British exports in the Americas, then the marked expansion in the sales of British manufactures across the Atlantic would have been accompanied by a deterioration in Britain's net barter terms of trade (i.e., the ratio of export to import prices would have declined).

Unfortunately, no satisfactory indices exist to allow historians to plot trends in Britain's terms of trade over the period 1688 to 1802. The data available for small samples of export and import prices suggest some improvement over the first half of the century followed by rough stability thereafter.[62] But aggregation and the imposition of trends on such small samples of prices, where they refer to a limited volume of trade, obfuscates complex changes through time. Fluctuations in import prices (c.i.f.) tended to be dominated by wars. Prices of domestic exports (f.o.b.) seem more stable and displayed little evidence of the trend that became such a familiar feature of British trade over the nineteenth century, namely, a tendency to decline continuously as the fruits of technical progress in British manufacturing were passed on as benefits to the rest of the world in the form of declining prices.[63] Before the Peace of Amiens, the secular deterioration in Britain's net barter terms of trade represented a trend of the future, succeeding, not preceding, the initial surges of industrialization.

Although continuous and marked improvement in Britain's net barter terms of trade would constitute presumptive evidence for export-led growth, the opposite tendency (for export prices to decline more rapidly than import prices) does not, prima facie, refute the possibility that increased sales overseas could theoretically be imputed to some combination of price and income effects, particularly if the

The Economy of Early America: The Revolutionary Period, 1763–1790 (Charlottesville, Va., 1988); and David Richardson, "The Slave Trade and Economic Growth in Eighteenth Century New England" (this volume).

[60] Pierre Vilar, *A History of Gold and Money 1450–1920* (London, 1976). We owe this suggestion to an unpublished paper by Stephen Fisher of Exeter University, "Latin American Precious Metals and Their Impact on Europe."

[61] Richardson, "The Slave Trade, Sugar, and British Economic Growth."

[62] Deane and Cole; for the United States, see Douglass C. North, *The Economic Growth of the United States, 1790–1860* (Englewood Cliffs, N.J., 1961).

[63] Albert Henry Imlah, *Economic Elements in the Pax Britannica: Studies in British Foreign Trade in the Nineteenth Century* (Cambridge, Mass., 1958); and W. W. Rostow, *The World Economy: History and Prospect* (Austin, Tex., 1978).

foreign income elasticity of demand for British manufactured exports happened to be high.

Finally, in debates about the endogenous or exogenous nature of British export growth, it seems impossible to distinguish initiating from sustaining forces behind cycles in exports. For example, it seems that autonomous increases in American and European demand initiated the export boom from the Peace of Paris to the Treaty of Amiens, but the growth of exports was sustained at a rate of 6% per annum for some two decades by investment and the diffusion of new technology in textiles and metals that, in the initial years of the upswing, represented a positive response to opportunities to satisfy the pent-up and growing demand for manufactures in the Americas and Europe.

Indeed, Crouzet's examination of that boom exposed a combination of forces behind the rapid expansion of British exports from 1783 to 1802. If we divide the data for this long cycle between a decade of peace, 1783–92, and a decade of war, 1793–1802, then interesting patterns appear in the rates of growth for British commodity exports. For example, although the growth rate for cottons (10.7% per annum) was well above the average for exports as a whole (6% per annum), relatively rapid rates of growth were also experienced by linens, metals, and metalwares, and the rate for woollens (at that time still the major component of manufactured exports) was only 1% below the rate for aggregate exports. These accelerated rates of growth were achieved despite rising prices for almost all exported commodities except cottons. (Cotton yarn prices halved between 1779 and 1799.) But the contribution of exports of the new fabric to the *increment* in total exports from 1783 to 1792 was (measured in current prices) approximately one-quarter. Over the second decade of the boom, when cotton invaded the markets for woollens, its incremental contribution came to about three-quarters.[64]

It looks as if this boom, over its first decade, was broadly based on a variety of manufactured exports, of which only cotton goods and yarn were offered at falling prices. During the war with revolutionary France, the rates of growth in export volumes for textiles other than cotton and for metals and metalwares decelerated. At a time when the Royal Navy kept open sea lanes to Europe and across the Atlantic, the expansion of industrial exports depended perhaps to a far greater extent than ever before on technical progress in cottons, effectively complemented by the use of naval power. Thus it was not until the

---

[64] Crouzet, "Toward an Export Economy."

1790s that the British trade entered a phase in which exports became less dependent on autonomous shifts in external demand than they surely had been during three earlier upswings in foreign trade: 1697–1714, 1744–60, and 1783–92. That move away from dependence on the growth of foreign demand coincided with an unfavorable trend in the net barter terms of trade that persisted down to the onset of free trade in 1846.[65]

VI

Recent calculations of the gains from trade are predicated upon perceptions and assumptions that mercantilists would find anachronistic. Modern views are exemplified by those of Thomas and McCloskey. "The end of economic activity," they pertinently observe, "is not production but consumption; exporting therefore is merely a lamentable sacrifice of resources consumable at home that is made worthwhile only by the importing it allows." The importance of trade can be measured by the potential it created for extra income and consumption. But, they add, because "domestic demand or supply within limits, could replace foreign demand or supply" and "because all things are substitutes the actual division of . . . British output between exports and domestic use, is an interesting fact but not one obviously significant for British economic growth."[66]

The authors do not proceed to estimate significance in terms of the social gains from exports, but they clearly suggest that the *net* benefits derived from using resources to produce goods sold to foreigners in order to consume imports could well have turned out to be a small fraction of national expenditure for 1800. At that juncture, the ratio of exports to national income stood at around 16% (compared to 25% in 1871 and half that proportion at the beginning of the eighteenth century). Nevertheless, the redeployment of resources involved in producing 16% of gross national output could not be represented as a "marginal adjustment," which is probably why Crafts, in his attempt to grapple with problems of measuring the incremental gains from trade, preferred to work with a more restricted counterfactual, namely, a hypothetical reduction of the ratio of British exports in 1841 down to the proportion that then prevailed in France.[67] Clearly, some counterfactual hypothesis is worth discussing; indeed, it is unavoid-

[65] Imlah.
[66] R. P. Thomas and D. N. McCloskey, "Overseas Trade and Empire, 1700–1860," in Floud and McCloskey, Vol. I, pp. 87–102.
[67] Crafts.

able if we are to examine the potential orders of magnitude representing benefits from trade.

What might the productivity of the labor, capital, management, land, and raw materials embodied in exports have been *if* some designated percentage of these resources had been reallocated to their second-best alternative use in the production of goods and services for the home market? By the late eighteenth century the adjustment process (as Napoleonic and American blockades of British trade demonstrated in 1808 and 1811–12) would have been painful and possibly politically difficult to contain without significant political changes.[68] Nevertheless, let us assume that such changes could have occurred piecemeal and involved no long-term political dislocation and possible losses of production beyond those contingent upon the reallocation of factors of production to alternative uses.

Modern economists are more inclined than either historians, their mercantilist predecessors, or even Adam Smith to assert that "domestic demand or supply within limits, could replace foreign demand or supply."[69] Contemporary observers were not impressed with either the potentialities of agriculture for sustained productivity growth or the prospective buoyancy of domestic demand.[70] Contrary observations, based perhaps on allowing for a different time horizon, emerge from the pens of those who analyze foreign trade in terms of the theory of comparative advantage.[71]

That theory (as it has evolved since Ricardo) has powerful insights to offer, but its application to eighteenth-century policy does not seem to be without question. When it is used to interpret commerce between Britain and the Americas from 1688 to 1802, trades effectively responsible for most of the long-run expansion in sales overseas during this period, arguments that lead to a derogation of the role of exports in the Industrial Revolution make several assumptions (or statements about the existing long-run economic conditions):

a. Britain's resources were given at a moment in time and were fully employed.
b. The function of trade was to reallocate resources efficiently between domestic production and exports.
c. The gains from trade measured by the extra consumption allowed through

---

[68] Crouzet, *L'Economie britannique* and "Impact of the French Wars."
[69] Thomas and McCloskey. Of course, the time period in which such replacements are to occur remains a crucial issue.
[70] Gomes.
[71] J. Mokyr, "Demand Versus Supply in the Industrial Revolution," in Mokyr (ed.), pp. 97–118.

the exchange of exports for imports emanated in large part from shifts to better positions on a given production-possibility boundary.

d. The internal transformation ratios involved in using domestic resources to produce exportables were economically superior, but not greatly superior, to their employment in the production of substitutes for importables – which implies that the degree and pattern of specialization adopted in relation to external opportunities, in regard to both exports and internally consumed imports, could have been reversed with no significant losses of output and welfare.

e. The externalities, technical progress, rates of capital formation, and incentive effects that flowed from the deployment of resources in foreign trade (exporting and its corollary set of activities, importing, reexporting, and servicing the international economy) would not have changed significantly *if* those same resources had been engaged in production for the home market.

f. British investment in the empire and in sea power to protect and service trade were dispensable elements in the growth of the Atlantic economy.

Such assumptions are certainly important to evaluate. How applicable are they to trade between Britain and the Americas as it evolved between 1688 and 1802 – a period of over one century?

Prima facie, the theory of comparative advantage seems to have more relevance for the analysis of trade between Britain and western Europe than for trade with the Americas. Import substitution had characterized the long-run evolution of British trade with Europe. Domestic resources were increasingly used to produce substitutes for textiles, bar iron, furniture, and metalwares purchased from the continent. Such manufactures were replaced, behind tariff walls, possibly without large consumption or production losses. But by 1750, when retained imports of industrial products accounted for only 14% of total imports, that process of "relatively costless" and effective import substitution was virtually over.[72] The domestic costs of producing comparable substitutes for foodstuffs and raw materials (imported from the Americas), as well as such "strategic" goods as copper, pitch, hemp, tar, and specific categories of timber (purchased from the Baltic), could have been far more expensive. These trades were clearly not based on marginal differences in internal transformation ratios between Britain and its American and Baltic suppliers.

"All things are substitutes," but the bulk of imports actually purchased with revenues from domestic exports and from increasingly essential reexports of tropical produce to the Baltic could not con-

---

[72] R. Davis, "The Rise of Protection in England, 1689–1786," *Economic History Review*, Vol. XIX (1966), pp. 306–17.

ceivably have been produced within the kingdom except at prohibi-
tively high costs.[73] This observation certainly applies to tropical groceries (sugar, tea, coffee, spices, and tobacco) and to raw materials such as cotton, dyestuffs, natural oils, silk, pitch, tar, and hemp.
Rather substantial adjustments in consumption and production would
have been required for a hypothetical British economy that had been
cut off from the possibilities of transforming its abundant resources
(labor and cheap fuels) into substitutes for the food, raw materials,
and military goods that it had procured through foreign trade. Although some fraction of manufactured exports might have been sold
in the home market with modest discounts in prices, it is difficult to
measure how far a greater switch from foreign to domestic markets
could have proceeded without reductions in prices drastic enough to
depress investment and slow up the diffusion of new technology
throughout industry.[74] Similarly, although some part of the resources
embodied in exports could perhaps have been reallocated to production for the domestic market, it was difficult for mercantilists to discern
just how this might have been achieved without rather drastic declines
in the productivity of labor employed in the export trades.[75]

Smith's vent-for-surplus theory seems to expose more of the essential character and dynamic properties of British trade as it was
perceived over the eighteenth century than Ricardo's more rigorous
and influential theory of comparative advantage. Smith saw the prime
function of trade as providing effective demand for the produce of
resources (particularly labor) and its secondary function as improving
and refining the division of labor from which, he believed, economic
growth would flow.

Foreign trade, as Smith saw it:

carries out that surplus part of the produce of their land and labour for which
there is no demand among them, and brings back in return for it something
else for which there is a demand. It gives a value to their superfluities, by
exchanging them for something else, which may satisfy a part of their wants,
and increase their enjoyments. By means of it, the narrowness of the home
market does not hinder the division of labour in any particular branch of art
or manufacture from being carried to the highest perfection. By opening a
more extensive market for whatever part of the produce of their labour may
exceed the home consumption, it encourages them to improve its productive

[73] Hans Chr. Johansen, "How to Pay for Baltic Products," in Wolfram Fischer, R.
Marvin McInnis, and Jürgen Schneider, (eds.), *The Emergence of a World Economy:
1500–1914, Part I,* "Trade and Growth." (Stuttgart, 1986), pp. 123–42.
[74] Findlay.
[75] Hutchison.

powers, and to augment its annual produce to the utmost, and thereby to increase the real revenue and wealth of the society.[76]

And turning specifically to trade with the Americas, Smith wrote:

By opening a new and inexhaustible market to all the commodities of Europe, it gave occasion to new divisions of labour and improvements of art, which, in the narrow circle of the ancient commerce, could never have taken place for want of a market to take off the greater part of their produce.... A new set of exchanges, therefore, began to take place which had never been thought of before, and which should naturally have proved as advantageous to the new, as it certainly did to the old continent.[77]

An appeal to the authority of Adam Smith over David Ricardo is mere rhetoric and does not constitute proof that British exporting might be better depicted in terms of a vent-for-surplus model of trade. Economic historians are required to investigate and, if possible, to measure the opportunity costs of labor employed in the export trades from 1688 to 1802. The argument for the presence of surplus productive capacity, or even resources with low opportunity costs, implies an inelastic domestic demand for goods exported and some degree of immobility and specificity among the factors engaged in their manufacture. At some set of commodity and factor prices, exportables could theoretically be transformed into production for the home market, but at what kinds of internal transformation ratios?

Incremental returns to capital goods and to some categories of professional and skilled labor might have been marginal. Is there, however, any evidence to support the notion that the majority of workers producing for export (comprising somewhere between 40 and 50% of the nonagricultural work force) could have been reabsorbed into alternative employment at other than radically reduced levels of productivity?

Most contemporaries saw exports as providing a net addition to employment not readily available elsewhere in the economy – especially for juvenile and female workers engaged in domestic and workshop production.[78] For Sir James Steuart, it was "a general maxim to discourage the importation of work and to encourage the export of it."[79] Full-employment assumptions hardly appealed to mercantilists at any time in this (or any other) period. They appealed even less when population growth accelerated and Malthusian fears emerged

---

[76] A. Smith, *The Wealth of Nations* (New York, 1937).
[77] Ibid.
[78] Hutchison.
[79] J. Steuart, *An Inquiry into the Principles of Political Economy*, 2 vols. (London, 1767);

to dominate discussions of poverty and employment in the late eighteenth century and again after the Napoleonic wars.[80]

Prospects for the easy reabsorption of labor into agriculture or production for the home market may even have declined over the eighteenth century. Enclosures and the reorganization of an increasingly commercialized agriculture into larger farms precluded the retention of underemployed labor in the agricultural sector. Population growth, which followed the breakdown of social controls on the age of marriage, at the same time created surplus labor and constrained the growth of working-class demand for its own output.[81] That tendency was reinforced by the growing concentration in the distribution of income and property for more than a century after 1688.[82]

Contrary trends emphasized in the historical literature operated both to widen the home market and to integrate labor markets. For example, investment in internal transportation, distribution, and information certainly created more opportunities and prospects for employment in activities connected with domestic demand. But recent research on the standard of living, poverty, and the position of labor in the eighteenth-century economy raises serious doubts about the short-run full-employment assumption implicit in Ricardian assessments of foreign trade.[83] In any case, to some extent the growth of foreign trade had its own impact upon the observed integration and expansion of the home market, which has attracted much attention from historians in recent years.[84]

Britain's productive agriculture, and the diversion of grain exports to domestic consumption together with increased food imports from Ireland, held subsistence crises at bay and allowed the population to grow, at first steadily and, after 1780, rapidly.[85] Foreign trade, in-

[79] J. Steuart, An Inquiry into the Principles of Political Economy, 2 vols. (London, 1767); and S. R. Sen, The Economics of Sir James Steuart (London, 1957).

[80] Reports of the Committee of the House of Commons, Report from the Committee to report and consider the returns made by the overseers of the poor, Vol. IX (London, 1803); and B. Hilton, Corn, Cash, and Commerce (Oxford, 1977).

[81] Robert C. Allen, "The Growth of Labor Productivity in Early Modern English Agriculture," Explorations in Economic History, Vol. 25 (1988), pp. 117–46.

[82] Jeffrey G. Williamson, Did British Capitalism Breed Inequality? (London, 1985).

[83] R. V. Jackson, "Growth and Deceleration in English Agriculture, 1660–1790," Economic History Review, Vol. XXXVIII (1985), pp. 333–51; L. D. Schwarz, "The Standard of Living in the Long Run: London 1700–1860," Economic History Review, Vol. XXXVIII (1985), pp. 24–41; and Peter H. Lindert, "English Living Standards, Population Growth, and Wrigley-Schofield," Explorations in Economic History, Vol. 20 (1983), pp. 131–55.

[84] Neil McKendrick et al., The Birth of a Consumer Society: The Commercialization of Eighteenth-Century England (London, 1982); and Lorna Weatherill, Consumer Behavior and Material Culture in Britain, 1660–1760 (London, 1988).

[85] Brinley Thomas, "Food Supply in the United Kingdom During the Industrial Revolution," in Mokyr (ed.), pp. 137–50.

vestment, and military expenditures created jobs outside agriculture and reinforced tendencies toward a productive division of labor both within the kingdom and between the kingdom and its possessions overseas. Given the nation's involvement in trade and the intensification of traditional outward-looking policies over the period 1688–1802, it is difficult to discern realistic alternatives for foreign policy and contingent options for development.[86] Indeed, opportunities to "delink" the British economy from trade may even have narrowed as populations, towns, and industries grew over that period. Whatever the theory of comparative advantage might suggest, the historical course and pattern of growth pursued from 1688 to 1802 do not expose alternative strategies for development, but may instead lead to a definite need to examine empirically the contention that resources embodied in exports possessed rather low opportunity costs. Furthermore, it is necessary to determine if supply curves for both unskilled and even skilled labor to the foreign trade sector may have been highly elastic.

The argument so far has been addressed to the possibilities and potential costs of transforming exportables and importables into domestic production and consumption. It could, in theory, be satisfactorily tested through a social savings exercise for foreign trade for, say, 1800, when exports amounted to 16% of national income. But unlike cost-benefit analysis for railways, steam engines, or the burdens of the Navigation Acts, the counterfactual of Britain cut off from trade in 1772 or 1802 may be too wide for satisfactory historical investigation. In any case, an estimate of the gains from trade at a moment of time (even if it could be measured empirically) would simply represent the movement along a production possibility boundary. The exercise would not address Adam Smith's perception of trade as a force that promoted outward shifts of the boundary and generated growth in that manner.

Over the long period 1688–1802, the British economy grew while becoming steadily more involved with international trade. Thus the issue that divides Ricardian from Smithian and mercantilist assessments of the contribution of foreign trade is not merely concerned with the real opportunity costs of resources allocated to international commerce but also with the question of how far forward some alternative strategy might have carried the economy by 1802. Again, it was difficult for contemporaries to envisage how the penumbra of

[86] Brewer; and D. Baugh, "Great Britain's 'Blue Water' Policy, 1689–1815," *The International History Review*, Vol. X (1988), pp. 33–58.

favorable spinoffs and externalities that flowed from involvement with the global economy might have emerged *if* Britain had radically constrained that involvement from the reign of William III onward.

Under what kind of alternative mix between exports and internal production could internal trade (between town and country, agriculture and industry) have provided comparable stimuli for the spread of markets, the growth of towns and communications, incentives for harder work, and the development of financial and legal institutions? Could an early delinking from foreign trade have provided equally efficacious mechanisms for the diffusion of technology, attractions for investors and entrepreneurs, demonstration effects, incentive goods, and a commercially minded aristocracy? There is, to complete the list, the large and unmanageable problem of modeling the state. Around 1800, something like one-third of tax revenue came from customs duties levied in large part on the imports of tropical foodstuffs and alcoholic beverages. Could the central government have funded a military establishment of sufficient capability to defend the integrity of the kingdom's boundaries without a tax base that included an array of imported commodities in inelastic demand?[87]

Finally, if a hegemonic power was required to lower transaction costs for world trade as a whole, a British state presiding over an economy less involved with trade would not have been willing to assume that role. Indeed, it would have lacked the surplus on current account necessary to guard the sea lanes and maintain a military presence in India, Africa, and the Americas. The geographical position, strategic policy, and military status of Britain within the system of competing European nation-states meant that the British, and perhaps only the British, were prepared to spend so much in the creation of an Atlantic economy from 1688 to the battle of Trafalgar in 1805.[88] Economically, this suggestion implies that the expansion of international trade depended in some degree on British investment in sea power and colonial expansion. *If* Britain had become less involved in trade and imperialism, then would world trade and the integration and growth of national economies within an international division of labor conceivably have developed more slowly under Dutch, Spanish, or French hegemony?

VII

Without denigrating the role played by other forces and by the domestic sectors of the economy, this chapter assesses some recent

---

[87] O'Brien, "Political Economy of British Taxation."
[88] Paul Kennedy, *The Rise and Fall of the Great Powers: Economic Change and Military*

attempts to minimize the contribution of foreign trade to the First Industrial Revolution. We confront the view that *if* the British economy had been constrained from increasing its dependence on foreign trade, then growth and structural change from 1688 to 1802 would have been roughly comparable to what actually occurred over that long period.

For that purpose, it is not logically necessary to settle the argument about the endogenous or exogenous nature of export growth in order to reinstate the historical significance of foreign trade. Certainly, the British state established and maintained the security required for expansion from 1688 to 1802. The development of an Atlantic economy is impossible to imagine without slavery and the slave trade. Beyond these large structural preconditions, the external or internal factors behind the growth of exports during particular phases of English commercial history are probably impossible to separate out and to weigh either theoretically or empirically. For example, it is extremely difficult to specify the forces that initiated upswings over particular cycles. Even when such forces are located, the argument is vulnerable in that some capacity to respond to an exogenous stimulus, however strong, has to be in place and capable of sustained momentum to move industry as a whole, or particular industries such as cotton, forward and upward to higher plateaus of production. This addresses the import of Davis's observation that the real growth of the cotton industry came only *after* it had conquered the home market, an argument that is questioned by Inikori's recent essay.[89] In this sense, it is the interaction of economies operating within a framework of imperial regulations, allowing for the rather free flows of capital, labor, and commodities across political boundaries, that created conditions for trade and growth. Domestic exports may then be simply designated in the traditional manner as clearly important and necessary components of the industrial growth that occurred in Britain over the eighteenth century.

Their significance can easily be minimized by expressing export revenues as proportions of national income.[90] But if one argues for the status of industry as the leading sector (that is to say, that it was that segment of the economy from which the growth of agriculture and services was basically derived), the analysis of national growth

    Conflict from 1500 to 2000 (New York, 1987); and Brewer.

[89] Davis, *The Industrial Revolution and British Overseas Trade*; and Joseph E. Inikori, "Slavery and the Revolution in Cotton Textile Production in England," *Social Science History*, Vol. 13 (1989), pp. 343–79.

[90] P. Bairoch, "Commerce International et Genere de la Revolution Anglaise," *Annales, E.S.C.*, Vol. 28 (1973), pp. 541–71.

should remain focused upon those forces promoting increases in the production of manufactured goods. On the demand side, something like 40% of the addition to industrial output from 1700 to 1800 took the form of exports. But even the obverse of that proportion simply emerges from an arithmetical exercise that classifies deliveries of industrial output among exports, investment, and domestic consumption. These ratios do not expose the interactions between these three categories of demand for manufactured goods. Exports were not, as the simple taxonomy suggests, independent of investment, nor was domestic consumption independent of exports. What is reasonably clear, however, is that the demand for industrial goods that emanated from productivity growth in agriculture accounted for a far lower proportion of the increment to the sales of industrial output from 1700 to 1800 than exports – particularly when connections between exports on the one hand and domestic consumption and investment (including investment in agriculture) on the other are taken into account.[91]

Interactions also flowed the other way. For example, buoyant domestic demand maintained the growth of industry when exports stagnated from 1760 to 1780.[92] High and rising productivity in British agriculture reduced potential demands for imported food and obviated potentially deflationary pressures emanating from deficits on the income account of the balance of payments. Agricultural development also mitigated against the tendency for the net barter terms of trade to turn sharply against Britain when population growth accelerated and the prices of exports (especially cottons) fell sharply at the end of the eighteenth century.[93] But it may equally be observed that the early commercialization of English agriculture owed much to its involvement in the export of wool. Its subsequent progress over the seventeenth and eighteenth centuries can be linked to grain exports, as well as to internal trade between towns and countryside.[94] On the supply side, the range and strength of externalities and demonstration effects from industries and commercial enterprises most heavily engaged in foreign trade were probably greater than the growth-promoting spinoffs that emanated from industries and ser-

---

[91] P. K. O'Brien, "Agriculture and the Home Market for English Industry, 1660–1820," *English Historical Review*, Vol. 91 (1985), pp. 773–800.

[92] D. E. C. Eversley, "The Home Market and Economic Growth in England, 1750–80," in E. L. Jones and G. Mingay (eds.), *Land, Labour, and Population in the Industrial Revolution* (London, 1967), pp. 206–59.

[93] Crafts.

[94] Ormrod.

vices catering to home demand. It was, after all, some export industries that demonstrated how productivity could be raised.

Between 1688 and 1802, as the economy became more involved with and more vulnerable to forces outside the Hanoverian kingdom, successive governments became more willing to tax and spend to maintain Britain's interests in the Atlantic economy and the Indian Ocean. Only Jacobite cranks fumed in the wilderness against Britain's "blue water" policy. Aristocratic politicians disdainful of "trade" entertained few doubts about promoting and protecting foreign commerce. Merchants and industrialists lobbied in order to have lower colonial tariffs and to persuade their colonial cousins to buy more and more British manufactured goods. Mercantilists wrote pamphlet after pamphlet extolling the pursuit of power and profit. Was all this expenditure of aristocratic time, bourgeois money, and intellectual energy merely a sufficient, but in no way a necessary, force behind British industrialization from 1688 to 1802?

CHAPTER 9

The slave and colonial trade in France just before the Revolution

PATRICK VILLIERS

THE production and consumption of colonial products increased considerably during the eighteenth century in the economies of France and the rest of Western Europe. Ernest Labrousse emphasized this in his thesis:[1]

Ce n'est ni le blé, ni le vin, ni le drap ni la toile qui soutiennent la fortune de notre pavillon mais le sucre et le café.

The statistics in money terms of French foreign trade between 1716 and 1772 corroborate such a view, as Table 1, produced by Bruyard, head of the Balance of Trade Office between 1756 and 1781, clearly shows.[2] Exports to the French colonies of America, as well as those of the slave trade, increased faster than other products in foreign trade. The goods coming from the colonies exceeded net imports, but above all – something contemporaries failed to notice – the French export trade to a large extent consisted in reexporting colonial products. Oriented by the mercantilist theory, the statistics of French foreign trade show a credit balance – but can we trust such estimates?

Ernest Labrousse and later Ruggiero Romano pointed out how important such statistical studies, begun in 1713, were.[3] All French merchants had to declare the goods they were exporting or importing at the offices of the *fermes* (customs). Such declarations were made in

---

[1] E. Labrousse, *La crise de l'économie française à la fin de l'Ancien Regime et au début de la Revolution*, 2 tomes (Paris, 1944), tome I, pp. 27–37.
[2] Archives Nationales, Paris, F12 1834 A. This table was established in 1780 by the Sieur Bruyard, who was in charge of the Bureau du Commerce. This source has been also published by Ruggiero Romano, *Documenti e Prime considerazioni interno alla "Balance du commerce" della Francia dal 1716 al 1780*, in *Studi in onore di A. Sapori* (Milan, 1959), pp. 1267–1300.
[3] Labrousse, p. 112; Romano, p. 1271.

Table 1. *French balance of trade, 1716–54, by Bruyard, head of the Balance of Trade Office*[a]

Year	General trade[b]		French West Indies[b]		Trade with Africa
	Imports	Exports	Imports	Exports	Imports
1716	33,386	47,059	4,484	2,106	—
1717	44,060	52,719	11,191	5,613	—
1718	42,288	71,407	13,445	7,357	—
1719	61,165	84,261	16,325	7,136	—
1720	62,297	158,031	20,884	13,170	—
1721	47,351	69,759	15,345	14,005	—
1722	61,359	90,412	20,949	19,508	—
1723	89,361	150,582	22,042	15,803	—
1724	102,962	91,391	17,852	13,459	—
1725	73,499	102,284	13,021	8,792	—
1726	68,541	95,431	12,901	12,699	—
1727	51,710	87,861	20,223	14,814	1,011
1728	66,554	105,390	17,983	17,926	221
1729	64,469	110,250	19,926	13,696	1,590
1730	70,985	103,741	20,117	9,868	2,302
1731	71,603	111,682	19,442	11,109	3,952
1732	78,647	113,248	18,219	11,951	1,285
1733	68,292	108,640	19,112	13,222	972
1734	60,300	104,227	22,501	10,820	285
1735	66,286	119,313	22,754	15,812	500
1736	75,256	119,773	30,178	17,953	959
1737	76,475	110,699	30,888	14,918	1,141
1738	88,632	126,056	31,824	19,177	1,913
1739	111,030	140,417	37,803	19,427	2,443
1740	112,279	180,265	45,961	21,904	2,421
1741	118,974	184,886	44,551	26,251	3,448
1742	103,615	177,609	50,354	27,408	2,691
1743	117,566	191,130	51,232	24,030	3,775
1744	87,820	148,476	32,307	16,008	1,106
1745	94,096	173,136	31,423	10,263	31
1746	91,584	156,010	21,994	18,442	44
1747	98,704	153,775	29,095	25,962	139
1748	114,496	149,040	20,625	26,428	1,484
1749	149,408	217,890	59,878	27,963	4,597
1750	141,949	213,253	62,034	30,449	3,471
1751	145,815	220,841	48,859	29,317	2,370
1752	166,524	230,915	61,080	47,168	4,840
1753	145,599	244,758	75,428	35,819	4,428
1754	150,230	248,521	76,891	37,436	6,126

[a]"Tabléau géneral contenant la progression annuelle de la valeur intrinsèque des marchandises estrangères de toutes espèces entrées en France comparée avec la valeur intrinsèque des marchandises de toutes espèces sorties pour l'Etranger formant la Balance du Commerce de la France avec l'Etranger depuis et compris l'année 1716, époque du travail ordonné par l'arrêt du Conseil du 29 février 1716.
[b]In thousands of pounds.

terms of volume. The collectors of customs and their clerks in each big harbor drew up a yearly detailed account in volume for each product and each foreign country. The directors of the Chambers of Commerce then indicated the yearly average price of each commodity. And all the calculations were eventually made in Paris by clerks who wrote the final document under the supervision of the director of the Balance of Trade Office.

E. Labrousse considered that the reliability of this document was already

ce que vaudront les statistiques douanières de la seconde moitié du XIXe siècle les chiffres absolus pêcheront tous par sous-évaluation, mais pourront être retenus au moins comme chiffres relatifs comme exprimant un mouvement à défaut d'un niveau.[4]

In his thesis, published in 1972, Jean Tarrade skillfully used this source again, more particularly studying the way the prices of colonial products were estimated. He estimated that the imports of colonial goods into France were subject to an ad valorem import duty of 4%, and the customs men kept a sharp eye on it. Smuggling, though possible, was limited. But the prices were negotiated every six months. Hence a certain discrepancy arose between the average price agreed upon by the customs men and the real prices. Tarrade also established that the prices were underestimated by at least 20%, and that this probably was true throughout the century. Therefore, the statistics on the imports of colonial goods in France are reliable, taking into account these underevaluations.[5] (Table 2).

These figures show the influence of the war on the foreign trade of France, and especially on the trade with India and the slave trade. Trade with the colonies was greatly dependent on the organization of convoys that would be established after 1780.[6]

The statistics of exports to the colonies and the slave trade are not as reliable as the ones concerning imports. There was no tax on those exports. The elaboration of the export statistics was based on the trust of the trader and the professional competence of the clerks of customs.

From 1763 to 1765, exports to the French West Indies and exports for the slave trade seem to have remained stable. The great historian

---

[4] Labrousse, p. 27.

[5] Jean Tarrade, *Le commerce colonial de la France à la fin de l'ancien Regime, l'évolution du régime de l'Exclusif de 1763 à 1789*, 2 tomes (*Paris* 1972). For comparison, see tome 2, pp. 747–9, tables of the imports and exports of colonial products in weight. Archives Nationales, F12 243–7. Balance du Commerce 1773–8.

[6] Patrick Villiers, *Le commerce colonial atlantique et la guerre d'Independance des Etats-Unis d'Amerique* (New York, 1977).

Table 2. *France: Balance of trade*

Year	General trade	Exports (in *livres tournois*) French West Indies	Africa	Indies
1773	278,951,036	32,850,862	16,387,302	5,520,452
1774	271,489,349	31,131,702	9,786,032	6,522,290
1775	283,072,130	28,220,077	11,915,732	8,834,978
1776	267,124,270	42,541,189	12,603,635	6,341,025
1777	311,544,475	43,338,849	12,536,392	2,952,232
1778	237,561,694	33,247,267	3,423,138	2,352,133
1779	207,635,473	26,832,169	58,152	440,731

General trade (without the French West Indies + Africa + the Indies)

Year	General trade	Imports (in *livres tournois*) French West Indies	Africa	Indies
1773	192,031,856	114,669,107	—	24,383,638
1774	168,397,432	107,040,257	—	20,205,234
1775	161,986,095	101,108,443	—	29,884,148
1776	198,590,264	136,092,942	—	36,214,773
1777	179,500,703	174,612,031	—	1,618,641
1778	175,532,168	178,328,417	—	45,186
1779	175,138,519	32,785,725	—	237,641

General trade (without the French West Indies + Africa + the Indies)

Source: Archives nationales, F 12 243–7, Commerce extérieur, Importations et exportations, pièces diverses.

of Nantes, Gaston Martin, working on the *registres des declarations de retours* of the slave traders, which unfortunately stop just before the American War of Independence, thought that the slave trade from Nantes was at its peak between the Seven Years' War and 1778. Father Rinchon, but mainly Jean Everaert and Jean Meyer, then showed that this was not true. Paul Butel from Bordeaux and Charles Carriere from Marseille confirmed that the colonial and slave trades increased from the War of Independence to the French Revolution.[7] But is it possible to elaborate statistics for all ports and to measure the French exports to the West Indies, knowing that those earlier estimates were made on only a few specific ports?

Statistics are available that allow a comparison between the years before the War of Independence and the years 1784–5 (Table 3).

This document is quite interesting, as it shows the average prices

[7] Paul Butel, *Les negociants bordelais, l'Europe et les Negociants marseillais au XVIIIe siecle*, 2 vols. (Marseille, 1973); Jean Everaert, "*Les fluctuations du commerce negrier nantais, 1763–1792*," *Cahiers de Tunisie*, Vol. 43 (1963), pp. 37–62; Jean Meyer, *l'Armement nantias dans la deuxième moitié du XVIIIe siècle*, (Paris, 1969).

Table 3. *Imports of colonial products to the harbours of Bordeaux, Nantes, Le Havre, Marseille, La Rochelle, and Dunkerque (thousands)*

	1774		1775		1784		1785	
	Quantity	Value	Quantity	Value	Quantity	Value	Quantity	Value
Raw sugar	57,409	15,116	47,749	13,423	55,256	16,768	80,318	26,418
White sugar	87,027	33,752	76,793	32,247	91,945	43,918	15,928	58,119
Coffee	61,945	31,213	64,844	29,511	65,337	50,914	72,478	58,055
Cotton	3,455	5,537	3,743	7,479	4,692	8,487	6,923	15,345
Indigo	13,961	13,147	12,627	9,210	8,600	7,236	16,851	15,114
Cacao	1,260	1,328	1,195	1,369	1,800	1,093	2,532	1,564
Total	213,037	100,697	195,596	93,240	220,653	135,238	279,876	174,618

Source: Archives Nationales, fonds Marine C5 53, f. 35, 28 October 1786. The "total" includes the value or weight of all the imported goods (including goods such as rocou, gayac . . . Quantities were measured in *livres pesant* (i.e., pounds). Value was measured in *livres tournois* (French money in the eighteenth century).

that had to be retained to go from the information given in volume to the information given in value. Unfortunately, it is only based on the results of goods for the period 1783–4. Those data emphasize the importance of colonial reexports in the French foreign trade.

In addition to these data sources, I demonstrate that by studying the French trading fleet (especially the colonial fleet from 1783 to 1792, with particular attention to the slave ship fleet between 1789 and 1792), we can improve our estimates of French trade. Data on the size and tonnage of vessels in the colonial trade, when properly interpreted, are a valuable new resource.

In 1784, the Maréchal de Castries, minister of the French Navy, wanted to know the consequences of the War of Independence for the French trade fleet. He asked his collaborators for numerous statistical inquiries. The shipbuilding inquiry was studied by Jean Meyer and T. G. A. Le Goff in a definitive paper illustrated with substantial tables.[8]

I briefly present the inquiry about the French trade fleet (Table 4). Before 1778, the Bureau des Classes conducted a yearly survey of trade ships that had sailed and classified them according to their destination and their *département* of origin. The purpose of this inquiry was to know the number of sailors available in case of war. The classification by maritime *département* is proof of this. The *département*

[8] Jean Meyer and T. G. A. Goff, "*Les constructions navales en France pendant la seconde moitié du XVIIIe siècle,*" *Annales E. S.C.,* Vol. 1, (1971), pp. 173.

Table 4. *Distribution of colonial ships (French West Indies)*

Destination	1774	1775	1776	1777
Saint-Domingue[a]	296	278	357	348
Martinique	123	137	116	132
Guadaloupe	67	79	80	42
Cayenne	6	5	15	12
Terre-Neuve	321	340	366	305
Coast of Africa	63	56	55	53
The Indies	27	44	39	18
Total	903	939	1,028	910

was the geographical basis of the census of the sailors. For instance, the *département* of Brest included the Lorient and Nantes port towns.

Some *Etats recapitulatifs* (statistics which were recapitulated yearly) still exist, but most of them are disappointing because they are too vague.

Although the tonnages were missing from these tables, a typology of French ports appears. Bordeaux, Marseille and, to a lesser extent, Le Havre traded with all the islands of the French West Indies and take part in all traffic. Thus, there the slave trade was a marginal activity practiced by only a few specialized shipowners. By contrast, Nantes, La Rochelle, and, on a small scale, Honfleur had a dominating slave trade activity. Only the slave trade allowed them to compensate for their incapacity to obtain cargoes capable of competing in the French West Indies with goods coming from Boreaux or Marseille. However, numerical analysis is too imprecise to explain the details of the patterns.

Castries sought new statistics that were better adapted to the commercial reality.[9]

Monseigneur est le premier ministre de la Marine qui ait désiré qu'il lui soit présenté des états généraux des batiments de commerce existant dans les différents ports et ce n'est qu'en 1784 qu'il en a fait la demande au Bureau de la Direction. Les plus anciens états de cette espèce remis de ce bureau à celui du Commerce Maritime sont en effet du mois de mars de ladite année. . . .

From this inquiry, I was able to establish a first table (Table 5).

However, this inquiry did not give precisely either the tonnages or the destination of the vessels. Fortunately, I have found other in-

[9] Archives Nationales, fonds Marine C5 53, p. 35, October 28, 1786.

Table 4 (*cont.*)

Ports	Departures to Saint-Domingue				Departures to Martinique			
	1774	1775	1776	1777	1774	1775	1776	1777
Le Havre	40	35	49	41	28	27	20	22
Honfleur	2	—	5	1	—	—	—	—
Cherbourg	4	—	4	3	6	3	8	7
Dunkerque[b]	1	7	14	3	7	1	2	3
Rouen	—	—	—	1	1	—	—	—
Caen	—	—	1	—	—	—	—	—
Nantes	68	61	87	71	2	9	3	5
St. Malo	4	5	5	9	—	1	1	1
Lorient	—	—	—	3	1	1	1	3
Rochefort	4	6	5	9	—	—	1	—
La Rochelle	7	3	4	7	2	2	—	—
Bordeaux	133	128	136	149	46	52	41	49
Bayonne	3	8	6	15	—	4	4	4
Toulon	—	—	1	—	—	—	1	—
Marseille	30	25	39	36	30	35	34	37
Cette	—	—	—	—	123	137	116	132

Ports	Departures to Guadeloupe				Departures to Africa			
	1774	1775	1776	1777	1774	1775	1776	1777
Le Havre	12	18	15	7	13	13	13	15
Honfleur	1	2	4	2	4	2	3	2
Cherbourg	1	3	2	2	—	—	—	—
Dunkerque	—	—	—	—	1	2	—	1
Fecamp	—	1	—	—	—	—	—	—
Nantes	14	10	11	5	14	16	19	21
St. Malo	—	—	—	—	4	3	4	6
Rochefort	1	2	—	—	1	—	—	—
Bordeaux	35	33	47	21	13	11	6	3
Bayone	1	—	1	—	—	—	—	—
Marseille	2	—	—	3	—	—	4	1
Total	296	278	357	346	123	137	116	132

[a]St. Dominguo.
[b]Dunkirk.
Source: Archives Nationales, fonds Marine C4 156, *Etat général des armements faits par le commerce 1774–1777.*

quiries from the Commisaires aux Classes that contain other data. These data are the ones used to establish those aggregate statistics.[10] These inquiries indicate more about the French Maritime trade re-

[10] Ibid., C4 156, August 1783, January 1785, October 1786.

Table 5. *Number of trade ships by department*

Year	Brest	Rochef.	Bordeaux	Le Havre	Dunker.	Toulon	Total
1780	1,054	533	589	914	228	1,125	4,443
1781	820	367	480	851	254	1,057	3,859
1784	1,278	493	717	865	403	904	4,660
1785	1,420	512	620	1,001	400	1,301	5,254
1786	1,478	499	542	1,067	383	1,417	5,306

Note: These statistics "were not published during last war, since they would not offer interesting or true data because of the number of ships that used neutral ensigns and did not have French passports.
Source: Archives Nationales, fonds Marine C5 53, p. 35, October 28, 1786.

covery from 1783 to 1787 by *département* and by tonnage. They had to be elaborated each month, but the only ones remaining date from the months of August 1783, January 1785, September 1785, July 1786, and October 1786. I first examine the distribution of the French fleet in terms of activity before studying it from in terms of tonnage. In order to limit data, I present only those of August 1783, January 1785, and October 1786 (Table 6).

The data quoted in Table 6 are to be compared with those established by Poujet, the *commissaire aux classes*, for the inquiry about shipbuiding in France from 1763 to 1786[11] (Table 7).

This table confirms that convoy organization and the neutralization of French ships protected the French trade fleet much more efficiently than they did in the Seven Years War. By 1785, the number of ships reached the level of 1775. The Castries' inquiry did not seem to be carried on after 1786. A table of the French fleet was published in the *Moniteur* of June 29, 1792, and for France indicates 5,535 vessels and a total tonnage of 733,000. This would tend to indicate that the growth of the French fleet had increased after 1786, but at a much slower pace.

These data show that the growth of the French fleet was mostly due to the colonial trade. In fact, from 1785 to 1786, the French fleet increased by 181 vessels, most of them colonial ships. This fact is partly disguised by the data of October 1786. At that time, many colonial vessels were at anchor; this is confirmed by the fact that such a large number of ships was ready to set sail. By comparison, the July 1786 *Etat* indicates 445 vessels in the ports and 697 ships trading with the West Indies.

[11] Ibid., C5 155, *Enquête Pouget*, 1762–86, undated paper.

Table 6. *Activities of the French fleet from 1783 to 1786*[a]

Département	Total	August 1, 1783 I	II	III
Brest	1,270	259	216	632
Rochefort	453	56	41	356
Bordeaux	694	223	351	120
Le Havre	815	316	188	311
Dunkerque	401	48	166	187
Toulon	887	187	494	206
Total	4,457	1,089	1,556	1,812

I = in the harbor, ready to sail or under construction.
II = colonial trade (boating, Europe) and codfish ship.
III = small coastal ship and coastal fish ship.

Département	Total	In the harbor A	B	Colonial trade Am.	Af.	In.	Boating Grand	Petit
Brest	1,420	40	220	131	33	34	84	618
Rochefort	512	42	48	23	18	6	11	321
Bordeaux	620	63	122	308	15	27	9	58
Le Havre	1,001	171	126	82	58	3	107	236
Dunkerque	400	106	15	36	2	—	39	94
Toulon	1,301	49	105	176	36	12	481	156
Total	5,254	221	636	756	162	82	731	1,483

January 1, 1785

A = ready to sail. B = shipbuilding or ship in repair. Am = West Indies. Af = slave trade. In = India + China. Trade with the Levant counts 197 vessels from the *département* of Toulon, 24 of Dunkerque, 21 of Le Havre, and 9 of Brest.
Fishermen were only taken in account in the total.

Départment	Total	In the harbor A	B	Colonial trade Am.	Af.	In.	Boating Grand	Petit
Brest	1,507	132	98	69	41	33	69	701
Rochefort	515	46	54	11	25	3	8	299
Bordeaux	542	63	87	296	32	18	7	20
Le Havre	1,121	139	168	51	43	—	85	376
Dunkerque	376	178	13	17	1	—	27	65
Toulon	1,374	78	88	160	42	18	583	94
Total	5,435	636	508	604	184	72	779	1,455

October 1, 1786

A = ready to sail. B = shipbuilding or ship in repair. Am = West Indies. Af = slave trade. In = India + China. Trade with the Levant counts 258 ships of the *département* of Toulon, 11 of Dunkerque, 9 of Le Havre, and 7 of Brest.
Fishermen were only taken in account in the total.
[a]These statistics were established by *département*, not by port.

Table 7. *Number of trade vessels in France*

Year	1773	1774	1775	1780	1781	1784	1785	1786
Number	4,294	4,651	4,970	4,443	3,859	4,660	5,254	5,306

Table 8. *Departures of colonial vessels, 1783*

Département	Americas		Africa		Indies	
	Number	Tonnage	No.	Tonn.	No.	Tonn.
Brest	76	25,677	41	8,387	22	7,830
Rochefort	17	4,378	15	3,838	3	1,210
Bordeaux	169	48,019	16	3,793	20	7,184
Le Havre	60	11,303	19	2,914	1	412
Dunkerque	16	3,195	3	420	—	—
Toulon	75	19,758	—	722	5	2,405
Total	413	112,330	97	20,074	51	19,041

An *Etat nominatif des navires coloniaux par port et en tonnage* allows us to complete the 1783 data and confirms the growth of the colonial fleet[12] (Table 8).

The second purpose of the 1784–6 inquiry is to give us a distribution of the fleet per tonnage. Again, I have selected January 1, 1783, January 1, 1785, and October 1 1786 (Table 9).

One must have the classification of vessels, according to their activity, tonnage, and departure in order to be able to interpret these data fully. Robert Richard studied the fleets of Le Havre port towns. Studying the *Matricule des navires de commerce*, he succeeded in separating the registered fleet (*flotte inscrite*) from the fleet in trade (*flotte en activité*). The comparisons are made on January 1 of each year,[13] (Table 10). This table confirms the growth of the French fleet and its stagnation after 1788. For the trade fleet, the decline begun in 1790. The colonial trade, and particularly the slave trade, were especially affected.

[12] Ibid., F2 81, *Etat nominatif des batiments armès pour Saint-Dominigue, la Martinique, la Guadeloupe, Cayenne, Tabago, Cote d'Afrique, Indes et Terre-Neuve, année 1783*, undated paper.

[13] Robert Richard, *La flotte de commerce du Havre (1751–1816), étude statistique d'après les archives des Classes de la Marine*, in *Aires et structures du commerce français au XVIIIE siècle* (Lyon, 1975), pp. 201–35.

Table 9. *Distribution of the French fleet per tonnage, 1783–6*

Tonnage	General total, January 1, 1783					
	Brest	Rochef.	Bordeaux	Le Havre	Dunker.	Toulon
500+	69	12	88	—	—	4
300–499	101	17	157	22	12	23
100–299	233	47	168	129	144	383
1–99	788	230	192	464	242	439
Total	1,191	306	605	615	398	849

General total: 4,064 ships.

Tonnage	General total, January 1, 1785					
	Brest	Rochef.	Bordeaux	Le Havre	Dunker.	Toulon
600+	36	12	27	—	1	4
500–599	17	2	72	3	1	6
400–499	45	8	103	7	3	6
300–399	73	15	101	37	9	30
200–299	105	9	115	101	44	100
100–199	174	41	128	226	113	419
1–99	970	425	74	627	229	736
Total	1,420	512	620	1,001	376	1,374

General total: 5,254 ships, 720,000 tons, and 64,800 sailors.

Tonnage	General total, October 1, 1786					
	Brest	Rochef.	Bordeaux	Le Havre	Dunker.	Toulon
600+	35	10	25	—	—	5
500–599	26	2	60	2	2	8
400–499	44	6	97	10	2	12
300–399	66	16	95	22	9	32
200–299	88	10	106	107	47	119
100–199	206	44	131	258	77	488
1–99	1,042	427	28	722	239	710
Total	1,420	512	620	1,001	376	1,374

Sailing: 4,147 ships, 550,000 tons, 49,500 sailors.

At this point, the problem is to determine precisely the part played by the colonial trade in the whole maritime activity, and then to evaluate the composition of the colonial fleet and its evolution. Statistics for 1783 and those elaborated by Jean Tarrade for 1773, 1783, and 1788 give us a first view of the issue. I have presented 1783 statistics as Jean Tarrade did.[14] (Table 11).

[14] Tarrade, p. 731.

Table 10. *Distribution of the fleet of Le Havre,*
1783–92

	Registered		Trade	
	Number	Tonnage	Number	Tonnage
1783	60	7,600	36	3,535
1784	122	17,789	113	16,474
1785	178	30,004	172	29,272
1786	196	33,663	179	31,507
1787	221	36,783	188	31,305
1788	241	40,306	197	33,307
1789	240	39,888	194	33,209
1790	235	40,100	174	29,618
1791	235	40,936	163	28,570
1792	235	40,190	161	26,931

Looking at Table 11, a few conclusions can be drawn.

1. *The importance of the colonial trade in the French maritime activities.* For instance, in 1783 the colonial trade used 509 vessels out of the 1,556 sailing in the colonial trade (*long cours*), offshore and coastal traffic (*grand cabotage*), and cod fishing (*pêche à la morue*), that is, 33% and 15% of the 3,368 boats in use. As for tonnage, the proportion was even higher. In 1788, the share of colonial trade was still increasing.

2. *The general growth of colonial trade* (see Table 12). In 1783, the slave trade was booming because ship owners wanted to meet the demand of plantation owners, as a consequence of the war, but 1788 turned out to be the peak year for slave trading. Colonial trade kept on growing.

3. *Classification of the destinations* (see Table 13). Trade with the *partie française de St. Domingue* increased, and that with Martinique and Guadeloupe improved in spite of questioning of the policy of the *exclusif colonial*. However, Saint-Domingue mostly harbored big vessels sailing from the largest French ports.

4. *Classification of French colonial ports* (see Table 14).

Average tonnage data are often researched by maritime historians, but they are misleading. The distribution of the port fleets may not be accurate. With the help of data from *l'état nominatif de 1783*, I have compiled a table (Tables 15 and 16) showing the distribution by capacity (tonnage) of colonial ships trading with Saint-Domingue.

The distribution in Gans curves of the port towns of Bordeaux and Nantes are very similar. The biggest ships were the most numerous,

Table 11. *Foreign destinations of the French fleet, 1773, 1783, and 1788*

Harbor	Foreign destination, 1773																
	St. Domingue		Martinique		Guadeloupe		Guyane		Total American			Africa			General tonnage		
	N	T	N	T	N	T	N	T	N	T	M	N	T	M	N	T	M
Dunkerque	11	1,431	—	—	—	—	—	—	11	1,431	130	—	—	—	11	1,431	130
Fécamp	—	—	—	—	1	45 tx	—	—	1	45	—	—	—	—	1	45	—
Le Havre	27	6,005	—	—	39	6,205	—	—	67	12,360	184	16	2,459	154	83	14,819	179
Honfleur	3	770	—	—	—	—	—	—	3	770	257	1	90	90	4	860	215
Cherbourg	1	120	—	—	7	747	—	—	8	867	108	—	—	—	8	867	108
St. Malo	6	1,570	1	80	1	30	5	430	13	2,110	162	3	630	210	16	2,740	171
Nantes	85	28,025	5	880	11	2,444	1	70	102	31,419	308	29	4,150	143	131	35,569	272
La Rochelle	5	1,300	—	—	—	—	2	380	7	1,680	240	4	600	150	11	2,280	207
Bordeaux	116	30,544	61	15,182	29	6,076	1	300	207	52,101	252	5	813	163	212	52,914	250
Bayonne	6	756	3	444	—	—	—	—	9	1,200	133	—	—	—	9	1,200	133
Marseille	36	8,473	36	8,106	7	1,125	3	500	82	18,294	223	2	345	173	84	18,639	222
Total	296	78,994	106	24,782 + 47	48	9,674 / 6,997 tx	13	1,830	510	122,277	240	60	9,087	151	870	131,364	230
M	267		206		141				240			151			230		

Windward Islands

222

Table 11 (cont.)

223

Harbor	St. Domingue N	St. Domingue T	Martinique N	Martinique T	Guadeloupe N	Guadeloupe T	Tabago N	Tabago T	Guyane N	Guyane T	Total American N	Total American T	Total American M	Africa N	Africa T	Africa M	General tonnage N	General tonnage T	General tonnage M
							Foreign destination, 1783												
Dunkerque	9	2,245	4	690	1	130	1	130	—	—	15	3,195	213	3	420	140	18	3,615	200
Dieppe	1	225	—	—	—	—	—	—	—	—	1	225	225	—	—	—	1	225	225
Fécamp	1	340	—	—	—	—	—	—	—	—	1	340	340	—	—	—	1	340	340
Le Havre	28	4,909	17	2,991	4	740	—	—	—	—	49	8,640	176	14	2,373	—	63	11,013	174
Rouen	1	200	—	—	—	—	—	—	—	—	1	200	200	—	—	—	1	200	200
Honfleur	4	849	—	—	—	—	—	—	—	—	4	849	212	5	54	—	9	1,390	154
Cherbourg	2	385	—	—	—	—	—	—	—	—	4	839	209	—	—	—	4	839	209
St. Malo	1	325	—	—	—	—	—	—	1	50	2	375	187	1	300	—	3	675	225
Morlaix	1	210	—	—	—	—	—	—	—	—	1	210	210	—	—	—	1	210	210
Lorient	1	600	—	—	2	220	—	—	1	80	4	900	225	4	690	—	8	1,570	196
Nantes	62	22,072	2	370	5	1,640	—	—	1	80	70	24,162	345	36	7,497	—	106	31,659	298
La Rochelle	10	2,158	—	—	—	—	—	—	—	—	10	2,158	215	15	3,543	—	25	5,701	228
Rochefort	6	2,150	—	—	—	—	—	—	1	70	7	2,220	358	—	—	—	7	2,220	358
Bordeaux	118	35,354	29	6,880	12	2,650	—	—	2	680	161	45,564	283	15	3,543	—	176	49,147	307
Bayonne	7	2,155	1	300	—	—	—	—	—	—	8	2,455	306	1	250	—	9	2,705	300
Marseille	42	7,615	23	4,773	5	950	—	—	2	260	72	13,618	189	3	722	—	75	14,340	191
Toulon	2	250	—	—	—	—	—	—	—	—	2	250	125	—	—	—	2	250	125
Total	297	82,292	77	16,004	30	6,784	1	130	8	1,120	412	106,200tx		97	20,074tx		509	126,274tx	
M		277		207		226		130		140		257			207			248	

Table 11 (cont.)

Harbor	Foreign destination, 1788																				
	St. Domingue		Martinique		Guadeloupe		Tabago		Guyane		Total American			Senegal		Africa			General tonnage		
	N	T	N	T	N	T	N	T	N	T	N	T	M	N	T	N	T	M	N	T	M
Dunkerque	10	2,360	12	3,050	2	510	6	1,541	—	—	30	7,261	242	—	—	—	—	—	30	7,261	242
Le Havre	65	15,705	24	5,196	10	1,982	7	1,555	1	110	107	24,548	229	12	1,988	19	4,300	226	138	30,836	223
Honfleur	6	1,110	—	—	—	—	—	—	—	—	6	1,110	185	—	—	10	2,791	279	16	3,904	244
St. Malo	9	2,160	—	—	—	—	—	—	—	—	9	2,160	240	—	—	2	1,364	682	11	3,524	320
Nantes	89	33,378	4	620	6	1,935	—	—	1	105	100	36,028	360	—	—	32	11,113	347	132	47,151	357
La Rochelle	6	3,681	—	—	—	—	—	—	—	—	6	3,681	614	—	—	6	5,065	844	12	8,746	729
Bordeaux	176	54,405	44	11,079	29	9,105	—	—	4	850	253	75,439	298	1	77	12	4,557	380	266	80,073	301
Bayonne	8	1,355	7	1,047	—	—	—	—	—	—	15	2,402	160	—	—	—	—	—	15	2,402	160
Marseille	89	22,935	43	11,514	6	1,385	—	—	3	365	141	36,199	257	—	—	7	1,987	284	148	38,186	258
Divers	7	1,535	2	230	1	150	—	—	—	—	10	1,915	192	1	497	3	1,485	495	14	3,897	278
Total	465	138,624	136	32,736	54	14,867	13	3,096	9	1,430	677	190,753		12	2,132	93	33,095		782	225,980	
M		298		241		275		238		159			282		178			356			289

N = number of trade vessels. M = average of tonnages.

Table 12. *Number of ships leaving French ports*

Trade with West Indies	1788 compared to 1783	164.3%
Trade with West Indies	1788 compared to 1773	132.5%
Slave trade	1788 compared to 1783	95.8%
Slave trade	1788 compared to 1773	155%
Total trade	1788 compared to 1783	153%
Total trade	1788 compared to 1773	137.2%

Table 13. *Trade with Saint-Domingue and Martinique-Guadaloupe*

Share of Saint-Domingue			
Number of ships	1773: 58%	1783: 72%	1788: 68.7%
Tonnage	1773: 64.8%	1783: 78%	1788: 72.8%

Share of the Martinique-Guadeloupe			
Number of ships	1773: 39.4%	1783: 25.9%	1788: 28%
Tonnage	1773: 33.9%	1783: 21.4%	1788: 24.8%

Table 14. *Trade with the West Indies (without the slave trade)*

	1773		1783		1788	
	Number	Tonnage	No.	Tonn.	No.	Tonn.
Bordeaux	40.5%	42.6%	39.0%	42.9%	37.4%	39.2%
Nantes	20.0%	25.4%	16.9%	22.7%	14.8%	18.8%
Marseille	16.1%	14.8%	17.4%	12.8%	20.8%	18.9%
Le Havre	13.1%	9.8%	11.8%	8.1%	15.8%	13.1%
La Rochelle	2.4%	2.0%	2.4%	2.0%	0.8%	1.9%

a consequence of the king's regulations in their favor as well as of convoy navigation during the War of Independence. The ship owners of Le Havre were the victims of their geographical situation. So, later, they preferred to invest in fast, mid-sized ships that they used as privateers and then as slave ships.

The case of Marseille was quite different. Shippers often entrusted their cargoes to their captains in order to avoid the forwarding agents of Saint-Domingue. Too big a ship implied too long a stay in the port of call.[15]

[15] Charles Carriere, *Négociants marseillais au XVIIIe siecle* (Marseille, 1973), pp. 594–602.

Table 15. *Distribution per tonnage toward Saint-Domingue in 1783*

Tonnage	Bordeaux	Nantes	Le Havre	Marseille
600 tx[a]	4	6	—	1
500–699 tx	11	11	—	—
400–499 tx	18	11	1	—
300-399 tx	30	12	1	3
200–299 tx	26	10	10	14
100–199 tx	15	9	12	16
0–99 tx	14	3	4	8
	118	62	28	42

[a] tx = tonneaux (French tons).

Table 16. *Distribution per tonnage toward Saint-Domingue in 1783*

Tonnage	Bayonne	Rochefort	La Rochelle	Honfleur	Dunkerque
600	1	—	—	—	—
500–599	2	—	—	—	—
400–499	—	3	—	—	2
300–399 tx	1	3	3	1	1
200–299 tx	1	—	3	1	2
100–199 tx	1	—	2	1	3
0– 99 tx	2	=	2	1	1
	8	6	10	4	9

tx = tonneaux (French tons)

Large ships required a very capitalistic commercial organization, because investments were large. Stops in ports of call had to be reduced so that large-scale economies could be justified. The use of large ships also revealed a growing integration between plantation owners, ship owners, and merchants.

The Nantes case differs from that of Bordeaux. Nantes mostly imported raw sugar for Orleans refineries, which were the first in France, whereas Bordeaux reexported 47% of French colonial products.[16]

What was the evolution of the ships' size from 1783 to 1789? To answer this question, the maritime historian can use a surprising source: the *registres de congés (passports) de droits d'ancrage et de balisage* of the accounts of the *Amiral de France's* chancellor. Since 1681, the owner of every ship leaving the French coasts had to buy a clearance

[16] Jean Butel, pp. 212–23, 229–45.

Table 17. *Distribution per tonnage of the fleets of Nantes, Bordeaux, and La Rochelle*

	Nantes										
	1773	1780	1781	1782	1783	1784	1785	1786	1787	1788	1789
−50 tx		2	2	2	2	—	3	1	1	—	1
50–100		10	11	12	6	9	3	4	7	3	—
100–150		9	6	7	9	11	8	4	7	3	6
150–200		4	4	5	9	10	7	8	4	10	11
200–250		2	1	4	8	12	7	9	9	4	3
250–300		2	1	6	12	9	11	10	16	8	9
300–350		4	1	2	14	14	18	11	13	18	20
350–400		5	1	4	10	15	18	14	14	9	11
400–500		6	1	8	13	19	27	23	26	23	31
500–600		7	3	6	6	10	16	17	14	12	22
600–800		2	3	5	4	8	11	12	7	8	8
800 +		—	—	—	—	3	—	1	1	2	2
Total		53	34	61	93	120	129	114	119	107	118

	Bordeaux										
	1773	1780	1781	1782	1783	1784	1785	1786	1787	1788	1789
−50 tx	2	—	1	2	—		—	1	3	2	—
50–100	4	11	8	12	15		8	7	8	6	15
100–150	11	8	14		12		11	14	12	13	17
150–200	24	15	9	12	18		19	27	22	30	19
200–250	45	11	13	6	19		23	29	24	22	24
250–300	37	7	11	2	13		25	24	20	25	16
300–350	36	18	22	9	14		30	28	21	28	30
350–400	19	19	24	9	20		38	37	34	39	25
400–500	17	16	25	17	27		43	42	34	42	28
500–600	1	3	11	3	8		10	7	9	6	6
600–800	—	1	5	3	2		3	4	1	1	2
800 +	—	—	—	—	—		—	—	—	—	—
Total	196	109	143	87	148		210	220	188	214	182

and pay taxes. He also had to pay anchor and buoy taxes, but most of these registers were lost. Fortunately, most of the *registres de congés* from 1780 to 1789 were preserved. Thus the name of the ship and of the captain, the destination, and the tonnage of the ship were known. From these archives, limiting myself to Bordeaux, La Rochelle, and Nantes, I have established Table 17.

Whatever the port town, the increase of tonnage is indubitable,

Table 17 *(cont.)*

	1773	1780	1781	1782	1783	1784	1785	1786	1787	1788	1789
					La Rochelle						
50–100 tx	2			5	3	3		—	—	2	1
100–150	4			2	—	3		2	—	—	1
150–200	1			2	3	5		—	—	—	—
200–250	1			3	2	4		3	3	2	2
250–300	4			—	—	2		—	—	1	—
300–350	2			5	2	5		2	—	1	
350–400	1			1	1	3		—	—	1	
400–500	—			3	1	3		3	—		2
500–600	—			—	1	1		1	2	2	3
600–800	—			2	—	4		3	2	2	—
800–1000	—			1	—	—		4	2	1	2
1,000 +	—			—	—	—		4	3	3	1
Total	15			24	13	33		22	12	15	12

Source: Archives Nationales, series G5.132, La Rochelle; G5.122, Nantes; and G5.45, Bordeaux.

especially for the over–400 *tonneaux* class. Unfortunately, a thorough study reveals that slave ships changed their tonnage declarations after 1784. Is it necessary to reject any analysis of tonnage from 1784 to 1792? Is it necessary to reject any source about tonnages, taking for granted that if there were a forgery of slaves ships' tonnages, this was also the case for any other kind of ship?

The answer is contained in the analysis of the documents about maritime practices of the eighteenth century.

In spite of the French government's efforts, ships carrying illicit merchandise were numerous in the French West Indies. Smugglers carrying slaves and sailing to Guadeloupe and Martinique were particularly numerous.

Thus, officially, 183 slaves a year would have landed in Martinique between 1775 and 1777. In fact, it was the English ships that provided these French islands with slaves. French shippers complained about unfair competition, and plantations owners accused the ship owners of selling slaves at outrageous prices.

Castries decided to put an end to this situation by regulating the arrival of foreign slave ships with a first act dated June 28, 1783. In the preamble of this act, the number of 19,700 slaves sold in 1776 is quoted and the annual needs are estimated at up to 25,000.[17] Besides, the French slave traders were know to avoid the French Leeward Islands. Consequently, foreign slave ships carrying more than 120 tons and 180 slaves were allowed to sail to these islands for three years on payment of a duty tax of 100 livres per slave. The duty was due to allow a premium of the same amount to the French slave traders laying anchor in the same ports. This measure was accepted by French ship owners, but it had only a small effect.

Its main purpose was to disclose the exact number of slaves brought in by foreigners: (1,180 in 1783, 913 in 1784, 0 in 1785, and 1,683 in 1786) and by the French (205 in 1783, 579 in 1784, 414 in 1785, and 191 in 1786).[18]

Facing this failure and seeking administrative simplification, Castries published a decree approved by the king's council on October, 26, 1784, which was enforced after November 10. The tax of 10 livres per slave introduced in French colonies was suppressed, as well as the *Acquits de Guinée*.

The *Acquits de Guinée* gave an exemption to the slaves traders of half the taxes on colonial goods introduced into France with the product of the sale of a slave cargo. As a counterpart of the suppression of the *Acquits de Guinée*, they received a premium of 40 livres per ton of cargo. Slave ships sailing to Martinique and Guadeloupe received 60 livres and 100 livres if they laid anchor at Cayenne.

This act was much discussed by Castries and Calonne, *Controleur général des Finances*, and especially the problems of tonnage and financial cost. The basis retained by Calonne was an average of 14,365 Africans brought in every year from 1768 to 1777, a yearly ship tonnage of 11,967 tons, and a yearly exemption of 950,636 livres. Dividing 950,636 livres by 11,967 tons gives a premium of 79.4 livres. The slaves shippers protested vigorously.[19]

Castries refused any compromise to modify the premium amount, but he allowed a new measure of ship tonnage on January 28, 1785, followed by another one in 1786, each of them more favorable to the ship owners. These two methods of measuring tonnage misled historians, most of whom believed in a general forgery. This was a mistake, as I demonstrate.

---

[17] Tarrade, pp. 517–20.
[18] Archives Nationales fonds Colonies C8B.18, Martinique, *Etats des noirs francais et étrangers introduits dans la Colonie de 1782 a 1786*.
[19] Tarrade, p. 552.

Measuring ship tonnage was a usual practice that the Maritime Act of 1681 had recalled:[20]

Tous navires seront jaugés incontinent après leurs constructions par les gardes-jurés ou prudhommes du métier de charpentier qui donnent leur attestation du port du batiment laquelle sera enregistreée au greffe de l'Amirauté.

In order to discourage shippers and captains who cheated, the Amiral de France created the position of state tonnage measurer in 1709. The clerk registered the certificate of tonnage measurement and stamped it. This certificate was attested to in every French port and was reported on insurance declarations and on official registers. The ship owners' aim was to diminish their measures of ship tonnage in order to pay less in taxes, but if the ship was sold to the king or particulars, this cheating worked against them. Moreover, when a dispute arose, it was inexpensive to have the tonnage measurer create a new certificate: only two or three livres. The difficulty rested mainly in establishing a clear rule of ship tonnage measurement:[21]

L'usage est de prendre la longueur de tête en tête du dehors de l'étrave au dehors de l'étambot, la largeur au fort, en dehors des préceintes, le creux du maitre-bau sur quille, de faire un produit des trois dimensions et de le diviser par 100. On obtient le port en tonneau.

In fact, the burden tonnage varied by up to 10 percent according to the shape of the ship – whether sharp built or Dutch built. A check of slave ships' tonnage shows that registered tonnage declared on the *Registres de congés de l'Amiral de France* are the same as tonnages declared on the *Registres de de soumission* of La Rochelle. Jean Mettas, in his *Répertoire*, noticed tonnage differences. In each case, they came from the data of the *Archives des Colonies* or private sources, particularly newspapers such as *Les Affiches américaines*. The *Etats de Commerce* established by Customs, such as those of the Nantes port town, did not mention the registered tonnage but the burden tonnage actually used in the journey of the ship coming from the West Indies. Therefore, the important differences found in research are easy to explain.

In the slave ship case, letters written by a French Navy shipwright of Rochefort harbor tell us how three slave ships of La Rochelle were measured (Table 18).

In a note, this shipwright mentioned that the *port en tonneaux de*

---

[20] Valin, *Commentaire sur l'Ordonnance de 1681*, Livre II, titre X, *Du navire...* (La Rochelle, 1766).

[21] Vial du Clairbois, *Encyclopèdie Marine* (Paris, 1783), tome 3, jauge p. 552.

Table 18. *Table about the burden of the ships*
La Fille Unique, *the* Forcalquier, *and the* Comte d'Hector

| | | | Main measures of the burden | | | | | |
	1	2	3	4	5	6	7	8
Fille Unique	116	104	110	31	28.6	19.6	12.5	4
Forcalquier	121.8	106.4	114	33	31.6	19.6	12.9	4.3
Comte d'Hector	108	98	103	27	25	17.3	9.9	4.7

1 = length of the lower deck
2 = length of the keel
3 = average of the length
4 = breadth extream

5 = breadth molded
6 = depth of the hold
7 = depth from the kelson to the first deck
8 = height of the between decks

(Translation from a dictionary of naval architecture of the 18th century.)

| | Burden when using internal measurement measures | | | General burden when using external measurement measures |
	Cale	Entrepont	Total	Cale + Entrepont
Fille Unique	850 tx[a]	381 tx	1,231 tx	1,455 tx
Forkalquier	786 tx	466 tx	1,247 tx	1,667 tx
Comte d'Hector	458 tx[a]	369 tx	827 tx	1,057 tx

[a] tx = tonneaux (French tons).
Source: Archives du Port de Rochefort, 2G⁴ No. 3.

poids (burden weight) was supposed to be 650 *tonneaux* for the *Fille Unique*, 680 *tonneaux* for the *Forcalquier*, and 300 to 350 *tonneaux* for the *Comte d'Hector*.

The study of Amiral de France registers reveals that the *Forcalquier* (also named the *Comte de Forcalquier*) had sailed toward Saint-Dominigue in 1784 with a declared tonnage of 700 *tonneaux* in 1785 as a slave ship with a registered tonnage of 1,350 *tonneaux*, and again in 1787 as a slave ship with a registered tonnage of 1,667 *tonneaux*. In 1788, in Nantes port town, back from the West Indies, it was registered as a 700-*tonneaux* ship.

On the La Rochelle books, the *Comte d'Hector* is registered as a 380-*tonneaux* cargo in 1783 on the G5 *serie*, as a 833-*tonneaux* slave ship in 1785, and as a 1,057-*tonneaux* slave ship in 1788.

The *Fille Unique* is mentioned only once in 1787 as a slave ship of 1,667 *tonneaux*, but it was considered to have a cargo of 650 *tonneaux* on its muster roll in the archives of Rochefort harbor.

All these data show that the changes of tonnage measurements in La Rochelle are not the result of an accident but come from two successive rules of tonnage measurements.

Ship owners were very sensible. Slave captains crowded the Africans in the area between decks and on the upper deck. The hold of the ship was entirely occupied by the water and the food for the middle passage. First, the shippers were permitted to include the area between decks in the measurement so that the maritime reality would be the same as the measurement rule. Second, the shippers emphasized that partial platforms, which were set on the decks for children and wives, reduced the volume allowed to the crew. As a consequence, the rule of external measurement is definitely the most accurate.

Of course, the government had to pay for the new subsidies resulting from these changes. The premium was paid when the ship left France and the measurement was then registered on the departure book, but on returning from the West Indies, the slave ship, a simple cargo carrier now, adopted cargo tonnage again.

To measure the French colonial fleet accurately, one should use only the measurements written in the *rules de desarmement* of 1785–92 – that is, the roll of laying up of the ship. Unfortunately, these registers are scarcely complete in the archives of French harbors and port towns. But a slave ship often sailed previously as a cargo, so its registered tonnage preceding 1785 indicates its nonslave ship tonnage. A study of the names of the French ships reveals that ships rarely changed names, even when they changed ownership. With the help of a computer, this problem should be soluble. I have tried to do so with handwritten notes for the La Rochelle port town. The result is given in Table 19.

A King's Council Act dated September 10, 1786, allowed, in addition to the subsidy of 40 livres per registered *tonneaux*, a premium of 160 livres per slave sold in the French colonies and 200 livres per slave sold in Saint-Dominigue. Necker, in his *Rapport au Roi*, mentioned that the premium allowed for slaves *"forment un objet de 2,400,000 livres"* The premium seems to have been paid correctly until 1789. In 1790, 105 ships were granted the premium, but only 31 in 1791 and 28 in 1792. The information is quite confusing. It seems that in 1792,

---

[22] Archives du Port de Rochefort, from manuscripts found by M. Boudriot of Paris, 2G⁴, No. 3; Jean Mettas, Serge Daget, and Michele Daget, *Répertoires des Expéditions négrières, Ports autres que Nantes*, (Paris, 1985), tome 2.

Table 19. *Slave ships of La Rochelle from 1783 to 1789*

Year	Name of Ship	Slave tonnage[a]	Cargo tonnage[b]	Estimated slaves[c]	Slaves carried[d]
1783	Marie-Louise	150	150	—	200
	Hirondelle	200	200	—	358
	Joli	350	350	—	403
	Belle Pauline	300	300	—	575
	Colombe	160	160	350	357
	Industrie	60	60	120	67
	Bonne Société	300	300	450	342
	Iris	60	60	60	—
	Euryale	300	300	—	400
	Utile	55	55	—	—
	Thetis	180	180	300	185
	Nisus	350	350	650	—
	Aimable Louise	350	350	700	577
	Nouvel Achille	400	400	800	380
	13 Cantons	500	500	700	520
	Elise	38	38	120	—
	Comte d'Hector	380	380	700	736
1784	Reine de Golconde	350	350	—	—
	Pauline	350	350	—	448
	Cigogne	160	160	—	—
	Iris	400	400	—	966
	Union des 6 freres	200	200	—	—
	Trois Frères	300	300	600	600
	Cerf-Volant	100	100	—	—
	Bellecombe	300	300	—	500
	Alerte	16	16	—	—
	Aurore	300	300	—	476
	Meulan	580	580	—	687
	Clameur ou Railleur	316	316	—	500
	Plaisanterie	18	18	—	—
	Caraibe	150	150	—	—
	Mercure	190	190	—	160
	Concorde	215	715	—	—
	Follette	50	—	—	—
1785	Aimable Suzanne	450	180	350	375
	Ebène	350	—	300	280
	Rosalie	280	—	399	370
	Joli	500	350	450	433
	Marquis de Voyer	700	300	500	605
	Lutin	179	—	—	194
	Comte de Forcalquier	1,350	700	376	138
	Concorde	375	215	—	376
	Argus	203	—	—	280
	Comte d'Hector	833	380	600	800
	Loudunois	792	400	300	—
	Duc de Normandie	446	240	—	459
	Reverseaux	1,179	—	—	425
	Fille Unique	1,232	—	600	—

Table 19 (*cont.*)

Year	Name of Ship	Slave tonnage[a]	Cargo tonnage[b]	Estimated slaves[c]	Slaves carried[d]
1786	Cigogne	493	—	—	400
	Réparateur	780	300	—	410
	Cacique	199	—	—	78
	Diamant	402	—	—	286
	Ville de Basle	441	150	—	300
	Aurore	800	300	400	—
	Prevost de Langristin	1,540	700	—	240
	Comte de Puysegur	1,253	600	—	370
	13 Cantons	1,021	500	—	440
	Plutus	807	450	—	525
	Comte d'Estaing	536	200	—	355
	Aunis	1,581	760	—	718
	Reine de Podore	316	150	—	118
	Bonhomme Richard	1,646	700	—	518
	Railleur	897	316	—	635
	Bien Aimee	681	300	—	316
	Reine de Golconde	831	—	—	251
	Amitie	781	300	—	224
	Comtesse de Puysegur	625	340	—	400
	Tigre	711	360	—	359
	Desiree	975	500	—	367
1787	Laboureur	795	350	—	—
	Victoire	827	350	—	300
	Bon Francais	1,519	—	—	334
	Nouvelle Betsy	529	200	—	342
	Comte de Forcalquier	1,667	650	—	779
	Bon Père	581	280	—	—
	Meulan	1,229	580	—	541
	Nouveau Joly	670	—	—	533
	Solide	810	—	—	242
	Frères	302	—	—	120
	Réparateur	734	300	—	514
1788	Duc de Normandie	517	240	—	429
	Aimable Suzanne	534	—	—	464
	Comte de Puysegur	1,253	600	—	540
	Trois Soeurs	609	—	—	205
	Comte d'Hector	1,057	380	—	672
	Desire	175	—	—	506
	Tigre	700	300	—	450
	Reverseaux	1,524	—	—	700
1789	Ville de Basle	447	150	—	155
	Bon Père	584	280	—	363
	Cigogne	809	—	—	409
	Nouvelle Betsy	529	200	—	353
	Meridien	92	—	—	—
	Duc de Normandie	517	240	—	376
	Sartine	1,259	600	—	450
	Victoire	827	—	—	288
	Deux Amis	402	—	—	—

Table 19 (*cont.*)

Year	Name of Ship	Slave tonnage[a]	Cargo tonnage[b]	Estimated slaves[c]	Slaves carried[d]
1790	*Comte de Puysegur*	1,253	600	—	500
	Comte de Forcalquier	1,667	650	—	530
	Bon Citoyen	92	—	—	—
	Réparateur	723	350	—	360
	Revanche	795	300	—	—
	Saint-Jacques	1,288	500	—	—
	Pauline	790	350	—	450
	Alcyon	—	—	—	—
	Bonhomme Richard	1,646	750	—	545
	Marie-Elisabeth	289	110	—	41
	Neptune	695	—	—	—
	Joly	670	—	—	—
	Reverseaux	1,524	—	—	—

[a] Registered tonnage from the Amiral de France's registers Archives Nationales, series G5.
[b] Registered tonnage in the *Registres de Soumission* de la Rochelle.
[c] Number of slaves estimated by the ship owners at the departure from La Rochelle.
[d] Number of slaves sold in the West Indies.[22]

at least 3,077 slaves were introduced into Martinique and 1,598 into Saint-Domingue.[23]

The 1791 budget did not plan any credit for the premium, but on the ship owners' demands, the *Comite des Finances* in March 1792 estimated the whole premium at 2,815,000 livres. Finally, the Assembly voted on August 16, 1792, the payment of the past due premium from January 1791 to August 16, 1792. The government offices were in no hurry to pay. Following the ship owners' claims, the premium was paid until July 1793: fifty-three vessels received 919,377 livres by virtue of the act of *40 livres par tonneau de jauge*. The premium for introducing slaves amounted to 795,120 livres, of which 319,000 was for Saint-Domingue. On July 27, 1793, the question was raised in the National Assembly. Bishop Gregoire vehemently intervened and

[23] In Jean Vidalenc, "La traite des nègres en France au début de la Révolution," *Annales historiques de la Révolution francaise*, (1957), p. 62.

stated that the premium should not be paid any longer, anticipating the law of the Convention pronouncing the abolition of slavery on February 15, 1794.[24]

---

[24] Archives Nationales, F12 1653, F12 1654; Patrick Villiers, *Traite des Noirs et Navires négriers* (Paris, 1985), pp. 113–22.

CHAPTER 10

Slavery, trade, and economic growth in eighteenth-century New England

DAVID RICHARDSON

In their recent study of colonial British America, McCusker and Menard bemoan the fact that, despite considerable research over the last
two decades on colonial New England's demography and society,
"[e]conomic issues have seldom commanded center stage in New
England studies." As a result, they claim, "recent work has as yet
failed to yield much insight into the operation of the economy."
Nevertheless, noting that New England "lacked a major staple commodity to export to the metropolis" but needed under the pressure
of rapid population growth "to import countless things from abroad,"
they argue that New Englanders became "the Dutch of England's
empire," creating "a well-integrated commercial economy based on
the carrying trade." It is, they conclude, "in the interactions between
the push of population growth and the pull of market opportunities
that answers to the central questions in New England social and
economic history are likely to be found."[1]

Seeking to integrate research on New England demography with
that on the region's economy, the approach advocated by McCusker
and Menard requires, as they themselves admit,[2] a fuller understanding of both the pattern of growth in the export sector and the relationship between trade and economic development in the region. A
comprehensive treatment of these issues cannot be attempted in this
chapter, not least because much of the detailed work required to trace
the patterns and levels of New England trade throughout the colonial
period remains to be done. However, there have been several recent
studies of trends in growth and wealth in the region, and by com-

---

[1] J. J. McCusker and R. R. Menard, *The Economy of British America, 1607–1790* (Chapel
Hill, N.C., 1985), pp. 91–2, 106.
[2] Ibid., p. 107.

bining these with available data on levels and patterns of trade, some new light can be shed on the dynamics of early New England economic development.

This chapter focuses primarily on the performance of the New England economy in the period from the end of the War of Spanish Succession to the American Revolution. Recent research has produced conflicting interpretations of wealth and growth trends in New England in this period, but the evidence now seems to be weighted in favor of a marked improvement in the growth rate of the New England economy over the period. The transition to higher growth occurred around midcentury and coincided with a general upturn in economic activity throughout the whole north Atlantic economy in the quarter-century before 1775. Centered largely on expanding trade between European nations and their slave-based colonies, this buoyant environment also stimulated the growth of New England trade, particularly with the Caribbean. Arguably, this expansion of trade helped in the short term to ease the Malthusian crisis that at least one historian has alleged New England society was facing by the middle of the eighteenth century.[3] And in the longer term, it created a solid foundation for the relatively rapid recovery of the New England economy from the damaging effects of the Revolutionary War.

This argument will be developed in three parts. Part I of the chapter provides a brief review of some of the recent literature on economic growth in colonial New England and seeks to establish the importance of trade in determining trends in the rate of growth in the prerevolutionary economy. In part II, the general patterns and levels of New England trade are examined with a view to tracing the significance of trade with slave-based economies for the region's changing economic fortunes. The main focus of this section is on the third quarter of the eighteenth century. Part III offers some reflections on the longer-term implications of the commercial changes that occurred in this period and some concluding remarks on the relationship between slavery and New England economic development.

I

Stimulated by a provocative paper in 1964 by Taylor,[4] a substantial literature has developed during the last quarter-century relating to

---

[3] K. Lockridge, "Land, Population, and the Evolution of New England Society, 1630–1790," *Past and Present*, Vol. 39 (1968), pp. 62–80.

[4] G. R. Taylor, "American Economic Growth before 1840," *Journal of Economic History*, Vol. 24 (1964), pp. 427–44.

the rates of growth and wealth of the thirteen mainland colonies that came to form the United States. Relying on trade data and back projection, Taylor proposed that growth was relatively limited during the seventeenth century but rather higher during the eighteenth century. Taylor's suggestions provoked a series of studies on the growth rates experienced in several regions or colonies. These included, in the late 1960s and early 1970s, studies by Davisson on growth in seventeenth-century Essex County, Massachusetts, and by Anderson on economic growth in New England between 1650 and 1710.[5] Relying heavily on probate records, both Davisson and Anderson suggested that considerably higher rates of growth occurred in seventeenth-century New England than Taylor had indicated. Thus Anderson claimed that economic growth in New England was, by most historical standards, relatively fast during the seventeenth century, averaging some 1.6% per year between 1650 and 1710. Similar rates of growth in Essex County were found by Davisson, with estimates of growth averaging about 2.0% per year between 1640 and 1682. Clearly, using these figures, Taylor's general article gave a misleading impression of the growth performance of the New England economy in the seventeenth century.[6] Average incomes in the region were apparently significantly higher at the end of the century than he had supposed.

One implication of this reinterpretation of seventeenth-century growth was, as Anderson himself later recognized,[7] that the growth of the New England economy in the eighteenth century was probably considerably lower than Taylor's article had indicated. In support of this pessimistic assessment of eighteenth-century growth rates, Anderson noted, among other studies, Egnal's estimate that the rate of growth in per capita income in the thirteen colonies was only 0.5% per annum between 1720 and 1775.[8] He also offered estimates of changes in real wealth and agricultural productivity in Hampshire County, Massachusetts, between 1700 and 1779. According to An-

---

[5] W. I. Davisson, "Essex County Wealth Trends: Wealth and Economic Growth in 17th Century Massachusetts," *Essex Institute Historical Collections*, Vol. 103 (1967), pp. 291–342; T. L. Anderson, *The Economic Growth of Seventeenth-Century New England* (New York, 1975).

[6] Work on other regions has also suggested higher growth rates than Taylor claimed and, together with studies on periods between 1700 and 1840, has led one historian to conclude that the "Taylor 'thesis' lies in shreds": J. A. Henretta, "Wealth and Social Structure," in J. P. Greene and J. R. Pole (eds.), *Colonial British America: Essays in the New History of the Early Modern Era* (Baltimore, 1984), p. 269.

[7] T. L. Anderson, "Economic Growth in Colonial New England: 'Statistical Renaissance,'" *Journal of Economic History*, Vol. 39 (1979), pp. 243–258.

[8] M. Egnal, "The Economic Development of the Thirteen Continental Colonies, 1720 to 1775," *William and Mary Quarterly*, third series, Vol. 32 (1975), pp. 191–222.

derson, real wealth in the county rose at an annual rate of only 0.54% during this period, and total factor productivity in agriculture fell by 0.8%.[9] However, these rates of change in wealth and productivity were not steady. On the contrary, they varied substantially over time. Thus, Anderson claims, real wealth per capita rose by up to 2.5% per annum during the first half of the century, but then fell by 1.0% or more per annum during the third quarter of the century. Similar undulations in growth rates were exhibited by agricultural productivity, though improvements were smaller and confined essentially to the very early part of the century, and declines after 1750 were even more pronounced than in the case of wealth estimates.

The fact that most New Englanders in 1775 were farmers makes Anderson's findings regarding agricultural productivity in Hampshire County, a western agricultural area with a rising share of the colony's population, particularly significant. Equally important, his rather pessimistic assessment of productivity and wealth trends in eighteenth-century New England has some support in the findings of other historians, notably Jones and Lockridge. Thus, following a detailed study of probate records for the early 1770s covering almost all the thirteen colonies, the late Alice Jones was led to conclude that New England "seemingly had the most dismal outlook of any region in 1774."[10] Similarly, according to Lockridge, rapid population growth in the region for over a century after 1630 seems to have resulted in a Malthusian crisis in many New England rural communities by the second half of the eighteenth century, with population pressure on the limited agricultural land resources leading to fragmentation of landholdings, growing rural poverty, and rising out-migration.[11]

Although various studies unite to paint a rather depressing picture of the state of the New England economy in the generation before the Revolution, there are major problems with such a pessimistic assessment. To envisage New Englanders as confronting a Malthusian crisis in the late colonial period, as Lockridge alleged, is, as McCusker and Menard note, "difficult to relate to the subsequent industrial and commercial development of New England's economy."[12] Their doubts about pessimistic assessments of the region's economy before 1775 are reinforced by trends in several economic indicators in the quarter-century before the Revolution. For instance, trade statistics indicate

---

[9] Anderson, pp. 251, 255.
[10] A. H. Jones, *Wealth of a Nation to Be: The American Colonies on the Eve of the Revolution* (New York, 1980), p. 141.
[11] Lockridge, p. 74.
[12] McCusker and Menard, pp. 105–6.

that, despite disruptions caused by nonimportation, exports of goods from Britain to New England failed to exhibit any real decline in per capita terms during this period; according to British customs figures, exports to New England rose in fact by some 130% over the third quarter of the century, an increase substantially greater than the population increase in the region.[13] A glance at available evidence on wages suggests one reason why this should have occurred: According to data provided by Warden, wage rates in Boston rose by up to 100% in money terms and by perhaps 50% in real terms during the twenty-five years before 1775.[14] Evidence relating to imports from Britain, most of which were manufactures, as well as to urban wages, tends to indicate that prosperity rather than crisis characterized the New England economy in the quarter-century that culminated in the Revolution.

The fact that most New Englanders in 1775 were still farmers largely engaged, according to some historians,[15] in subsistence production invites some skepticism about such a reappraisal of the condition of the New England economy in the late colonial period. However, the latest research on probate records of Connecticut and Massachusetts by Gloria and Jackson Main suggests that Anderson's description of trends in wealth and growth in the eighteenth-century New England economy may well have been misleading. According to the Mains' findings, average real male wealth in southern New England rose by less than one-quarter between the 1640s and the mid-eighteenth century but then rose considerably in the two decades before the Revolution, from about £276 per capita in 1735–54 to £365 per capita in 1765–74.[16] Contrasting sharply with Anderson's findings, this acceleration in the rate of increase in the region's wealth was led by rising land values but appears to have characterized most areas, whether rural or urban, of southern New England in this period, the one notable exception being the upland district of Hampshire County, Massachusetts. It was this county that, it will be recalled, Ander-

---

[13] Figures on imports may be found in U.S. Bureau of the Census, *Historical Statistics of the United States: From Colonial Times to 1970* (Washington, D.C., 1975), part 2, pp. 1176–8. Available estimates suggest that New England's population grew from almost 371,000 in 1750 to over 596,000 in 1770, an increase of some 61%; Bureau of Census, p. 1168.

[14] G. B. Warden, "Inequality and Instability in Eighteenth-Century Boston: A Reappraisal," *Journal of Interdisciplinary History*, Vol. 6 (1975–6), p. 590.

[15] R. E. Mutch, "Yeoman and Merchant in Pre-industrial America: Eighteenth-Century Massachusetts as a Case Study," *Societas*, Vol. 7 (1977), pp. 279–302.

[16] G. L. Main and J. T. Main, "Economic Growth and the Standard of Living in Southern New England, 1640–1774," *Journal of Economic History*, Vol. 48 (1988), p. 36.

son used to assess trends in New England wealth in the eighteenth century.

An explanation of the differences in wealth trends revealed by Anderson's and the Mains' work is beyond the scope of this chapter, but a comparison of Anderson's findings and those of the Mains suggests that estimates of trends in real wealth derived from probate records may be sensitive to the price index used to deflate probate valuations.[17] The more buoyant impression of economic conditions in late colonial New England given by the Mains' analysis is, however, consistent with the trade and wage data noted earlier. It is also supported by evidence on changes in rural diet and in the consumption of amenities. In a recent study of rural diets based largely on probate material, Sarah MacMahon has argued that by the mid-eighteenth century New England farmers, although primarily subsistence oriented, were nevertheless beginning "to adopt new methods that suggest an unwillingness to accept traditional seasonal limitations on the quantity and variety of their food supply."[18] Such changes, in MacMahon's view, reflected not only a response to "declining agricultural conditions in the early eighteenth century or *to growing market opportunities after the revival of economic activity at mid-century*" but also to "changing cultural expectations about both the daily fare and the composition of diet through the year."[19] Such arguments are corroborated by an index of amenities compiled by the Mains. Consisting primarily of goods "associated with eating and drinking" such as imported foods, household linen, and tableware, their index demonstrates substantial increases during the decades after 1730, with peak levels of usage by all income groups in almost every region of New England surveyed occurring in the years just prior to 1776. It seems, therefore, that New Englanders on the eve of the Revolution, in the Mains' words, "were suffering less from bleak houses than from great expectations."[20]

It is evident that not all localities or social groups shared equally in this rising wealth and consumption, but the weight of evidence

---

[17] There appear, for instance, to be significant differences in the trends of livestock and crop prices during the eighteenth century assumed by Anderson and the Mains. For Anderson, livestock and crop prices rose through the 1740s and then fell back in the 1750s and 1760s (p. 252) whereas for the Mains, they fell between 1713 and the 1730s but then revived thereafter (p. 35).

[18] S. F. McMahon, "A Comfortable Subsistence: The Changing Composition of Diet in Rural New England," *William and Mary Quarterly*, third series, Vol. 42 (1985), p. 46.

[19] Ibid., p. 48 (italics added).

[20] Main and Main, pp. 39–45.

clearly points toward a much more optimistic assessment of economic conditions and living standards generally in New England in the quarter-century after 1750 than some recent studies have claimed. This reappraisal of trends in the region's economy has important implications for our understanding of the dynamics of New England growth in the eighteenth century. For if, as the latest findings suggest, New England experienced very slow growth in the first half of the century and significantly faster growth and rising prosperity in the final quarter-century of colonial rule, then the trend in growth and consumption in the region was very similar to that in most other sectors of the north Atlantic economy that comprised the old colonial system of Britain. According to Kulikoff, economic growth in the Chesapeake colonies was very modest during the first half of the eighteenth century but was fairly pronounced during the third quarter of the century.[21] It is also evident that after a prolonged period of slow growth, there occurred a significant upturn in the rate of activity in the British economy after the War of Austrian Succession.[22] Available figures suggest that this was associated primarily with an expansion in industrial output. Of this, a sizable proportion was apparently exported, mainly to markets in Africa and the colonies in the West Indies and North America. Such exports were, in turn, related to substantial growth in sugar production in the British Caribbean during the third quarter of the century, growth stimulated primarily by rising consumption in Britain itself of imported foods and beverages such as sugar and tea.[23] An upsurge in economic activity, underpinned by rising incomes and consumption of manufactures and colonial products, thus seems to have occurred throughout the British Atlantic empire during the third quarter of the eighteenth century.[24]

---

[21] A. Kulikoff, "The Economic Growth of the Eighteenth-Century Chesapeake Colonies," *Journal of Economic History*, Vol. 39 (1979), pp. 275–88.

[22] N. F. R. Crafts, "British Economic Growth, 1700–1831: A Review of the Evidence," *Economic History Review*, second series, Vol. 36 (1983), p. 187.

[23] D. Richardson, "The Slave Trade, Sugar and British Economic Growth, 1748–1776," in B. L. Solow and S. L. Engerman (eds.), *British Capitalism and Caribbean Slavery* (Cambridge, 1987), pp. 103–33.

[24] For an analysis of consumer behavior in colonial America and the significance of consumption patterns for political action, see T. H. Breen, "An Empire of Goods: The Anglicization of Colonial America, 1690–1776," *Journal of British Studies*, Vol. 25 (1986), pp. 467–99; idem., "Baubles of Britain: The American and Consumer Revolutions of the Eighteenth Century," *Past and Present*, Vol. 119 (1988), pp. 73–104. This transatlantic pattern of growth seems to have extended as far as the Canadian parts of the empire, with cod exports from Halifax rising substantially between 1749 and 1775. See L. Fischer, "Revolution without Independence: The Canadian Colonies, 1749–1775," in R. Hoffman, J. J. McCusker, R. R. Menard, and P. J. Albert

New England had well-developed trading links with most parts of this empire by the mid-eighteenth century, importing manufactures from Britain and tropical foodstuffs from the Caribbean and exporting in return a variety of goods, including whale products, livestock, fish, and building and packaging materials. Faced with chronic trade deficits with Britain, New Englanders had developed from an early date a significant trade in fish to southern Europe, seeking to use the credits thereby earned to meet some of their debts to Britain.[25] The pursuit of this trade as well as trade with the Caribbean had, in turn, encouraged the rise of powerful merchant communities in Boston and other New England ports and the growth of a local shipbuilding industry of significant dimensions. By the middle of the eighteenth century, therefore, New Englanders were not only important freighters of goods but also major suppliers of ships to the British merchant fleet.[26]

Several recent studies have tended to downgrade the importance of trade and New England's merchant class as factors in shaping the evolution of the region's economy. Such an approach is clearly reflected in a paper by Mutch in which he seeks to minimize the impact of merchants and markets on rural life in eighteenth-century Massachusetts.[27] It is also essentially implicit in Lockridge's analysis of an emerging crisis in New England rural communities by the middle of the eighteenth century. It has been long understood, of course, that New England lacked a major export staple comparable to West Indian sugar or Chesapeake tobacco and that per capita exports overseas from the region were among the lowest in the eighteenth-century north Atlantic world.[28] Yet levels of imports per capita into New England at this time were not greatly dissimilar to those attained

(eds.), *The Economy of Early America: The Revolutionary Period, 1763–1790* (Charlottesville, Va., 1988), p. 118.

[25] J. G. Lydon, "Fish and Flour for Gold: Southern Europe and the Colonial American Balance of Payments," *Business History Review*, Vol. 39 (1965), pp. 171–83; idem., "Fish for Gold: The Massachusetts Fish Trade with Iberia, 1700–1773," *New England Quarterly*, Vol. 54 (1981), pp. 539–82.

[26] On the estimates of New England earnings from sales of ships to Britain, see J. M. Price, "A Note on the Value of Colonial Exports of Shipping," *Journal of Economic History*, Vol. 36 (1976), pp. 704–24. The origins of the New England merchant class have been comprehensively studied in B. Bailyn, *The New England Merchants in the Seventeenth Century* (Cambridge, 1955).

[27] Mutch, pp. 281, 297. Even Mutch acknowledges, however, that the West Indian market was not unimportant to "northern farmers" (p. 281).

[28] S. L. Engerman, "Notes on the Patterns of Economic Growth in the British North American Colonies in the Seventeenth, Eighteenth and Nineteenth Centuries," in P. Bairoch and M. Levy-Leboyer (eds.), *Disparities in Economic Development since the Industrial Revolution* (London, 1981), p. 48.

elsewhere, and when allowance is made for coastwise trade and invisibles, per capita earnings from trade compared reasonably well with those of other mainland regions.[29] Moreover, the fact that improved growth and rising prosperity in New England in the quarter-century before the Revolution coincided with an Atlantic-wide economic expansion reinforces doubts about the claims of those who would deny trade a major influence on the region's economic development. At the very least, it requires a reappraisal of the relationship of trade to New England economic growth in the late colonial period. It is to that issue that I now turn my attention.

II

Among historians of New England, there is a long tradition of focusing upon overseas trade as a significant factor in the economic development of the region in the seventeenth and eighteenth centuries. For various reasons, a particularly large amount of attention has been given to New England's involvement in the slave trade and its impact on the region's economy. For some historians, the importance of this trade lay simply in the stimulus it gave to the growth of certain ports. DuBois, for instance, suggested that it was principally the slave trade "that raised Newport to commercial importance in the eighteenth century."[30] Such claims have been endorsed more recently by Crane, who, in an article specifically related to Newport, argued that the triangular trade in molasses, rum, and slaves was "a crucial element in the economy" of the city in its golden days just prior to the Revolution.[31]

Several other historians, however, have regarded the trade as having had a much more pervasive impact on New England's economy; they see it, in fact, as shaping the whole fabric of the region's commercial and industrial life in the eighteenth century. Thus, in 1887,

---

[29] According to Shepherd and Walton, New England earnings from commodity exports overseas and invisibles averaged some £1.56 per capita in 1770: J. F. Shepherd and G. M. Walton, *Shipping, Maritime Trade and the Economic Development of Colonial North America* (Cambridge, 1972), p. 102. These estimates exclude earnings from coastwise trade, which were particularly significant for New England (see later text). As computed by Shepherd and Walton, New England earnings from trade were only £0.29 per capita or 16% lower than the estimated earnings of the southern plantation colonies in 1770 and were equivalent to about 14% of estimated per capita incomes in New England at this time (Jones, p. 63).

[30] W. E. B. DuBois, *The Suppression of the African Slave Trade to the United States of America 1638–1870* (New York, 1973), p. 28.

[31] E. F. Crane, "'The First Wheel of Commerce': Newport, Rhode Island and the Slave Trade, 1760–1776," *Slavery and Abolition*, Vol. 1 (1980), p. 179.

Weeden claimed that, although slaving was "a small constituent in itself," it nevertheless "exercised a great influence in the whole commerce of the first half of the eighteenth century."[32] Weeden's words were echoed some sixty years later in Greene's classic study, *The Negro in Colonial New England*. Anticipating the claims made by Eric Williams in his *Capitalism and Slavery* about the relationship between the slave trade and British industrialization, Greene argued that on the eve of the American Revolution the slave trade "formed the very basis of the economic life of New England: about it revolved, and on it depended, most of her other industries." Among the industries "dependent on the slave traffic," Greene listed the "vast sugar, molasses and rum trade," as well as shipbuilding, the distilleries, and "a great many of the fisheries."[33]

Although the slave trade may have contributed substantially to the growth of cities such as Newport, the more grandiose arguments of historians such as Weeden and Greene have met with little sympathy among most modern historians of colonial New England. It has been pointed out that slaving voyages were only a very small fraction of New England's overseas trading activities in 1768–72, when, arguably, the number of African ventures fitted out by the region's merchants was approaching its prerevolutionary peak.[34] Similarly, though rum was unquestionably the major New England export to Africa, constituting perhaps three-quarters of the cargoes dispatched to the coast,[35] the slave trade appears to have consumed only a small part of the total output of New England's many distilleries in the colonial period. Most of the distillers' production was sold, in fact, either locally or in other North American markets. Finally, despite assertions that the slave trade "often yielded high returns,"[36] a close study of the profitability of the trade and its relationship to the growth of merchants' fortunes in New England still remains to be carried out. It is clear, however, that, as in the British trade, returns on New England slaving voyages were highly variable, and it is quite likely

[32] W. B. Weeden, "The Early African Slave-Trade in New England," *American Antiquarian Society Proceedings*, new series, Vol. 5 (1887–8), p. 109.

[33] L. J. Greene, *The Negro in Colonial New England* (New York, 1942), pp. 68–9.

[34] Shepherd and Walton, p. 97. For a general assault on the importance attached to the slave trade by historians such as DuBois, Greene, and Weeden, see G. M. Ostrander, "The Making of the Triangular Trade Myth," *William and Mary Quarterly*, third series, Vol. 30 (1973), pp. 635–44; J. J. McCusker, *Rum and the American Revolution: The Rum Trade and Balance of Payments of the Thirteen Continental Colonies*, 2 Vols. (New York, 1989), pp. 492–7.

[35] J. Coughtry, *The Notorious Triangle: Rhode Island and the African Slave Trade, 1700–1807* (Philadelphia, 1981), p. 86.

[36] Crane, p. 185.

that profits from the trade made a more modest contribution to wealth accumulation in the region than has sometimes been suggested.[37]

It is evident that, in isolation, the slave trade cannot bear the responsibility for promoting general economic development in colonial New England that some earlier historians sought to place upon it. Yet, to dismiss the slave trade as having been of only marginal significance to New England, as most recent historians have tended to do, may be hasty, for closer attention to the chronology of the New Englanders' participation in this notorious trade helps to shed light on some wider structural changes taking place in the region's overseas trading pattern, particularly after 1750.

Detailed evidence regarding the scale of New England's total involvement in the slave trade is unavailable, but it is generally accepted that the overwhelming majority of voyages before 1776 were probably dispatched from Boston and Newport.[38] For these two ports we have relatively solid evidence regarding clearances to Africa, especially for the quarter-century before the Revolution.[39] What this suggests is that about ten ships a year cleared from these two ports for Africa in the early 1750s; this figure was, apparently, only a little higher than that for the 1730s.[40] The outbreak of war in 1755 led to some disruption in the trade, but following the return of peace in 1763, combined

---

[37] Some of the difficulties associated with the pursuit of the slave trade by New Englanders are indicated in J. B. Hedges, *The Browns of Providence Plantations: Colonial Years* (Cambridge, Mass., 1952), pp. 70–85; V. B. Platt, "'And Don't Forget the Guinea Voyage': The Slave Trade of Aaron Lopez of Newport," *William and Mary Quarterly*, third series, Vol. 32 (1975), pp. 601–18. Evidence on returns from slaving, based on relatively small numbers of voyages, is presented in Crane, p. 186, and Coughtry, p. 20.

[38] E. Field (ed.), *The State of Rhode Island and Providence Plantations at the End of the Century: A History*, 2 vols. (Boston, 1902), Vol. I, p. 404; J. A. Rawley, *The Trans-Atlantic Slave Trade* (New York, 1981), pp. 323–84; R. Anstey, "The Volume of the North American Slave-Carrying Trade from Africa 1761–1810," *Revue Francaise d'Histoire d'Outre-Mer*, Vol. 62 (1975), p. 50. There is evidence of some involvement in slaving by other New England ports before the Revolution. One voyage is known to have taken place from Providence in 1736 (Hedges, p. 71), and one vessel, appropriately named the *Africa*, is recorded as having cleared Salem for the coast in October 1764: *Early Coastwise and Foreign Shipping of Salem: A Record of the Entrances and Clearances of the Port of Salem, 1750–1769* (Salem, Mass., 1934), p. 5.

[39] Figures for Newport are provided in Coughtry, appendix; figures for Boston may be found in M. G. Lawson, "Routes of Boston's Trade, 1752–1765," in *Publications of the Colonial Society of Massachusetts*, (Boston, 1947–51), Vol. 38, pp. 81–120, as well as E. Donnan (ed.), *Documents Illustrative of the History of the Slave Trade to America*, 4 vols. (Washington, 1930–5), Vol. III, pp. 70–6. Lawson's figures have been adjusted to allow for incomplete coverage of Boston's clearances in certain years.

[40] It should be noted that there are only figures on Newport clearances to Africa in the 1730s; it is conceivable, therefore, that annual clearances from Newport and Boston in the early 1750s were lower than in the 1730s.

clearances from Boston and Newport for Africa rose sharply, averaging about twenty a year in the first five years after the Peace of Paris and reaching twenty-five a year in the early 1770s. New England's involvement in the slave trade thus seems to have more than doubled in size over the third quarter of the eighteenth century.[41]

It is evident that even at its prerevolutionary peak around 1770, New England's slave trade remained modest by British standards.[42] What is interesting, however, is that the expansion of New England's slaving after 1750 paralleled a substantial growth in Britain's slave trade over the same period. As I have argued elsewhere,[43] increased slaving activity by the British in the quarter-century before 1775 was closely related to a more general expansion of trade with the British Caribbean in the same period. Between 1750 and 1775, Britain's trade with its Caribbean possessions increased substantially, not only in absolute terms but also relative to other areas. In Britain's case, therefore, a rising level of slave trading was a barometer of change in the country's overall pattern of trade, signaling a growth in dependence on trade with slave-based economies, especially those of the West Indies. Furthermore, such trade, together with the trade to Africa, provided a more than marginal stimulus to industrial change and growth in Britain itself. The question to be explored here, then, is: How far did the growth of New England slaving in the quarter-century before 1775 reflect similar changes in the region's overseas trade, leading to both greater dependence on trade with slave-based economies and increasing prosperity within New England itself? In order to begin to answer this question, it is necessary to examine general trends in New England trade after 1750.

Analyzing trends in trade is not easy, for the only comprehensive data on New England's overseas trade that have been produced to date are confined to the five-year period from 1768 to 1772. Compiled by Shepherd and Walton, these data are summarized in Table 1. Trade patterns in these years may be somewhat distorted by the nonim-

---

[41] A similar increase in slaving activity seems to have occurred also at New York in this period; see J. G. Lydon, "New York and the Slave Trade, 1700 to 1774," *William and Mary Quarterly*, third series, Vol. 35 (1978), p. 378.

[42] Available figures suggest that, on average, over 150 ships a year cleared from British ports for Africa for slaves between 1760 and 1775. This was six times the level of clearances from Newport and Boston in the early 1770s. Moreover, New England slave ships were smaller in general than their British counterparts, so Newport's and Boston's slave-carrying capacity was even smaller relative to the British trade than clearance data indicate. For British figures see D. Richardson, "The Eighteenth-Century British Slave Trade: Estimates of Its Volume and Distribution," *Research in Economic History*, Vol. 12 (1989), appendix.

[43] Richardson, "Slave Trade, Sugar and British Economic Growth."

Table 1. *New England overseas trade, 1768–72 (thousands £)*

	Britain		Southern Europe		West Indies		Africa		Total	
Year	(1)	(2)	(1)	(2)	(1)	(2)	(1)	(2)	(1)	(2)
1768	89	441	62	15	252	258	13	—	416	714
1769	90	228	70	26	281	362	23	—	464	616
1770	96	457	62	14	318	350	20	—	496	821
1771	88	1,446	78	15	319	322	15	—	500	1,783
1772	78	912	59	20	347	403	25	—	509	1,335
Annual Average	88	697	66	18	303	339	19	—	477	1,054

Notes: Col. 1: New England exports; col. 2: imports. Britain includes Ireland; Southern Europe includes the Wine Islands.
Source: J. F. Shepherd and G. M. Walton, *Shipping, Maritime Trade and the Economic Development of Colonial America* (Cambridge, 1972), p. 115.

portation policies adopted by the colonies at this time. It is evident, moreover, that in some instances Shepherd and Walton's estimates of trade between New England and certain overseas areas in this five-year period may be low.[44] Nevertheless, the overall picture of trade that emerges from these data seems fairly clear. The figures underline certain common conceptions about New England trade, notably the substantial trade deficit. They also help to put trade with particular overseas areas into perspective. Three points may be noted. First, trade with Africa and southern Europe, often the focus of attention because of their potential for generating trade surpluses, was a relatively small sector of New England overseas trade in 1768–72. Together, exports to the two areas averaged about £85,000 a year and comprised less than 18% of total New England exports overseas at this time.[45] Second, despite nonimportation in certain years, New

[44] Estimates made recently by Lydon suggest that exports of fish from Massachusetts to southern Europe averaged some £81,500 sterling annually in 1768–72 (Lydon, "Fish for Gold," pp. 562–3). Fish apparently dominated New England's exports to southern Europe at this time, and Massachusetts evidently controlled the bulk of these exports. Lydon's estimate of fish exports is, nevertheless, still some 24% greater than Shepherd and Walton's estimate of the average annual value of all of New England's exports to this region in this period.

[45] It is perhaps worth noting that Africa's share of New England exports was 4% in this five-year period. Exports to Africa comprised an almost identical proportion of total British exports during the second half of the eighteenth century: D. Richardson, "West African Consumption Patterns and Their Influence on the Eighteenth Century British Slave Trade," in H. A. Gemery and J. S. Hogendorn (eds.), *The Uncommon Market: Essays in the Economic History of the Atlantic Slave Trade* (New York, 1979),

England imports in 1768–72 were dominated by Britain, with almost two-thirds of them coming from the mother country. In this respect, the pattern of New England's imports was similar to that of other mainland areas. What also emerges from Table 1, however, is that most of the remaining imports of New England in 1768–72 came from the West Indies. Furthermore, the share of West Indian products in New England imports was substantially greater than that of other mainland colonies.[46] These imports were a vital prop for New England's trade to Africa and also had, as we will see, considerable significance for New England's coastwise trade with its mainland neighbors. Finally, in terms of exports, the West Indies dominated New England trade around 1770 almost as much as Britain controlled the region's imports. Averaging some £303,000 a year and growing rapidly, exports to the Caribbean comprised almost 64% of total New England exports in 1768–72. The remaining 36% of the region's exports were largely shared more or less equally by Britain and southern Europe. On the export side at least, trade with the West Indies seems, therefore, to have been, in Morison's phrase, "the cornerstone" of not only Boston's but New England's export trade in the years just prior to the outbreak of war with Britain.[47]

If the Caribbean was central to New England's trade about 1770, how important was it two decades earlier? As indicated previously, detailed information relating to all of New England's trade before 1768 is unavailable. The most solid evidence we have relates to trade with Britain, but there are indications of the level of trade with other regions in the 1750s. Evidence on trade with Britain derives from British customs records. Covering both imports and exports, the figures on British trade with New England are presented in Table 2. It should be noted that these figures are official values and differ, particularly in terms of exports to Britain, from the estimates of the current value of New England's exports to the home country in 1768–72 constructed by Shepherd and Walton.

Three features of trade between Britain and New England in the third quarter of the eighteenth century emerge from the figures in Table 2. First, both imports and exports grew substantially and at

---

p. 305. In this respect, the slave trade was perhaps just as important to New England's economy as it was to the British.

[46] According to Shepherd and Walton, total mainland imports from Britain "dwarfed imports from all other overseas areas," amounting to "over four times the value of commodity imports from all other areas combined" in 1768–72 (p. 112).

[47] S. E. Morison, "The Commerce of Boston on the Eve of the Revolution," *American Antiquarian Society Proceedings*, new series, Vol. 32 (1922), p. 39.

Table 2. *British trade with New England, 1748–74 (£)*

Year	Average annual imports from New England	Average annual exports to New England	Average annual deficit of New England
1748–52	68,503	276,371	207,868
1753–7	65,752	360,615	294,863
1758–62	49,404	438,376	388,972
1763–7	133,042	412,780	279,738
1768–72	157,330	664,958	507,628
1773–4	133,579	554,313	420,734

Note: Import figures exclude sales of ships.
Sources: U.S. Bureau of the Census, *Historical Statistics of the United States, Colonial Times to 1970*, 2 vols. (Washington, D.C., 1975), Vol. II, pp. 1176–8.

more or less the same rate over this period. Thus, between 1748 and 1772, annual imports into Britain from New England rose from some £68,500 to over £157,000, or by almost 130%, and exports to New England rose from about £276,000 to almost £665,000, or by 141%. Second, New England had a substantial trade deficit with Britain throughout this period. This was, of course, a problem for New England throughout the colonial period and reflected in part the lack of a New England staple suitable for large-scale export to the mother country. It was also the root of the long-standing general overseas trade deficit of the region. What Table 2 suggests, however, is that the trade gap with Britain actually grew after 1750, rising from almost £208,000 a year around 1750 to over £507,000 twenty years later, an increase of some 144%. Third, comparing trade figures with population estimates, it appears that both imports and exports grew faster than the population in New England during the period covered by Table 2. Available population data suggest in fact that per capita exports to Britain from New England rose from £0.18 to £0.26 in this period, whereas imports rose from £0.74 to £1.12. Given that imports largely consisted of manufactured goods, these import trends may be seen, as noted earlier, as an important indicator of rising living standards in New England in these years.

It is quite evident, then, that there was a marked increase in trade, both overall and in per capita terms, between Britain and New England over the final quarter-century of the colonial period. But what of other overseas trades, such as the African, southern European, and West India trades? To my knowledge, no attempt has been made to estimate the value of New England's exports to Africa before 1768.

Figures on clearances of ships noted earlier suggest, nevertheless, that increases in exports to Africa probably kept pace at least with increases in trade with Britain, growing by perhaps about 150% between 1750 and 1770. Specific attempts to estimate the value of New England's trade with southern Europe and the Caribbean before 1768 have been made by Lydon and by Shepherd and Walton. Using various sorts of records, notably local customs reports and newspapers, Lydon estimated that fish exports from Massachusetts to southern Europe averaged about £58,400 a year in 1752–6, whereas figures compiled by Shepherd and Walton on the basis of shipments of certain key commodities gleaned from colonial naval office lists indicated that in the 1750s New England's exports to southern Europe perhaps averaged around £45,000 a year and exports to the West Indies averaged around £75,000 a year.[48]

Shepherd and Walton concede that their estimates of trade values in the 1750s are very tentative and inevitably subject to some error. And from Lydon's figures for fish exports from Massachusetts, it seems that they may well have understated the level of New England's exports to southern Europe throughout the third quarter of the eighteenth century. However, although their estimates of export levels differ, the trend in fish exports from Massachusetts described by Lydon is very similar to the trend in exports to southern Europe revealed by Shepherd and Walton's figures. In view of this, it is perhaps reasonable to use their export estimates for the 1750s and 1768–72 as a guide to the general trend in New England's trade with southern Europe and the Caribbean in the third quarter of the eighteenth century.

The data of Shepherd and Walton indicate, on the one hand, that exports from New England to southern Europe grew only modestly in absolute terms over this period and may have barely maintained their 1750s levels in per capita terms. Their figures suggest in fact that exports to southern Europe rose by only about £20,000 a year between 1750 and 1770 and remained at about £0.12 per capita. Based

---

[48] Lydon, "Fish for Gold," pp. 562–3; Shepherd and Walton, pp. 167–75. In using Shepherd and Walton's figures, I relied simply on their estimates of fish exports to derive estimates of exports to southern Europe. For estimates of the West Indian trade, I used their estimate of overall mainland exports to the Caribbean and apportioned 36% of these exports to New England, the latter being the region's share of North American trade with the Caribbean suggested by their data for the 1750s. Since their regional breakdown of exports excludes trade from colonies such as New York and Pennsylvania, this procedure is likely to inflate estimates of New England trade with the Caribbean around 1750 and therefore to understate the growth of trade with the region over the ensuing two decades.

on these calculations, therefore, trade between New England and southern Europe was in the doldrums in the quarter-century after 1750.

The figures for the West India trade, on the other hand, paint a very different picture. Following Shepherd and Walton's estimates, it appears that exports from New England to the Caribbean roughly quadrupled in value between the 1750s and the early 1770s, rising from about £75,000 a year to over £300,000 a year. The rise in exports was not quite so sharp in per capita terms, but the figures still show an impressive rise in exports of about 150%, or from about £0.2 per capita in the 1750s to £0.5 per capita around 1770. This was, on the available evidence, a far superior performance to that achieved in exports to southern Europe and Britain in these years and indicates that trade with the Caribbean, together with the associated though much smaller trade with Africa, was the most dynamic sector in New England overseas trade in the period after the War of Austrian Succession. The figures suggest in fact that the growth in exports to the West Indies accounted for perhaps two-thirds of the increase in New England's exports overseas between 1748 and 1772. At the same time, the West Indies' share of New England exports seems to have risen substantially, from less than 40% in the early 1750s to around 55% or more on the eve of the Revolution.[49] Colonial overseas trade may well have been characterized over the long term by continuity in terms of products and markets, as some historians have recently observed,[50] but significant changes in the market structure of New England's export trade were apparent in the late colonial period. In the final twenty-five years of British rule, growth in New England's overseas trade seems to have rested largely on dealings with slave-based economies in the Caribbean.

The tentative nature of the pre-1768 trade statistics requires one to be cautious about accepting too literally the precise calculations just made. It is possible, however, to attempt to verify the broad trends in overseas trade implied by the available figures by examining evidence on the numbers and tonnages of vessels clearing from New England ports. Unfortunately, clearance data are not available for

[49] These calculations assume that exports to Africa were £5,000 a year around 1750 and rely on the export data to Britain set out in Table 2. It will be noted that the figures in this table suggest higher levels of exports to Britain in 1768–72 than the current value estimates compiled by Shepherd and Walton. This largely explains the fact that the West Indian share of New England exports around 1770 given here is lower than that revealed by Table 1.

[50] McCusker and Menard, pp. 107–9.

Table 3. *Number and tonnage of vessels clearing Boston, Salem, and Newport for various destinations in certain years, 1714–74*

	Africa		Britain		Europe		Caribbean		North America	
	No.	Tons	No.	Tons	No.	Tons	No.	Tons	No.	Tons
Boston										
1714–17	—	—	48	3,985	19	1,185	191	10,897	145	4,475
1753	4	171	42	3,552	20	1,678	154	10,535	261	11,453
1764	9	670	54	5,303	14	937	126	8,490	240	11,267
1772	5	420	58	6,348	11	555	178	10,703	584	24,295
Salem										
1714–17	—	—	1	69	39	3,041	24	891	10	235
1751	—	—	6	559	44	3,298	78	4,561	58	3,182
1766	—	—	—	—	40	3,437	112	7,765	92	4,880
Newport										
1763	13	—			18	—	131	—	230	—
1764	19	—			14	—	127	—	359	—
1773	14	—			6	—	197	—	460	—
1774	30	—			20	—	200	—	526	—

Notes: 1. Figures for Boston and Salem in 1714–17 are annual averages. Figures for Newport relate only to numbers of clearances; the sources used include clearances for Britain within the total clearances for Europe.

2. The Caribbean includes both British and foreign colonies; North America includes Newfoundland as well as other mainland British colonies. Clearances to Europe were essentially to southern Europe, except for Newport figures, which also include Britain. *Sources:* Boston, 1714–17, E. B. O'Callaghan (ed.), *New York Documents Relative to Colonial History* (Albany, N.Y., 1855), Vol. V, p. 618; 1753, 1764, M. G. Lawson, "Routes of Boston's Trade, 1752–1765," *Publications of the Colonial Society of Massachusetts*, Vol. 38 (Boston, 1947–51), table 1; 1772, Bureau of the Census, *Historical Statistics*, Vol. II, p. 1180. Salem, 1714–17, *New York Historical Documents*, Vol. V, p. 618; 1751, 1766, *Coastwise and Foreign Shipping of Salem.* Newport, all years: Crane, "Wheel of Commerce," p. 182.

every New England port throughout the quarter-century before 1775, but there are some series of statistics for several major ports, notably Boston, Salem, and Newport. These are presented in Table 3. There are, in addition, some figures of total clearances from each of the New England colonies in 1760–2 and 1768–72.[51] These fail to distinguish the particular destinations of ships clearing New England, but inferences about changes in the importance of particular overseas markets may perhaps be drawn by relating total clearance data for colonies to descriptive evidence as well as statistics for individual ports.

It has to be emphasized at the outset that interpreting the data in

[51] J. F. Shepherd, "British America and the Atlantic Economy," in Hoffman, McCusker, Menard, and Albert, pp. 42–3.

Table 3 poses a number of problems. The total clearances from colonies in 1760–2 and 1768–72 suggest that, even over fairly short periods of time, the relative importance of individual colonies in overall New England trade could alter quite significantly. In general, it appears that Rhode Island and Connecticut trade increased in the 1760s relative to that of Massachusetts; this reflected the continuance of a trend evident before 1760 and obviously affects the weight that should be attached to shipping data for individual ports.[52] The picture is further complicated by the fact that the relative standing of ports within individual colonies also shifted over time. In Table 3, the most notable feature is the growth of Salem, Massachusetts, relative to Boston.[53] As the shipping patterns of individual ports differed, changes in the relative positions of ports had important implications for assessing shifts in the overall pattern of shipping activity. Finally, the numbers and tonnages of vessels clearing New England for particular destinations are, at best, an imperfect indicator of the economic significance of individual trades. One obvious problem is that voyage times associated with trades varied; as a result, annual clearance figures tend to give an inflated impression of the numbers and tonnages of ships employed in short-distance trades such as the coasting or Caribbean trades compared to those employed in longer distance trades such as those to Africa and Europe.[54] A further difficulty is that average outlays in cargo varied among ships engaged in different trades, with ships bound for Africa and Europe normally carrying much more valuable cargoes than those sailing to the Caribbean or to other North American ports.[55]

Bearing these problems in interpreting shipping statistics in mind, what do the figures on clearances presented in Table 3 suggest? Al-

---

[52] The figures provided by Shepherd show, in fact, that the tonnage of ships clearing each year from New Hampshire and Massachusetts fell slightly between 1760–2 and 1768–72, whereas tonnages from Rhode Island and Connecticut rose by 40 and 122% respectively. As a result, the share of these last two colonies in New England clearances rose from about 16% in 1760–2 to 26% in 1768–72.

[53] The relative decline of Boston is discussed in J. M. Price, "Economic Function and the Growth of American Port Towns in the Eighteenth Century," *Perspectives in American History*, Vol. 7 (1974), pp. 140–9.

[54] This is a point that Crane seeks to use to underline her claim that the slave trade was of greater significance to Newport than clearance data would seem to suggest (p. 183).

[55] W. I. Davisson and D. J. Dugan, "Commerce in Seventeenth-Century Essex County, Massachusetts," *Essex Institute Historical Collections*, Vol. 107 (1971), pp. 131–42, show that though clearances from Salem to the Caribbean in 1715 outnumbered clearances to southern Europe, trade with the latter was much more valuable because fish dominated exports to this area, whereas low-value timber products dominated trade to the Caribbean.

though the figures are obviously fragmentary, they suggest a pattern of clearances that is broadly consistent with the trade statistics discussed earlier. Among New England ports, Boston clearly remained throughout the colonial period preeminent in trade with Britain. The fact that annual clearances to Britain from Boston rose over the third quarter of the century, and were apparently supplemented by increasing clearances from other ports such as Newport, confirms therefore the healthy growth of trade with Britain in this period. Similarly, the discovery that annual clearances to southern Europe from Salem stagnated between 1751 and 1766 and fell at Boston reinforces the impression given by Shepherd and Walton's trade estimates, as well as by Lydon's calculations of Massachusetts's fish exports, that the southern European trade from New England grew sluggishly after 1750.

The trend in overseas clearances that emerges most forcefully from Table 3, however, is the rise in clearances of vessels employed in the Caribbean trade. The growth in clearances to the sugar islands was particularly marked after 1750 at Salem and Newport, and in both cases maintained an upward trend in clearances to the Caribbean established during the previous two or three decades.[56] The picture of increasing shipping activity between New England ports and the West Indies created by the Salem and Newport data is reinforced to some extent by an apparent resurgence in Boston clearances to the islands after 1763. And it is further strengthened by the rise in the tonnages of ships clearing from Connecticut ports after 1760, for, as Jonathan Trumbull, the colony's governor, noted in 1774, "[t]he principal trade of this colony is to the West India islands, excepting now and then a vessel with Ireland with flaxseed, and to England with lumber and pot ashes, and a few to Gibraltar and Barbary."[57] Overall, therefore, the available shipping data strongly suggest that the Caribbean was the most vibrant sector of New England overseas trading activity during the third quarter of the eighteenth century.

Although both shipping and overseas trade statistics point toward the same conclusion, it is likely that both sets of evidence understate the real significance of trade with the West Indies as a factor contrib-

---

[56] Evidence of the earlier growth of Rhode Island trade, including trade with the West Indies, is to be found in the reports of governors summarized in Field, Vol. I, pp. 396–8.

[57] *Massachusetts Historical Society, Collections*, first series, Vol. VII (1800), p. 234. Trumbull went on to explain that the trade to Barbary involved shipments of mules from the north African coast to the West Indies, where they were sold for bills of exchange (p. 235).

uting to economic prosperity in New England after 1750. There are several reasons for this, but in the context of this chapter, two merit particular attention. The first relates to merchants' earnings from shipping and other commercial services, the second to the role of West Indian products and their derivatives such as rum in the coastwise trade between New England and the other mainland colonies.

Recent studies have shown that, as the so-called Dutch of British America, New England merchants earned considerable sums from freight and other commercial services in the late colonial period. Shepherd and Walton have conservatively estimated that between 1768 and 1772 New England earnings from invisibles averaged some £427,000 a year, with the bulk of these coming from freight.[58] Such earnings appear to have outstripped quite comfortably those earned by any other group of mainland traders from similar activities, and provided New Englanders with their largest single source of revenue from overseas trade; earnings from invisibles are estimated to have exceeded, for instance, the value of New England exports to the West Indies by about £100,000 a year in 1768–72. Amounting to £0.71 per capita around 1770, invisible earnings were a vital lubricant for the New England economy in the late colonial period, enabling the region's population to pay for increasing amounts of imports from Britain and the West Indies.

Closer inspection of Shepherd and Walton's figures reveals, however, that some £280,000, or two-thirds of New England's invisible earnings in 1768–72, arose from trade with the Caribbean. These earnings were only about £20,000 a year less than New England's commodity exports to the West Indies. Moreover, they were proportionately higher than the West Indies' share of New England's total commodity trade with overseas areas; this probably reflected the higher level of New England ownership of vessels employed in the Caribbean trade compared to other trades and the higher utilization rates of ships on Caribbean routes.[59] Given that New England trade with the Caribbean appears to have expanded absolutely and relative to other areas, it is quite probable that the region's earnings from invisibles experienced unusually rapid growth after 1750, thereby boosting urban incomes and perhaps providing a substantial stimulus to local shipbuilding. The increase in Caribbean-related invisible earnings between 1750 and 1775 cannot be calculated exactly. But if one

---

[58] Shepherd and Walton, pp. 128, 134.

[59] Based on the figures presented in Table 1 earlier, trade with the West Indies accounted for some 42% of total New England exports and imports in 1768–72. On ownership patterns and utilization rates, see Shepherd and Walton, pp. 122, 126.

assumes that invisible earnings rose pro rata with New England exports to the Caribbean, then per capita earnings from freight and other services associated with Caribbean dealings may have risen from about £0.2 in 1750 to about £0.5 in 1770. This, in turn, would have raised estimated total New England earnings from their Caribbean commercial activities at these two dates to £0.4 and £1.0 per capita, respectively.[60] As available estimates suggest that average incomes in New England were about £10–12 around 1770,[61] earnings from commodity exports and shipping to the West Indies may thus have been equivalent to almost 10% of per capita incomes in New England on the eve of the Revolution.[62]

The commercial dealings with the West Indies not only boosted New England's incomes, they also played a vital role in enabling New Englanders to purchase the foodstuffs needed to sustain the populations of the port towns of Massachusetts and Rhode Island. Recent studies have shown that there occurred large increases in imports of grains and other foodstuffs into New England during the eighteenth century; most of these imports came from other mainland areas, notably New York, Pennsylvania, Maryland, and Virginia. Figures compiled by Klingaman from naval office lists indicate that food imports into Massachusetts were negligible in 1714–17 but had risen to some 250,000 bushels of grain and 38,000 barrels of flour per year by the early 1760s. Such imports cost, according to Klingaman's calculations, about £75,000 a year.[63] Further evidence of "New England's deficit in cereals" in the late colonial period is provided by Shepherd and Williamson.[64] Relying on data culled from Customs 16, they calculate that net imports of grain, bread, and flour into the four New England

---

[60] It was estimated earlier that per capita exports to the Caribbean averaged £0.2 and £0.5 in 1750 and 1770, respectively.

[61] Jones, p. 63.

[62] These calculations do not include earnings that New Englanders achieved by shipping produce directly from the Caribbean islands to Britain. Such shipments were perhaps greater than Shepherd and Walton assumed (p. 129), but were still likely to be small relative to earnings from trade between the mainland and Caribbean colonies. For examples of New England earnings from freighting produce from the Caribbean to Britain, see the accounts of the sloop *Abigail* and the brig *Diana* for 1771 in Aaron Lopez papers, box 6, American Jewish Historical Society Library, Brandeis University, Waltham, Massachusetts.

[63] D. C. Klingaman, "The Coastwise Trade of Colonial Massachusetts," *Essex Institute Historical Collections*, Vol. 108 (1972), pp. 231–4. Klingaman employs some of this material in his "Food Surpluses and Deficits in the American Colonies, 1768–1772," *Journal of Economic History*, Vol. 31 (1971), pp. 553–69.

[64] J. F. Shepherd and S. Williamson, "The Coastal Trade of the British North American Colonies, 1768–1772," *Journal of Economic History*, Vol. 32 (1972), pp. 783–810 (quotation, p. 797).

colonies of Connecticut, Rhode Island, Massachusetts, and New Hampshire averaged some £94,000 a year in 1768–72; the bulk of these imports were shipped from the Middle Atlantic colonies of New York and Pennsylvania and were particularly important in helping to feed the urban populations of Rhode Island and Massachusetts.[65] Reflecting the inability of New England farmers to meet the growing demand for food in urban New England, such imports may be regarded as symptomatic of the Malthusian crisis that is alleged by some to have threatened the region by the middle of the century. The growing need to import foods also potentially exacerbated the long-standing overseas trade deficit of the region.

The studies that have highlighted New England's mounting dependence on food imports have also shown, however, that payment for such imports was largely accomplished by coastwise shipments of West Indian products or of rum manufactured in New England from imported molasses. According to Klingaman, shipments of rum, molasses, and sugar to other mainland colonies constituted over 90% of the £36,500 of goods that Massachusetts' merchants are estimated to have sent coastwise each year in 1761–5.[66] Dispatched mainly to Pennsylvania, Maryland, and Virginia and valued f.o.b., these exports were equivalent to 45% of the cost, c.i.f., of Massachusetts's annual coastwise imports of grain and flour in these years. Figures computed by Shepherd and Williamson suggest that the contribution of West Indian produce and New England rum to the payment of Massachusetts's food import bill in 1768–72 was even greater, for net exports of such products to other North American ports are estimated to have averaged some £72,100 annually in this period and just exceeded net imports of basic grains, bread, and flour.[67] Moreover, taking New England as a whole, coastwise shipments of the same produce comfortably covered the food import bill of the region, yielding, it seems, a useful surplus of some £40,000 annually over imported foodstuffs during these years. It is hardly surprising, therefore, that Shepherd and Williamson conclude that, as New England's dependence on food imports grew, "the West India connection" came to be "even more important" for the New England colonies.[68] Slave-

---

[65] Klingaman has calculated that New England's deficit in grains and meat was equal to about 11% of its requirements in 1768–72, with Massachusetts having "a much higher basic deficit than did the rest of New England." Klingaman, "Surpluses and Deficits," pp. 562–3. Klingaman excluded Connecticut from these calculations.

[66] Klingaman, "Coastwise Trade," p. 234.

[67] Shepherd and Williamson, appendix II, pp. 808–9.

[68] Ibid., p. 804.

produced molasses, sugar, and rum seem in fact to have contributed significantly to averting the alleged Malthusian crisis of late colonial New England.

Trade with the slave plantation economies of the Caribbean seems to have been a major factor, both directly and indirectly, in stimulating and sustaining economic expansion and rising per capita incomes in New England in the quarter-century that culminated in the Revolutionary War. However, one question remains: Although New England's prosperity in this quarter-century was part of an Atlantic-wide economic expansion based on growing trade between free-labor societies and slave-based colonies, why did New England's trade with the Caribbean grow relative to that with other overseas areas in this period?

By the mid-eighteenth century, New England's trading network was highly diverse and complex. Changes in the level and pattern of the region's trade were bound to be affected, therefore, by shifts in production and consumption within the various components of the whole north Atlantic economy.[69] A detailed investigation of these changes would necessitate a separate chapter. But a brief survey of price trends shows that, compared with the previous quarter-century, the period from 1750 to 1775 was marked by a movement in the terms of trade between the northern mainland colonies and the West Indies that was distinctly favorable to the former. In particular, the prices of basic foodstuffs, notably grains, and timber products rose quite appreciably after 1750, whereas the price of molasses, though not of sugar, remained relatively stable or even fell. Thus, as Pares reminds us, whereas a bushel of wheat at Boston was exchanged for two to three and a half gallons of molasses before 1748, by the early 1770s it fetched five gallons or even more.[70] As far as mainland merchants were concerned, wheat was a minor product in trade with the Caribbean, but trends in wheat prices after 1750 broadly mirrored those of certain other goods that figured much more prominently in New England's dealings with the sugar islands. These included beef and

---

[69] Changes in consumption and production in this period were undoubtedly determined primarily by the private sector, but the impact of government spending should not perhaps be totally ignored; see J. Gwyn, "British Government Spending and the North American Colonies 1740–1775," in P. Marshall and G. Williams (eds.), *The British Atlantic Empire before the American Revolution* (London, 1980), pp. 74–84.

[70] R. Pares, *Yankees and Creoles: The Trade between North America and the West Indies Before the American Revolution* (Cambridge, Mass., 1956), p. 129. Similar movements in the prices of flour, molasses, and rum may be observed at Philadelphia: A. Bezanson, R. D. Gray, and M. Hussey, *Prices in Colonial Pennsylvania* (Philadelphia, 1935), pp. 212–14.

pork, as well as hogshead and barrel staves. The prices of all these products were noticeably higher in the third quarter of the century than earlier.[71] Pares himself sought to explain the movement of wheat and molasses price relativities largely by reference to variations in the rate of growth of production of goods on the continent and in the sugar islands in the Caribbean, arguing that the depreciation of West Indian products such as molasses in terms of grains from the late 1740s on was perhaps attributable to "the ever-increasing intercourse between British North America and the French sugar colonies, which provided new markets for northern produce and new supplies of sugar and molasses."[72]

In focusing on the illicit trade between the northern colonies and the French sugar islands, Pares undoubtedly drew attention to a key factor in promoting New England prosperity after 1750.[73] But more recent studies suggest that his analysis of movements in price relativities was probably incomplete. In particular, it seems that the climb in grain prices throughout the north Atlantic in the quarter-century before 1775 may also have been influenced by the growth of grain and flour exports from the mid-Atlantic colonies to New England and Europe, with exports to the latter being triggered by Britain's decline as a major grain exporter from the late 1750s on.[74]

Although the explanation of the shift in the terms of trade between North America and the West Indies was more complex than Pares assumed, the improvement in the mainland's terms of trade was surely a powerful encouragement to greater commerce with the Caribbean in general and the French colonies in particular during the generation before the Revolution. The latter was, of course, a source of mounting political conflict with Britain. But as Pares himself concluded, trade with the sugar islands, legal or otherwise, "helped to

[71] For price evidence see Bezanson et al., pp. 98–9, 121–3.

[72] Pares, p. 129.

[73] Figures provided by Goebel show that exports from Martinique and Mole St. Nicholas, St. Domingue, to the British North American mainland colonies amounted to about 5.7 million livres (or £240,000) in 1768 and 2.2 million livres (or £95,000) in 1769. These figures exclude exports from Guadeloupe, which in 1765–6, at least, averaged over 1.2 million livres (£50,000) a year. Comparing these figures with Shepherd and Walton's, the French islands may have supplied in some years almost one-half of the imports into British North America from the Caribbean. It appears that New England ships handled a substantial part of this trade. See D. B. Goebel, "The 'New England Trade' and the French West Indies, 1763–1774: A Study in Trade Policies," *William and Mary Quarterly*, third series, Vol. 20 (1963), pp. 352–3, 366, 369; Shepherd and Walton, p. 230.

[74] On changes in Britain's grain trade, see A. H. John, "English Agricultural Improvement and Grain Exports, 1660–1765," in D. C. Coleman and A. H. John (eds.), *Trade, Government and Economy in Pre-Industrial England* (London, 1972), pp. 45–67.

keep the wheels of American commerce turning" and, in addition,
"made an original and independent contribution to the formation of
American capital."[75] The indications are that for no group of North
American colonists were such claims more relevant than for the residents of New England after 1750. For them, West Indian products
and trade not only provided the benefits described by Pares; they also
provided the means to pay for essential food imports from the neighboring mainland colonists.

III

In his autobiography published in 1845, Frederick Douglass described
his escape from slavery in Maryland in 1838 and his flight to New
Bedford, Massachusetts. He expressed surprise "at the general appearance of things" in the New England seaport; he was particularly
struck by "the strongest proofs of wealth" he found there.[76] He noted
"ships of the finest model"; "granite warehouses of the widest dimensions, stowed to their utmost with the necessaries and comforts
of life"; and "splendid churches, beautiful dwellings, and finely-
cultivated gardens." All this, he argued, evinced "an amount of
wealth, comfort, taste, and refinement, such as I had never seen in
any part of slaveholding Maryland."

Douglass's surprise at the discovery of such wealth in New Bedford
reflected, as he himself admitted, the fact that, as a slave, he had
"somehow imbibed the opinion that, in the absence of slaves, there
could be no wealth, and very little refinement." As "northern people
owned no slaves," he had naturally believed that "they were about
upon a level with the non-slaveholding population of the south."
Seeing the latter as "exceedingly poor," he expected to encounter in
the north "a rough, hard-handed, and uncultivated population, living
in the most Spartan-like simplicity, knowing nothing of the ease,
luxury, pomp, and grandeur of southern slaveholders." Life in mid-
nineteenth-century New Bedford clearly contradicted Douglass's expectations and seemed to offer convincing evidence that wealth
accumulation without slavery was not impossible.

However, to infer from Douglass's description of New Bedford, a
seaport grown rich on whaling, that wealth accumulation in New
England in general was historically unconnected with slavery would

---

[75] Pares, pp. 161, 163.
[76] F. Douglass, *Narrative of the Life of Frederick Douglass, an American Slave: Written by Himself* (New York, 1968 Signet edition), p. 115. All other quotations from Douglass are from the same volume, pp. 115–16.

be misleading. Two qualifications to Douglass's remarks need to be made. First, though slave owning had effectively disappeared in New England by the time of Douglass's arrival there, blacks, most of them slaves, had constituted a small segment of the region's population throughout most of its earlier history. Available figures suggest, in fact, that blacks composed some 3% of New England's population on the eve of the Revolution.[77] Furthermore, the ownership of slaves in certain parts of New England was quite widespread; in 1774, for instance, some 14% of households in Rhode Island contained at least one slave, reflecting, as one historian has recently claimed, "a substantial commitment to the institution" of slavery in the colony.[78] This commitment was reinforced by the fact that the richer, commercial, and politically dominant sections of society tended to own disproportionate numbers of slaves. Slave ownership may have been a much weaker source of wealth accumulation in New England than elsewhere on the mainland, but wealth and slaveholding were still quite regular companions in the region in the late colonial period.

A second, and more important, point is that many of the wealthy in prerevolutionary New England, whether slaveowners or not, derived significant portions of their wealth, directly or indirectly, from trade with slave-based economies such as the Caribbean sugar islands. This chapter has argued in fact that the expanding trade with the West Indies was the pivot on which New England trade developed during the third quarter of the eighteenth century, and that this, in turn, was a major factor in the resurgence of general economic activity and wealth accumulation in the region in that period. Moreover, it appears that the benefits that New Englanders derived from greater commerce with the sugar islands were not confined to the twenty-five years preceding the War of Independence. Recent studies have shown that although independence triggered the development of trade with new areas overseas, such as the East Indies, it was the slave economies of the European powers in the Caribbean and South America that continued to exercise the most powerful influence over New England's trade in the decades immediately after 1783. Indeed, it appears that reviving trade with the Caribbean after the war allowed most New England states to achieve higher per capita exports than they had attained before 1776 and to recover more rapidly from the war's effects than most other parts of the newly formed United

---

[77] J. Potter, "Demographic Development and Family Structure," in Greene and Pole, p. 138.

[78] L. P. Masur, "Slavery in Eighteenth-Century Rhode Island: Evidence from the Census of 1774," *Slavery and Abolition*, Vol. 6 (1985), pp. 140–2.

States.[79] New England may never have been a slave society in the conventional sense of the term. But trade with slave-based economies, whether within or outside the British Empire, evidently played a far more significant role in promoting the growth of wealth in late colonial and early national New England than Frederick Douglass's impressions of New Bedford and some historians' studies of the region's eighteenth-century trade led them to believe.

[79] G. C. Bjork, *Stagnation and Growth in the American Economy, 1784–92* (New York, 1985), pp. 31–7, 86–9. Bjork's evidence is largely confined to Massachusetts; for evidence on trade levels and per capita exports for other New England states after 1783, see J. F. Shepherd and G. M. Walton, "Economic Change After the American Revolution: Pre- and Post-War Comparisons of Maritime Shipping and Trade," *Explorations in Economic History*, Vol. 13 (1976), p. 413; Shepherd, pp. 25–9. A further boost to New England trade with slave-based economies in the New World came after 1793, when with the outbreak of war in Europe, North Americans became major carriers of goods between the European powers and their colonies in America. D. C. North, *Economic Growth of the United States, 1790–1860* (New York, 1962), pp. 38–45.

CHAPTER 11

Economic aspects of the growth of slavery in the seventeenth-century Chesapeake

DAVID W. GALENSON

THE 169 years that elapsed between the establishment of the first successful English settlement in North America and the declaration by the American settlers of their independence from Great Britain witnessed many dramatic changes and momentous developments in the colonies that stretched from the Chesapeake Bay to the South. The harsh demographic regime of the early settlements, which caused negative rates of natural increase in the Chesapeake during much of the seventeenth century, was transformed over time, eventually producing rapid population growth in the southern colonies and life expectancies as great as those of the English population of the day.[1] Material life in the early southern colonies was meager; even well-to-do planters in the mid-seventeenth century lived in crude wooden houses with plain furnishings and few luxuries. However, the next

I am grateful to Bernard Bailyn, Stanley Engerman, Joseph Ferrie, Robert Fogel, Robert Gallman, Farley Grubb, Peter Hill, Allan Kulikoff, Daniel Levy, Russell Menard, Jacob Price, Barbara Solow, Theodore Schultz, Daniel Scott Smith, Peter Temin, and Lorena Walsh for discussions of the issues treated in this chapter and comments on an earlier draft. Earlier versions were presented to seminars at the Murphy Institute of Political Economy of Tulane University, and the University of Chicago. Financial support was provided by a grant from the Alfred P. Sloan Foundation.
[1] On the early mortality, see Carville V. Earle, "Environment, Disease, and Mortality in Early Virginia," in Thad W. Tate and David L. Ammerman (eds.), *The Chesapeake in the Seventeenth Century: Essays on Anglo-American Society* (Chapel Hill, N.C., 1979), pp. 96–125, and Lorena S. Walsh and Russell R. Menard, "Death in the Chesapeake: Two Life Tables for Men in Early Colonial Maryland," *Maryland Historical Magazine*, Vol. 69, No. 2 (1974), pp. 211–27. On subsequent improvement, see Jim Potter, "Demographic Development and Family Structure," in Jack P. Greene and J. R. Pole (eds.), *Colonial British America: Essays in the New History of the Early Modern Era* (Baltimore, 1984), pp. 123–56, and Daniel S. Levy, "The Life Expectancies of Colonial Maryland Legislators," *Historical Methods*, Vol. 20, No. 1 (1987), pp. 17–28.

century was quite different; their counterparts in the late eighteenth century lived in elegant brick houses and enjoyed such luxuries as imported furniture and tableware.[2] From a position of support for the English monarchy in the early colonial period, the elite of the southern colonies in the late eighteenth century produced a group of men – Washington, Jefferson, Monroe, Madison, and others – who became the leaders of the American republican movement that opposed the monarchy.[3] And these were only a few of the more prominent elements of the process by which a few struggling colonial settlements evolved into the wealthiest region of what would be a powerful new nation.

Yet of all the changes that occurred in the southern colonies of mainland British America, perhaps none was more important for both its impact on the conditions of life in the region at the time and its implications for the future than the growth of slavery. For this reason, the early history of slavery in the southern colonies has received considerable attention from historians. Recently some elements of a convincing economic explanation for the growth of slavery have emerged. This explanation remains incomplete in some respects, however. This chapter considers some significant questions that have not yet been addressed and extends the scope of the answers that have been offered to some others.

The Chesapeake Bay colonies were one of the major regions of colonial America. Their experience offers us the opportunity to trace in detail the process by which variation in the streams of voluntary and coerced labor produced fundamental changes in the social and economic organization of the colonies. As Barbara Solow stresses, the task is of the first importance, for this is clearly one of the central issues of the American past.[4]

WHY DID THEY WAIT SO LONG?

The first region in mainland British America to adopt slavery on a large scale was the area around the Chesapeake Bay, and as a result, that area has been intensively studied by social and economic historians. These historians' interest in this episode has also been stim-

---

[2] Compare Gloria L. Main, *Tobacco Colony: Life in Early Maryland, 1650–1720* (Princeton, N.J., 1982), chaps. 2, 4, and 6, with Alice Hanson Jones, *Wealth of a Nation to Be: The American Colonies on the Eve of the Revolution* (New York, 1980), chaps. 6 and 9.

[3] On the historiography of the evolution, see John M. Murrin, "Political Development," in Greene and Pole, pp. 408–56.

[4] Barbara L. Solow, "Slavery and Colonization" (Chapter 1, this volume).

ulated by the substantial lag in time between the rise of a staple crop to domination of the Chesapeake's economy and the rapid growth of slavery: Although Virginians began to concentrate on growing tobacco during the 1620s, slaves did not become their primary source of bound labor until after 1680. In 1975 Edmund Morgan raised a question about this experience: "Why . . . did Virginians not furnish themselves with slaves as soon as they began to grow tobacco? Why did they wait so long?"[5]

Research published since Morgan's inquiry has revealed that important changes in the conditions of supply of both English indentured servants and African slaves occurred during the 1680s, and that together these changes caused the majority of the Chesapeake's bound labor force to shift from white to black. These discoveries have made a major contribution to our understanding of colonial history by identifying the economic forces responsible for the most dramatic surge in the growth of slavery in the Chesapeake region. Yet the resulting concentration on the final two decades of the seventeenth century has caused the relative neglect of another intriguing issue: the more gradual growth of slavery during the two decades before 1680. For although slaves came to dominate the Chesapeake's bound labor force only after 1680, they were already present in significant numbers earlier. Thus, for example, in 1680 slaves made up 37% of the bound laborers on Maryland's lower Western Shore.[6] This level

---

[5] Edmund S. Morgan, *American Slavery, American Freedom: The Ordeal of Colonial Virginia* (New York, 1975), p. 297. For a discussion of the answer he suggests in *ibid.*, pp. 297–9, see David W. Galenson, *White Servitude in Colonial America: An Economic Analysis* (Cambridge, 1981), pp. 152, 266.

[6] Russell Menard, "From Servants to Slaves: The Transformation of the Chesapeake Labor System," *Southern Studies*, Vol. XVI, No. 4 (1977), p. 369. The growth of slavery relative to servitude did not occur at precisely the same time and at the same rate everywhere in the Chesapeake. The following evidence on the share of slaves among all bound workers listed in probate inventories in selected locations can be drawn from *ibid.*, pp. 360–1:

Year	Lower Western Shore, Maryland	All Maryland	York County, Virginia
1674–9	27%	20%	34%
1680–4	39	42	34
1685–9	35	39	79
1690–4	69	78	93
1695–9	61	75	98

This evidence shows that slaves made up one-third or less of bound labor during the 1670s, with generally higher shares during the 1680s and still higher shares during the 1690s. The most obvious differences are the earlier sharp increase in the share

had been reached after two decades of sustained growth in the area's slave population, from 8% of the bound labor force in 1660 to 16% in 1665 and to 23% in 1675. Although less dramatic than the years after 1680 because of the lesser quantitative importance of slaves in the Chesapeake's labor force, this earlier growth is nonetheless of considerable interest. Many attitudes and practices involving the use of slaves in the Chesapeake originated in this earlier period. Furthermore, it was during this time that Chesapeake planters first gained access to a supply of slaves directly from Africa. The causes of the gradual growth of slavery in the decades prior to 1680, and of the timing of the establishment of a transatlantic slave trade from West Africa to the Chesapeake, constitute a significant problem that remains to be explored.

An early expression of interest by Chesapeake planters in the purchase of African slaves appeared in a law enacted by Virginia's Assembly in 1660. The law provided that Dutch and other foreign traders were to pay a duty of ten shillings per hogshead on all tobacco they carried from Virginia, with one exception:

... *Allwaies provided,* That if the said Dutch or other forreiners shall import any negro slaves, They the said Dutch or others shall, for the tobacco really produced by the sale of the said negro, pay only the impost of two shillings per hogshead, the like being paid by our owne nation.[7]

This act does not appear to have succeeded in promoting the delivery of slaves to the Chesapeake, but the region's planters' interest in slaves continued. A revealing expression of this interest appears in a letter written in 1664 by Maryland's Governor Calvert to his father, Lord Baltimore, in England. The letter indicates that Lord Baltimore had made inquiries about the prices the newly chartered Company of Royal Adventurers into Africa would require to contract for ship-

---

of slaves in York County than in Maryland, during the late 1680s, and the continuing growth of slave shares to higher levels in York County than in Maryland during the 1690s. For a discussion of the possible sources of these differences, see ibid., pp. 382–5. For the purposes of this investigation, however, the significant feature of this evidence is that all the areas demonstrate relatively low shares of slaves before 1680, with slaves rising to much higher shares in the course of the following two decades.

[7] William Waller Hening (ed.), *The Statutes at Large: Being a Collection of all the Laws of Virginia,* (New York, 1823), Vol. 1, p. 540; also see Wesley Frank Craven, *White, Red, and Black: The Seventeenth-Century Virginian* (Charlottesville, Va., 1971), p. 92, and Robert McColley, "Slavery in Virginia, 1619–1660: A Reexamination," in R. Abzug and S. Maizlish (eds.), *New Perspectives on Race and Slavery: Essays in Honor of Kenneth M. Stampp* (Lexington, Ky., 1986), p. 20.

ments of slaves to the Chesapeake and expresses his son's disappointed response to the information:

I have endeavored to see if I could find as many responsable men that would engage to take a 100 or 200 neigros every yeare from the Royall Company at that rate mentioned in yr. Lopps [Lordship's] letter but I find wee are nott men of estates good enough to undertake such a businesse, but could wish wee were for wee are naturally inclin'd to love neigros if our purses would endure it.[8]

Calvert's letter leaves little doubt that in 1664 slave prices were too high to enable him and his fellow planters to guarantee a market for even one small shipload a year in order to establish a direct trade in slaves from Africa to the Chesapeake. The precise timing of the eventual establishment of this trade is not known with certainty. It is known, however, that it had begun by 1674, as in that year the Royal African Company scheduled two ships to carry 650 slaves to the Chesapeake. Another two shipments occurred in the following year, and a steady transatlantic trade in slaves to the Chesapeake appears to have continued thereafter.[9] The forces that permitted this initial establishment of the slave trade to the Chesapeake have never fully been explored. In part, as noted earlier, this has been because historians have tended to focus their attention on the more dramatic period that followed, during the final two decades of the seventeenth century, which witnessed the large-scale adoption of slavery in the region. Yet the origins of the transatlantic slave trade to the Chesapeake are nonetheless of interest, for they appear to hold the key to understanding the necessary preconditions for the later growth of slavery in the region.

In 1664, the Chesapeake's planters were "nott men of estates good enough" to purchase 100 slaves a year; a decade later, apparently, they regularly bought considerably more than that number. Examination of some obvious variables that might have been expected to affect the planters' demand for slaves does not reveal evidence of any significant movement in this period that would have produced this change. The planters' wealth apparently changed little: One study found that the mean wealth of decedents on Maryland's lower West-

---

[8] Maryland Historical Society, *The Calvert Papers*, Peabody Publication Fund, No. 28 (Baltimore, 1889), p. 249.

[9] Menard, p. 366. Records of cargoes brought to the Chesapeake by the Royal African Company during the 1670s have not been found, so it is not possible to establish the numbers of slaves delivered with precision. Menard concludes that "it is almost certain that the Company delivered at least 500 slaves to the Chesapeake between 1674 and 1679, and the number may have been well over 1000."

ern Shore was no higher in the 1670s than during the preceding decade.[10] Nor does it appear that the price of slaves changed significantly; although evidence on slave prices in the Chesapeake is lacking, it is known that slave prices in the English West Indies did not fall – and may have increased moderately – in the ten years after 1664.[11] The cost of indentured servants, the alternative source of bound labor, did not rise from the mid–1660s to the mid–1670s.[12] Nor was there any significant change in the composition or price of the Chesapeake's output, or in the techniques of its production, that might have prompted an increase in the demand for slaves.[13]

Yet a change did take place in the Chesapeake in the course of the later 1660s and early 1670s that may have had a major effect on the demand of the region's planters for slaves. This took the form of a series of laws that served to define the institution of slavery by clarifying the extent of the property rights of masters in bound black workers. Winthrop Jordan has concluded that the practice of slavery existed in the Chesapeake at least as early as 1640.[14] Yet statutory recognition of slavery lagged behind practice, and it was not until 1661 that a Virginia law referred to the fact that some blacks were held for lifetime service.[15] In 1664, Maryland's Assembly passed "An Act Concerning Negroes & Other Slaves," which stated that "all Negroes or other slaves already within the Province And all Negroes and other slaves to be hereafter imported into the Province shall serve Durante Vita."[16]

Unsettled questions nonetheless remained, however, concerning

[10] Russell R. Menard, P. M. G. Harris, and Lois Green Carr, "Opportunity and Inequality: The Distribution of Wealth on the Lower Western Shore of Maryland, 1638–1705," *Maryland Historical Magazine*, Vol. 69, No. 2 (1974), Table 1, p. 173.

[11] David W. Galenson, *Traders, Planters, and Slaves: Market Behavior in Early English America* (Cambridge, 1986), pp. 66–7.

[12] Russell R. Menard, "Economy and Society in Early Colonial Maryland" (unpublished Ph.D. dissertation, University of Iowa, 1975), p. 342.

[13] Tobacco prices were generally lower in the 1670s than during the preceding decade; Menard, "Farm Prices of Maryland Tobacco, 1659–1710," *Maryland Historical Magazine*, Vol. LXVIII (1973), pp. 80–5.

[14] Winthrop D. Jordan, "Modern Tensions and the Origins of American Slavery," *Journal of Southern History*, Vol. XXVIII, No. 1 (1962), pp. 18–30; idem., *White Over Black: American Attitudes Toward the Negro, 1550–1812* (Baltimore, 1969), pp. 73–5.

[15] Hening, Vol. 2, p. 26; Jordan, *White Over Black*, p. 81.

[16] William Hand Browne et. al. (eds.), *Archives of Maryland* (Baltimore, 1883), Vol. 1, p. 533. The act further specified that the children of slaves would also be slaves.

For a listing of the groups the colonists considered eligible for slavery, see footnote 23. Concerning whites, Abbot Emerson Smith's statement that "there was never any such thing as perpetual slavery for any white man in any English colony" remains authoritative: *Colonists in Bondage: White Servitude and Convict Labor in America, 1607–1776* (Chapel Hill, N.C., 1947), p. 171.

the absoluteness of property rights in slaves in the Chesapeake. In Virginia in 1656, for example, Elizabeth Key, the illegitimate daughter of a slave woman, had successfully sued for her freedom from slavery on grounds that included the fact that she had been baptized.[17] In 1667, the Virginia Assembly eliminated this possibility in "An act declaring that baptisme of slaves doth not exempt them from bondage":

Whereas some doubts have risen whether children that are slaves by birth, and by the charity and piety of their owners made pertakers of the blessed sacrament of baptisme, should by vertue of their baptisme be made free; *It is enacted*... that the conferring of baptisme doth not alter the condition of the person as to his bondage or ffreedome; that diverse masters, ffreed from this doubt, may more carefully endeavour the propagation of christianity by permitting children, though slaves, or those of greater growth if capable to be admitted to that sacrament.[18]

Although this act was intended to encourage masters to have their slaves baptized, its language clearly indicates that at least some planters feared that baptism of a slave might destroy their property rights in the worker.[19] The desire of legislators to stimulate planters' demand for slaves by guaranteeing that baptism would not free their workers was made explicit in the very title of the parallel law enacted by the Maryland Assembly in 1671: "An Act for the Encourageing the Importacon of Negroes and Slaves into this Province." The act stated the assembly's concern and its resolution:

---

[17] Warren M. Billings, "The Cases of Fernando and Elizabeth Key: A Note on the Status of Blacks in Seventeenth-Century Virginia," *William and Mary Quarterly,* third series, Vol. XXX, No. 3 (July 1973), pp. 467–74; for the surviving records of this case, see Billings (ed.), *The Old Dominion in the Seventeenth Century: A Documentary History of Virginia, 1606–1689* (Chapel Hill, N.C., 1975), pp. 165–9. Twelve years earlier, in 1644, a mulatto named Manuel, who had been purchased "as a Slave for Ever," was "by the Assembly adjudged no Slave and but to Serve as other Christian servants do and was freed in September 1665": *Virginia Magazine of History and Biography,* Vol. XVII, No. 3 (July, 1909), p. 232; for discussion see Helen Tunnicliff Catterall (ed.), *Judicial Cases Concerning American Slavery and the Negro* (Washington, D.C., 1926), Vol. 1, pp. 58–9.

[18] Hening, Vol. 2, p. 260; also see A. Leon Higginbotham, Jr., *In the Matter of Color: Race and the American Legal Process, The Colonial Period* (Oxford, 1978), pp. 36–7; Joseph Boskin, *Into Slavery: Racial Decisions in the Virginia Colony* (Philadelphia, 1976), p. 45.

[19] This fear apparently stemmed from a belief that under English law baptism would result in freedom from slavery; Catterall, Vol. 1, p. 55; also see William Darrell Stump, "The English View Negro Slavery, 1660–1780" (unpublished Ph.D. dissertation, University of Missouri, 1962), pp. 108–14; Paul C. Palmer, "Servant Into Slave: The Evolution of the Legal Status of the Negro Laborer in Colonial Virginia," *South Atlantic Quarterly,* Vol. LXV, No. 3 (1966), pp. 360–1. Billings speculates that a proliferation of suits by blacks may have led to the Virginia act of 1667: "The Cases of Fernando and Elizabeth Key," pp. 470–1.

Whereas Severall of the good People of this Province have been discouraged
to import into or purchase within this Province any Negroes or other Slaves
. . . upon a mistake and ungrounded apprehension that by becomeing Christians they and the Issues of their bodies are actually manumited and made
free from their servitude and bondage be itt declared and Enacted . . . That
where any Negro . . . Slave being in Servitude or bondage is . . . or shall become Christian . . . the same is not . . . to amount to a manumicon. . . . [20]

The extension of the property rights of masters in slaves did not
stop with these laws. Within two years of its treatment of the relation
between slavery and baptism, Virginia's Assembly extended masters'
property rights in their black workers to their eventual limits in a law
of 1669 called simply "An act about the casuall killing of slaves." The
act declared:

if any slave resist his master . . . and by the extremity of the correction should
chance to die, that his death shall not be accompted ffelony, but the master
. . . be acquit from molestation, since it cannot be presumed that prepensed
malice (which alone makes murther ffelony) should induce any man to destroy his owne estate.[21]

In 1664, Charles Calvert had found that it was the high price of
slaves, rather than any skepticism about their capacity for labor, that
prevented him and his fellow planters from being able to guarantee
a market for one shipload a year. In 1664, however, the unwillingness
of some Chesapeake planters to meet that high price might have
resulted from uncertainty about their ability to hold the Africans in
servitude for life. No such uncertainty existed in Barbados, the major
destination for Africans in English America at the time, where thousands of slaves arrived annually to grow sugar on great plantations.
Nearly three decades earlier, in 1636, that colony's Council had declared that "Negroes and Indians, that came here to be sold, should
serve for Life, unless a Contract was before made to the contrary,"
and this act appears subsequently to have been enforced without
exceptions.[22] Although Maryland's "Act Concerning Negroes & Other
Slaves," quoted earlier, gave an assurance of this kind to that colony's
planters in 1664, it was not until 1670 that Virginia's legislature produced such a guarantee when it declared that "all servants not being
christians imported into this colony by shipping shalbe slaves for their

---

[20] Browne, Vol. 2, p. 272.
[21] Hening, Vol. 2, p. 270; also see Higginbotham, p. 36.
[22] Richard S. Dunn, *Sugar and Slaves: The Rise of the Planter Class in the English West
Indies, 1624–1713* (New York, 1973), p. 228.

lives."[23] An important part of the answer to the question of why Chesapeake planters hesitated to invest heavily in slaves during the 1660s may be that during that decade they lacked the statutory assurance concerning the security of their investments that their counterparts in Barbados had received thirty years earlier.[24]

A possible objection to this conclusion is that the causation suggested here could be the reverse of the truth: Rather than the extension of the legal definition of property rights stimulating the growth of

[23] The quotation is from Hening, Vol. 2, p. 283. The title of this act as given by Hening was "What tyme Indians to serve." Yet the use of "servants" rather than "Indians" in the passage quoted would appear significant, and it would equally appear applicable to Africans imported into the colony.

Interestingly, even this act of 1670 left a gap that apparently became troublesome. In 1682, the Virginia Assembly declared the earlier act void, noting the problem raised by its application to the status of "negroes, moores, mollatoes and others" who had been purchased as slaves but baptized as Christians sometime prior to their importation into Virginia; at that time, the owner could "sell him here for noe longer time then the English or other christians are to serve, to the great losse and damage of such master or owner, and to the great discouragement of bringing in such slaves for the future." The new act eliminated this loophole, declaring that all servants, "whether Negroes, Moors, Mollattoes or Indians, who and whose parentage and native country are not christian at the time of their first purchase of such servant by some christian, although afterwards, and before such their importation and bringing into this country, they shall be converted to the christian faith . . . shall be adjudged, deemed and taken to be slaves to all intents and purposes": Hening, Vol. 2, pp. 490–2.

[24] It might be asked why legislative action would be taken to encourage planters to purchase slaves. In part, of course, legislators may have wanted to protect their own (actual or potential) investments in slaves, and so supported laws to do this. Yet this might not fully explain a statement like that of Governor Calvert, quoted earlier: Since Calvert was probably sufficiently wealthy that his own economic status would not be greatly jeopardized by the uncertainties surrounding slaves as property, his complaint of 1664 appears to have been motivated by a desire for his fellow planters to buy slaves. To the extent that legislators were buying slaves, why would they have supported laws that would induce other planters to adopt this cheaper form of labor and potentially reduce their own profits? Apart from a possible desire to act for the good of the colonists even at their own expense, the answer may lie in a perceived externality. Planters already committed to the use of slaves may have believed that they would gain access to a supply of slaves of higher quality, and at lower cost, if the Chesapeake could gain access to the direct transatlantic trade from Africa. That an increase in demand by their fellow planters was necessary to gain this access is indicated by Calvert's statement. Although this argument is speculative in the absence of testimony concerning the motivations of Chesapeake legislators of the 1660s, it might be noted that planters in the West Indies strongly believed that the quality of the slaves available to them was higher when they received shipments directly from Africa, as opposed to indirect shipments through other colonies; for example, see Galenson, Traders, Planters, and Slaves, pp. 37, 183–4. Another motive of wealthy legislators in strengthening statutory property rights in slaves could have been a desire to increase the cooperation of poorer planters, who lacked a direct economic interest in the institution, in protecting the property of slave owners. By clarifying the legal basis of slavery, the legislators might have intended to increase its perceived legitimacy, and consequently to increase the willingness of poorer planters to help in such activities as capturing runaways.

slavery, the legislation of the 1660s and 1670s could have been merely a symptom of the increasing quantitative importance of blacks in the Chesapeake, and may have constituted no more than a recognition of practices that were already firmly established.[25] Yet Elizabeth Key's success in gaining her freedom from slavery in 1656 would appear to argue against the view that property rights in slaves were secure in practice even before the legislative actions. That Maryland's act of 1664 "Concerning Negroes & Other Slaves" was a response to a real need is furthermore suggested by the description of its origin contained in the journal of the colony's upper house for Monday, September 19, 1664:

Then came a Member from the lower house with this following paper (vizt) Itt is desired by the lower house that the upper house would be pleased to draw up an Act obligeing negros to serve durante vita they thinking it very necessary for the prevencon of the damage Masters of such Slaves may susteyne by such Slaves pretending to be Christned And soe pleade the lawe of England.[26]

The upper house of the legislature drafted the act before adjorning the same day, and within the week it had been approved by both houses and enacted as law. A similar indication of legislative action responding to need is afforded by the reference of the preamble to Virginia's law of 1667 to the doubts that had arisen about the effects of baptism on slave status. Interestingly, also, the passage of Virginia's law concerning baptism occurred in September 1667, just a month after a slave identified only as Fernando had sued for his freedom at the August sitting of the Lower Norfolk County Court, claiming that "hee was a Christian and had been severall yeares in England." Fernando's suit was dismissed by that court, but he appealed that decision to the General Court; the proximity of the act to his suit further

---

[25] For example this appears to be the position taken by the Handlins in an influential paper on the origins of slavery. They wrote of the seventeenth-century Chesapeake that "by mid-century the servitude of Negroes seems generally lengthier that that of whites; and thereafter the consciousness dawns that the Blacks will toil for the whole of their lives, not through any particular concern with their status but simply by contrast with those whose years of labor are limited by statute. The legal position of the Negro is, however, still uncertain; it takes legislative action to settle that." They then proceeded to summarize the laws discussed earlier: Oscar Handlin and Mary F. Handlin, "Origins of the Southern Labor System," *William and Mary Quarterly*, third series, Vol. VII, No. 2 (1950), pp. 211–13.

[26] Browne, Vol. 1, p. 526; also see Catterall, Vol. 4, p. 1, who notes in regard to this act that "in 1772 England's lack of a positive law to support slavery justified Lord Mansfield in discharging Somerset."

suggests that the doubts referred to in the act's preamble might have been a serious cause of current concern.[27]

Yet the question of whether the legislation of the late 1660s and early 1670s was a cause or a symptom of the growth of slavery in the region most likely presents a false dichotomy. The two need not have been mutually exclusive, for the legislation might have ratified the practices of some planters while having an independent influence on the actions of others. The argument proposed here is that a number of pieces of evidence point to the conclusion that the latter at least comprised a sizable group. The gradual and piecemeal adoption of the legislation that eventually served to define the property rights of masters in slaves suggests not only that the legal enactment of slavery was less a matter of external example in the Chesapeake than elsewhere, as Winthrop Jordan has suggested, but also that each element of the definition responded to a perceived need of planters otherwise eager to purchase African workers; indeed, as noted earlier, the very language of some of these acts states this directly.[28] The timing of the establishment of the slave trade from Africa to the Chesapeake in the mid–1670s, and the acceleration of the growth of the region's slave population after that time, further point to the likelihood that the increased precision of the legal definition of masters' property rights in slaves of the late 1660s and early 1670s was an important factor in increasing the demand for Africans and making possible the large-scale growth of slavery in the Chesapeake in the following decades.[29]

---

[27] The record of the case appears in Billings, *The Old Dominion in the Seventeenth Century,* p. 169; for discussion see Billings, "The Cases of Fernando and Elizabeth Key," pp. 467–70. Billings notes that "as long as local justices of the peace recognized baptism as a reason for changing a black's status from slave to servant or as a basis for releasing him outright, and as long as unfavorable lower court decisions in such matters could be appealed, there were neither means to forestall such lawsuits nor assurances that a planter could retain his slaves. No matter how the courts decided these cases, the planter sustained losses of time and money. If he lost, he had to pay costs; if he won, the slave could not make restitution" (ibid., pp. 471–2). Thus, until the possibility of such litigation was eliminated, the attractiveness of slaves as a form of bound labor was lessened considerably.

[28] Jordan, *White Over Black,* p. 81. Interestingly, Wesley Frank Craven used precisely the legislative record of the development of slavery to illustrate the considerable independence of individual colonial governments: "The colonial legislators were left remarkably free to settle as they saw fit all questions arising from the presence of the Negro. Indeed, the development of the institution of Negro slavery in the North American colonies has to be viewed as an especially impressive example of the extent to which these communities were self-governing": *The Colonies in Transition, 1660–1713* (New York: Harper & Row, 1968), p. 295.

[29] Russell Menard observed that rapid growth of the slave population on Maryland's lower Western Shore began in the mid-1670s: "The Maryland Slave Population, 1658

DETERMINANTS OF THE RELATIVE COSTS OF
SERVANTS AND SLAVES

As mentioned earlier, recent research has shown that the decisive period in the growth of slavery in the Chesapeake centered on the decade of the 1680s: In Maryland, planters' holdings of bound labor shifted from a ratio of 3.9 indentured servants for each slave in the late 1670s to nearly the reverse, 3.6 slaves for each servant, in the early 1690s.[30] This dramatic change in the composition of the bound labor force appears to have been the result of changes in the conditions of supply of both servants and slaves.

The supply of servants to the Chesapeake appears to have fallen sharply during the 1680s.[31] A number of factors might have contributed to this situation. The 1670s and 1680s may have been a period of some improvement in labor market conditions in England.[32] This would have tended to make Englishmen less likely to emigrate in general, and the available estimates of migration to all the American colonies do suggest declining levels during the 1680s.[33] Yet perhaps more damaging for the Chesapeake was a decline in the attractiveness of the region for those who did migrate. Migration estimates suggest that Maryland and Virginia suffered a much larger reduction in immigration than did the American colonies in general, as the Chesapeake's share of total English migration to America fell from about 40% during the 1660s and 1670s to 25% in the 1680s.[34] An obvious reason for this was the rise of competition from Pennsylvania during the 1680s, as the excitement caused by the opening of that colony, and the liberal land grants that quickly gave it the reputation of being

---

to 1730: A Demographic Profile of Blacks in Four Countries," *William and Mary Quarterly*, third series, Vol. XXXII, No. 1 (1975), p. 30.

[30] Menard, "From Servants to Slaves," p. 360.

[31] Ibid., pp. 362–3.

[32] Ibid., p. 379; Henry Phelps Brown and Sheila V. Hopkins, *A Perspective of Wages and Prices* (London, 1981), p. 30.

[33] Henry A. Gemery, "Emigration From the British Isles to the New World, 1630–1700: Inferences from Colonial Populations," *Research in Economic History*, Vol. 5 (1980), p. 215; Galenson, *White Servitude in Colonial America*, pp. 216–18. For estimates of total net migration from England that also show a decline in this period, see E. A. Wrigley and R. S. Schofield, *The Population History of England, 1541–1871: A Reconstruction* (Cambridge, Mass., 1981), p. 219.

[34] Galenson, *White Servitude in Colonial America*, pp. 216–18. Alternative estimates made by Russell Menard show a smaller decline in the Chesapeake's share of British migration to the Americas, from 43% in the 1670s to 36% in the 1680s and 1690s: "British Migration to the Chesapeake Colonies in the Seventeenth Century" (unpublished paper presented to the Economic History Workshop, University of Chicago, 1980), Table 5.

the best poor man's country, raised its share of the immigration to English America from negligible levels in the 1670s to a quarter of the total in the next decade.[35] By the 1680s, some prospective migrants to the Chesapeake may also have been aware of a trend that has been documented by recent studies, as economic opportunities for poor immigrants to the region deteriorated substantially during the second half of the seventeenth century.[36] This could have led them to avoid the older region and contributed to the shift of migration to Pennsylvania.

The result of the declining supply of indentured servants to the Chesapeake in the 1680s was a considerable increase in their price; probate valuations of male servants with four or more years to serve rose from average levels of £8–10 during the 1670s to £10.5–12 in the 1680s.[37] At the same time, slave prices were falling in English America. The mid–1680s witnessed the lowest point of a secular decline in slave prices in the West Indies that appears to have been the result of a downward trend in world sugar prices that had continued for four decades. With their traditional markets in the sugar colonies depressed, and with no obvious end in sight to the falling slave prices, slave traders appear to have looked for new markets during the 1680s.[38] One result of this was an increased supply of slaves to the Chesapeake, as the decade saw a substantial increase in the number of slaves imported into the region.[39]

---

[35] Galenson, *White Servitude in Colonial America*, pp. 216–18. It is interesting to note that total estimated white migration to Pennsylvania and the Chesapeake together increased from about 15,600 during the 1670s to 18,300 in the following decade. Yet Pennsylvania's share of that total rose from only 4% in the 1670s to one-half in the 1680s. For evidence on servant ownership in early Pennsylvania, see Jean R. Soderlund, *Quakers and Slavery: A Divided Spirit* (Princeton, N.J., 1985), pp. 59–61; on economic opportunity for former indentured servants there, see Sharon V. Salinger, *"To Serve Well and Faithfully": Labor and Indentured Servants in Pennsylvania, 1682–1800* (Cambridge, 1987), chapter 2; also see the review of ibid. by Farley Grubb, *Journal of Economic History*, Vol. XLVIII, No. 3 (1988), pp. 772–4.

[36] Russell R. Menard, "From Servant to Freeholder: Status Mobility and Property Accumulation in Seventeenth-Century Maryland," *William and Mary Quarterly*, third series, Vol. XXX, No. 1 (1973), pp. 37–64; Lois Green Carr and Russell R. Menard, "Immigration and Opportunity: The Freedman in Early Colonial Maryland," in Tate and Ammerman, pp. 206–42; Lorena S. Walsh, "Servitude and Opportunity in Charles County, Maryland, 1658–1705," in Aubrey C. Land, Lois Green Carr, and Edward C. Papenfuse (eds.), *Law, Society, and Politics in Early Maryland* (Baltimore, 1977), pp. 111–33; idem., "Staying Put or Getting Out: Findings for Charles County, Maryland, 1650–1720," *William and Mary Quarterly*, third series, Vol. XLIV, No. 1 (1987), pp. 89–103; John J. McCusker and Russell R. Menard, *The Economy of British America, 1607–1789* (Chapel Hill, N.C., 1985), pp. 137–8.

[37] Menard, "From Servants to Slaves," p. 372.

[38] Galenson, *Traders, Planters, and Slaves*, pp. 64–7.

[39] Menard, "From Servants to Slaves," p. 372; Galenson, *White Servitude in Colonial*

Rising prices for indentured servants and falling prices for slaves therefore combined to produce the rising relative cost of servants that has been used convincingly to explain Chesapeake planters' rapid substitution of slaves for servants during the 1680s.[40] The decline in the supply of servants evidently forced planters to switch to slaves, and the evidence suggests that many planters may initially have done so reluctantly, for the increase of nearly 60% in the purchase price of servants relative to slaves between 1675 and 1690 placed their cost far above past levels. Once the planters had gained experience with slaves, however, their reluctance apparently diminished, for they continued to import large numbers of slaves in the 1690s and subsequent decades in spite of a combination of falling servant prices and rising slave prices that restored the relative prices of the two types of labor to levels that had prevailed in the 1670s.

Evidence on the relative purchase prices of servants and slaves may actually understate the true magnitude of the increase in the relative cost of servant labor to planters that occurred during the 1670s and 1680s. There are two effects that are not captured in these data on prices that would lead to this conclusion. One is the result of possible changes in the quality of the servants over time. If the average productivity of servants arriving in the Chesapeake had declined during the 1670s and 1680s, the trend of observed prices of servants would be biased downward relative to the trend for servants of constant productivity and would therefore understate the true increase in the real cost of servant labor over time. Although the evidence is not conclusive, it is very possible that the 1680s did witness a decline in the average quality of the servants bound for the Chesapeake, for the shortage of servants there may have prompted English merchants to

---

America, p. 217. Although too much confidence should not be placed in the precision of these estimates, it is interesting to note that the estimated increase in black immigration to the Chesapeake between the 1670s and the 1680s, of 5,600, was nearly equal to the estimated decline in white immigration, of 5,800.

[40] For example, see Menard, "From Servants to Slaves," pp. 373–5. A logical qualification of Menard's interpretation of the price evidence might be noted. He writes that "the price of servants rose as the supply declined and blacks replaced whites as the majority among bound laborers in the Chesapeake. This is a strong criticism of the traditional argument [that planters' demand for servants had fallen]: the supply of servants did not fall in response to a decline in planter demand" (ibid., p. 373). Logically, an increase in the price of servants does not imply that the demand for servants did not decline: It implies only that if any decline in demand did occur, it was smaller in magnitude than a concurrent decline in supply. Although not logically necessary, however, it appears likely that Menard's rejection of a decline in the demand for servants is correct. The most telling evidence in favor of this belief is a striking lack of contemporary testimony that would indicate a decline in the desire of planters for servants.

extend their efforts at recruitment among groups of workers previously considered undesirable.[41] Time series evidence for these decades is lacking, but surviving English servant registrations do indicate that a much smaller proportion of servants bound for the Chesapeake during the mid–1680s possessed occupational skills than had been the case three decades earlier.[42] The declining skill level of the average servant would imply that over time planters were receiving less productive workers for the increasingly higher prices.

A second reason why the true relative cost of servants to planters might have been higher than shown in the relative purchase prices follows in part from the discussion earlier in this chapter of the legal status of slaves. For whereas during the 1660s and 1670s masters were increasing their control over their slaves, the same was not true for servants. Servants had many basic legal rights and enjoyed important legal protections. Servants had the right to sue their masters for mistreatment. In an extreme instance in 1663, the court of Charles County, Maryland, freed a servant after summoning his master to explain why the servant "hath bin so ill treated in his hows in so much that the voyce of the People Crieth shame thereat."[43] Although it was not easy for servants to win their liberty, county courts frequently granted some measure of redress in response to their complaints, often ordering that masters improve the diet or clothing they provided their servants.[44] Masters who caused the death of a servant were to be tried for murder "as near as may be to the law of England," and in two well-documented cases in Maryland in 1657 and 1664, the death sentence was imposed on masters convicted of murdering their servants.[45]

Although severe punishments were given to masters for abuse of their servants only in extraordinary cases, minor improvements in the conditions of servants were more commonly ordered by colonial courts, and the threat of suits resulting from the legal rights and protections of servants imposed a constraint on masters in the su-

---

[41] Ibid., p. 380. For a description of the methods by which servants were recruited, see Bernard Bailyn, *Voyagers to the West: A Passage in the Peopling of America on the Eve of the Revolution* (New York, 1986), Chapter 9.

[42] Galenson, *White Servitude in Colonial America*, p. 93.

[43] Browne, Vol. L111 (Baltimore, 1936), pp. 410–11.

[44] Richard B. Morris, *Government and Labor in Early America* (New York, 1946), pp. 484, 488–90, 502–3; Abbot Emerson Smith, *Colonists in Bondage: White Servitude and Convict Labor in America, 1607–1776* (Chapel Hill, N.C., 1947), p. 243; Susie M. Ames, *Studies of the Virginia Eastern Shore in the Seventeenth Century* (Richmond, Va., 1940), pp. 85–6.

[45] Morris, pp. 485–6; Raphael Semmes, *Crime and Punishment in Early Maryland* (Baltimore, 1938), pp. 122–7.

pervision and treatment of their bound white workers that – as seen earlier – was altogether lacking for slaves by the 1670s.[46] Thus in 1705, when the council of Virginia issued an act detailing the legal rights of servants and defining the obligations of masters to them, the act made no mention of parallel rights of slaves; they had none.[47] The full cost of the labor of a bound worker to a planter would include both the initial purchase price of the worker and all costs of maintaining and employing the worker during his service to the planter. The greater rights of servants might have forced masters to treat them with greater care than slaves, thus raising the cost of maintenance and the care taken in supervision.[48] The difference in the legal protections of servants and slaves could therefore have resulted in higher costs for masters in employing servants than slaves, and these would not be apparent simply from consideration of the changing relative purchase prices of the two types of bound worker.

[46] This discussion is not intended to indicate that colonial courts afforded servants complete protection from maltreatment by their masters. As Richard Morris noted, English law was recognized to be one-sided on the subject of labor relations (p. 470), and it would be surprising if colonial court officials had not often favored their fellow planters in disputes with servants; for example, see Ames, pp. 86–7, T. H. Breen and Stephen Innes, *"Myne Owne Ground": Race and Freedom on Virginia's Eastern Shore, 1640–1676* (New York, 1980), pp. 62–3; and Joseph Douglas Deal, "Race and Class in Colonial Virginia: Indians, Englishmen, and Africans on the Eastern Shore During the Seventeenth Century" (unpublished Ph.D. dissertation, University of Rochester, 1981), pp. 122–4. The argument here is rather that the access of servants to the courts gave them an advantage over slaves in the degree of their protection against the abuses of masters, and the evidence provided in the secondary sources cited in footnotes 43–5 suggests that this was a real advantage that would have been evident to colonial planters.

[47] Higginbotham, pp. 53–7; Palmer, pp. 366–8. For a qualification, see Raphael Cassimere, "The Origins and Early Development of Slavery in Maryland, 1633 to 1715" (unpublished Ph.D. dissertation, Lehigh University, 1971), pp. 146–7.

[48] Lois Carr and Lorena Walsh refer to the growing differences in the treatment of servants and slaves in this period: "So long as slaves were few and intermingled with servants, work rules for whites probably also applied to blacks. But once slaves became dominant in the bound labor force, late in the seventeenth century, the experiences of slaves and servants began to diverge. Slaves had no claims to English workers' customary rights to food of reasonable quantity and quality, adequate clothing and shelter, and a certain amount of rest and leisure": "Economic Diversification and Labor Organization in the Chesapeake, 1650–1820," in Stephen Innes, ed., *Work and Labor in Early America* (Chapel Hill, N.C., 1988), p. 157.

Evidence on the relative cost of maintaining servants and slaves is difficult to find. Ralph Gray and Betty Wood have estimated that the annual cost of feeding and clothing servants was substantially higher than for slaves in Georgia about 1740: "The Transition from Indentured to Involuntary Servitude in Colonial Georgia," *Explorations in Economic History*, Vol. 13, No. 4 (1976), pp. 367–8. Although consistent with the argument made here, however, this does not bear on the issue of possible changes in the relative costs of using the two types of bound labor over time.

Table 1. *Percentages of householders who owned servants and slaves by total estate value, lower Western Shore, Maryland, 1658–1705*

Total estate value	1658–9	1660–9	1670–9	1680–9	1690–9	1700–5
£0–19.9						
Servants	0	0	0	2	2	0
Slaves	0	0	0	0	1	2
No. of householders	4	21	82	94	127	63
£20–39.9						
Servants	0	17	28	9	9	9
Slaves	0	2	1	0	0	0
No. of householders	1	46	79	75	107	58
£40–59.9						
Servants	0	61	40	36	8	27
Slaves	0	0	0	2	5	2
No. of householders	1	23	63	50	78	45
£60–99.9						
Servants		74	47	49	30	50
Slaves		5	7	11	9	14
No. of householders	0	19	55	71	46	36
£100–149.9						
Servants	100	88	89	66	69	76
Slaves	0	6	11	9	31	33
No. of householders	1	17	28	35	32	33
£150+						
Servants	100	100	84	88	65	85
Slaves	0	37	38	54	70	72
No. of householders	1	27	91	68	96	78

Source: Probate inventories from Calvert, Charles, St. Mary's, and Prince George's Counties, Maryland.

WEALTH AND THE GROWTH OF SLAVERY IN THE CHESAPEAKE

Recent research has disclosed other interesting features of the early growth of slavery in the Chesapeake that have not been fully explained. One of these concerns the characteristics of the planters who purchased slaves during the early period. Several historians have observed that wealthy planters, the owners of large estates, were the first in the region to hold slaves.[49] This is borne out by Table 1, which

[49] Menard, "From Servants to Slaves," pp. 385–7; Main, pp. 102–3; McColley, p. 18; Deal, pp. 207–8; Bernard Bailyn, *The Peopling of British North America: An Introduction* (New York, 1986), p. 102.

Table 2. *Mean numbers of servants and slaves owned by householders who owned any of the respective type of labor, by total estate value, lower Western Shore, Maryland, 1658–1705*

Total estate value	1658–9	1660–9	1670–9	1680–9	1690–9	1700–5
£0–19.9						
Servants				1	1.5	
Slaves					1	1
£20–39.9						
Servants		1	2	1.1	1.1	1.2
Slaves		1	1			
£40–59.9						
Servants		1.5	1.2	1.2	1.3	1.3
Slaves				1	1.3	1
£60–99.9						
Servants		1.9	2	1.5	1.4	3.2
Slaves		1	1.5	2.4	1.5	1.9
£100–149.9						
Servants	2	2.9	2.5	1.8	1.8	2.1
Slaves		1	1.7	1.8	2.3	2.6
£150+						
Servants	2	4.6	3.6	4.6	2.7	3.7
Slaves		4.3	3.5	5.7	5.9	8.2

Source: See Table 1.

shows that the ratio of estates with slaves to those with servants was positively related to the level of wealth for decedents in four countries on Maryland's lower Western Shore during the second half of the seventeenth century. Table 2 further shows that the average number of slaves held by those decedents who had any also rose with wealth.

Table 3 presents another view of this evidence on labor holdings that further underscores the difference in the behavior of poorer and wealthier planters. This tabulation includes the estates only of those decedents who held at least three servants or one slave, and therefore effectively eliminates the question of whether a planter could afford to own a slave: Virtually all those included in the table had in fact invested an amount in bound labor that was sufficient to buy at least one slave.[50] Table 3 shows that during the 1660s, planters worth less

[50] See the price ratios for servants and slaves in Menard, "From Servants to Slaves," p. 372; also Paul G. E. Clemens, *The Atlantic Economy and Colonial Maryland's Eastern Shore: From Tobacco to Grain* (Ithaca, N.Y., 1980), p. 62. I am grateful to Russell Menard for providing me with abstracts of the probate inventories on which Tables 1–4 are based.

Table 3. *Ratios of servants to slaves on selected estates, by total estate value, lower Western Shore, Maryland, 1660–1705*

Total estate value	1660–9		1670–9		1680–9		1690–9		1700–5	
	n	Ratio	*n*	Ratio	*n*	Ratio	*n*	Ratio	*n*	Ratio
£0–100	8	10.5	12	3.4	11	2.3	12	0.4	9	1.8
101–200	20	14.2	28	9.5	20	2.3	21	0.6	27	1.2
201–400	9	1.9	29	2.1	22	1.5	25	0.7	29	0.8
401–1,000	2	2.8	10	2.1	15	1.7	21	0.3	16	0.5
1,000+	2	1.4	3	0.5	7	1.0	6	0.2	10	0.3

Note: Estates were included in this tabulation only if they contained at least three indentured servants or at least one slave. The ratios were calculated as the total number of servants held by decedents in a given wealth category divided by the total number of slaves held by those decedents.
The entries under *n* for each decade refer to the number of estates tabulated.
Source: See Table 1.

than £200 owned more than 10 times as many servants as slaves, whereas for those worth more than £200 this ratio was less than 3. The difference declined during the 1670s but remained sizable, as the ratio of servants to slaves was over 9 for planters worth £100–200 and again under 3 for those worth more than £200. As slaveholding became more common in the 1680s the difference became smaller, as planters worth less than £200 held just over twice as many servants as slaves, compared with ratios below 2 for those worth more than £200. In the 1690s, planters in all wealth categories held fewer servants than slaves, and the ratio of servants to slaves remained higher for poorer than wealthier planters only because the latter had both increased their slave holdings and reduced their servant holdings over time.

The evidence of Table 3 therefore makes it clear that even when consideration is restricted to those planters capable of owning slaves, during the early stages of the growth of slavery in the Chesapeake poorer planters held slaves in much smaller numbers relative to servants than did their wealthier counterparts. This difference in behavior, which was very marked during the 1660s, declined steadily in the decades that followed; although it had not disappeared completely by the 1690s, that it had become so much smaller by then suggests that for the most part its causes must have been transitory.

Beyond the observation that less wealthy planters could not afford slaves, there has been little detailed inquiry as to why it was the wealthiest planters who substituted slaves for servants earlier than others. If slaves had become a better buy than servants during the 1680s – if the rate of return on the ownership of slaves exceeded that on servants – why didn't all planters with sufficient wealth to own bound laborers attempt to substitute slaves for servants at the same time? There are many possible reasons for this difference; several factors that seem likely to have contributed to it will be discussed here. Although the evidence to determine their relative importance is not currently available, further research can produce evidence that would bear on this issue and improve our understanding of this episode.

One possibility is that the relative profitability of buying slaves varied among purchasers owing to financial conditions. One reason for this could have been differences in access to credit by wealth. Although relatively little is known of the role of credit in the purchase of slaves in the early Chesapeake, it is known that virtually all purchases of slaves in the West Indies at the time involved credit. Each transaction was negotiated individually between buyer and seller, and it seems likely that different interest rates were charged to different buyers, with the lower default risk of wealthier planters resulting in access to credit on better terms.[51] In general, the lower the interest rate, the higher the present value of a longer-lived asset relative to one of shorter life, because more distant services are discounted less heavily. An inverse relationship between interest rates and planters' wealth would therefore have served to make the profitability of purchasing slaves relative to servants an increasing function of the wealth of the purchaser.

The relative profitability of purchasing slaves and servants could also have differed among planters for another reason that involved commercial practices. A recent analysis of the records of a British firm trading in the Chesapeake found that during the 1690s servants were normally bought with tobacco, but slaves were bought with bills of exchange.[52] This meant that servants were available to all purchasers on the same terms, but slaves could most easily be purchased by planters able to draw bills of exchange on accounts with British merchants or by those who could buy bills of exchange. This practice

---

[51] K. G. Davies, *The Royal African Company* (London, 1957), p. 317. The hypothesized difference in interest rates among purchasers is the obvious reason why actual auctions could be held only for cash; for discussion, see Galenson, *Traders, Planters and Slaves*, chapter 4.

[52] Jacob M. Price, "Sheffeild v. Starke: Institutional Experimentation in the London–Maryland Trade c. 1696–1705," *Business History*, Vol. XXVIII, No. 3 (1986), pp. 19–39.

would therefore have given an advantage in purchasing slaves to the larger planters who were more likely to consign tobacco to British merchants.

A second possibility is that even if the expected rates of return to holding servants and slaves had been the same to all planters, considerations of risk might have led less wealthy planters to buy servants. These planters might have chosen to forego the higher average returns from buying slaves in order to reduce the variance of the return from their investments in labor. In the high-mortality environment of the seventeenth-century Chesapeake, less wealthy purchasers of bound labor might have wished to avoid the concentration of a large share of their wealth in one or two slaves, preferring instead to reduce their risk by owning larger numbers of less expensive servants. In contrast, wealthier planters might more easily have afforded to bear the risk of holding slaves, and might therefore more often have opted for the more profitable type of labor.[53]

A third factor that could have led to the earlier purchase of slaves by wealthier planters is possible differences in information. The early growth of slavery in the mainland colonies may have been slowed by planters' doubts about the productivity of African slaves. Such doubts might have been less prevalent among wealthier planters, however, who would generally have been better informed about the successful use of black slaves by English planters in the West Indies. In fact, some very wealthy planters who were among the early large slaveholders in the Chesapeake had migrated there directly from the West Indies. Thomas Notley, for example, arrived in Maryland from Barbados in 1662, and went on to serve as personal attorney to Charles Calvert and to hold a series of political offices, including deputy governor of the colony. At his death in 1679, Notley left an estate that included twenty-nine slaves in addition to several thousand acres of land. Jesse Wharton arrived in Maryland from Barbados in 1670 and, like Notley, held a series of offices that included deputy governor of Maryland; he left eleven slaves as well as more than 3,000 acres at his death in 1676.[54] No systematic study has yet been done of the

---

[53] For a discussion of this point, and variations on the theme, see Darrett B. Rutman and Anita H. Rutman, *A Place in Time: Middlesex County Virginia, 1650–1750*, 2 vols. (New York, 1984), Vol. 1, pp. 180–4.

[54] See the entries for Notley and Wharton in Edward C. Papenfuse, Alan F. Day, David W. Jordan, and Gregory A. Stiverson, *A Biographical Dictionary of the Maryland Legislature, 1635–1789*, 2 vols. (Baltimore, 1985), Vol. 2 pp. 616, 880–1. I am grateful to Russell Menard for these references.

relationship between early large-scale slaveholding in the Chesapeake and connections with the West Indies, but the political prominence of men like Notley and Wharton makes it likely that their examples would have been widely known, particularly among their wealthy associates.

A fourth factor concerns possible variation in planters' attitudes toward the purchase of African slaves as a result of differences in living and working conditions. Smaller planters generally could not afford separate dwellings for their bound workers, and the latter typically lived in the same houses as the planters and their families.[55] In contrast, wealthier planters more often had separate living quarters for their laborers.[56] As a result of this greater physical separation, wealthier planters may have been less reluctant to purchase Africans, who were culturally more alien to them than their own countrymen. Wealthier planters were also more likely to have hired overseers, who would do the work of training and supervising their bound laborers.[57] Because the wealthy were less likely than their poorer counterparts to have to perform these jobs themselves, they may have been less concerned with the problems involved in overcoming language barriers and teaching African slaves farming methods that many English servants already knew.

As noted earlier, the significance of each of these effects remains to be determined through further investigation. They are, of course, not mutually exclusive. It might also be pointed out that all of them could have declined in force over time, leading to the reduction in the difference among wealth categories observed in Table 3. Thus an increase in the importance of slave markets in the Chesapeake could have led to improvements in the efficiency of credit markets for slave purchases and a reduction of interest rate differentials among planters. Improvements in life expectancies in the region in the late seventeenth century could have reduced the riskiness of holding slaves.[58] Information about the productivity of slaves would have diffused to planters at all wealth levels as the region's black population grew. And the barriers of language and skills between colonists and slaves

---

[55] Carr and Menard, p. 228; Lorena Seebach Walsh, "Charles County, Maryland, 1658–1705: A Study of Chesapeake Social and Political Structure" (unpublished Ph.D. dissertation, Michigan State University, 1977), p. 176.

[56] Main, pp. 160–2; Walsh, p. 178; Garry Wheeler Stone, "St. John's: Archaeological Questions and Answers," *Maryland Historical Magazine*, Vol. 69, No. 2 (1974), p. 147.

[57] For example, Main, pp. 112, 131–2; Walsh, p. 178.

[58] For an indication of improvements in the life expectancies of whites in the region at the time, see Levy, pp. 18–19.

Table 4. *Frequency distributions of slaveholdings by size, lower Western Shore, Maryland, 1660–1705*

Number of slaves	1660–9	1670–9	1680–9	1690–9	1700–5
1	4	20	17	25	16
2	1	11	10	15	12
3	3	7	5	10	2
4	1	2	4	4	9
5	2	1	4	8	1
6	1	2		3	7
7			2	3	5
8				4	5
9			2	1	2
10		1	2	1	2
11		1	2	1	
12				2	2
13	1			1	1
14			1		
15					
16				1	2
17			1		1
18					
19				1	
20				1	1
21				1	
23					1
26					1
29		1			1
30				1	
31					1
39					1
40			1		
41				1	
Total	13	46	51	84	73

Source: See Table 1.

would have diminished over time as a larger American-born slave population emerged.

Although wealthy planters played an important role in bringing slavery to the Chesapeake, genuinely large slaveholdings were rare in the region during the seventeenth century, and most slaveholdings remained quite small.[59] This is clearly demonstrated by Table 4, which presents the size distribution of the slaveholdings of decedents on the lower Western Shore of Maryland during 1660–1705. Although these data do show a tendency for the size of slaveholdings to increase

[59] This point was made by Craven, *The Colonies in Transition*, p. 301.

over time, the typical holding remained quite small throughout the period: The median number of slaves held by slave owners rose only from two during the 1670s and 1680s to three during the 1690s and to four during 1700–5. The proportion of slave owners with more than ten slaves remained under 10% until the 1690s, and such men still made up less than one of six slave owners during 1700–5. This contrasted sharply with the situation in the West Indies. For example, in Barbados as early as 1680, more than 30% of all property holders owned twenty or more slaves; nearly half of these large planters held more than sixty slaves.[60] Yet although few Chesapeake planters owned extremely large numbers of slaves, Table 4 does indicate an increase in the importance of large holdings at the turn of the eighteenth century. The proportion of slaveowners with more than twenty slaves rose from 2% in the two decades before 1690 to nearly 7% during 1700–5. The proportion of slaves in estates held by owners with more than twenty slaves similarly rose from less than 22% during each of the last three decades of the seventeenth century to 30% in 1700–5.

The increasing significance of larger slaveholdings is also indicated by calculating from the distributions of Table 4 what Lewis Gray called the "median average" holding, defined such that half of all slaves would reside on estates of the median average size or greater. The median average holding on the lower Western Shore rose from five in the 1660s and four in the 1670s to nine during the 1680s and 1690s and to twelve in 1700–5. Plantation sizes continued to increase during the later colonial period and the early nineteenth century; for 1860, for example, Gray found median average plantation sizes ranging from twenty-four to twenty-eight slaves in tobacco-growing areas of Virginia and North Carolina.[61]

Another interesting feature of the growth of slavery in the Chesapeake was its gradual nature: In a common comparison, it has been noted that the interval between the introduction of slaves and their quantitative domination of the bound labor force was much longer in the Chesapeake than in the West Indies.[62] Much of the literature to date has explained this as a consequence of differences in the supply

---

[60] Dunn, p. 91.

[61] Lewis Cecil Gray, *History of Agriculture in the Southern United States to 1860*, 2 vols. (Washington, D.C., 1933), Vol. I, pp. 529–31; for additional discussion, see Robert William Fogel and Stanley L. Engerman, *Time on the Cross: Evidence and Methods* (Boston, 1974), pp. 143–9. For some evidence on the increasing sizes of slaveholdings in the eighteenth century, see Allan Kulikoff, *Tobacco and Slaves: The Development of Southern Cultures in the Chesapeake, 1680–1800* (Chapel Hill, N.C., 1986), p. 137.

[62] For example, see Richard S. Dunn, "Servants and Slaves: The Recruitment and Employment of Labor," in Greene and Pole, p. 166.

of white labor to these regions, emphasizing that English servants avoided the West Indies after the middle of the seventeenth century but remained more willing to go to the Chesapeake. A variety of evidence supports this view, including the fact that indentured servants bound for the West Indies received substantially shorter terms than those alike in other respects who traveled to the Chesapeake.[63] The latter result, which points to an implicit wage premium that compensated servants for their choice of a less attractive destination, cannot have arisen solely from differences in the demand for servants among the colonies and therefore demonstrates the influence of the servants' preferences on the indenture bargains.[64]

Other authors have offered quite different accounts of the causes of the growth of slavery, emphasizing instead the influence of factors on the demand side of the labor market.[65] Part of the reason for the differing speed of the growth of slavery in the West Indies and the Chesapeake may in fact lie on the demand side, in a combination of differences in the technology of the cultivation of sugar and tobacco and, as discussed earlier in this chapter, differences in the extent of planters' control over servants and slaves.

In the West Indies, it was apparently recognized very early that sugar cultivation could be done most efficiently by the use of gang labor.[66] Turning the ground, planting the sugar, weeding the fields,

---

[63] Galenson, *White Servitude in Colonial America*, chap. 7.

[64] If conditions of servant supply had not varied by colony – if servants had had no preferences concerning (or influence in determining) their destinations – there would have been no differences in the length of contracts of servants bound for different destinations, i.e., the (implicit) wages of servants would not have varied across colonies. Differing levels of demand for servants across colonies would instead have caused differences in the relative numbers of servants bound for the various colonies; differing contract lengths by destination could occur only as a result of differences in supply facing the colonies.

It might be noted that this evidence on servants' contract lengths contradicts the contention of some recent historians that the determination of servants' destinations was done by merchants, with little or no regard for the servants' desires; see, e.g., James Horn, "Servant Emigration to the Chesapeake in the Seventeenth Century," in Tate and Ammerman, p. 92, and Gary B. Nash, *The Urban Crucible: Social Change, Political Consciousness, and the Origin of the American Revolution* (Cambridge, Mass., 1979), p. 111. Yet it might have been less surprising to Abbot Emerson Smith, who remarked that the "most striking of all evidences [of the servants' knowledge concerning the bargains they entered] is that which shows servants preferring one colony over another" (p. 57).

[65] For example, Barbara L. Solow, "The Transition to Plantation Slavery: The Case of the British West Indies," in *De la Traite à l'Esclavage* (Paris, 1989), pp. 89–110. The following argument appears to be consistent with that given by Solow.

[66] Richard Pares, *Merchants and Planters, Economic History Review* Supplement No. 4 (Cambridge, 1960), pp. 19–20; K. G. Davies, *The North Atlantic World in the Seventeenth Century* (Minneapolis, 1974), p. 183; Gary A. Puckrein, *Little England: Plantation Society and Anglo-Barbadian Politics, 1627–1700* (New York: New York University Press,

and cutting the cane were operations requiring heavy work that could be performed effectively by large gangs of regimented workers forced to work rapidly. The gang labor was not as important in the Chesapeake, however, for in contrast, a number of steps in the cultivation and harvesting of the more delicate tobacco plants had to be done with greater care if the final product was to be of high quality.[67] A critical feature of successful use of the gang system was discipline of the workers: The system economized on supervision by having all the members of a gang work in unison, and it was therefore important for the overseer to maintain strict control of the workers. As in the Chesapeake, the latitude permitted masters in the West Indies in disciplining slaves was greater than that for servants. Masters might therefore have found it inefficient to mix servants and slaves in the same work gangs. No such problem may have existed in field work in the Chesapeake, however, for tobacco workers worked more independently than the laborers of the West Indies, and in consequence, servants and slaves may have been used more readily in mixed groups. The result may have been that slaves could be brought into the Chesapeake's labor force more gradually than in the West Indies without sacrifice of productive efficiency.

THE ATLANTIC ECONOMY AND THE GROWTH OF SLAVERY IN AMERICA

Early in this century, historical studies of indentured servitude and slavery in the colonial period tended to treat those subjects in isolation in a number of respects; not only was each typically studied without reference to the other, but both were normally treated as American phenomena, without consideration of their economic connections to

---

1984), pp. 83–4; David Brion Davis, *Slavery in the Colonial Chesapeake* (Williamsburg, Va., 1986), pp. 5, 18.

[67] Lois Carr and Lorena Walsh have recently argued that many slaves in the colonial Chesapeake did work in gangs while cultivating tobacco. This view appears to contrast with some other statements, e.g. Gray, Vol. I, p. 552; Pares, p. 21; Gerald W. Mullin, *Flight and Rebellion: Slave Resistance in Eighteenth-Century Virginia* (London, 1972), p. 49; Davis, pp. 18, 30; William A. Green, "Race and Slavery: Considerations on the Williams Thesis," in Barbara L. Solow and Stanley L. Engerman (eds.), *British Capitalism and Caribbean Slavery: The Legacy of Eric Williams* (Cambridge, 1987), p. 37. The precise nature of the work done in the gangs referred to by Carr and Walsh remains to be compared to that of gang laborers in the West Indies at the time, however; the gang labor that was done on tobacco plantations in the Chesapeake may have been less arduous and less regimented than the work done by slaves in the large gangs used to cultivate sugar in the West Indies. For a suggestive statement, see Gray, Vol. I, pp. 550–1.

Europe and Africa. Subsequently, increasing interest in the origins of slavery in colonial America led to a growing awareness of the need to consider the two types of labor simultaneously, to compare their advantages and disadvantages in order to understand the decisions made by colonial planters in choosing between them. More recently still, interest in understanding the timing of planters' choices between servants and slaves in more detail, and in explaining the differences in those decisions across colonies, has led to a recognition of the need to examine the determinants of the supply of servants and slaves, and consequently to study the trades that connected America with the places of origin of the workers who came to the colonies.

One major result of research on colonial economic history during the past decade has been the discovery that transatlantic markets for bound labor worked far more efficiently than had previously been realized.[68] The shipment of indentured servants was not an irregular, haphazard trade but a considerable business, many outcomes of which can be understood as the results of a competitive industry; the same was true of the slave trade, which was a highly organized business run by professional traders. These findings imply that the numbers of workers brought to America year by year, and their costs to colonial planters, should have depended systematically on economic conditions in Europe and Africa and on the trade routes across the Atlantic. Recent quantitative research has begun to confirm this prediction, and both quantitative and qualitative evidence have been used in beginning the task of delineating the channels of trade throughout the Atlantic economy that made these adjustments possible.[69] Improving labor market conditions in England in the last

---

[68] For a summary of this research, see David W. Galenson, "Labor Market Behavior in Colonial America: Servitude, Slavery, and Free Labor," in Galenson (ed.), *Markets in History: Economic Studies of the Past* (Cambridge, 1989), pp. 52–96.

[69] The operation of the internal African slave trade and the dealings between African traders and European merchants and captains have both recently been the subject of considerable attention. On the former, see Philip D. Curtin, "The Abolition of the Slave Trade from Senegambia," in David Eltis and James Walvin (eds.), *The Abolition of the Atlantic Slave Trade: Origins and Effects in Europe, Africa, and the Americas* (Madison, Wis., 1981), pp. 83–97; on both, see Paul E. Lovejoy, *Transformation in Slavery: A History of Slavery in Africa* (Cambridge, 1983), chaps. 2–6. The specific cooperation between European and African traders that produced the African slave supply responses to changing American demands is described in detail in such documents as the journal of the captain of a ship sent to West Africa by the Royal African Company in 1667. On February 11, he recorded: "This day aboutt nine in the morninge Came on Board the Kinge of New Callabarr with some others of his generals and after a Long discourse Came to Agreemtt," and went on to report the prices at which the company agreed to buy slaves, specified by age and sex: Public Record Office, London, Treasury 70/1213. Later the central Royal African Company

David W. Galenson

quarter of the seventeenth century appear to have raised the cost of indentured servants in the colonies and pushed Chesapeake planters toward the use of slaves. At the same time, a slump in European sugar prices lowered the value of African slaves in the Caribbean and South America and made slaves an increasingly attractive substitute for servants in the Chesapeake.

The significance of these interconnections appears to have been critical for the development of the colonial labor market – as for the colonial economy in general – and it is now clear that future research on the size and composition of the colonial labor force will continue to be informed by an appreciation of the influence of conditions in other parts of the Atlantic economy. Indeed, an improved understanding of the colonial economy will require further research on other sectors of the Atlantic economy, for many linkages remain to be identified and measured more precisely. An obvious example concerns the supply of slave labor to America, for recent studies have only begun the task of constructing and testing models of the determinants of the supply of slaves to European traders on the west coast of Africa.

Yet this chapter has also suggested that in order to improve our understanding of the outcomes observed in colonial labor markets, this work on the linkages among distant parts of the Atlantic economy must not be pursued to the exclusion of the consideration of the local conditions of specific places. The growth of slavery in the early Chesapeake depended not only on the transatlantic trades that governed the supply of English servants and African slaves, but also on conditions internal to the societies of Maryland and Virginia. Both collective actions, as seen in the changing legal definition of the extent of property rights in slaves, and the material circumstances, information, and attitudes of individual planters appear to have had a profound influence on the relative demands of the planters for servants and slaves, and therefore on the evolution of the labor system of the colonial Chesapeake. A fuller understanding of the growth of slavery in the early Chesapeake, or in any other part of the Atlantic economy, will consequently depend on a blend of research on forces general to that wider economy and those specific to the particular region.

office in London corresponded directly with African chieftains, sending them descriptions of the demographic composition of the slave cargoes they desired. The detail of the requests suggests the care devoted by both parties to the transactions, and the cordial tone suggests the mutual benefits. For example, in a letter of 1702 addressed to the "Great King of Bandie," the company prefaced its specifications by acknowledging that "Wee take very kindly your inviting us to send our ships to trade in your country": PRO, T70/51, f. 150; also see f. 103v. On the quantitative effects of these adjustments, see Galenson, *Traders, Planters, and Slaves*, chap. 5.

CHAPTER 12

Credit in the slave trade and plantation economies

JACOB M. PRICE

INTRODUCTION

A few years ago, I was invited to prepare for this conference a paper on credit in the slave trade. Over the years, I had accumulated some scraps of data on this topic, as well as bibliographic references to the vast and ever-growing library of scholarly books on slavery. After accepting this deceptively easy assignment, I proceeded through a very long shelf of publications on the slave trade – including many by those here today – only to discover that most of these erudite works had relatively little to say about credit. Thus, of necessity, this chapter is not a rich synthesis of existing scholarship but an exploratory essay suggesting some questions and answers hinted at by our still scrappy evidence.

We can perhaps usefully start with a generalized if simplified way of thinking about the problem of credit in the slave trade and slave economies. In the seventeenth and eighteenth centuries the dynamic areas of the slave economies, the principal destinations of the slave trade, were in most cases what can be described from a European perspective as initially frontier areas, underpopulated territories of new settlement. In such areas, land is characteristically abundant and cheap, whereas capital and labor are scarce and, by European standards, expensive. Such almost valueless land can be made productive and valuable – a process succinctly expressed is the French phrase *mettre en valeur* – only by the application of capital and labor. In those centuries, capital was generally slightly more mobile than labor. Thus, in such frontier areas with almost free land but a constraining shortage of labor, the successful entrepreneurial settler was likely to be one who could scrape together some capital to be used to obtain labor through the purchase of either indentured servants or slaves. In tropical and other areas unattractive to indentured servants, this usually meant slaves. A poor settler might acquire an indentured servant with the product of as little as one year of his own labor, but the product of several years' labor by a settler, servant, or slave would be needed to buy a slave. Thus the process of building up a labor force by reinvesting the yields of the labor of existing servants and slaves could be very slow. The prospects for the entrepreneurial agricultural settler with little capital were therefore not too attractive.

However, where credit was available, the linked processes of labor acquisition, capital investment, and land improvement could be speeded up significantly. Slaves bought on credit could not only pay for themselves but, provided that they lived long enough, by their labor could soon provide the wherewithal to purchase other slaves. Credit did not so much change the fundamental character of slave cultivation as accelerate the processes of initiation and expansion of slave systems.

Popular mythology associates credit and debt with the needs of the less advantaged competitors in the market. But in the early modern plantation world, credit was unlikely to benefit equally all would-be slave owners, least of all the poorest. Those in a position to lend money or sell on credit normally preferred to minimize their risks. Larger planters with more improved land, capital equipment, and bound labor should have appeared better risks for credit than their smaller competitors or beginners just starting out. Thus the readier availability of credit to the creditworthy should have tended to favor the growth of larger productive units and of social systems dominated by larger planters. Of course, these larger planters did not always have to buy on credit. But, for most of them, to buy four slaves on credit rather than one for cash appeared a rational and not unduly risky investment decision.

Cash, it should be remembered, did not necessarily mean coin. Most often, "cash purchases" were in fact paid for in colonial commodities or in bills of exchange. The bill, in turn, might be drawn against a credit balance of the planter with a metropolitan merchant but, more likely, was a claim against the anticipated value of commodities shipped to market but not yet sold or even landed when the bill was drawn. Only rarely was the bill a pure credit instrument drawn against nothing but the good will of the metropolitan merchant; such bills were more often returned unaccepted. Although any thrifty planter could expect some day to be able to buy a slave with the produce of his land, only the more substantial planter was likely to have a metropolitan correspondent who would accept and pay his bills of exchange. Thus, in cash as much as in credit purchases, the trading system favored the larger over the smaller planter.

Few areas remained frontiers indefinitely. But, on the terra firma of North or South America, as zones of initial settlement filled up, inland areas still worth settling retained the frontier characteristics of cheap land, scarce capital, and dear labor. If slavery was a viable option in such new frontier zones, then credit there too served to speed up both settlement and the development of slave plantation cultures. By contrast, in Barbados and other smaller islands, cheap land and underdevelopment very soon disappeared and with them the ostensible need for development credit. However, the slave populations in those islands did not reproduce themselves, and the importation of replacement slaves remained necessary down to the end of the slave trade. A well-managed plantation could perhaps be expected to finance the purchase of replacement slaves out of current earnings. But all plantations were not well managed in this sense, and so credit on slave purchases remained extremely useful to large and small planters down to the end of slavery.

Credit for slave purchases was not uniformly available over time. It was a market phenomenon whose availability and terms were governed by supply and demand conditions both in the slave trade and in the trade in the products produced by the slaves. When the prices of a slave-grown commodity (sugar, tobacco, coffee, indigo, rice, etc.) were high and the planters "in funds," then demand for slaves would be keen, resulting in higher prices and shorter credits. When those same commodity prices fell, planter demand for additional slaves would slacken and slave sellers would have to offer lower prices and easier credit terms, that is, longer delays before payment. Similarly, when the supply of slave imports was reduced, particularly by war, sellers could insist on higher prices and shorter credits. When, however, several consecutive years of peace facilitated cumulatively large slave imports in any particular area, the market might well become glutted and sellers who did not want to look elsewhere would have to offer lower prices and easier credit terms.

The length of credit offered to slave buyers was a significant cost and potential restriction of activity for those engaged in the slave trade. Where slaves could be sold for cash, commodities, or short-term bills of exchange, the venturers in that trade could expect to realize the returns for their venture in perhaps fifteen or eighteen months. Counting on this, they could move without too much imprudence from one year's ventures to the next. However, when slaves were sold on what amounted to two or three years' or longer credit, the turnover of risk capital was much slower. With much of their capital tied up in debts owed in remote plantation colonies, the slave traders had to plan on higher interest payments over time for the sums they may have borrowed, as well as on a more encumbered financial position that could make their dealings with their own suppliers and other creditors more difficult and probably more costly. As we shall see later, a strong preference for liquidity forced English slave traders in particular into rather complex and costly institutional experiments.

Although many of the conventions of purely mercantile credit appear to have been rendered relatively homogeneous across state boundaries by the "custom of merchants," the same does not appear equally true for credit arrangements that touch on the laws of landed and other property. Though no legal historian, I have tried in my reading to sort out the ways in which different legal systems facilitated or hindered the use of credit in slave sales. It may be useful to distinguish between two models describing the effect of the law on credit. In what I shall call the "Latin model," the law in the situations observed protected the integrity of the plantation as a working unit. Creditors could seize crops but could not use the courts to seize nonlanded accoutrements of the plantation or sugar mill – such as agricultural equipment, livestock, or slaves – and thus diminish its productive capacity. Opposed to this was an Anglo-Saxon or "creditor defense model." Where it prevailed, efforts by colonial legislatures to protect the productive integrity of the plantation were usually thwarted by the central or metropolitan government, which preferred to protect the interests of the creditor or credit seller.

Not all credit or debt was equally necessary to develop or maintain the productive capacity of a plantation. To clarify this distinction in a plantation economy, we may usefully distinguish between what I shall term "primary," "secondary," and "tertiary" credit or debt. "Primary" credit/debt refers to obligations incurred by the plantation to obtain replacement or additional labor, livestock, or tools and machinery absolutely necessary for its ongoing or expanding operations. "Secondary" credit/debt refers to the heavy obligations incurred, usually under a mortgage, when a plantation was sold by one owner to another. Such credit neither added to nor sustained the productive capacity of the plantation, but its availability undoubtedly encouraged investment in plantations. (An intelligent entrepreneur investing in the development of a plantation would take into consideration the degree to which the availability of mortgages would facilitate or enable him to sell out advantageously if and when he chose to do so.) "Tertiary" credit/debt refers to all other burdens assumed by the proprietors unrelated to either the ownership or productive capacity of the plantation (e.g., borrowing for dowries, family settlements, residential building, or luxury consumption).

BRAZILIAN ANTECEDENTS

In the main part of this chapter, I concentrate on the English and French colonies in the seventeenth and eighteenth centuries. It is useful, however, to start with a few remarks on Brazil, the first exemplar and seedbed in the Americas of the slave sugar system later transplanted to the British, French, Dutch, and Spanish colonies. When the Dutch invaded northeastern Brazil in the 1620s, they found in the areas they occupied a significant population of Portuguese planters using slave labor to produce sugar for export sale. This was the most productive sector of the local economy but depended on the continuing importation of slaves not just to expand but merely to sustain production, for there was a constant loss of slave labor through death and flight into the interior. Thus, the Dutch West India Company, after establishing itself in Brazil, was also obliged to seize many of the Portuguese stations on the Guinea and Angola coasts and enter into the slave trade systematically. Almost at once, the company found that the Brazilian planters were keen to acquire its slave imports but could do so in numbers only if assisted by credit such as they had received from their previous Portuguese suppliers. The Dutch company (and probably independent merchants as well) obliged with easy terms, and soon the Brazilian planters were reported to be heavily in debt to their slave suppliers. With earnings cut by bad weather and poor crops, the situation soon became so difficult that the Dutch West India Company in 1644 ordered its agents to cease slave sales on credit. The next year, 1645, the Brazilians rose in revolt against the Dutch. At least one contemporary Dutch observer thought that it was the desire to escape from the burden of debt that persuaded many Portuguese Brazilian planters to join the revolt. By 1654 the Dutch empire in Brazil was gone.[1]

With the departure of the Dutch, the Portuguese Brazilian sugar industry entered upon a half-century of only modest growth (down to ca. 1710) and of stagnation and decline thereafter. Much of the difficulty arose from the combination of stagnant or declining prices

---

[1] C. R. Boxer, *The Dutch in Brazil 1624–1654* (Oxford, 1957), pp. 81–4, 106–7, 138–9, 144, 164, 173; Ernst van den Boogaart and Peter C. Emmer, "The Dutch Participation in the Atlantic Slave Trade, 1596–1650," in Henry A. Gemery and Jan S. Hogendorn (eds.), *The Uncommon Market: Essays in the Economic History of the Atlantic Slave Trade* (New York, 1979), pp. 353–75, esp. pp. 358, 369–70.

for sugar and steadily rising prices for slaves, both ascribable in part to the development of slave sugar cultivation elsewhere in the Americas. Although the institutions of the Brazilian sugar industry are not within the scope of this chapter, I should like to emphasize one feature of those institutions noted in the recent work of Stuart Schwartz. As is well known, colonial Brazilian sugar production was characterized by the interdependence of the larger, heavily capitalized plantation with substantial investment in a sugar mill (*engenho*), slaves, and livestock and the smaller, dependent nearby plantations of the *lavradores* who did not have their own mills. The money for setting up a mill or *engenho* was frequently borrowed on mortgage from ecclesiastical and other lenders. For slaves, however, the owners of both the mills and lesser plantations were dependent on local merchants who conducted a largely bilateral slave trade with the Gulf of Guinea and Angola. The slaves were apparently sold to planters and mill owners on relatively short credit. Should the debtor not pay in time and the merchant attempt to recover what was owed him by seizing slaves or livestock, such action could interrupt the complex operation of the mill and the dependent plantations. To prevent this, the Portuguese authorities fairly early recognized what was termed earlier the Latin principle of the integrity of the plantation. A law of 1663 (frequently renewed) prohibited the "piecemeal attachment of parts of an *engenho*." Action could be taken only against the entire mill-plantation, and then only when the debt was roughly equal to the value of the whole. Otherwise, only the income (crops), and not the capital stock, could be attached. This protection was extended in 1723 to the holdings of the *lavrador* as well. As total Brazilian slave imports remained high throughout the eighteenth century, we can only speculate on the degree to which these restrictions on the rights of creditors may have diverted slave imports away from sugar toward other, less protected sectors of the Brazilian economy, particularly mining.[2]

THE ENGLISH COLONIES AND MONOPOLY

The Portuguese Brazilian planter revolt of 1645 led to the almost immediate suspension of Dutch slave sales in Brazil but not to the end of the Dutch slave trade. Almost at once the Dutch redirected part of their slave shipments toward the English colony of Barbados,

---

[2] Stuart B. Schwartz, *Sugar Plantations in the Formation of Brazilian Society: Bahia, 1550–1835* (Cambridge Latin American Studies, Vol. 52) (Cambridge, 1985), pp. 168, 186, 190, 192, 195–6, 204–12, 343; Philip D. Curtin, *The Atlantic Slave Trade: A Census* (Madison, Wis., 1969), pp. 207, 216.

where some Dutchmen had already been active in the introduction of Brazilian methods of sugar refining.[3] The Dutch traders helped develop this market, as Dalby Thomas pointed out, by giving "credit to those islanders, as well as they did to the Portugalls in Brasile, for black slaves, and all other necessaries for planting, taking as their crops throve, the sugar they made." But, as another contemporary pointed out, Dutch credit for slaves and the equipment of the sugar mill was restricted to the "most sober [i.e., substantial] inhabitants." These mandates of prudent credit help explain the emergence of the large sugar planters as the dominant social element in Barbados. The inability of the less "sober" inhabitants to get equivalent credit contributed to their decline in sugar-producing areas.[4]

After the restoration of Charles II in 1660, the implementation of the acts of trade and navigation eliminated the Dutch as suppliers of slaves to the English colonies. Their place was taken during 1660–72 by the monopoly Company of Royal Adventurers of England Trading into Africa and after 1672 by its successor, the Royal African Company. Almost from the start, the Royal Adventurers found that it could not supply as many slaves as the West Indian colonists wanted and was forced to license some "private traders" to supplement the flow. The Royal African Company had better luck defending its monopoly down at least to 1688, but thereafter lacked the effective legal powers to enforce its claims on the high seas. Thus, from 1689 the company had to share its trade with "interlopers" whose position was legalized from 1698 subject to the payment to the company of a 10% toll on goods exported to Africa. By the late 1720s the interlopers had in effect taken over the trade, though the Royal African Company wasn't formally wound up until 1750–2.[5] In his discussion of the failure of the company, David Galenson emphasizes its inability –

---

[3] For the Dutch role in the introduction of sugar cultivation in Barbados, see Richard S. Dunn, *Sugar and Slaves: The Rise of the Planter Class in the English West Indies, 1624–1713* (Chapel Hill, N.C., 1972), pp. 60–6.

[4] David Watts, *The West Indies: Patterns of Development, Culture and Environmental Change since 1492* (Cambridge Studies in Historical Geography, Vol. 8) (Cambridge, 1987), p. 188; William A. Green, "Supply versus Demand in the Barbadian Sugar Revolution," *Journal of Interdisciplinary History*, Vol. XVIII (1988), pp. 403–18, esp. pp. 416–17; [Sir Dalby Thomas], *An Historical Account of the Rise and Growth of the West-India Colonies . . .* (London, 1690), pp. 13–14, 36–7; Richard B. Sheridan, *Sugar and Slavery: An Economic History of the British West Indies 1623–1775* (Baltimore, 1973), pp. 272–3.

[5] For general accounts, see George F. Zook, "The Company of Royal Adventures of England Trading into Africa, 1660–1672," *Journal of Negro History*, Vol. IV (1919), pp. 134–231, esp. pp. 134–41 (also published separately); K. G. Davies, *The Royal African Company* (London, 1957); David W. Galenson, *Traders, Planters, and Slaves: Market Behavior in Early English America* (Cambridge and New York, 1986).

almost from the beginning – to enforce its monopoly.[6] K. G. Davies appears to attach somewhat more importance to the company's inability to collect with reasonable promptness the large sums owed it by the planters who bought its slaves on credit.[7]

The companies found credit a significant feature of the slave trade both in America and in parts of Africa. At the northern end of the slave trading coasts of West Africa, particularly in what is now termed Senegambia, the English and French companies frequently found it useful as early as the 1670s to make merchandise advances to African and Portuguese slave traders to be repaid in slaves at six months or so. Such arrangements made it easier to plan ahead and increase shipping efficiency by accumulating slaves at coastal shipping points before the arrival of the slaving vessels from Europe. In the earlier decades of the eighteenth century, this practice appears to have been geographically limited to Senegambia. However, by the second half of the century, there were a number of British merchants settled on the coast who also supplied slaves to the slave traders in arrangements that sometimes involved advances of trading goods. By the end of the century, a number of the largest British slave trading firms had established their own stations on the coast and very likely made credit advances to those who supplied them with slaves. However, there is no firm evidence to suggest that total credits outstanding on the coast from goods advanced were anything but a fraction of the sums outstanding in America from slave sales on credit.[8]

Almost from their start, the two English monopoly companies found it necessary, or at least commercially advisable, to sell slaves to the planters of Barbados and the other sugar islands on credit. The procedure worked out by the Royal African Company by the 1680s was built on the expectation that the sales would procure only a small fraction of their total value in cash or sugar or other goods. For the balance, the factors or commission agents of the company would take penalty bonds from the planter-buyers for payment in three, six, nine, or twelve months. The time allowed would carry the planter through

---

[6] Galenson, chap. 7.

[7] Davies, pp. 316–25, 335–43.

[8] Philip D. Curtin, *Economic Change in Precolonial Africa: Senegambia in the Era of the Slave Trade* (Madison, Wis., 1975), pp. 302–8; Davies, 216–18, 284–5. For credit advances to British traders on the coast, see J. H. Hodson, "The Letter Book of Robert Bostock, a Merchant in the Liverpool Slave Trade, 1789–1792," *Liverpool Libraries, Museums and Arts Committee, Bulletin*, Vol. III, Nos. 1 and 2 (1953), pp. 41, 53–5. For the trading station era, see J. E. Inikori, "Market Structure and the Profits of the British African Trade in the Late Eighteenth Century," *Journal of Economic History*, Vol. XLI (1981), pp. 745–76.

the next crop year. Most planters more or less paid when their bonds became due. But a substantial minority of them were very tardy in paying, and the agents of the company were reluctant to cut off the credit of substantial planters and good customers.[9] Sir Dalby Thomas, writing in 1690, argued that the debt problems of the slave buyers were exacerbated by changes in the market in recent decades. Since the 1660s, he reported, prices of slaves had risen considerably while prices of sugar had declined. West Indian planters had to buy replacement slaves, but the fall in sugar prices prevented them from paying.[10] Whatever the ultimate cause, the amounts owed the company in the West Indies kept rising, reaching £120,000 in 1680, £136,000 in 1684, and a peak of £170,000 in 1690. Though worrisome to the company, this rise in debt is not surprising, since the company's American deliveries grew steadily down to 1686–7.[11] To help carry these "accounts receivable" and the other requirements of its trading stock, the company itself had to borrow on bond in England. By 1708–10 its bonded debt was reported to be in the vicinity of £300,000–400,000.[12] This bonded debt is but one way in which the capital resources of the country were made available to the African slave trade by persons not otherwise involved therein.

The surge during the 1680s in the amounts owed the company in the West Indies occurred despite its frequent warnings to its factors against imprudent credit and neglect of collections. In some of the colonies the company could claim interest of up to 10% on these balances, but in others such interest was forbidden by law. Nor was the company satisfied ca. 1690 that its factors were doing all that they might to collect the interest permitted by law. Ultimately, in 1697, the company was forced to follow the lead of some interlopers and alter contractual arrangements with its factors. The latter's commissions were raised from 7 to 10% but they were made responsible for all credit extended to planters and "were obliged to undertake to remit to the company the entire proceeds of a cargo of slaves within twelve months." This was to be a crucial innovation for the institutional evolution of the trade in the next century. It was enforceable when introduced because the factors, like all senior employees and agents of the company, were required to give "security" and performance

---

[9] Davies, pp. 316–19; Galenson, p. 191.
[10] Thomas, pp. 38–40.
[11] Davies, pp. 319, 363.
[12] Elizabeth Donnan (ed.), *Documents Illustrative of the History of the Slave Trade to America,* 4 vols. (Washington, D.C., 1930–5), Vol. I, pp. 265 and n., 266n; Vol. II, pp. 89–90, 98, and n.

bonds countersigned by well-to-do figures, usually merchants in England.[13]

Because the Royal African Company had such difficulties in collecting the sums owed it in the West Indies for slave purchases by planters, it was interested during 1672–89 in experimenting with other sales arrangements, particularly contract deliveries tried earlier by the Royal Adventurers. A group or ad hoc syndicate of merchants in London would contract with the company in advance to purchase a number of slaves at a price of so much per head delivered. When the slaves were received in the colony specified or on the African coast, the local representative of the purchasing syndicate would give the agent of the company a bill or bills of exchange for the amount due drawn on a merchant in London designated by the syndicate. This system was used for the relatively few deliveries by the company to Virginia, where it did not attempt to sell slaves on its own before the 1690s. Syndicates of independent London merchants trading to Virginia were formed in the 1670s and 1680s, under the leadership of prominent merchants (such as John Jeffreys, his nephew Sir Jeffrey Jeffreys, Micajah Perry the elder, or Alderman Richard Booth), to contract with the company for the purchase on delivery in Virginia (or Africa) of about 100 slaves at a time. On such delivery, the agent of the syndicate would give the representative of the Royal African Company sets of bills of exchange drawn on the head of the London syndicate. One-third of the sale amount would usually be covered by a bill at "sixty days' sight" (payable sixty days after presentation to the addressee in London for acceptance), another third at four months' sight, and the final third at six months' sight. In such transactions, the Royal African Company accepted a smaller book profit per slave in return for an assured and not too prolonged schedule of payment. The syndicate, of course, most likely resold the slaves to Virginia or West Indian planters on credit, but the merchants in the syndicate had ongoing credit relationships with such planters, whose tobacco or sugar they marketed, and presumably were better able than the company to collect what was due from them.[14] The system

---

[13] Davies, pp. 296–7, 320–1; Galenson, 191. For registers of security bonds given to the Royal African Company, see PRO T.70/1428 and 1432. T.70/57 f. 127 (February 23, 1696–7) indicates that the company's 1697 innovations were based on practices used by the separate traders. See also ff. 127–9v, 132v–34.

[14] Davies, pp. 294–5; Donnan, 54–5; PRO T.70/269 (7 July 1676, 20 Aug. 1678); T.70/271 (16 Sept. 1684); T.70/273 (7 Sept. 1687). In the 1684 contract, John and Jeffrey Jeffreys took delivery on the African coast with payment in three- and six-month bills. See also Susan Westbury, "Slaves of Colonial Virginia: Where They Came

of staggered bills of exchange tried by the Royal African Company in the 1670s and 1680s was to become a marked feature of the slave trade in the next century.

Market conditions in the slave trade changed noticeably during the long wars of 1689–97 and 1702–13. The dangers of war and the rationing of sailors during the 1690s reduced the number of slaving vessels that could be sent to the African coast, and some of those that did depart were captured by enemy privateers and never reached the English colonies in America. These same wartime difficulties reduced the flow of sugar and tobacco from the colonies to England and led to significant increases in European prices.[15] Thus the inflow of slaves to the colonies[16] was reduced at the very time when higher European prices put more money or credit balances into the hands of consigning planters that they might well use for slave purchases. In these changed markets, sellers of slaves could be much less generous in offering credit. The Royal African Company was quick to sense the changed market conditions and in 1690 instructed its agents in the West Indies to sell only by auction and only "for money, Goods or Bills of Exchange with Securitie [endorsers or bonds] and not give further Creditt." These orders were repeated in 1691, but the next year the company found buyer resistance too strong and retreated, leaving the details of sales to the discretion of its factors. Even so, the balances owed the Royal African Company, which had been rising steadily in the 1680s, peaked at £170,000 in 1690, and declined in the ensuing decade to somewhere between £120,000 and £140,000 and in 1708, at £160,000, were still below their 1690, at peak. The private slave traders in the West Indies went further in the 1690s and were reported ca. 1698–1700 to be insisting on immediate payment (in cash or commodities) or offering only the most limited credit.[17] However, the very tight credit reported by our evidence for the 1690s does not appear to have persisted through the different market conditions of

From," *William and Mary Quarterly*, third series, Vol. XLII (1985), pp. 228–37, esp. pp. 229–30.

[15] For tobacco prices in Europe, see Nicolaas Wilhelmus Posthumus, *Inquiry into the History of Prices in Holland*, Vol. I, *Wholesale Prices at the Exchange of Amsterdam 1585–1914* (Leiden, 1946), pp. 199–206, and Jacob M. Price, *France and the Chesapeake: A History of the French Tobacco Monopoly, 1674–1791* . . . , 2 vols. (Ann Arbor, Mich., 1973), p. 852. For sugar prices in Europe, see Posthumus, pp. 119–46, and Sheridan, pp. 404–11, 496–7. For sugar and slave prices in the West Indies, see Davies, pp. 363–6; Galenson, pp. 63, 65.

[16] Davies, p. 363; PRO T.70/1205/A.43; C.O.388/10/H.105, H.108; Walter Minchinton, Celia King, and Peter Waite (eds.), *Virginia Slave-Trade Statistics 1698–1775* (Richmond, Va., 1984), pp. x–xiii.

[17] Davies, pp. 319, 325; Galenson, pp. 82, 84.

the later stages of the war of 1702–13. Despite reduced shipments, by 1710 both company and interloping sources report the return of longer credits in the West Indies.[18]

The 1690s saw a significant increase in the activity of interlopers or "separate traders" in the slave trade to the Chesapeake, as well as in the trade to the West Indies. From the records of an Exchequer lawsuit, we get a rather detailed picture of the activities of one of them, Thomas Starke of London. Starke had been trading to Virginia and Maryland as a conventional merchant in the 1670s and 1680s. Observing that no slaves had been imported into those colonies since the start of the European war in 1689, he and others applied to the Privy Council in 1692 for permission to send a slaving vessel to the Guinea Coast and Virginia. Permission was granted, though the number of sailors authorized was deducted from the wartime quotas allowed to the Virginia trade and the individual venturers. Starke remained active in both the slave and Chesapeake trades down to his death in 1706, with the slaves he sent to Virginia being entrusted at first to his chief factor there, Henry Fox of King and Queen County (York River). Fox apparently sold such slaves on credit, just as he did the other goods sent him. By 1696, Starke had become dissatisfied with the large balances owed him in the Chesapeake and decided to send his apprentice, John Sheffeild, to manage his affairs in Maryland and to take charge of any slaves sent to Virginia. Sheffeild found on arrival that it was then normal in the Chesapeake to pay for indentured servants in tobacco but to pay for slaves in bills of exchange. He appears to have been able to dispose of all the slaves Starke sent him during 1698–1702 for bills of exchange of rarely more than thirty days' duration (sight). This is consistent with what we read of the activities of the independent slave traders in the West Indies at that time and confirms the suggestion that during the wars of 1689–1713, longer credits on slave sales were much less necessary or common than they had been before 1689 and were to be again after 1713.[19]

We have thus seen that, before its role in the slave trade faded

---

[18] Donnan, Vol. II, pp. 132, 147. For activity during war down to 1708 see Davies, pp. 143, 363, and PRO C.O.388/11/I.8. For French privateering during war, see J. S. Bromley, "The French Privateering War, 1702–13," in H. E. Bell and R. L. Ollard (eds.), *Historical Essays 1600–1750 Presented to David Ogg* (London, 1963), pp. 203–31.

[19] Jacob M. Price, "Sheffeild v. Starke: Institutional Experimentation in the London–Maryland Trade, c. 1696–1706," *Business History*, Vol. XXVIII (July 1986), pp. 19–39, esp. pp. 27–8, 31–5; reprinted in R. P. T. Davenport-Hines and Jonathan Liebenau, *Business in the Age of Reason* (London, 1987), pp. 19–39. Based on original firm records in PRO E.219/446.

away, the Royal African Company had by 1700 evolved certain effective mechanisms for sale of slaves on credit: (1) Planters buying slaves on credit were expected to give bonds for payment at stated dates. (2) Merchants buying large shipments of slaves were expected to pay in bills of exchange, though these could be staggered, for example, with due dates in tranches of two, four, and six months after acceptance. (3) From 1697, the company's factors were made personally responsible for the collection of the proceeds of all slave sales on credit. (4) The last was enforceable because the factors had long been required to give the company security bonds for their right handling of the valuable property entrusted to them. Our evidence on the separate traders and their factors is much thinner, but, like Starke, most of them appear frequently to have had to let their factors sell on credit. During the war years 1689–1713, the separate traders, dealing on a smaller scale than the company, were at times able to restrict credit much more than the company. However, in the changed market conditions after 1713, the four credit practices developed by the company and the interlopers before 1700 were to be developed further by the separate traders and integrated by them into a coherent long-term credit system.

THE BRITISH SLAVE TRADE, 1713–75

In the years following their legalization in 1698, the separate traders steadily pulled ahead of the Royal African Company in the slave trade. Between June 24, 1698, and December 3, 1707, the private trade sent 376 vessels to Africa from London alone, whereas the company sent only 128.[20] In every colony for which we have data of any sort, the interlopers led the company: In Jamaica, for example, they imported 35,718 slaves in that same period, whereas the company imported only 6,854; in Virginia, the private trade accounted for 5,692 slave imports, whereas the company brought in only 679; in Maryland the total was 2,938 for the former and nil for the latter.[21] Conditions became even better for the separate traders de facto, if not de jure, when the legislation requiring them to pay a 10% toll on exports to Africa lapsed in 1710.

As they took over more and more of the trade, the burden of supporting its credit structure fell increasingly on the separate traders. Though they had boasted in 1711 of their "generosity" in this re-

---

[20] PRO C.O.388/11/I.8.
[21] PRO T.70/1205/A.43.

spect,[22] it would not appear that the burden of debt was too heavy in the years immediately following the war. These were years of good prices for growers of both sugar and tobacco,[23] and a good part of the higher disposable income of their estates went into the purchase of additional slaves. (These were the years of the triumph of the slave plantation in Virginia.) In South Carolina, the bounties paid by the British crown for imports of naval stores had the same stimulative effect on slave purchases.[24] Against this background of relative prosperity, we hear comparatively few complaints about the burden of debt.

Market conditions changed, however, in the late 1720s and 1730s, with falling and eventually abysmally low prices in Europe for both sugar and tobacco.[25] With their incomes thus reduced, slave owners understandably found it very difficult to support and clear the debt they had incurred for slave purchases. In such a trap, the planters inevitably turned for relief to the colonial legislatures they dominated. In colony after colony, bills were passed sheltering debtors, including debtor slave owners, from the claims of creditors.

In no colony did the legislature attempt to establish the full Latin principle of the integrity of the plantation that we saw recognized in Portuguese Brazil as early as the 1660s. But the trend was clearly if hesitatingly in that direction. As early as the 1660s, we find the Royal Adventurers complaining of the laws of Barbados, which made it almost impossible for them to sue for recovery of debts incurred by slave purchases.[26] K. G. Davies and Richard B. Sheridan have surveyed the legislative and other legal impediments to the collection of debts in the West Indian slave colonies. Typical legislative measures altered the ratio of the local money of account to the Spanish silver dollar, to the disadvantage of creditors, or required creditors to accept payment in commodities at more than their current market value. (An act to the latter effect was also passed in South Carolina in 1719.)[27]

---

[22] Donnan, Vol. II, p. 132.

[23] See footnote 15.

[24] Donnan, Vol. IV, pp. 265–6. Cf. Converse D. Clowse, *Economic Beginnings in Colonial South Carolina 1670–1730* (Columbia, S.C., 1971), pp. 129, 131–2, 203–4, 222, 230–1.

[25] See footnote 15. For the credit problems of the South Sea Company selling slaves in the Spanish colonies at this time, see Colin Palmer, *Human Cargoes: The British Slave Trade to Spanish America 1700–1739* (Urbana, Ill., 1981), pp. 126–7.

[26] Zook, p. 210; Donnan, Vol. I, pp. 165n–166n, 165–6. The Barbados legislature refused to make land liable for such debts. The most objectionable Barbados law was repealed in 1677.

[27] Davies, 319–23; Sheridan, 274–8; Donnan, Vol. IV, pp. 265–6 and n.; Richard Pares, *Merchants and Planters* (Economic History Review Supplements, 4) (Cambridge, 1960), pp. 45–7, 88–90.

These measures tended to affect all merchant creditors equally and were not specifically aimed at slave traders. In fact, a clause in one Antigua law specifically permitted creditors to recover slaves not paid for. However, the Royal African Company did not like the rest of the law, which, on their petition, was disallowed by the crown.[28]

Technical bills might have relevance to the slave trade that at first glance is not self-evident. In 1709–10 the merchants of London trading to Maryland obtained the disallowance by the crown of three measures passed by the Maryland legislature. One of these, "An Act for the Relief of Poor Debtors," would have exempted future earnings from the claims of current creditors (as is true of modern bankruptcy laws). The merchant creditors objected "Because the Merchants have given the Planters Credit to buy Negroes[,] to Cloath and Support their Familyes not upon any known or Supposed Stock they had, but [upon] their [sense of] Justice & [the] future Crops they should make." The law deprived the creditor of any claims upon "their future Labour ... which alone was that foundation on which the Credit was solely given, & by which Credit those plantations have been supported & peopled & ye trade itself sustained & without which it had been altogether Unable to have been Carryed on & can't long without it be supported but by Credit." They also objected to the law reducing the penalty on protested bills of exchange from 15 to 10%. Since the bill of exchange was a common medium for paying for slaves, a planter anxious to get more slaves might well try paying for purchases with bills he knew would be refused acceptance and protested, calculating that 10% was not an excessive interest and penalty to pay to get the labor he needed.[29]

Tensions between creditors and debtors – and hence between debtor-dominated colonial legislatures and the creditor-influenced metropolitan government – so conspicuous during the price fall of ca. 1660–90 became pronounced again with the new fall in commodity prices in the late 1720s.[30] Many sugar and tobacco colonies experi-

---

[28] Davies, p. 320.

[29] PRO C.O.5/716/67; C.O.5/717/15; *Journal of the Commissioners of Trade and Plantations, 1704–1708/9*, pp. 36, 70, 75–6, 81, 82, 84, 96, 97, 181, 186. For protested bills in the slave trade, see Walter Minchinton, "The Virginia Letters of Isaac Hobhouse, Merchant of Bristol," *Virginia Magazine of History and Biography*, Vol. LXVI (1958), pp. 278–307.

[30] See the sources cited in footnote 14 and Jacob M. Price, "Glasgow, the Tobacco Trade, and the Scottish Customs, 1707–1730," *The Scottish Historical Review*, Vol. LXIII (1984), pp. 1–36, esp. pp. 34–5; and John M. Hemphill II, *Virginia and the English Commercial System 1689–1733:* ... (New York, 1985), pp. 311–14 (for tobacco prices in Virginia).

enced this heightened tension but it was particularly apparent in Jamaica and Virginia, which merit our attention. In 1728 both houses of the Jamaica legislature passed a bill "to oblige creditors to accept of the produce of the Island in payment of their debts" at fixed prices. This was an oft-tried ploy (analogous to the South Carolina act of 1719) usually disallowed by the London authorities. This particular bill was strongly objected to by the merchants and traders of Kingston and at least one member of the council. Governor Hunter, on the advice of his council, decided that assenting would be contrary to his instructions and so referred the bill to the Board of Trade in London, where it died.[31]

In Virginia the legislative reaction to the decline in European prices for their commodity was more energetic. At first the legislature saw the problem as one of overproduction. In 1728, for the last time, they passed a stint act restricting production. That same year, they tried to discourage the growth of the labor force by introducing a bill taxing imports of slaves; this was disallowed by the Privy Council, as was a bill of 1726 prohibiting shipments of North Carolina tobacco through Virginia. More successful was the 1730 bill sponsored by Governor Gooch for the compulsory warehousing and inspection of all tobacco before shipment out of the colony. Tobacco that failed inspection was to be burned.[32] Inevitably, the Virginia legislature's attention was also drawn to the debt problem. When Gooch went out to Virginia in 1727, he received the standard instructions to ask the legislature for a bill enabling creditors to recover sums owed in Virginia to British bankrupts. The legislature did not think that such a bill was needed but, as a slight concession, passed a law in 1728 weakening previous legislation declaring slaves to be real property and thus unavailable to satisfy certain types of debt. The merchants of London now took the initiative and complained against a 1705 Virginia act setting time limits for legal actions for the recovery of sums owing by judgment, bond, bill, note, or open account. The Board of Trade, on the advice of counsel, recommended the disallowance of the 1705 act on the ground that it ran counter to an English act (21 James I) by which rights created by judgment or bond were unlimited in time. This disallow-

---

[31] *Calendar of State Papers Colonial: America and West Indies, 1728–1729*, pp. 167–9 (no. 344), 243 (no. 469); *Journal of the Commissioners of Trade and Plantations, 1722/3–1728*, p. 434.

[32] Jacob M. Price, "The Excise Affair Revisited: The Administrative and Colonial Dimensions of a Parliamentary Crisis," in Stephen B. Baxter (ed.), *England's Rise to Greatness, 1660–1763* (Berkeley, Calif., 1983), pp. 257–321, esp. pp. 272–3; Hemphill, pp. 150–73.

ance created new problems, for there were other clauses in the 1705 act useful to the merchants, including one by which a merchant creditor resident in Britain but party to a suit in Virginia could prove his accounts by swearing to them before the chief magistrate of his place of residence. Gooch tried to persuade the legislature to reenact the desirable clauses of the 1705 act, but the resultant bill did not include the clause for proving accounts in Britain.[33]

Concerned about their weakened legal position in litigation for debt collection, the merchants of London and Bristol trading to Virginia joined with their fellows trading to Jamaica to petition the crown for help. Their memorial complained not only of the Virginia laws just mentioned but of equivalent discriminatory legislation in Maryland, including one measure that also made it impossible there for British creditors or receivers to collect sums owed bankrupts, and of the laws of Jamaica and some other colonies by which lands and houses were not liable to pay ordinary debts, though by the laws of England "estates in the Plantations are deemed Chattel." The merchants' petition was referred to the Board of Trade, which reported that legislation would be necessary. The resulting Colonial Debts Act of 1732, supported by the active solicitation of merchants of London, Bristol, and Liverpool, met some of the merchants' complaints. A uniform system applying to all the colonies was established for proving accounts in Britain for use in colonial debt litigation. More sensitively, the act declared that the *lands, houses, chattels, and slaves* of debtors in the American colonies were liable for the satisfaction of debts "in the like Manner as Real Estates are by the Law of *England* liable to Satisfaction of Debts due by Bond or other Specialty."[34]

The Colonial Debts Act of 1732 was deeply offensive to many slave-owning planters in the West Indies and North America. Those in the

---

[33] Price, "Excise Affair," pp. 277–8; Leonard Woods Labaree (ed.), *Royal Instructions to British Colonial Governors 1670–1776*, 2 vols. (New York, 1935, 1967), Vol. I, p. 338; *Calendar of State Papers Colonial . . . 1728–1729*, nos. 45, 190, 241, 351, 593, 606, 614, 637, 722, 730–1; *1730*, no. 289; *1731*, no. 434iii; PRO C.O.5/1321/R.76; C.O.5/1337/75; William Waller Hening, comp., *The Statutes at Large; being a Collection of all the Laws of Virginia, from the First Session of the Legislature*, 13 vols. (Philadelphia, 1823; Charlottesville, Va., 1969), Vol. III, pp. 377–81 (4 Annae c. 34), Vol. IV, pp. 222–8 (1 Geo. I, c. 11); Hemphill, pp. 175–80.

[34] 5 Geo. II c. 7 (*Statutes at Large*, ed. Ruffhead, Vol. VI, pp. 74–5; Price, pp. 278–9; Bristol, Merchants Hall Archives, Minutes of Proceedings, V, 23 February 1730–1; 14 December 1731; *Calendar of State Papers Colonial . . . 1731*, nos. 367, 401, 406, 434, 473; *1732*, nos. 22, 24, 32, 36, 55, 136, 176, 196, 197; PRO C.O.5/1322 ff. 187–91v; 194–9v, 216–17v; Leo Francis Stock (ed.), *Proceedings and Debates of the British Parliament Respecting North America*, 5 vols. (Washington, D.C., 1924–41), Vol. IV, pp. 128, 130, 145, 150, 153–5, 160; Hemphill, 180–9.

Virginia legislature were so offended that they sought revenge against the merchants by petitioning for what became Walpole's abortive excise scheme.[35] However, planter wrath may have been misplaced. The act did not in fact hurt the slave trade or undermine the slave plantation system. It did, however, clear up many questions touching debts for slave purchases. In particular, it made a very effective legal instrument of the *bond* given by planters buying slaves on credit. With this legal protection in place, the credit-based slave trade in many colonies could and did expand significantly in the ensuing decades.[36]

If the 1732 act did not adversely affect slavery as an institution, the same cannot be said for its impact on slaves as individuals and members of families. Under the act, slaves could be seized and sold for the payment of certain classes of their owners' debts, separating them thereby from their friends and families. In the changed moral climate at the end of the century, such separations were no longer acceptable; Bryan Edwards was able to obtain an act of Parliament in 1797 abrogating so much of the 1732 act as made slaves "chattels for the payment of debts." But the slave trade was almost over by then. While it lasted unscathed, the act could "truly be called the Palladium of Colony credit, and the English Merchant's grand security".[37]

The first clear evidence of the reorientation of the trade following the act of 1732 comes from South Carolina. Planters there had been buying slaves for rice and giving bonds when credit was involved. As long as the law was weak on suing on such bonds, the merchant-factors in the colony were inclined to be lenient with overdue bonds, particularly as they could make such bonds with their penalties earn them 10% interest. After the 1732 act, however, the whole system was tightened up. Since the merchant-factors in the colony were now in a stronger position vis-à-vis the planters in collecting bonded debt, the English slave traders, in turn, sought to improve their position vis-à-vis the factors. They now insisted on formal contracts that obliged the factor to give security in England and to assume legal liability for the value of all slaves received and sold by him. Some contracts further obliged the factor to remit two-thirds of the sale

---

[35] Price, "Excise Affair," pp. 279, 284–8, 306–7.

[36] In Virginia, slave imports were quite buoyant in the years following the 1732 act, averaging 2,141 in 1733–7 compared with 173 in 1728–31 (Minchinton, King, and Waite, xv). The act was much less effective in facilitating debt recovery actions against land in Jamaica. See Edward Long, *The History of Jamaica*, 3 vols. (London, 1774), Vol. I, p. 546.

[37] 37 Geo. III c. CXIX (ed. Ruffhead, *Statutes at Large*, Vol. XVII, pp. 656–7); Sheridan, p. 289; [William Cobbett], *The Parliamentary History of England*, 36 vols. (London, 1806–20), Vol. XXXIII, pp. 261–3, 831–4.

proceeds within one year of the date of sale and the remainder within two years. To assume such contractual obligations, the factor had to be sure that he could collect from the planter. The initial sale was secured with credit of up to eighteen months; if the planter could not pay then, a new bond was taken for another year's credit with 10% interest or penalty.[38]

When Henry Laurens of the Charleston firm of Austin & Laurens entered the slave selling business ca. 1749, he approached a number of slave-trading firms in Bristol, Liverpool, and Lancaster, soliciting consignments. He proposed arrangements similar but not identical to those just enumerated, which had emerged in South Carolina in the 1730s. In return for a 10% commission, Laurens would give security in England and assume full responsibility for collecting all slave sale debts, but he insisted that he be given discretion in the length of credit and thus could not commit himself to remittance within any certain time limits – though he later claimed that he was usually able to remit in six to nine months in bills of exchange payable in England thirty or forty days after presentation (sight).[39] By 1755, however, some of the big slave traders in England were no longer satisfied with the uncertain timing of payment implied by such terms and transferred their consignments from Laurens's company to newer firms in Charleston that undertook *immediate remittance*, or what contemporaries called "bills in the bottom." That is, when a slave-trading vessel left the colony for home, it would carry whatever had been thus far received for the slave sales (commodities, specie, and planters' bills of exchange), with the balance (the greater part of the whole) covered by the factor's own bills of exchange on his surety (called the "guar-

[38] Donnan, Vol. IV, pp. 291–4, reprinted from *South Carolina Gazette* of March 9, 1738. For the use of bonds in slave sales in South Carolina before 1720, see ibid., Vol. IV, p. 266n. Advertisements for slave sales in the *South Carolina Gazette* in the 1730s sometimes mentioned credit of up to six months but at other times indicated that "Good Encouragement will be given ready Pay in Currency, Rice, Pitch and Tar." However, a merchant's letter of September 12, 1735, refers to the 2,400 slaves imported at Charleston that year, "which have sold very well tho' the greatest part upon Credit." Ibid., Vol. IV, pp. 276–80n (and pp. 302n, 311, for similar advertisements in 1749–52), 412n. The high rates of interest mentioned in the text were presumably based on the penalty clauses in the bonds and thus circumvented colonial usury laws.

[39] Ibid., Vol. IV, pp. 303, 317–18; Philip M. Hamer et al. (eds.), *The Papers of Henry Laurens*, 11+ vols. (Columbia, S.C., 1968–), Vol. I, pp. 202–6, 211–12, 226–7, 254–7. For the high frequency of three- to six-month credits in slave sales at Charleston, see Donnan, Vol. III, pp. 153–5, 161. Slaves were imported into North Carolina in smaller shipments from the West Indies, supported in part by six- to nine-month credits from West Indian slave dealers. North Carolina State Archives AB58/14 Hogg and Campbell invoice book.

antee") in England. These last were generally drawn in three or four
tranches, or clusters payable – for example, at three, six, and nine
months' "sight," that is, three, six, or nine months after presentation
to the addressee or drawee in England for acceptance. The guarantee
in England was prepared to accept these bills drawn on him because,
if all went as arranged, he expected to receive remittances from the
factor before the accepted bills became due for payment, and, if not,
to be reimbursed for anything for which he was "out of pocket."[40]

How in fact were the guarantees reimbursed for both expenses and
risks? In a letter in 1773 to a young slave factor in South Carolina,
Henry Laurens, visiting England, wrote that, as far as he could find
out, the guarantee received only the usual 0.5% commission both on
bills accepted (and paid) by him and on bills sent him for collection.
If he did not receive remittances in time and had to use his own funds
to pay the bills he had accepted, he was entitled to charge interest at
5% per annum.[41] (As the guarantees were substantial merchants, they
should have been able to borrow for less than 5% in peacetime, and
so should have made from 0.5 to 1% on such interest charges.)[42]
Richard Pares could not find any hint in the records of Lascelles &

---

[40] In 1755–6, Laurens lost the sale of at least two slave ships to Charles Mayne, who
undertook to return bills in the bottom. On one occasion, Richard Oswald & Company of London was prepared to consign a shipload of slaves to Laurens without
security in England. Laurens's principal correspondent in England was Devonsheir,
Reeve & Lloyd, of Bristol. When a London guarantee was needed, he could use
Augustus & John Boyd & Company, for which he bought rice for shipment to the
West Indies. The Charleston supply of bills of exchange on England was created by
rice sales. With the advent of war, discouraging to the rice trade, and the new
payment system, Austen & Laurens withdrew from slave selling in 1756: Hamer et
al., Vol. II, pp. 37, 42–7, 169–70, 185–6, 239–43, 294–5, 451, 522. See also Vol. I,
pp. 257–9, 269–76; Vol. II, pp. 47–50, 169, 217–19, 283; Donnan, Vol. IV, pp. 319–
22, 334–5, 348–9. See also Donnan, Vol. III, p. 161, for the length of credit (six-nine
months) of a consignment of sixty-three slaves sold in Charleston for a Rhode Island
firm. On the share of the guarantee, see the following discussion in text. In exceptional cases, it was possible for the guarantee to reside in America. In such cases,
he had a correspondent in England accept the bills. Hamer et al., Vol. VII, p. 503.
For the continuation of the immediate remittance system in South Carolina during
1763–75, see Donnan, Vol. III, pp. 268–9; Vol. IV, pp. 391–4, 399, 414, 424–6, 431–
2, 440, 451–2, 457–8, 460–2, 469; Hamer et al., Vol. VI, pp. 87–91. Around 1772 there
appears to have been an effort to reduce the time of the planter-buyer's credit:
Donnan, Vol. IV, pp. 446–9, 451–2. See also S. G. Checkland, "Finance for the West
Indies, 1780–1815," *Economic History Review*, second series, Vol. X (1958), pp. 461–
9, esp. pp. 466–7; Leila Sellers, *Charleston Business on the Eve of the Revolution* (Chapel
Hill, N.C., 1934), chap. VII, esp. pp. 138–42, 145–6; Elizabeth Donnan, "The Slave
Trade into South Carolina before the Revolution," *American Historical Review*, Vol.
XXXIII (1928), pp. 804–28, esp. pp. 812–13.
[41] Hamer et al., Vol. VIII, pp. 638–9.
[42] Cf. Jacob M. Price, *Capital and Credit in British Overseas Trade: The View from the
Chesapeake, 1700–1776* (Cambridge, Mass., 1980), Chap. 4.

Maxwell, which accepted bills for West Indian slave factors, that they received any more.[43] However, George Buchanan, a Glasgow merchant, wrote to his Maryland correspondent, George Maxwell, that he understood that "the Suretys in Britain generally gett one half" of the 10% commission earned by the slave-selling factor in America.[44] I have found only one confirmatory example – in Maryland in 1718 – of a slave-selling factor sharing half his commission, but it is probable that others in that line had to offer some sort of special consideration to get solid people to act as guarantees. Of course, in most cases the guarantees were firms trading to America as commission houses (like Lascelles & Maxwell) and were willing to help the slave-selling factors in America because they received other remunerative business from them.[45]

The immediate remittance or bills in the bottom system that was introduced into South Carolina ca. 1755 was almost certainly developed first in the West Indies, whence it was imported into Charleston. There were, however, significant differences in the system in the two areas. At Charleston in the generation before the American Revolu-

[43] Richard Pares, "A London West-India Merchant House 1740–1769," in Richard Pares and A. J. P. Taylor (eds.), *Essays Presented to Sir Lewis Namier* (London, 1956), pp. 75–107, esp. pp. 103–4. I am not sure that what Pares wrote about contracted prices represented normal practice in the trade. The records of this firm were largely destroyed by bombing in 1940.

[44] Scottish Record Office, C.S.96/507 pp. 47–9, G. Buchanan to G. Maxwell, 6 December 1761.

[45] Henry Laurens arranged for the London firm of Bourdieu & Chollet to act as a guarantee for his protégé, John Lewis Gervais, in Charleston. This was a firm with activities all over the Atlantic world but was only beginning in the Charleston trade when approached. On them, see Price, *France and the Chesapeake*, Vol. II, pp. 687–8 and index. In the papers of James Rogers, a Bristol slave trader, there are a number of letters of credit from British merchants guaranteeing acceptance and payment of bills of exchange drawn by factors in the West Indies to remit the proceeds of the sale of Rogers' slaves. See, e.g., PRO C.107/7(i) Bridgman, Combe & Bridgman (London, 1 Jan. 1793); Alex. Houstoun & Company (Glasgow, 19 Apr. 1787); C.107/7(ii) Thomas Daniel & Son (Bristol, 19 July 1788); C.107/9 Lindo Aguilar & Dias (London, 19 Feb. 1789); C. 107/10 Turner Gammell & Company (London, 16 Feb. 1792); John Campbell Sr. & Company (Glasgow, 30 July 1792). For the correspondence of a Bristol guarantee, see Kenneth Morgan (ed.), "Calendar of Correspondence from William Miles to John Tharp 1770–1789" in Patrick McGrath (ed.), *A Bristol Miscellany* (Bristol Records Society's Publications, Vol. XXXVII) (Bristol, 1985), pp. 84–121. There are also references to letters of credit from guarantees in Richard Pares's transcripts from the (destroyed) Lascelles & Maxwell letterbook (Bodleian Library), boxes I and IV. On the relations between the slave-selling factors in the West Indies and their merchant correspondents/guarantees in London, see Richard B. Sheridan, "The Commercial and Financial Organization of the British Slave Trade, 1750–1807," *Economic History Review*, second series, Vol. XI (1958), pp. 249–63, esp. pp. 260–3. The 1718 example is in Georgetown University Library, James Carroll letter book, fo. 97, with at least one of the sharers living in Maryland.

tion, merchant buyers of rice and indigo (regardless of whom they were buying for) normally paid with bills of exchange on London. This created a regular if not always adequate supply of London bills that planters could use to help pay for their slave purchases when due and that the slave-selling factors could acquire for the necessary remittances to their guarantees in England. In the West Indies, by contrast, the larger planters did not normally sell their sugar locally but shipped it to consignment merchants in England to be sold on commission. They then could draw bills against these consignment earnings but ran the risk of nonacceptance and "protest" if they drew too much without permission. Charleston bills normally drawn by merchants were therefore less likely to be protested than West Indian bills drawn by planters.[46] This was a particularly sensitive point, for West Indian planters buying slaves, instead of giving buyer's bonds, sometimes paid at purchase with long bills on London payable up to eighteen months after acceptance. Through the immediate remittance system, however, the risk of such long bills fell not on the English slave traders but on the West Indian factor and his guarantee.[47] Even the new Liverpool intruders after 1750 found it wiser, therefore, to sell through factors (with sureties) rather than through their ship captains, as before.[48] Some Liverpool firms went even further and tried to get the factors to guarantee them in advance a minimum sale price – but there is no evidence that this became a common practice.[49]

At the beginning of the American Revolution, though, when the North American market was cut off, something of a slave glut appears to have developed in the West Indies, and the factors reportedly could sell the slaves they received only by giving planters up to five years' credit secured by bond, instead of taking the previously normal twelve- to eighteen-month bills of exchange. Such bonds, unlike the

---

[46] For the nonacceptance of planters' bills, see Donnan, *Documents*, Vol. III, pp. 248–9, 297–8.

[47] Ibid., Vol. III, pp. 248–9, 255, 259, 272n–273, 291–2, 295–302; Vol. IV, p. 418.

[48] Francis E. Hyde, Bradbury B. Parkinson, and Sheila Marriner, "The Nature and Profitability of the Liverpool Slave Trade," *Economic History Review*, second series, Vol. V (1953), pp. 368–77, esp. p. 369n.

[49] Gomer Williams, *History of the Liverpool Privateers and Letters of Marque with an Account of the Liverpool Slave Trade* (London, 1897), pp. 486–8, 550. With the threat of war in 1775, some smaller-scale Rhode Island slave traders attempted to sell a whole cargo at a flat price per head. We do not know how common this attempt was; at other times, the Rhode Islanders also used the bills in the bottom system. Jay Coughtry, *The Notorious Triangle: Rhode Island and the African Slave Trade 1700–1807* (Philadelphia, 1981), pp. 180–2; Virginia Bever Platt, "'And Don't Forget the Guinea Voyage': The Slave Trade of Aaron Lopez of Newport," *William and Mary Quarterly*, third series, Vol. XXXII (1975), pp. 601–18, esp. p. 613.

previous bills, were not negotiable in England, and this sudden loss of liquidity forced some English firms into bankruptcy.[50] In the 1790s another glut developed (perhaps reflecting the loss of the St. Domingue market); the length of credit on slave sales in the West Indies is reported to have been distinctly longer than before 1776, with the factors' bills on their guarantees allegedly averaging three years' sight, but still fully acceptable for discount or circulation on the credit of the signatures of the acceptors and endorsers. Planters needing longer credit were reportedly giving bonds then at 6% with such interest retained by the factor and available to reimburse the guarantee in case he did not get returns in time to cover his acceptances.[51]

In summary, the immediate remittance system had two major features that must be clearly understood: (1) It involved two separate streams of bill of exchange operations. The first stream was bills drawn by slave-selling factors on their guarantees in England and remitted to the slave traders immediately after the American sale as returns on their ventures. The second stream consisted of bills drawn by sugar planters or rice-purchasing agents on their correspondents in England, acquired by the slave-selling factors and remitted by them to their guarantees in England to reimburse the latter for accepting and paying the bills in the first stream. (2) The first stream of bills drawn by the factors on their guarantees were long bills normally drawn in three or four tranches, with intervals between the payment dates of at least three months. The timing of the tranches changed over time with market conditions. At first, we read of three tranches at three, six, and nine months' sight. Later we read of durations of up to eighteen and twenty-four months and longer.[52] Whatever their lengths, to serve their remittance function the bills had to be negotiable, that is, acceptable for discount or circulation. That is what the English slave traders meant when they "said that Bills in the bottom kept the wheel in motion."[53]

[50] Donnan, *Documents*, Vol. II, p. 553n.
[51] Ibid., Vol. II, pp. 625–9. In the Rogers papers, the maximum length of bills drawn in the West Indies in the late 1780s and early 1790s appears to have been thirty months. PRO C.107/8, 9, 10, 12.
[52] For three-, six-, and nine-month tranches, see Hamer et al., Vol. II, pp. 47–8, Vol. VI, pp. 87–91; Donnan, *Documents*, Vol. III, p. 286, Vol. IV, p. 399. For twelve- to fifteen-month tranches, see Hamer et al., Vol. II, pp. 46–7, Vol. VI, pp. 87–91, Vol. VIII, pp. 636, 637; Donnan, *Documents*, Vol. III, 298–302, Vol. IV, pp. 391–4, 424–6. For eighteen-month tranches, see Donnan, *Documents*, Vol. III, pp. 295–6, 305. For twenty-four-month tranches, see Donnan, *Documents*, Vol. III, p. 305; James A. Rawley, *The Transatlantic Slave Trade: A History* (New York, 1981), p. 188; PRO C.107/8, 9, 10, 12.
[53] Hamer et al., Vol. VI, pp. 89–90.

The immediate remittance system thus understood was particularly suited to the needs of the Liverpool slave traders who increasingly dominated the trade from the 1740s. In London, Bristol, or Glasgow, local bills of exchange with two months or less to run before maturity could be discounted at local banks or passed in some branches of trade. (Glasgow or Bristol merchants receiving bills on London would send them to their correspondents in the capital, where they also could be discounted within two months of maturity.) Accepted bills of longer maturities, however, normally had to be kept until they were within two or so months of payment, when they became negotiable.[54] However, in South Lancashire a local practice had developed of passing longer bills in trade with an appropriate discount. (These were normally accepted bills on London.) This was of special use to the Liverpool slave traders, who could use the bills they received from the West Indies of whatever length to pay for their export goods (purchased on about twelve months' credit) and some of their ships' gear.[55] David Richardson's analysis of the accounts of the slave-trading firm of William Davenport of Liverpool shows that almost all the bills of exchange received (90% of total returns) were disposed of before maturity with a discount.[56] There would thus appear to have

---

[54] For normal practice, cf. Price, *Capital and Credit*, chap. 5, esp. pp. 89–95. The "bill book" of Buchanan & Simson of Glasgow makes it clear that longer local bills (up to one year's sight) were normally kept in the firm's strong box but that bills with less than sixty days to maturity could be discounted or passed in trade. Scottish Record Office, C.S.96/508.

[55] Alfred P. Wadsworth and Julia de Lacy Mann, *The Cotton Trade and Industrial Lancashire 1600–1780* (Manchester, 1931), pp. 96, 249; L. S. Pressnell, *Country Banking in the Industrial Revolution* (Oxford, 1956), pp. 19–20, 77, 170–3; T. S. Ashton, *An Economic History of England: The 18th Century* (London, 1955), pp. 185–8; Henry Thornton, *An Enquiry into the Nature and Effects of the Paper Credit of Great Britain (1802)*, ed. F. A. Hayek (London, 1939), p. 94n; B. L. Anderson, "Financial Institutions and the Capital Market on Merseyside in the Eighteenth and Nineteenth Centuries," in B. L. Anderson and P. J. M. Stoney (eds.), *Commerce, Industry and Transport: Studies in Economic Change on Merseyside* (Liverpool, 1983), pp. 26–59. For other contemporary references to the circulation (at discount) of slave factors' bills on their sureties, see Donnan, *Documents*, Vol. II, p. 629, Vol. IV, pp. 418, 457–8.

[56] David Richardson, "Profits in the Liverpool Slave Trade: The Accounts of William Davenport, 1757–1784," in Roger Anstey and P. E. H. Hair (eds.), *Liverpool, the African Slave Trade, and Abolition . . .* (Historic Society of Lancashire and Cheshire, Occasional Papers, Vol. 2) (s.l., 1976), pp. 72–3; idem., "Profitability in the Bristol–Liverpool Slave Trade," in *La Traite des Noirs par l'Atlantique: Nouvelles approches* (Bibliothèque d'Histoire d'Outremer, Nouvelle Série, Etudes, 4) (Paris, 1976), pp. 301–8, esp. pp. 304–5. See also B. L. Anderson, "The Lancashire Bill System and Its Liverpool Practitioners . . . ," in W. H. Chaloner and Barrie M. Ratcliffe (eds.), *Trade and Transport: Essays . . . in Honour of T. S. Willan* (Manchester, 1977), pp. 59–77; and [James Wallace], *A General and Descriptive History of the Ancient and Present State of . . . Liverpool* (Liverpool, 1795), pp. 232–3.

been a most singular organic connection between the South Lanca-shire bill circulation system and the rise of Liverpool as a slave-trading port from the 1740s. Every businessman in that area who sold export goods on long credit or who received and passed American bills of exchange was in a sense helping to finance the slave trade.

However, in seeking to comprehend the handling of the very long bills of exchange produced by the slave trade, one should be wary of overemphasizing the importance of the Lancashire bill system to the relative neglect of the London and other money markets. Davenport's bill book of the 1770s shows that only 21% (by value) of bills received from the West Indies were disposed of in Liverpool and vicinity; 75% were sent to London to a rather large group of merchants with whom Davenport dealt.[57] Some of these were clearly merchants from whom Davenport purchased textiles, ironmongery, and other goods for his African voyages. Thus West Indian bills could be passed (with an appropriate discount) to pay at first hand for goods purchased. Other bills, however, may have been sent to London for discount in what were essentially financial as distinct from commercial transactions. Since we do not have Davenport's correspondence, we cannot be ab-solutely sure of the underlying character of his London bill trans-actions.[58]

We are fortunate, however, in having a considerable surviving cor-respondence dating from the 1780s and 1790s of the Bristol slave trader James Rogers. As a return of the proceeds of the sale of his slaves, he also received from his factors in the West Indies the familiar "sets" of bills in tranches of twelve, eighteen, and twenty-four months, or some variant thereof. He does not appear to have passed these bills to his suppliers in the reputed Lancashire fashion but instead sought to get cash for them. His London bankers, including the Quaker firm of Smith, Wright & Gray, and its successor, Sir James Esdaile & Com-pany, would discount bills sent them when within two months of maturity, but this did not help with the longer bills.[59] Rogers was,

---

[57] Keele University Library, William Davenport bill-book, 1769–85, omitting the atypical war years, 1776–82.

[58] An earlier bill and letterbook of Davenport at Keele shows that in the early 1750s he sent bills to his London banker, Hoare & Company, for collection and deposit. It is not possible to tell from this source or from an examination of Davenport's account in the ledgers of Messrs. Hoare & Company, Fleet Street, whether or not they discounted for him.

[59] PRO C.107/3 to Smith, Wright & Gray, 2 Oct. 1790, 3, 13 June 1792; C.107/9 from same (many letters). Rogers was informed that "nothing is discountable here [Lon-don] that has more than 2 Months to Run." C. 107/10 from John Hallett, 10 Mar. 1785.

however, in touch with a number of West Country provincial bankers (particularly in Bath) who would take bills at four months from maturity and give him in exchange two-month bills, charging him two months' discount for the time saved. He could send these shorter bills to London for immediate discount at his bankers.[60] For the much longer bills characteristic of the slave trade, Rogers had to make private discount arrangements. There were men in Bristol (most likely retired merchants) who would discount them, but Rogers, his correspondence would suggest, most often went outside. In at least two cases, the London merchants or guarantees who had accepted some of his West Indian bills agreed to discount or prepay their own acceptances. This was a very safe way for a semiretired merchant to earn the best market interest on his capital.[61] In other cases, country bankers with idle cash at places such as Bradford (Wilts), Chepstow (Monmouth), and Worcester discounted Rogers's long bills. These slave paper discountings were large transactions, sometime £3,000–5,000 at a time.[62] Rogers's varied experience suggests that each active slave trader had to develop his own circle of affluent acquaintances with available liquid resources who would help him with large, longer-term discounts as needed. Through such discounting, remote pockets of capital were made available to the slave trade.

In Virginia there was nothing strictly comparable to the immediate remittance system characteristic of the slave trade in the West Indies and South Carolina after 1750. However, Chesapeake factors were expected to give sureties too, and the same results (speedy and secure remittances) were achieved by slightly different practices. Remittances for slave purchases in Virginia had commonly been made in bills of exchange from the late seventeenth century.[63] The sale of slaves for credit secured by bonds was known there before 1732,[64] but we have no way of determining how widespread the practice was. However,

---

[60] PRO C.107/10 from Atwood Abraham & Company, Bath, 1791.

[61] The two semiretired merchants were Robert Cooper Lee and Robert Shedden, both of whom lived in or near Bedford Square, not a neighborhood for active businesses. See PRO C.107/9 from R. C. Lee, 5 June 1789, 16 Oct., 3 Nov., 16, 18 Dec. 1790; C.107/10 from R. Shedden, 2 Feb. 1792; from R. C. Lee, 25 Mar. 1791.

[62] PRO C.107/3 to Glover, Embury & Cross, Worcester, 17 Nov. 1789; C.107/10 from D. Clutterbuck, Bradford (Wilts), 12 Dec. 1785, 2 Jan., 10 Feb. 1786; from Lewis, Stoughton & Company, Chepstow, 5 Dec. 1791.

[63] For problems arising from the nonacceptance of planters' bills in England, see Minchinton, "Isaac Hobhouse," *Virginia Magazine of History and Biography*, Vol. LXVI (1958), pp. 278–307. For earlier attempts to get Virginia slave selling factors to assume collection responsibility without English surety, see Bank of England Archives, B48 (H. Morice Papers) invoice and instructions for Anne-Galley, 25 Mar. 1725.

[64] Donnan, *Documents*, Vol. IV, pp. 94–5.

after the passage of the Colonial Debts Act, the use of bonds in such transactions became almost universal. There was an active local market in the colony for the sale of Virginia-born slaves by owners, executors, administrators, receivers, or trustees. An examination of several dozen advertisements for such sales published in the *Virginia Gazette* in 1772 shows that, where terms were specified, these almost always included credit (for ca. six to twelve months) secured by bond with security. That is, the bond had to bear the signature not only of the debtor (slave buyer) but also of one or two cosigners who stood surety for him.

However, when slaves newly imported from Africa were advertised for sale in the *Virginia Gazette*, different modes of settlement might be demanded. Five notices of such sale appeared there in 1772: One of these gave no terms, and another specified only that credit would be given with security, probably meaning that bonds would be taken; the other three announced that payment was to be made in "merchants' notes" payable at the next "merchants' meeting."[65] In Virginia before the Revolution, the principal merchants (and managers for British firms) met four times a year at Williamsburg at the time of the regular meetings of the province's General Court (April and October) and Oyer and Terminer Court (June and December). At these meetings they settled accounts among themselves after agreeing on a rate of exchange on London for that session. At such meetings, holders of merchants' notes could therefore expect to receive payment, if desired, in the form of bills of exchange on London at the agreed-upon rate.[66] Where slaves were sold for merchants' notes only, purchases could be effected only by merchants or by the substantial planter who could get such notes as needed. Merchants who bought slaves at such sales undoubtedly planned to resell them on credit to

---

[65] The first mentioned in the text was the *Prince of Wales*, with 400 slaves (*Gazette*, 24 Sept.); the second was the *Thomas*, with 200 slaves (30 July); the last three were the *Polly*, with 430 slaves (4 June), the *Nancy*, with 250 (9 July), and the *Union*, with 280 (20 Aug.). Cf. also Donnan, *Documents*, Vol. IV, p. 160; Minchinton, King, and Waite, p. 185. Payments were not necessarily punctual where bonds were taken. Advertisements also appeared reminding slave buyers at specific sales that their bonds were overdue. See *Virginia Gazette*, March 20 and October 1, 1772. It is possible that *merchants' notes* came to be insisted on in Virginia because an unacceptable proportion of the planters' bills of exchange were refused acceptance and returned protested. Cf. Donnan, *Documents*, Vol. IV, pp. 147–8. In Maryland, sales seem to have been handled by slave factors on a system comparable to that described by H. Laurens for South Carolina in 1749–55. Planters' bills of exchange were accepted as cash. Ibid., Vol. IV, pp. 26, 38–40, 43.

[66] On merchants' meetings, see James H. Soltow, "The Role of Williamsburg in the Virginia Economy," *William and Mary Quarterly*, third series, Vol. XV (1958), pp. 467–82.

planters at a profit, presumably taking bonds for the security of the credit. From the standpoint of the English slave traders, sales by factors for merchants' notes meant a slightly slower return than expected under the immediate remittance system but should have been just as secure. And they didn't have to worry about the nonacceptance of planters' bills.

The slave sale advertisements in the 1772 *Virginia Gazette* include one instructive shipload for which no mode of payment was specified. In September 1772 there was entered in the Upper District of the James River the ship *Prince of Wales*, containing 400 African slaves consigned by John Powell & Company of Bristol to their local agents, John Wayles and Colonel Richard Randolph.[67] Wayles was a successful lawyer (and planter) with extensive experience representing British firms, including Farell & Jones of Bristol.[68] Richard Randolph of Curles came from a distinguished Virginia family – his father had been treasurer of the colony earlier in the century – and represented Henrico County in the House of Burgesses from 1766 to 1772. (The fact that he was unseated on petition in 1772 suggests, however, that all was not absolutely well with his affairs.) He also had a Bristol connection, his cousin William Randolph being a partner in Stephenson, Randolph & Cheston, a merchant firm there.[69] Wayles's friends, Farell & Jones, were the guarantees enabling Wayles and Randolph to get this consignment. Neither Wayles nor Randolph was a professional merchant, but leading people in Virginia – including Governor Spotswood – were more than interested in receiving such consignments, both for the 10% commissions and for the air of importance they gave.

The immediate remittance system did not normally operate in Virginia, but, to get their consignment from Powells, Wayles and Randolph undertook – with Farell & Jones guaranteeing their performance – to remit half the proceeds of the sale in six months and the balance in twelve months. Their slave cargo was advertised for sale in the *Virginia Gazette* of September 24, rather late in the year for such business, as planters ordinarily preferred to buy slaves early in the summer so that their new hands could do some work and be "seasoned"

---

[67] *Virginia Gazette*, September 21, 1772; Minchinton, King, and Waite, 185.

[68] John M. Hemphill II, "John Wayles Rates His Neighbours," *Virginia Magazine of History and Biography*, Vol. LXVI (1958), pp. 302–6.

[69] Cynthia Miller Leonard, comp., *The General Assembly of Virginia . . . A Bicentennial Register of Members* (Richmond, Va., 1978), pp. 95, 97, 100, 103; William G. Stanard, "The Randolph Family," *William and Mary Quarterly*, first series, Vol. VII (1898–9), pp. 122–4, 195–7, Vol. VIII (1899–1900), pp. 119–22, 263–5, Vol. IX (1900–1), pp. 182–3, 250–2; *Sketchley's Bristol Directory* (Bristol, 1775).

before the advent of cold weather. With not enough planters coming forward, large lots of these slaves had to be sold to merchants intending to resell them. No terms of sale were given in the advertisement but, in the light of what happened subsequently, they were likely to have been fairly generous, explainable in part by the lateness of the season, by the previous arrival of four other slave ships that year, and perhaps by Randolph's desire to do favors to rebuild his local political position. Had they insisted on merchants' notes in payment – as did at least three other slave ships that summer – Wayles and Randolph would have had no difficulty meeting their obligations to Powell & Company. But they obviously did not and missed both their remittance deadlines, forcing their sureties, Farell & Jones, to pay for them. Wayles died in 1773, leaving an estate estimated at £30,000. In a codicil to his will, he directed that his executors (his three sons-in-law) not distribute his effects to his heirs until his slave accounts with Farell & Jones were cleared. But the sons-in-law (including Thomas Jefferson) ignored this provision and in 1774 divided the estate among the heirs (mostly their wives and themselves). Since Randolph, the surviving partner, could not pay by himself, Farell & Jones could only seek redress at law, but the closing of the courts in 1774–5 and the Revolution obstructed this course for many years. Although the peace treaty of 1783 and the Jay Treaty of 1794 recognized the validity of claims for such prewar debts, the heirs of Farell & Jones were unable to recover much until Jefferson's administration, when, in accordance with a bilateral convention of 1802, the United States paid the British government £600,000 sterling to be quit of claims against it relating to the treaty provisions on prewar debts. The British government turned this money over to a commission, which in 1811 paid the estates of Farell & Jones about 46% of their claim (without interest) after almost forty years. The case is interesting not only because it involved Jefferson but also because it gives some indication of the strategic role of the guarantees in financing the trade and suggests some of the risks they ran.[70]

---

[70] Price, *Capital and Credit*, 138; Farell & Jones claim, PRO T.79/9 and 30; Somerset Record Office, DD/GC 62. The slaves were sold for £8,537, of which £6,017 (without interest) was still owing in 1783. For an analogous case of 1733 in which Lyde and Cooper, another Bristol firm of guarantees, was forced to pay when the slave-selling factor, Henry Darnall, Jr., defaulted, see Maryland State Archives, Chancery Records, Vol. 8, ff. 9–75. For British debt claims after the war and the compensation of 1802–11, see Jacob M. Price, "One Family's Empire: the Russell–Lee–Clerk Connection in Maryland, Britain and India, 1707–1857," *Maryland Historical Magazine*, Vol. LXXII (1977), pp. 165–225, esp. pp. 201–14; idem., "The Maryland Bank Stock Case: British–American Financial and Political Relations Before and After the American

The planned credit emphasis of this chapter should not, of course, mislead the reader into thinking that *all* slave sales were for credit. In every colony there were a few well-to-do planters and merchants who could buy for cash but who expected substantial reductions in price in return for their coin, notes, or bills. The seller needed much skill to steer between the Scylla of reassuring "cash" sales at unacceptably low prices and the Charybdis of easier sales at strikingly higher prices with unacceptably long credits and attendant risks. In a letter of 1773 to a young man starting out as a slave seller in Charleston, Henry Laurens advised:

... I would by no means encourage you to give Credit to every Man who may offer to deal with you merely for the Sake of a high price & a flaunting Average, which must end in the prejudice of your Constituents & your own Ruin. Yet on the other hand if you Consult only your own Safety by Selling to Monied Men who are always careful to obtain full abatement for Cash, you will depreciate your prices to Such a degree as will Injure your Friends, the Owners of Cargoes consigned to you ... & greatly undervalue your Own Credit & Reputation.[71]

It is not within the scope of this chapter to explore at length the North American slave trade after the American Revolution. Published work does, however, suggest that there was some continuity in credit arrangements. Perhaps the single most significant interstate slave trade affecting the United States after the abolition of the import trade in 1807 was the coastal trade from the Chesapeake to New Orleans. The newspaper advertisements published by Bancroft indicate that professional slave buyers in Virginia had to offer hard cash for their purchases. However, at the New Orleans end, the advertisements on the eve of the Civil War announce that these same traffickers would sell for "good town bills," that is, accepted bills of exchange on mer-

Revolution," in Aubrey C. Land, Lois Green Carr, and Edward C. Papenfuse (eds.), *Law, Society, and Politics in Early Maryland* (Baltimore, 1977), pp. 3–40. For the sale of slaves to merchants in lots of ten to thirty-one, see Virginia State Library, *Jones, Surviving Partner of Farell and Jones v. Wayles exors*, 1797 Circuit Court Cases, as cited in Michael L. Nicholls, "Competition, Credit, and Crisis: Merchant–Planter Relations in Southside Virginia" (unpublished paper presented at the Conference on Merchant Credit and Labour Strategies in the Staple Economies of North America, Memorial University of Newfoundland, August 1987), p. 6.

[71] Hamer et al., Vol. VIII, pp. 671–2. In an earlier letter on the same subject, Laurens advised young Gervais to "take Collateral Security from every Person whose Circumstances are doubtful" (ibid., p. 637). Comparable advice was given by Samuel and William Vernon, Rhode Island slave traders, to their captain in the West Indies in 1771–3 (Donnan, *Documents*, Vol. III, pp 248, 272).

chants in New Orleans.[72] In this way, the sellers gave several months' credit to buyers, whether planters or inland dealers, without running the risk and burden of collecting such debts. This is functionally just what the sellers in prerevolutionary Virginia achieved by demanding merchants' notes.

In summary, the English slave trade started in the seventeenth century without any clearly established credit conventions of its own. Slaves were sold to planters more or less like any other trade goods. But planters were hungrier for slaves than they were for almost any other conceivable purchase and pushed the existing system of agricultural credit to its limits in their greedy effort to get as many slaves as possible. The slave traders thus found it much easier to sell slaves on credit than to collect debts – and the planter-dominated colonial courts and legislatures were not much help. By the end of the seventeenth century, both the Royal African Company and the separate traders normally found it necessary to require their factors to assume responsibility for the payment of all their credit sales. The factors could undertake such commitments only if they could, in turn, require planter-buyers to give bond or equivalent security. The credit control practices introduced in the last quarter of the seventeenth century were further developed by the private traders in the opening decades of the new century, with the planter's bond becoming a much more effective debt instrument after the passage of the Colonial Debts Act of 1732. Thus, by the 1730s and 1740s, English slave traders were fairly certain of eventually receiving the proceeds of credit sales, but they still were not certain about *when* they would see their money. As such uncertainty could be fatal for a business, in the 1750s slave traders to both the West Indies and South Carolina turned increasingly to the immediate remittance system by which their factors were required to send back on the slave-importing vessel the total net receipt of the slave sales, most of it in the form of bills of long maturity drawn by the factors on their guarantees in England. Since such bills could often be discounted or passed into circulation in England, the slave traders gained substantially in liquidity. This arrangement made the factors' guarantees, or sureties, the linchpins of the trade's credit structure. In this, the guarantees were in effect performing a role anticipating that of the Victorian "accepting house."

---

[72] Frederic Bancroft, *Slave Trading in the Old South* (New York, 1959). For offers to buy for cash, see pp. 22, 24, 25, 28n et passim; for the New Orleans sale, see facing p. 316. The New Orleans *Picayune* slave sale advertisements show the use of other credit merchanisms, including bonds, in earlier years.

THE PROBLEM OF MORTGAGES

Thus far, we have been discussing what is essentially short- and medium-term credit – but important credit nevertheless. At the level of the planter buying a slave, the extent of credit was set by the market. There may not have always been as much credit available as ambitious planters would have wished, but there was always enough to sell all slaves. The development of the immediate remittance or bills in the bottom system shifted the burden of carrying this credit from the slave trader to the factor and his guarantee, with the slave trader receiving full remittance on sales (in the form of discountable bills) on the return of his vessel, normally within eighteen months of departure. By the 1790s, we are told, the average length of the bills accepted was three years. With bills of this duration, the guarantees would have had acceptances (obligations) outstanding that far exceeded the average annual return from the trade. Even if the average acceptance was only two years, they would very likely have been at least equal to the annual returns.

But was there no long-term credit? What about the mortgages that loom so large in some popular accounts of the plantation economy of the West Indies? In considering such questions, we can usefully start with the last work of Richard Pares, who, with a few others, laid the foundations of the post–World War II study of the slave economy of the West Indies. For the purposes of this chapter Pares made several major points: (1) Except for the relatively modest sums that some emigrants brought with them, there was (*pace* Adam Smith) no significant long-term movement of capital from the mother country to the colonies. (2) The credit that was available from the mother country was largely short-term commercial credit. As the West India houses of London and Bristol prospered, they reinvested part of their profits in further advances to their planter and merchant correspondents in the Caribbean, so that their outstanding balances grew at least as fast as their capital. (3) The great fortunes we find in the West Indies were built up by reinvesting profits and utilizing to the fullest available commercial credit. (In a few cases, profits of office also helped.) (4) Where we do find mortgages, they are unlikely to represent independent capital movements and are more likely to be only the last stage in the ontogeny of debt: book debt, bond, judgment, mortgage. In his dealings with a merchant (in the colony or in Britain), a planter ran up a debt on the trader's books too large to be cleared by the next crop or two. To assuage the merchant and gain more time, the planter entered into a bond for the debt. When the bond was not cleared in the time specified, the merchant or his representative went to court and obtained a judgment against the planter. To forestall action on the judgment, the planter gained more time by giving the merchant a mortgage on some or all of his real estate and slaves.[73]

Although I tend to agree with the main thrust of Pares's generalizations, I do not find them equally applicable to all the slave economies in the old or Atlantic British Empire at all stages of their existence. Pares's formulation is probably truer of the continental colonies before 1776 than it is of the West Indian colonies if we carry their story down to 1833. Although we have only vague estimates of West Indian debt, we have quite precise information about preindependence debt in the thirteen colonies. Much of it wasn't repaid because of the Revolution and caused considerable legal and diplomatic difficulties thereafter that have left a useful subsidence in the archives.

British merchants trading to the thirteen colonies in the generation before 1776 generally operated in one (or more) of three modes: (1) They were factors acting on commission for planters in the Chesapeake who consigned them tobacco for sale and ordered goods for them to purchase. These arrangements were very similar to those connecting West Indian sugar planters to commission houses in London or Bristol. (2) They corresponded in normal merchant fashion with independent merchant houses in the colonies, north and south, with each side buying and selling for the other as requested, charging the usual commissions. (3) They operated "stores" (a new word) in the interior of Maryland, Virginia, and North Carolina, serving small and middling planters in particular. Although the first mode has attracted the most attention in writings on the Chesapeake, it was probably the least important by the 1770s where debts were concerned.

So far, I have been able to discover the balance sheets of only two English firms trading to the Chesapeake in the generation before the Revolution: James Buchanan & Company and John Norton & Son(s). Both dealt with American merchants and planters, though planters were slightly more important in Norton's business than in Buchanan's. Dealings with American merchants were generally in the mode then called the "cargo trade." The American merchant ordered a "cargo" of goods (possibly worth £5,000 or more), which his London or Bristol correspondent purchased for him on one year's credit from

[73] Pares, pp. 45–50.

the great wholesalers in those ports, the American correspondent undertaking to remit goods or bills of exchange to pay for the same before the year's credit had expired. In 1768, the peak year for Buchanan & Company, about 60% of the amount owing the firm in Virginia was from merchants and only 38% was from planters. Despite their greater involvement with planters, Norton's debt figures for 1773 were not too different: 54% owed by merchants and other traders and 42% owed by planters.[74] In the stores run by Glasgow, Whitehaven, and other firms, we should expect naturally to find a higher percentage of planter debt, but even there some large wholesale transactions with local merchants appear.[75]

The total commercial debt owed by the thirteen colonies to Britain tended to rise in the century along with the rise in population and trade, reaching a peak of ca. £6 million sterling in 1774. As the American Revolution approached and imports from Britain were stopped in 1775, the debt outstanding was cut back by perhaps one-half. One merchant claimed that during 1775 merchant-to-merchant debt (as in the cargo trade) was cut by at least two-thirds. However, net collections were much less impressive from the small and middling planters who patronized the stores in the interior of Virginia, Maryland, and North Carolina. Hence, with the peace, prewar debts outstanding were disproportionately those of the southern colonies (84.1%), particularly Virginia and Maryland (57.7%).[76]

However, in the mass of paper left behind by the debt problem,

---

[74] Jacob M. Price, "The Last Phase of the Virginia–London Consignment Trade: James Buchanan & Co., 1758–1768," *William and Mary Quarterly*, third series, Vol. XLIII (1986), pp. 64–98, esp. p. 91; Price, *Capital and Credit*, chap. 6; on Nortons, see also Frances Norton Mason, *John Norton & Sons, Merchants of London and Virginia . . . 1750 to 1795*, new ed. (Newton Abbot, 1968), with an introduction by Samuel M. Rosenblatt.

[75] For examples of local merchants owing substantial amounts to the local stores of Glasgow firms, see PRO T.79/24, Cuming, Mackenzie & Company's Nansemond store; T.79/25 Archibald & John Hamilton & Company (Virginia and North Carolina).

[76] Price, *Capital and Credit*, chap. 1. For the reduction in merchant-to-merchant debt, see Richard Champion, *Considerations on the Present Situation of Great Britain and the United States of America*, 2nd ed. (London, 1784), p. 269n. The planter debt reduction was much less in the Chesapeake and North Carolina during the nonimportation year, 1775. There was some collection of debts during that year, but new debts were created by the sale of merchandise in the stores at the beginning of the year. Thus the British firms' total effects (merchandise and debts) in those colonies may have been reduced by as much as a third, although total debts remained much as before. The Alston accounts in PRO T.79/33(10) show no reduction in debts owed at four North Carolina stores between August 1774 and August 1775. At the Nomony store (in Virginia) of John Ballantine, the net total investment of the company was reduced 40% between September 1774 and August 1775, whereas the customer debt was reduced only 11.7%. PRO T.79/31.

we find mortgages appearing less frequently than we should expect. There are, of course, conspicuous examples: On the eve of the war in 1774–6, Daniel Dulany had entered into two mortgages (totalling £12,121) to Osgood Hanbury & Company of London to cover debts owed that firm by his late father, Walter Dulany.[77] This is a classic example of what I have termed Pares's "ontogeny of debt." We can find the same process at work among the smaller planters of Southside Virginia in the depressed years 1772–4, when many were obliged to give mortgages to appease their creditors. Michael Nicholls has shown that mortgages and deeds of trust recorded in seven Southside Virginia counties increased from 31.3 per annum in 1768–70 to 145.3 per annum in 1771–3 as tobacco prices fell. However, the total amounts involved were small, with the total recorded for the seven counties in the peak year 1772 being only £22,117 in Virginia currency (ca. £17,700 sterling), or less than the estate of John Wayles.[78] The infrequent mention of mortgages in the postwar debt claims would seem to reinforce the impression that in the thirteen colonies mortgages were, at most, a tactic to collect old debts and not a vehicle for independent transatlantic capital movements. The planters of Virginia and Maryland could avoid the worst pitfalls of debt because they did not have to buy replacement slaves as urgently as did their West Indian counterparts. Their slaves, by contrast, tended to grow more numerous over time, even without new purchases. With both their speculative landholdings and their slaveholdings growing steadily more valuable, they could, in a pinch, get out of serious debt by selling land or slaves – or so the advertisements in the *Virginia Gazette* would suggest – and thus normally avoid the threatening grasp of the mortgage.

In the West Indies, the mortgage situation tended to become markedly different, particularly after 1763. Even there, Pares's paradigm of the ontogeny of debt would appear to hold true for the older settled areas. However, Richard Sheridan has pointed out that after 1763 there was an increased demand for new credit associated with buying and developing estates in the islands ceded by France, as well as with improving the as yet undeveloped areas of Jamaica and Demerara.[79] This demand came to the surface in the pressures behind two acts of

---

[77] Price, "The Maryland Bank Stock Case," pp. 16–18.

[78] Nicholls, pp. 20–1. Nicholls's aggregation does not distinguish British from local creditors or primary obligations from obligations protecting cosigners to bonds, etc. Nicholls's paper has been published in Rosemary E. Ommer, ed., *Merchant Credit and Labour Strategies in Historical Perspective* (Fredericton, Canada, 1990).

[79] Sheridan, "Commercial and Financial Organization," p. 258.

Parliament on colonial mortgages passed in the early 1770s. The first (1773) recognized the right of Dutch and other foreigners to lend money on mortgage in the British West Indian colonies at the British legal maximum interest rate of 5% – provided only that, in case of foreclosures, the land so seized was to be sold at auction and not retained by the foreigner.[80] The second act (1774) regularized the legal standing of persons resident in Britain (where the legal maximum interest rate was 5%) who had been lending large sums on mortgage in Ireland and the colonies at the 6% rate permitted in those jurisdictions.[81]

In the debate on the bills in the House of Commons, it was asserted that the first measure was opposed by those interested in the fully developed, smaller island colonies but pushed by those desiring to develop the ceded islands and the undeveloped sections of the larger colonies. Although the legal rate of interest in most of the colonies was then 6%, it was alleged without explanation that it was impossible to borrow in the islands for less than 8% – a rate considered prohibitive for many improvements. Outside mortgage money at lower rates was therefore desired to encourage the development of the more backward areas of the colonies.[82]

Of special interest in the debates is the leading role in steering both acts through the House of Commons played by William Pulteney (né Johnstone), a private member. William Johnstone, who took his wife's family name on marrying the heiress to the vast Pulteney fortune, was one of the four remarkably adventurous (in the eighteenth-century sense) Johnstone brothers of Westerhall, Dumfriesshire, Scotland. One of his brothers, John, was a survivor of the Black Hole of Calcutta; another, George, was a naval officer and governor of West Florida from 1763 to 1767. From brother George, Pulteney could have found out some of the difficulties of developing newly acquired lands in or near the Caribbean. More relevant, perhaps, were Pulteney's close connections with the Alexander brothers of Edinburgh, who had bought large plantations on Grenada and Tobago from their former French owners but were having trouble paying for their purchases in the difficult aftermath of the crash of 1772. The Alexanders were

---

[80] 13 Geo. III c. 14 (*Statutes at Large*, ed. Danby Pickering, Vol. XXX, pp. 22–6). Jamaica subsequently permitted 6 percent interest on such mortgages. Long, Vol. I, pp. 556–7, 577n, 578n.

[81] 14 Geo. III c. 79 (*Statutes at Large*, ed. Pickering, Vol. XXX, pp. 542–5).

[82] Cobbett, *The Parliamentary History of England*, Vol. XVII, pp. 482–3, 642, 686–8, 690. On interest rates, see Pares, p. 44; Long, Vol. I, pp. 555–6; *Considerations on the State of the Sugar Islands, and on the policy of enabling foreigners to lend money on real security in those colonies . . . by a West Indian Planter* (London, 1773).

interested in getting a Dutch or other mortgage on their West Indian estates, and Pulteney, in pushing his bills, most likely had in mind their needs, as well as those of broader interests.[83]

One wonders, though, whether Pulteney's success in getting these bills through with relatively little trouble was due solely to the support of those interested in developing new areas in the West Indies. By the 1770s, the absentee West Indian plantation owner had become a conspicuous feature of British social life. There were thirteen "West Indians" in the house that passed the acts of 1773–4.[84] Many others in Parliament must have been connected to West Indians by blood, marriage, or friendship. Most should have known that it wasn't easy to manage a West Indian estate from afar for very many years. One solution was to sell the estate if one could find a buyer who could pay an attractive price. But such buyers were rare, particularly when large fresh mortgages (as distinct from mortgages converted from older debts) were needed but difficult to obtain in the islands or at home. For many an absentee, fearing that no mortgage meant no sale, the acts opened new possibilities.

In the longer run, what difference did the mortgage acts of 1773–4 make? The 6% rate should have been attractive in peacetime, when the yield on the government "funds" in Britain hovered around 3.5 percent, but less so in wartime, when yields on the funds and British mortgages were around 5%.[85] One therefore wonders whether the colonies were entirely wise in setting their maximum rates of interest as low as 6%.[86] One picks up chance references to the Dutch lending on mortgages in both the British and French islands after this time, but it is difficult to assess the weight of such lending. Van de Voort has studied Dutch mortgage records but does not distinguish between the periods before and after 1773; his data show, however, that during 1753–94, the British islands received only 4.9% of Dutch mortgage loans to the West Indies.[87] In the British islands, we are told, mortgage lending from all sources increased substantially both in the prosper-

---

[83] All four Johnstone brothers were in Parliament at one time or another between 1768 and 1805. Sir Lewis Namier and John Brooke, *The History of Parliament: The House of Commons 1754–1790*, 3 vols. (Oxford and New York, 1964), Vol. II, pp. 683–7, Vol. III, pp. 341–3. On the Alexander–Pulteney connection and the Alexanders' interest in the West Indies, see Price, *France and the Chesapeake*, Vol. II, pp. 693–700.

[84] Namier and Brooke, Vol. I, p. 157.

[85] T. S. Ashton, *Economic Fluctuations in England 1700–1800* (Oxford, 1959), pp. 85–8, 187.

[86] On interest rates, see footnote 82.

[87] J. P. Van de Voort, "Dutch Capital in the West Indies During the Eighteenth Century," *The Low Countries History Yearbook: Acta Historiae Neerlandicae*, Vol. XIV (1981), pp. 85–105, esp. p. 105.

ous times following the return of peace in 1783 and the removal of St. Domingue competition after 1790 and in the distressed times following the ending of the slave trade in 1807 and the decline of sugar prices after 1815. We have already noted the process by which merchant advances to planters had to be protected by bonds and judgments and, ultimately, mortgages. The final step came when the mortgage was foreclosed and the merchant house became the plantation owner. To gain some liquidity, the merchants, in turn, sometimes had to take out a new mortgage in Britain on the estate.[88]

What did it all add up to? When St. Lucia changed from French to English land law, more than £1 million in 2,000 unrecorded mortgages had to be registered ca. 1833.[89] Sheridan and others suggest that when slavery was abolished after 1833, much of the £20 million sterling in compensation paid to the former slave owners had to be repaid by them to clear their mortgages.[90] But I have as yet seen no hard data on the total burden of such mortgages ca. 1830, and wonder whether anyone has gone through the registries of deeds in the various West Indian islands and analyzed the registered mortgages. Until this is done, we can only speculate on the relative importance of local, British, and European lenders, or on what changes, if any, are noticeable after the mortgage acts of the 1770s or the abolition of the slave trade in 1807. On the financial side, at least, much still needs to be done in historical research on the economics of the West Indian slave plantation.

The pre-1807 slave trade, of course, was normally financed by short-term and not by long-term credit secured by mortgage or otherwise. However, the need for replacement slaves could push the running debt of a plantation so high that a first or additional mortgage became inevitable, just as could a plantation owner's desire for large numbers of new slaves to open up hitherto undeveloped lands. Thus, the difference between short-term and long-term debt may be clearer as

---

[88] Richard B. Sheridan, "The West India Sugar Crisis and British Slave Emancipation, 1830–1833," *Journal of Economic History*, Vol. XXXI (1961), pp. 539–51; Pares, pp. 48–9. On the difficulty of obtaining outside mortgages in the 1820s, see Lowell Joseph Ragatz, *The Fall of the Planter Class in the British West Indies: A Study in Social and Economic History* (New York, 1928), pp. 381–2. On mortgages from merchant houses, see also Michael Craton and James Walton, *A Jamaican Plantation: The History of Worthy Park 1670–1970* (Toronto and Buffalo, 1970), pp. 119, 159. On bank mortgages, see L. S. Pressnell, *Country Banking in the Industrial Revolution* (Oxford, 1956), pp. 307–8.

[89] Ragatz, p. 382.

[90] Sheridan, "West India Sugar Crisis," pp. 547–9; Pares, p. 49.

abstractions than as realities in the demanding world of tropical agriculture.

THE FRENCH ANTILLES:
A COMPARATIVE APPROACH

I propose to discuss the slave trade in the French Antilles rather briefly, emphasizing those key features of the credit system that can be compared or contrasted with those prevailing in the British West Indies. There is a rich body of erudite modern scholarship on the French slave trade.[91] Unfortunately, little of it concentrates on the specific questions I raised earlier in this chapter. However, Father Dieudonné Rinchon has published several volumes of documents that furnish some valuable clues to the precise commercial practices facilitating the use of credit in France's slave trade.[92] His important publications enable us at least to ask of the French record some of the questions raised by British experience – though the answers often prove different.

At the beginning of this chapter, I suggested two models describing the attitude of the law toward the availability of plantation slaves to satisfy creditors' claims against a plantation owner. On the one hand, there was the Latin model, which placed great emphasis on protecting the functioning integrity of a plantation and made it almost impossible for a creditor to seize slaves, livestock, or equipment. On the other hand, there was the Anglo-Saxon model, giving primacy to the rights of creditors, particularly when reinforced by bond or judgment. We have seen the Latin model at work in Portuguese Brazil and the Anglo-Saxon model at work both in the Board of Trade's review of colonial legislation and in the Colonial Debts Act of 1732.

In the French colonies, policy was at first ambiguous, with one colony giving primacy to the integrity of the plantation and another

---

[91] See in particular the valuable bibliographies in Robert Louis Stein, *The French Slave Trade in the Eighteenth Century: An Old Regime Business* (Madison, Wis., 1979); Jean Meyer, *L'Armement nantais dans la deuxième moitié du XVIII° siècle* (Ports-Routes-Trafics, Vol. XXVIII) (Paris, 1969); and P. Dieudonné Rinchon, *Les armements négriers au XVIII° siècle d'après la correspondance et la comptabilité des armateurs et des capitaines nantais* (Académie royale des sciences coloniales, Classe des sciences morales et politiques, Mémoires, Vol. VII, 3) (Brussels, 1956).

[92] See P. Dieudonné Rinchon, *Le trafic négrier, d'aprè les livres de commerce du capitaine gantois Pierre Ignace Liévin van Alstein* (Bruxelles, 1938); idem., *Pierre-Ignace-Liévin van Alstein, capitaine négrier* (Memoires de l'Institut Français d'Afrique Noire, 71) (Dakar, 1964), and his work cited in the previous footnote.

paying more attention to the rights of creditors. This ambiguity even crept into the *Code Noir* of 1685, the legal foundation of the slave system in the French colonies for the next century and more. Articles 44 and 46 of the code declared slaves to be *meubles*, personal property or chattels, hence divisible among heirs and as subject to seizure as any other personal property. However, article 47 declared that in seizures and sales, slave "wives" were not to be separated from their "husbands" or small children (under age seven, in practice) from their mothers; article 48 provided further that slaves aged fourteen to sixty working on sugar, indigo, or other plantations could not be seized for debts unless the whole plantation or farm was seized. However, within this exception, a further exception was made to permit the recovery of recently sold slaves if the price of their purchase had not been paid. This last concession does not appear to have been much used and, in practice, the integrity of the plantation was respected in the French colonies as much as in Brazil. This meant that creditors could seize crops but could not seize anything that would diminish the productive capacity of a plantation.[93] Thus, although French law knew documents (*contrats d'obligation*) analogous to an English bond, in practice these did not give the recourse against slaves that British bonds enjoyed under the Colonial Debts Act of 1732. Persons selling slaves for credit were thus ordinarily in a weaker legal position in the French colonies than in the English ones.

In the British colonies, the general tendency in the late seventeenth and eighteenth centuries was for the proceeds from the sale of slaves to be remitted with increasing frequency in bills of exchange rather than in commodities. French slave traders had also experimented with bills of exchange (*lettres de change*) but found a discouraging proportion of nonacceptances in France of bills drawn by planters and therefore tended, with some exceptions, to avoid using bills.[94] English slave traders also had troubles with the nonacceptance of planters' bills and therefore preferred bills drawn by merchants and factors, such as

---

[93] Lucien Peytraud, *L'esclavage aux Antilles Francaises avant 1789* (Paris, 1897), pp. 160, 164, 245, and n, 247–65. See also Alain Buffon, *Monnaie et crédit en économie coloniale: Contribution à l'histoire économique de la Guadeloupe 1675–1919* (Basse-Terre, 1979); Louis-Philippe May, *Histoire économique de la Martinique (1635–1763)* (Paris, 1930), pp. 264–6; Adrien Dessalles, *Histoire générale des Antilles*, 5 vols. (Paris, 1847–8), Vol. III, pp. 243–9; [Michel René Hilliard d'Auberteuil], *Considérations sur l'état présent de la colonie française de Saint-Domingue*, 2 vols. (Paris, 1776), Vol. I, pp. 111–29.

[94] Gaston Martin, *Nantes au XVIIIᵉ Siècle: L'ère des négriers (1714–1774)* (Paris, 1931), p. 133. For an exception in which 226,498 livres were remitted in twenty-one bills of exchange by the Cap Français (St. Domingue) firm of de Russy, Gauget & Cie to the Nantes slave trader François Deguer, see Rinchon, *Les armements négriers*, p. 64.

they obtained in the immediate remittance system. There does not appear to have been anything precisely corresponding to this system in the French slave trade, even though eighteenth-century France was familiar with the assignment of bills of exchange by endorsement and with discounting. The chief difficulty may have been in finding rich merchants and bankers at home who could be persuaded to act as guarantees for trustworthy slave-selling factors in the West Indies and to accept their long bills. French firms appear to have had difficulty finding strong, independent correspondents in the West Indies and, when they needed factors there, often found it necessary to set up branches (*succursales*) under junior partners or client firms in which they retained a major interest (*sociétés en commandite*). Since such branches or client firms could draw heavily only on their partners in France, such drawing would hardly have been a useful channel for their remission of the proceeds of slave sales to those same partners.[95]

There are, of course, always exceptions or partial exceptions. In a letter of 1770, François Deguer, a big Nantes slave trader, described the existence of certain large houses in Le Cap (St. Domingue) who, for the high commission of 12%, would agree to guarantee all collections on credit sales of slaves and would send back in the slave ship the proceeds of the sale paid for then or payable within six months. The proceeds of credit sales payable beyond six months would be remitted as received.[96] This is little more than Henry Laurens of Charleston offered to do for a 10% commission in 1749. It differed from the Liverpool immediate remittance system in that the French slave trader had no guarantee or even firm knowledge of when he was going to get remittances for sales with more than six months' credit. Though Deguer and a few others may have experimented with such guaranteed sales through the big merchants of Le Cap, the existing literature would seem to suggest that most French slave traders stayed with more traditional methods.

British slave traders, we have seen, preferred selling through factors

---

[95] For example, four-fifths of the capital of the Saint-Marc (St. Domingue) firm of Reynaud Frères & Cie was held by the partners in the Bordeaux slave-trading and West Indies firm of Henry Romberg, Bapst & Cie, which they represented in the colony. Françoise Thésée, *Négociants bordelais et colons de Saint-Domingue: . . . la maison Henry Romberg, Bapst et Ce 1783–1793* (Bibliothèque d'Histoire d'Outre-mer, Nouvelle Série, Travaux, 1) (Paris, 1972), pp. 29–32. For the use of bills of exchange in France then, see Charles Carrière, *Négociants marseillais au XVIIIe siècle*, 2 vols. (Marseille, 1973), Vol. II, pp. 845–74; Charles Carrière et al., *Banque et capitalisme commercial: La lettre de change au XVIIIe siècle* (Marseille, 1976). For the mercantile community in the French Antilles, cf. Dessalles, Vol. IV, p. 592; May, pp. 208–9.

[96] Rinchon, *Les armements négriers*, p. 53.

rather than ship captains even in the late seventeenth century. Where captains were sometimes used, especially in the West Indies, there was a tendency to change to factors by the mid-eighteenth century.[97] By contrast, many French slave traders appear to have continued to make heavy (though not exclusive) use of ship captains in slave sales throughout the eighteenth century. A typical large French slave trade vessel (with 250 to 400 slaves) would be staffed with two captains. As soon as the slaves were disposed of and return cargo taken on board, the ship would depart for France under the command of the second captain, with the first remaining in the islands for up to a year to collect the debts arising from the slave sale. The first captain had a strong interest in staying behind because he collected a substantial commission (5 to 7%) on the slave sales he completed.[98] If on departure he had had to leave the collection of some debts in the hands of a firm in the island, he would have had to share his commission with it.

A substantial portion (10–35%) of French slaves sales were paid in *comptant*, or current effects. These took the form of the worn Spanish coins that circulated in the islands for more than their intrinsic worth, or *mandats* (drafts or sight bills) on local traders, or promissory notes (*billets*) from the buyer given with the understanding that they would be almost immediately converted into commodity deliveries. In whatever form, the *comptant* were speedily converted into commodities for the slave vessel's return cargo. The unpaid balances earned by the slave sales were acknowledged by the buyers' personal notes (*billets*) payable ordinarily at two to twelve months, but sometimes at up to eighteen or twenty-four months. These notes were usually paid off in commodities at the current market price. The commodities so acquired were freighted back to the slave-trading firm in France in whatever vessels were available. After about twelve months, when most but not all the *billets* had been redeemed by the slave purchasers, the captain returned to France, leaving any unsettled notes in the hands of his employer's factor for collection. Substantially the same procedures were followed when the sales were made by factors.[99]

Contemporary commentators and modern scholars agree that the

---

[97] Hyde et al., pp. 368–77, esp. p. 369n.

[98] Rinchon, *Van Alstein*, pp. 120, 212–13.

[99] Ibid., pp. 89–92, 114–15, 120, 194–7, 200–1, 203–5, 215, 217, 243–4, 282 passim; idem., *Le trafic négrier*, pp. 129–30, 222–23; idem., *Les armements négriers*, pp. 67, 93–4, 101, 107, 109, 116. It is possible that because the Van Alstein papers are those of a ship captain, they exaggerate the relative importance of sales by captains. In *Les armements négriers*, Rinchon gives more details of sales through factors. See also Paul Butel, *Les Négociants bordelais, l'Europe et les îles au XVIIIᵉ siècle* (Paris, 1974), pp. 222–35.

chief weakness of the French system was that buyers of slaves (particularly planter buyers) did not clear their notes at the times promised. (Here the difference between the French and British debt laws are relevant.) We regularly find indications of ventures taking five and six years to be settled, and some reportedly took up to ten years.[100] As a result, many slave-trading firms accumulated large balances owed them in the Antilles. In 1785, eight large firms in Nantes were owed over 8 million livres in the islands.[101] (If these were *livres tournois*, they would have been the equivalent of ca. £333,445 sterling.) On collections, therefore, the French slave traders were working under a significant disadvantage compared with the Liverpool slavers, who after 1750 usually received the product of their American sales "in the bottom" on the return of their vessels, either in goods or in negotiable bills.

We need not, however, be overly concerned about the balance sheets of French slave traders, nor ought we to take too seriously the tales of their great losses from uncollectable debts. Whatever misfortunes may have befallen individual slave traders, the great growth of the French slave trade in the eighteenth century[102] can only mean that the trade as a whole was most attractive. The profit margins of the French slave traders had to be large enough to absorb the costs, delays, and losses of debt collections.

CONCLUSION: THE ECONOMIES AND COSTS OF CREDIT

Credit, with all its difficulties, was just one of the necessary transaction costs that the slave trade could support and still be attractive. We can conceive of a slave trade conducted entirely for cash, but it

---

[100] Rinchon, *Les armements négriers*, pp. 62–3, 72, 92, 101–2, 110, 124–6; Martin, pp. 131, 375–6; Meyer, pp. 227–231; Thésée, pp. 85–6, 96–7, 101; Perry Viles, "The Slaving Interest in the Atlantic Ports, 1763–1792," *French Historical Studies*, Vol. VII (1972), pp. 529–43, esp. p. 532; Stein, 113–16, 149–50; H[ervé] du Halgouet, *Au temps de Saint-Domingue et de la Martinique d'après la correspondance des trafiquants maritimes* (Rennes, 1941), pp. 63–84.

[101] Rinchon, *Van Alstein*, p. 215. At the time of the Seven Years War, it was estimated that all the Nantes slave traders had 10 million livres owed them in St. Domingue, alone. Martin, pp. 131, 309. Even so, the share of their total indebtedness owed by Antilles planters to merchants, local and metropolitan, was less (40%) than the share (53%) owed to other West Indians for land purchases and family settlements. Christian Schnakenbourg, *Les sucreries de la Guadeloupe dans la second moitié du XVIII*e *siècle (1760–1790)* (Thèse pour le doctorat d'état, Paris II, 1973), pp. 146–56; Alain Buffon, *Monnaie et crédit en économie coloniale: Contributiion à l'histoire économique de la Guadeloupe 1635–1919* (Basse-Terre, 1979), p. 111.

[102] Stein, pp. 207–11.

would undoubtedly have been a much smaller trade: With markedly less effective demand, profit margins on sales should have been significantly lower, and in the aggregate such a trade should have been less profitable.

We must therefore take credit into account when we calculate the profitability of the trade. Since I have been able to examine the original business records used by only a few of the scholars who have attempted to make such calculations, I refrain from commenting on their individual works and instead confine myself to some general remarks on the problem of the relationship of credit to profits.

Slave traders in both Britain and France tended to keep separate records for each "adventure"; this was necessary in part because the adventure was sometimes an ad hoc association of persons who were not otherwise partners. In their accounts they debited the adventure with all charges relating to the *mise-hors* or "outfit" and cargo of the venture (cost of buying or chartering the vessel, expenditure for sails, cables, and repairs, trading goods, provisions, wages of crew, etc.) and credited it with net receipts realized from the remittances for the slave sales. Such calculations showed whether or not the individual venture was profitable, but not the return on capital invested, inasmuch as the outfit and cargo were not necessarily identical to the capital ventured by the adventurers.

Between 1741 and 1810, approximately 61,000 slaves were transported annually from Africa to the American plantations of the various European colonial powers. If over these years the outset and cargo expenditure of the slave ventures in peacetime had averaged £20 per slave landed, the annual ventures would have been about £1,220,000 sterling. The total at risk would have been perhaps double this figure, since the returns for one year's venture would not in most cases have come home before it was time to send out the next year's venture (except in Brazil). Where did these large sums come from? Slave traders did not usually start out as rich men and had therefore to act together to mobilize the resources necessary for their speculations. Their ventures could be conducted by ongoing partnerships but were often, as noted, an activity of ad hoc and temporary groups of co-venturers. In England, the participants in any given venture were usually recruited from the same port, though we find evidence of nonlocal participation (e.g., Glasgow merchants taking shares in Liverpool slaving ventures).[103] Outside money (particularly from Paris)

---

[103] Price, "Buchanan & Simson," pp. 29–31; Curtin, *Atlantic Slave Trade*, p. 216. The £20 figure is a crude and arbitrary estimate, given the fluctuations in costs over this

was more in evidence in French slave trading ventures, a mobilization facilitated by the French limited partnership (*société en commandite*). Merchant firms in Britain frequently supplemented their capital by medium- or long-term borrowing on bond from persons with money who wanted a better rate of return than they could get from the public funds.[104] I know less about practices in France but find evidence of a slaving firm in Bordeaux borrowing on *contrats d'obligation* (bonds) both from its own inactive partners (*commanditaires*) and from other merchants in its port.[105] References also occur to slaving firms or syndicates borrowing on bottomry bonds (*contrats à la grosse aventure*), a practice more likely exceptional rather than routine. French slave traders are also reported to have obtained substantial advances from Paris bankers. English slave traders rarely got much help from banks (almost unknown in the outports before 1750) except in the discounting and collecting of short-term bills of exchange. (The Bank of England normally did not discount bills of more than sixty days' duration, and private banks were only slightly more helpful.)[106] All borrowing – including discounting – reduced, of course, the amount that the participants had to put "up front".

A further level of credit appears in the terms on which the outward-bound trading goods were purchased. David Richardson reports that, in the outport firm records he has examined, 40 to 50% of such goods were normally purchased on credit.[107] However, we must distinguish between expenditures for trading cargo and expenditures for the ship's outfit or "outset." For the outset, some cash was needed for advances on sailors' wages and certain port charges and services. Other outset items, including victuals and drink for the ship and some ship's supplies, such as sailcloth, could only be purchased for cash or very short credit. By contrast, most cargo items could be purchased

---

long period. It is close to the figure given in Rinchon, *Armements négriers*, p. 52, and not inconsistent with the data given by Richardson (footnote 56), though higher figures are suggested by Stein, pp. 137, 140, 144. At the other extreme, Brazilian outsets should have been much lower than French.

[104] Price, *Capital and Credit*, chap. 4.

[105] Thésée, pp. 86–7.

[106] Stein, 148–9; Sir John Clapham, *The Bank of England: A History*, 2 vols. (Cambridge, 1966), Vol. I, pp. 124–5; Bank of England Archives, Court Minutes, passim; Price, *Capital and Credit*, chap. 5. On bottomry loans, see Butel, 196–7. In a *bottomry bond*, the master or owner of a vessel gave security for a loan made to him by pledging the keel or hull of his vessel. If the vessel was lost at sea within the time contracted, the bond was voided. Analogous was the *respondentia bond* secured against all or part of the cargo of a vessel.

[107] David Richardson, "West African Consumption Patterns and Their Influence on the Eighteenth Century Slave Trade," in Gemery and Hogendorn, pp. 303–30, esp. p. 315n.

on long credit. (The big exceptions were beads and guns.) The usual
export credit in Britain, particularly on textiles and hardware, was
twelve months, but many suppliers would by the 1780s grant up to
eighteen months to the African trade.[108] Of course, since sellers allowed a discount or rebate calculated at up to 10% per annum for
early payment, firms in funds also had a strong incentive to repay
export credits early. These long credits were a distinctive British institution that did not exist in Holland, where almost all trade goods
were sold for payment within six weeks and the buyers were left to
arrange their own financing.[109] Long credits were known in France,
but I do not know whether they were available in all export trades.
Three to six months may have been more typical in French ports.[110]
The relevant point here is that if the slave-trading firm did not have
to pay cash for its outbound trading goods, the capital requirements
of the trade were somewhat reduced, with *possibly* beneficial effects
on profits expressed as returns on venture capital.[111] Such credit was,

---

[108] Price, *Capital and Credit*, pp. 101–18, 156–7. The Rogers papers are filled with letters,
particularly from London and Manchester, offering goods on credits of twelve to
eighteen months. PRO C.107/3, 7(i), 7(ii), 9, 15. But the cargo notes in C.107/10
show shorter credits for perishables and sailcloth. The Davenport ship accounts
(Keele University Library) show that on outfit expenditures, cash disbursements
always exceeded credit notes by a good margin, but that on cargo items there was
greater irregularity. Presumably, when cash was tight, Davenport took full advantage of credits on purchases, but when cash was easy, he used cash obtainable at
no more than 5 percent to obtain discounts of 10 percent and up on his purchases.

[109] Price, *Capital and Credit*, p. 119.

[110] Cf. Butel, pp. 258–9, C. F. Gaignat de L'Aulnais, *Guide du Commerce* (Paris, 1791),
pp. 27, 368–84.

[111] A careful examination of surviving accounts and correspondence reveals several
ways in which payment mechanisms reduced the amount of cash that slave trade
adventurers had to advance or "put up front". Humphry Morice's journal (Bank
of England Archives B19) suggests that about 1710, shares in slaving voyages were
paid to the managing partner in cash. However, the William Davenport papers
(Keele University Library) show that by midcentury, participants in his ventures
did not pay their full subscriptions in cash. Instead, Davenport of Liverpool, as
manager, divided most (not all) of the bills or "shopnotes" that came in from
suppliers among the individual participant-adventurers according to their shares.
Each was thereby free to take full advantage either of credit or of discounts for early
payment on his share of the bills. A different but equivalent system is revealed by
the papers relating to the ventures managed in the 1780s by James Rogers of Bristol,
who obtained most of his textiles from London. Shortly before the year's credit on
purchases had expired, the London credit seller would sometimes write Davenport
for the "divisions" (shares of the several venturers) so that he could send out a bill
for his share to each venturer. Since this practice was not general, it presumably
was a technique by which some big London textile houses sought to get more of
the slave trade business. See, e.g., PRO C.107/7(ii) from Ludlam Parry & Son,
London, 16 July 1788; C.107/8 from Sargent, Chambers & Co., 15 Oct. 1785. However, whether or not such divisions were made, the long credit offered by suppliers

of course, expensive, as the firms recognized when they repaid their suppliers early to save on interest.

However, the most important effect of credit on the profitability of the slave trade arose from the length of credit with which slaves were sold. Jean Meyer has pointed out that profits impressive at first glance could waste away to less than ordinary interest if the adventurers had to wait too many years to collect the proceeds of their slave sales.[112] The Liverpool slave traders escaped from this dilemma by insisting on immediate remittances, which ideally would have enabled them to close their books on an adventure in eighteen to twenty-four months – though at the cost of higher commissions to their factors and substantial discounts on the bills remitted. The French slave traders, who did not have this institutional option, had to wait for returns. To get a sharper picture of the profitability of the slave trade, we must also consider the opportunity costs of the capital tied up in that trade for such long but varying periods of time.

Despite individual cases of planter mortgages foreclosed, slaves seized, and slave trader bankruptcies, we have been dealing with a system that, in its own narrow bookkeeping terms, worked. Through various credit mechanisms, the external resources of bankers, bill negotiators, accepting/guaranteeing houses, merchant and manufacturer suppliers, and lenders on mortgages and bonds were in varying ways added to those of slave traders and planters to make possible the continuous expansion of the British and French slave plantation economies from the 1660s to 1790 or 1807. As a Liverpool slave trader put it, the right sort of credit "made the wheel turn."

reduced the amount of cash participants had to advance at the beginning of an adventure.
[112] Meyer, pp. 227–34.

Index

Africa, 15, 166; in Atlantic system, 20, 76, 97–119, 122; credit in slave trade of, 300; economy of, 139; New England trade with, 248, 249, 251–2, 253; imports into, 105–10; slave trade, 4, 7–8, 57–8, 61, 66, 69, 73, 116–18, 136–43, 144–5, 149–50, 174–5; slavery in, 48; trade with Spain and Portugal, 9, 67, 68–70, 71, 73; trading networks, 43–4; value of total trade, 99–103, 111, 115

agricultural productivity: New England, 239–40

agriculture: Brazil, 6; and labor supply, 2–3; England, 208; export, 79; slaves employed in, 89–90

Alcaçovas, treaty of, 166

alcohol: imported into Africa, 7, 105, 107, 110

Alencastro, Luiz Felipe de, 9–11, 19, 20, 151–76

Alexander brothers, 328–9

Alfonso V, king of Portugal, 167

Alfoso X, king of Castile and Leon, 71

Almeida, Francisco de, 153

Alvares de Almada, André, 170

amenities index: New England, 242

America(s): Atlantic economy and growth of slavery in, 290–2; Old World background of slavery in, 43–61; slavery in, 145–6; *see also* Latin America; North America; South America

American colonies: in Atlantic system, 20, 27–30; debt to Great Britain, 326–7; foreign trade, 21, 196–7; settlement of, 22–6; slavery in, 43n2; slaving in, 149

American Revolution; *see* War of Independence (U.S.)

Amerindians, 47, 95; efforts of Spanish crown to protect, 44–5; impact of disease on, 4, 45–7; as labor supply, 43–5, 46, 47; missionary work among,

162; as slave labor, 70, 71, 159, 169, 171–2, 175–6; slave trade in, 44, 54; struggle over control of, 152–4

Amsterdam, 87, 94, 147

ancien regime, 13, 76

Anderson, T. L., 30, 239–40, 241–2

Andrews, Charles M., 22

Anglo-Dutch War of 1780–4, 94

Anglo-French Treaty of 1713, 190

Anglo-Saxon model (credit), 19, 296, 331–2

Anglo-Spanish wars, 22

Angola, 9, 83, 84, 99, 105n16, 171; colonization of, 152, 159; commodity trade, 140–1; Inquisition in, 163; slave trade, 123–4, 128–32, 133–4, 135, 137–8, 140–1, 142, 145, 153, 154, 159, 167, 170, 173, 297, 298; struggle over control of natives in, 153–4

Antigua, 307

Aragón, 58

Arawaks, 70n24

Arguim island, 63

aristocracy, landowning, 3, 36–7

artisanal slavery, 3, 4, 47, 48, 56

Aruba, 91

Asia, 1, 15, 144; Dutch trade with, 81, 82, 88–9; indentured laborers from, 113; Portuguese trading network with, 9–10, 166–7

ascientos (licenses), 70, 78, 126, 164, 167

Atlantic, 1, 4; Dutch role in, 95; Portuguese slave trade in, 120–50

Atlantic economy: African slaving from periphery of, 138–43; England in, 181–2, 206, 209; and growth of slavery in America, 290–2; and New England trade, 260–1; precolonial western Africa and, 97–119; slave labor in, 168–9; slave trade in development of, 57, 181–2, 207; *see also* Americas

Atlantic islands: Portuguese colonies, 64;

341

Printed in the United States
84292LV00003B/94-102/A

9 780521 457378